Rev. Kathryn Rust
W9570 County Road, F
Antigo, WI 54409-9131

The Minister's Annual Manual
for Preaching and Worship Planning
2010-2011

Logos Productions Inc.
6160 Carmen Avenue
Inver Grove Heights, MN 55076-4422
1-800-328-0200
www.logosproductions.com

First Edition
Twenty-fourth Annual Volume

Compiled and Edited by Suzanne L. H. Olson

Published in the US by Logos Productions Inc.
6160 Carmen Avenue
Inver Grove Heights, Minnesota 55076-4422
Phone: 800-328-0200
Fax: 651-457-4617
www.logosproductions.com

ISBN: 978-1-885361-37-0
ISSN: 0894-3966

Contents

Children's Time

Appendices

FREE Children's Sermon Index

Your paid subscription now includes FREE access to the *Children's Sermon Index* – a database of children's sermons based on the Revised Common Lectionary for each Sunday of the year. You can search by theme, season of the church year, or keyword.

- **Your activation code is MA880.**
- **In the US visit www.logosproductions.com** and click on "Online subscriptions."
- **In Canada visit www.woodlakebooks.com** and click on "Church resources."
- Follow the instructions to receive FREE access to the *Children's Sermon Index* for as long as you subscribe to *The Minister's Annual Manual.*

How to Use This Book

A Note about the Lectionary

If you have used this book in the past, you are accustomed to seeing the lectionary listings referred to as:

> RCL – Revised Common Lectionary
> Roman Catholic
> Episcopal (BCP)
> Lutheran

Beginning with this edition, you will see the following terms used instead:

> RCL – Revised Common Lectionary
> SC – Semi-continuous
> C – Complementary
> RC – Roman Catholic

During the Season after Pentecost, lections marked Semi-continuous are used by most mainline congregations. Lections marked Complementary are used by Lutheran congregations. If you have any questions, please contact us at feedback@ LogosProductions.com.

Dear Readers of
The Minister's Annual Manual,

This book contains planning materials for 63 worship occasions from August 2010 through July 2011.

What You Will Find in This Resource

The following materials are included for each worship experience:

- Lessons, assigned for liturgical preaching
- Speaker's Introduction for the Lessons
- Theme materials
- Thought for the Day, related to the theme
- Sermon Summary, noting key points of sermon
- Call to Worship, to begin community praise and worship
- Pastoral Prayer, a general prayer for the worshiping community
- Prayer of Confession, a prayer of community contrition and repentance
- Prayer of Dedication of Gifts and Self, an offering prayer
- Hymn of the Day, a suggested hymn with background information
- Children's Time for conversation with children
- The Sermon, a reflection on one of the texts for the day
- Hymns, suggestions for opening, sermon, and closing hymns

The brief speaker's introductions for the lessons may be read aloud during worship or used as notes in the worship bulletin.

The Children's Time suggestions can be used by pastors or others who lead a time for children during worship, or offered to those who lead Sunday school worship.

The sermon materials may be used as devotional reading or thought-starters for your own sermon preparation.

Lection Guidelines

Not all preachers use the lectionary lessons on a regular basis. If you don't base worship on the lectionary, the materials in this book may still be useful in providing sermon ideas and illustrations on specific texts appropriate for the time of year. On the other hand, if you are accustomed to using the lectionary lessons, you will find these materials especially suited to your preaching needs.

Many denominations now follow the Revised Common Lectionary, the organizing basis for the resources in this book. You should have no difficulty adapting these materials to your own church calendar. The Consultation on Common Texts asks that we include the following information:

For the Sundays following Pentecost, the Revised Common Lectionary provides two distinct patterns for readings from the Old Testament. One pattern offers a series of semicontinuous Old Testament readings over the course of these Sundays. The other pattern offers paired readings in which the Old Testament and Gospel reading for each Sunday are closely related. In adopting the Revised Common Lectionary, the Presbyterian Church U.S.A., United Church of Christ, and United Methodist Church elected to use the pattern of semicontinuous Old Testament readings. The other pattern of paired readings is found in The Revised Common Lectionary (Nashville: Abingdon Press, 1992).

- The Revised Common Lectionary, 1992 Consultation on Common Texts (CCT)

Hymn Resources

Many of the hymns suggested may be reproduced if you obtain a license. A copyright cleared music license for churches is available through LicenSing at www.licensingonline.org.

More Planning Resources

To assist in your planning, a four-year church year calendar is included in the appendices, as well as calendars for the years 2010 and 2011.

For even more worship planning helps, you may wish to use the May/June 2010 planning issue or the regular monthly issues of *The Clergy Journal*. These resources include additional sermons and hymn selections.

The planning issue also includes more ideas for children's time. Preachers who use *The Minister's Annual Manual 2010-2011* and also subscribe to *The Clergy Journal* will have valuable resources for worship planning that include:

- Three sets of preaching helps for every Sunday of the year. The materials are cross-referenced so that you will know at a glance which publication to use for a particular text.
- Two sets of children's time ideas.
- Hymn suggestions to support the lectionary texts.
- A variety of prayers and calls to worship.

It is our hope that *Minister's Annual Manual* will enrich your worship preparation throughout the year.

– Suzanne L. H. Olson, editor
Spring 2010

Using the CD-ROM

Although the book may be the easiest way to read weekly material, if you wish to reprint prayers or worship material in your Sunday bulletin, using the CD-ROM will save you time and effort. As a purchaser of *The Minister's Annual Manual 2010-2011,* you have permission to use and reprint the entire contents of this book. (When quoting portions from the sermons, please credit the author.) Following are some simple hints for using the CD-ROM:

- This CD can be used in both IBM-compatible and Macintosh computers.
- Insert the CD into your computer's CD-ROM drive and select your preferred word-processing application. Click on "File" and then "Open." Be sure the "List Files of Type" drop-down menu says "All Files (*.*)." For additional help, refer to your software manual.
- Select the week of materials you are interested in viewing or copying and double-click on that file.
- Once the file has opened, you will see a plain text version of the manuscript. You may highlight any or all of the information, then copy and paste it into another document – for example, into your worship bulletin.
- Once the material is in place, change the type font and size to match the document.

How Preachers Become Disciples
Rev. William L. Mangrum

The week I accepted this assignment, a long-time church member sent a letter saying, "The pastor's sermons are fluff."

A couple of weeks later, a new elder resigned saying, "The pastor talks too much and puts me to sleep."

The very next Sunday I received an enthusiastic embrace from a visiting elder. "I was headed back to my church to resign," she said. "Your sermon gives me hope enough to continue." She then asked, "Do these people know what they have here?"

As I finish this article, our session voted to employ a conflict mediator *and* a church consultant. Both! The fear, distrust, and hurt are so palpable that only immediate and specially trained assistance from beyond us holds promise for us. All of this, and I must preach tomorrow.

Across three decades of pastoral work I have learned this much: this is a steep and hair-pinned roller coaster I ride but not one I ride alone. Even the best preachers have their critics and the worst preachers have their devotees. One thing, however, unites us all. No matter what transpires during the week, come Sunday morning we preachers must "stand and deliver."

How do we do this? How do we stay with reading ancient texts and scrutinizing contemporary culture with hearts divided – sometimes drawn by wondrous praise and often wounded by sneer and scorn? How do we avoid bending – to one way or the other – our Sunday sermons?

How do we stay on task when weekly urgencies crowd our calendar? How do we stay focused when the critic sits up front and those who love us are on vacation – again? Given Saturday's *accidie*, how do we "stand and deliver" God's Word on Sunday?

Growing Calm, Staying True

Reading famous sermons and deconstructing our own sermons – these we do routinely. In our study, we engage a venerable crowd. We listen well and ask thoughtful questions. We muse and delight to the delight of poets and the musings of scholars. We plunder obscure narratives for wisdom and holy oil. All the while we dream of the big game. There is not a preacher who does not want to score the season-saving touchdown. We imagine knocking home the winning run. We work feverishly, preparing for competition. We study and write and ponder the morrow – then we go home and to bed early.

Early Sunday morning before the bathroom mirror, while the shower runs out cold, we match hand motions with metaphors. We dream success. Seeing in our mind's eye their faces and remembering with our hearts their needs, we run over our game plan for reaching our people. We fix our smiles, and clear our throats. We mutter prayers.

Then, we "stand and deliver."

This weekly cycle is gut wrenching. Hard-purchased words go out and so does our soul. Blood drains from our bodies. With every breath, with every push of syllable, with every wild look of eye – we sweat. Saturday is Lamaze. Sunday we give birth. And all the church watches from pillowed pews, then comments on our hair.

When young to our calling, Sunday suppers are depressing. No one wants to be with us – fatigued and often angry. Did they listen? Do they care that each week we strip our souls bare for them to see? We are spent and not sure the cost was appreciated. No one, we whisper, catches our insight and profundity.

If we dwell in this preacher-adolescence, we go septic. We rot. But not before we spew poison. Not before we spread filth and not health.

However, in spite of our congregation's denseness, in spite of their failure to admire our gifts, we can learn to practice our craft faithfully. In even isolated places our souls will flourish if we grow calm and stay true. If we do, our eyes and voice across the decades will manifest the deepening of our *own* Christian faith.

After many years of this discipline – if we are true to it – people will want to sup with us on Sundays. Not because they want to feed on us or because they want to disagree with us. Rather, because they simply want to be with us. Only by taxing circumnavigation do we get here – to these calm waters from there at the falls' edge. However demanding and often demeaning this weekly cycle is for us as preachers, it is possible to grow by means of this torment and torture into someone different than ourselves yet more truly ourselves than we ever imagined. Indeed, quite possibly, the greatest beneficiaries of our calling to preach will be us.

And I do not think this statement selfish, only realistic and biblical. Jesus said that those who seek their lives will lose them. He also said those who give their lives away will find a way of being in the world beyond their imagination. Some of us give our lives away in preaching only to find a wild and precious way of living beyond our own making.

Two Practices for Avoiding Failure, Three for Health and Life
How do we find life through the practice of preaching? Here are several habits I cultivate – habits staving off preacher-despair; habits heightening my soul's awareness of God's everlasting goodness for me through my calling.
1. **Make a specific Bible your Bible.** Most preachers have more Bibles than are present in entire Chinese villages and districts. We luxuriate in commen-

taries and monographs and translations. As I write in my bedroom, I count six Bibles within reach – four versions – and more downstairs and in my pastor's study.

Yet having many Bibles and purchasing a Bible with your life are not the same. I am speaking of something fundamental, primitive. Laugh if your will, but I am speaking of tattooing the scriptures with your life – etched in green, blue, and black. I am speaking of purchasing every page with prayers and names and dates and memories.

Manuscript scholars tell us some texts are corrupted by scribal interpolations. It seems comments were written into parchment margins and later crept into *textus receptus.* The notations of devout readers were later judged as faithful by astute readers and preserved.

Today we neatly package and sell the same. We call them "Study Bibles" and I bet you have at least three. Chuck them all; write your own. Make one specific Bible *your* Bible.

2. **Memorize the text – the biblical text.** As much as I need a Bible recording my struggles, I need a heart that records the Bible. I need the text *in* me.

Many preachers were trained to memorize sermon outlines so as to speak unencumbered by a manuscript. Some were trained to preach entirely without notes. This is not as difficult as it may seem.

Thousands move in this direction following seminary. The demands of parish life dictate doing so. Often they are guided by other pastors or stand-up comics. For many, however, it isn't an image of Jonathan Edwards pitched low over a New England pulpit, reading aloud in dim candle light that inspires them to "stand and deliver." It's Leno. It's Letterman.

Yet for all this working up our own words, we often fail to store up the Word. One sinful tendency I fight as a preacher by memorizing the Word is the tendency to cherish my words about the Word above the Word. Memorizing scripture, I indwell it and it dwells in me.

When I memorize the scriptural text, when I carry it inside me through the week, I feed continually. An ancient Native American saying gets it right: *"Now the story has made camp in you – if you permit it, it will hunt meat for you; at night its fires will keep you warm."*

The Imitation of Christ contains over 700 biblical quotes and allusions. Yet Thomas à Kempis gives not a single reference in his manuscript. He had copied scriptures so regularly and chanted them daily – he became scripture.

What does it say that we preachers memorize our *own* words each week, but leave the Word un-assumed into our flesh?

3. **On Saturday, turn off the email.** Phones still work and parishioners know where we live. If we are needed, they will find us. Turn off your email.

Protect your solitude. Knowledge of God flourishes in solitude. In solitude before God, God loves us over with a healing love. Preachers need this on Saturday.

Checking email on Saturdays disrupts solitude. We expose our souls to attack and risk fatal distractions. Those who would never call on Saturday morning to complain of trash left in the Fellowship Hall will, on Saturday night, email dozens that we aren't doing our job. Others will weigh in with their dissatisfactions. Then, more.

The deluge comes every week. Every word on the Internet is true on Saturday night and there is no more vulnerable moment in the life of a preacher. The wise preacher hiding inside the Word stays away from the many words of others on Saturdays.

And Sunday too! While writing this article, after a memorable service, I broke routine and checked my email before heading home. Disaster struck. At 10:17 a.m. while I served Eucharist, an elder sent a resignation letter from his home. We all got it. No one missed the sad juxtaposition. At supper I felt young again: vulnerable and horrible.

Email is a great help for introverts – and fraught with danger. If we are to let the Word settle into our souls Saturday night, and let God love us into preaching shape for Sunday morning – we had best turn it off.

One Wild and Precious Life

There is nothing new here. There is just a simple plea that we preachers become disciples of Jesus Christ. For all of our skills and training, this is not a given, but learning to preach can help.

Unless we become disciples through the discipline of our craft, we haven't a prayer for surviving this roller coaster ride we purchased. Yet if we cultivate a few good habits, even the worst sermon on the worst week will still feed our people and save our own souls.

To preach is not a way of life many understand. It is not a popular way of becoming more human. It is one way, however, that God restores to some the *imago dei,* working our frailty into the image and likeness of the Triune God.

"Tell me," says the poet Mary Oliver, "what is it you plan to do with your one wild and precious life"?

For some of us the only answer is, "Preach."

August 1, 2010

10th Sunday after Pentecost (Proper 13 [18])
RC/Pres: 18th Sunday in Ordinary Time

Lessons (See p. 10 for guidelines)

Semi-continuous (SC)	Complementary (C)	Roman Catholic (RC)
Hosea 11:1-11	Ecc 1:2, 12-14; 2:18-23	Ecc 1:2, 2:21-23
Ps 107:1-9, 43	Ps 49:1-12	Ps 95:1-2, 6-9
Col 3:1-11	Col 3:1-11	Col 3:1-5, 9-11
Lk 12:13-21	Lk 12:13-21	Lk 12:13-21

Speaker's Introduction for the Lessons
Lesson 1
Hosea 11:1-11 (SC)

Hosea likens the actions of God toward the divided kingdoms of Israel and Judah as a parent toward rebellious children.

Ecclesiastes 1:2, 12-14; 2:18-23 (C); 1:2, 2:21-23 (RC)

The teacher of wisdom considers what it feels like to spend your whole life building a fortune only for it to be left to someone who may or may not know how to manage it.

Lesson 2
Psalm 107:1-9, 43 (SC)

The psalmist teaches us that when we cry out to God, God hears us and answers.

Psalm 49:1-12 (C)

The psalmist reminds us that no matter how rich and wealthy one gets, we all die and there is no amount of money we can pay that stops death from coming.

Lesson 3
Colossians 3:1-11 (SC/C); 3:1-5, 9-11 (RC)

When you accept Jesus as Lord and Savior there is a whole new life that awaits you as Jesus helps you walk away from destructive behaviors.

Gospel
Luke 12:13-21 (SC/C/RC)
Jesus teaches that greed for the things of this world is not the key to treasures in heaven.

Theme
One way to build a treasure in heaven is by building relationships based on love.

Thought for the Day
I don't believe an accident of birth makes people sisters or brothers…
Sisterhood and brotherhood is a condition people have to work at.
– Maya Angelou

Sermon Summary
The sermon consists of stories about two different sets of brothers. One story tells of a man who demands Jesus tell his brother to divide their inheritance equally; the other story tells of two brothers who reach out in love to each other. How will you build your relationships?

Call to Worship
One: Friends, let us love one another, for love comes from God.
All: Anyone who loves is a child of God and knows God.
One: But anyone who does not love does not know God, for God is love.
All: God showed how much he loved us by sending his Son.
One: This is real love – not that we loved God, but that he loved us and sent his Son as a sacrifice to take away our sins.
All: Since God loved us that much, we ought to love each other and God. Come let us worship the God of love.
– Adapted from 1 John 4:7-11 NLT

Pastoral Prayer
Dear God, so often we come to you complaining that life is unfair. We did not get the things that we wanted; we were not treated the way we thought we ought to be treated; we were not loved the way we desired to

be loved. Guide us this day, Lord, to give the way we want to be given to; to treat others the way we want to be treated; to love as we want to love. Touch our lives this day. Heal those who need healing in body, soul, mind, and spirit. Guide those who do not know which way to turn but need to take a decisive step in their lives. Use us to reach out to those in need and to help bring your peace in our homes, our neighborhoods, our communities, our country, and our world. Hear the prayers we raise to you our God and help us to hear your answers. Amen.

Prayer of Confession

Dear God, forgive us when we lose sight of what is really important in life, when instead of following the law of love we follow the law of greed. When instead of reaching out in love to those around us we reach out to grab the most we can get for ourselves. Help us, Lord, to trust that as we follow you and live your law of love, you will provide for all of our needs, big and small. Teach us to love. Amen.

Prayer of Dedication of Gifts and Self

Creator of the universe, giver of life, thank you for all you give to us, seen and unseen. Help us to understand and experience firsthand that it is in giving that we receive. Help us to be willing to give in love. Bless these gifts we now give to you that they may reach those most in need. In Jesus' name we pray. Amen.

Hymn of the Day
All My Hope on God Is Founded

Poet Robert Bridges created the versification for this text from a table grace by Joachim Neander. It was first published in 1899. In 1986, Fred Pratt Green wrote a new translation, "All My Hope Is Firmly Grounded," which is a closer version to the original text. The tune, MICHAEL, by British composer Herbert Howells, is a wonderful match for the text. The tune is named for Howells's son, who died of polio at the age of nine. If this hymn is new to your congregation, spend some time with the text, especially the Pratt Green translation. Allow time to discover the rich allusions and imagery. While the tune gives strength to the text, reading it in unison as a statement of faith and thanksgiving is a wonderful alternative to singing it.

Children's Time: Too Much Stuff

(Option: Bring a large number of items such as golf clubs, a musical instrument, a CD player, etc. They should be large and, ultimately, too many to carry.)

Talk with the children about things. What are some things they like to do? How many like to play games? Tell them you like to play games, and clutch the golf clubs – or other sports equipment – to your chest.

How many like to listen to music? Grab the CD player. Play music? Grab the instrument. The point is to gather so much "stuff" toward you that you are overwhelmed, and/or you can no longer really see the children, or the church. You might even drop an item or two.

Talk with the children about Luke 12:13-21. Someone once had lots of stuff, and he decided that the best thing to do would be to build bigger barns so that he could store more and more stuff. But God said something very important to the person: "What's the point of having so much 'stuff' that you lose sight of God? You could die tonight, and you'd be all alone."

Put down the items. Explain that you like having things, but maybe you don't need as much as you thought. Trying to get and have too many things can keep us from seeing what God wants us to have and do in life.

Prayer: Thank you, God, for taking care of us. Help us not to want so many things that we lose sight of you. Amen.

The Sermon: The Gift of Relationships
Scripture: Luke 12:13-21

(For sermon materials on Colossians 3:1-11, see the March/April 2010 issue of *The Clergy Journal*; for sermon materials on Luke 12:13-21, see the May/June 2010 planning issue of *The Clergy Journal*.)

This summer we are going on a treasure hunt together, you and me. We are going to search for the treasure the Gospel text chides us about this week, those who store up treasures for themselves but not with God and not in heaven. We know the treasures of this age will rust, burn, crash, and become worthless at the end. So what are those treasures we can store up in heaven? What are the ways we can be rich toward God? I propose to you the treasures we need to store in heaven start with the gifts God has already given us. We just need to be willing to reach out, freely accept them, and start to use them.

Let us start with today's Gospel lesson, and the question I have is this, what would you do if you were in Jesus' shoes? What would you do if a friend sent you a tweet, or a text, or a message on Facebook, or an email, or called you on your cell phone, or worse yet, actually visited you and talked to you face-to-face and wanted YOU to talk with their brother or sister because they were not willing to divide up the family inheritance? What would you say? How would you handle it?

It is unfortunate in both the biblical world and our own world that we have the problem of greed. In fact for a while there, or at least until the latest economic recession, people were trying to sell the idea that greed was good. The Gordon Gekko speech to the Teldar paper shareholders in the movie *Wall Street* became the rallying cry of greed being good. It is only because there is strong evidence that greed caused this latest recession that we are re-evaluating how good greed really is.

You see, in Jesus' time, the oldest brother usually got at least twice what all of his siblings inherited, and in certain cases could keep it all for himself. In our own day we read about parents leaving all their money to their favorite son or daughter or maybe even their favorite dog or cat and cutting everyone else out of the will. For us that grates against our ideals of what is fair. In the Gospel lesson today we would expect Jesus to rally to the cause and demand an equal and fair distribution, but that is not what happens.

In the scripture text it is a classic case of what we would call triangulation. The brother went to Jesus rather than going to his brother. The text does not tell us if he tried to work things out with his brother before he went to Jesus or if he sidestepped his brother altogether and went directly to Jesus and tried to tell Jesus what to tell his brother. Ever get triangulated? It actually happens a lot in life, sometimes knowingly and other times quite by accident. Someone comes up to you with a concern about someone else and instead of allowing that person to take their concerns directly to the person in question, you step in and try and correct everything for both parties. It rarely works. What usually happens is you get caught in the middle and often manage to get both parties angry at you.

Notice how well Jesus sidesteps this question and how quickly he turns the tables. Jesus refused to take responsibility for their disagreement and focuses their attention on what the brother is really concerned about, greed. How many collectible cards do you own? How big is your 401(k) plan? Do you have the biggest house on the block? Is your pension plan making as much money as you hoped it would? How many clothes does your closet hold and is it full? How many pairs of shoes do you own? Do you own the fastest car on the block? Do you own the most up-to-date gadgets?

So let's say you found out you were going to die tomorrow; how much would all of that matter? What would matter to you? For all our society teaches us we would think we would learn from those who we consider lucky enough to hit it big. They win the lottery and you would think they should be the happiest people in the world, but they are not.

Did you ever wonder in this text what kind of relationship these two brothers had that this brother is asking Jesus to step in and referee? I doubt very highly it was built on love. I propose to you that the first building block of having treasure in heaven and being rich toward God is love. Consider the example of these two brothers in a story by an anonymous author:

Two brothers worked together on the family farm. One was married and had a large family. The other was single. At the day's end, the brothers shared everything equally, produce and profit.

Then one day the single brother said to himself, "It's not right that we should share equally the produce and the profit. I'm alone, and my needs are simple." So each night he took a sack of grain from his bin and crept across the field between their houses, dumping it into his brother's bin.

Meanwhile, the married brother said to himself, "It's not right that we should share the produce and the profit equally. After all, I'm married, and I have my wife and children to look after me in years to come. My brother has no one, and no one to take care of his future." So each night he took a sack of grain and dumped it into his single brother's bin.

Both men were puzzled for years because their supply of grain never dwindled. Then one dark night the two brothers bumped into each other. Slowly it dawned on them what was happening. They dropped their sacks and embraced one another.

When it comes to relationships, we have a choice as to how we will relate to one another. The question becomes, which type of relationship do you want and are you willing to step out in love? Amen.

– Deborah Spink Winters

Hymns
Opening Hymn
Love Divine, All Loves Excelling

Sekai no Tomo/Here, O God, Your Servants Gather
Sermon Hymn
Won't You Let Me Be Your Servant?

They Asked, "Who's My Neighbor?"
Closing Hymn
Born of God, Eternal Savior

Listen, Sisters! Listen, Brothers!

August 8, 2010

11th Sunday after Pentecost (Proper 14 [19])
RC/Pres: 19th Sunday in Ordinary Time

Lessons (See p. 10 for guidelines)

Semi-continuous (SC)	Complementary (C)	Roman Catholic (RC)
Isa 1:1, 10-20	Gen 15:1-6	Wis 18:6-9
Ps 50:1-8, 22-23	Ps 33:12-22	Ps 33:1, 12, 18-22
Heb 11:1-3, 8-16	Heb 11:1-3, 8-16	Heb 11:1-2, 8-19 or 11:1-2, 8-12
Lk 12:32-40	Lk 12:32-40	Lk 12:32-48 or 12:35-40

Speaker's Introduction for the Lessons
Lesson 1
Isaiah 1:1, 10-20 (SC)
Isaiah uses the infamous cities of Sodom and Gomorrah to teach what kind of worship God wants from humanity.
Genesis 15:1-6 (C)
After complaining to God about his situation, Abraham was willing to believe God heard him and had an answer. Do we?
Wisdom 18:6-9 (RC)
Through the exodus experience, God separated those who were willing to follow God from those who would not. How does God separate us today?

Lesson 2
Psalm 50:1-8, 22-23 (SC)
The psalmist reminds us that it is God who judges our acts of worship. What kind of grade would our worship receive?
Psalm 33:12-22 (C); 33:1, 12, 18-22 (RC)
The psalmist reminds us that it is not our latest military weapons that will save us; only God can save us.

Lesson 3
Hebrews 11:1-3, 8-16 (SC/C); 11:1-2, 8-19 (RC)
Faith is the fundamental building block of our relationship with God. These ancestors of faith show us what that means.

24

Gospel
Luke 12:32-40 (SC/C); 12:32-48 (RC)

Jesus teaches his disciples that it is not the things of this world that are most important in life, rather it is our relationship with God and the treasures we store up in heaven.

Theme
God overwhelms us with extravagant generosity.

Thought for the Day
You have not lived until you have done something for someone who can never repay you.

– John Bunyan (1628-88)

Sermon Summary
Three stories are shared where people experienced generosity and then two questions are explored: have you experienced generosity and have you ever been a generous giver? God offers us extravagant generosity through his son Jesus Christ. The question is whether we are going to accept the gift or not.

Call to Worship
One: We have come today to worship the Giver of Life.
All: We have come this day to give thanks to the Creator of all.
One: We have come today to worship Jesus, who gave his life for us.
All: We have come this day to sing praises to our Risen Savior.
One: We have come this day to worship the God who loves.
All: Come let us worship in spirit and in truth and in love.

Pastoral Prayer
Dear God, we are overwhelmed by the many ways you show us your love. We see it in the beauty of nature. We hear it in the laughter of children, and we feel it in a hug of a loved one. Scripture tells us you have every hair on our head counted. Because of your love we ask you to hear our prayers and answer them. Bring peace to our world so all soldiers can safely come home. Guide those who have decisions weighing on their hearts. Bring wholeness to those whose lives are in strife. Heal those who need your special touch. Touch all of our lives so we can be extravagant givers in you name. Amen.

8/8/10

Prayer of Confession

Dear Lord, so often we are takers instead of givers. We horde all we can, fearful of what might happen in the future. We live by fear instead of faith. Help us to learn from our ancestors of faith and trust that you want to be a part of our lives, guiding and leading us in the ways we should walk. Forgive our unbelief, help us to believe. Amen.

Prayer of Dedication of Gifts and Self

Thank you, God, for your extravagant generosity toward us. Everything we have is from you: our life, the earth, our families and friends, the gifts and talents we possess, the ability to use them to earn a living, and the gift of eternal life through your son, Jesus. Teach us to be extravagant givers of your love. Bless these gifts we now give, and use them to touch the lives of those who need extravagant givers in their lives. Amen.

Hymn of the Day
Come, We That Love the Lord

Isaac Watts's hymn of praise was a favorite in early American singing schools and was set to a variety of early fuguing tunes. It needs to be sung with energy and great conviction – quiet mumbling does not work! The tune MARCHING TO ZION by Baptist preacher Robert Lowry is an excellent match. Sing this hymn in unison or parts. Use of the piano, improvising in a gospel style, will greatly enhance the presentation of this hymn. An alternate setting with the tune ST. THOMAS provides a less boisterous but still joyful setting for the Watts hymn. This setting leaves out the chorus "We are marching . . . " and is therefore more of a hymn than a song of revival.

Children's Time: Being Ready

Ask the children: How many of you like to sleep in? How about on Saturdays, when there's no school or church? A lot of people do like to grab a chance to sleep in a little later.

How many of you like to stay up late? How does that make you feel in the morning?

A friend of mine, when he was little, was planning on going fishing with her dad. The dad said, "You'd better get to bed early tonight; we're leaving at 4 in the morning." Do you think she listened? No. She stayed up and watched a TV show and then went to bed. She was *not* in the mood to get up in the morning. In fact, her dad almost left without her.

Jesus tells us to be ready. "Be dressed for action and have your lamps lit," Jesus says (Luke 12:35).

It's not that we're going out fishing, but rather that Jesus wants us to be ready to serve – to spread the message of God's love. Falling asleep on the job is not very helpful; nor is not being awake and ready.

Prayer: God, we know you want us to be disciples, ready to share the good news of your love. Help us to do that, and always to be ready. Amen.

The Sermon: The Gift of Extravagant Generosity
Scripture: Luke 12:32-40
(For sermon materials on Hebrews 11:1-3, 8-16, see the March/April 2010 issue of *The Clergy Journal*; for sermon materials on Luke 12:32-40, see the May/June 2010 planning issue of *The Clergy Journal*.)

Did you ever have someone give you a gift that blew you away? A gift so generous it took you by surprise? I have a friend who worked and saved all of her money to be able to fly to audition for the music school she dreamed of attending. The day came for her audition and she drove to the airport, took the plane she needed, hired a taxi cab that was more expensive than she was expecting, got to the school on time, and had a wonderful audition. After her audition she took a taxi back to the airport and due to a mixup on her ticket, an extra fee was applied, and she was short the money she needed to fly home. She tried to no avail to get them to wave the fee, or let her fly home where she would get someone to meet her with the money (this took place in the time before they allowed students to have credit cards and way before cell phones!), or she would mail them the money when she got home. Nothing she suggested worked, and they would not let her on the plane. She left the counter, sat on a bench and started to cry when a man asked her what was wrong. She told him her predicament and he gave her the money to fly home. Simply gave her the money. She was accepted into the school, got the scholarship, earned her college degree there, and to this day she remembers the stranger who freely gave her the money so she could go home.

Have you ever experienced generosity like that? There is a mission group in the United States that raises money for students to be able to go to school in Liberia. One of the students wrote in her thank-you note to the person paying for her education how overwhelmed she was that a person who did not know her would pay for her education. She was overwhelmed that anyone would be that generous to her. She wrote how hard she was studying to live up to the gift and this opportunity to get an education and make something of herself so she could help her country. In my own life as I was scrimping to try and get enough of a down payment for a condo, my eccentric uncle out of the blue gave me the money I needed for the down payment and told me that every year I was to buy a savings bond made out to myself until I paid the full payment back in bonds to myself. Not only did he help me with the down payment, but he forced me to start a savings fund for my future needs. What a generous gift!

What is your response when someone is that generous to you? Have you ever experienced extravagant generosity in your life? When I have been overwhelmed by someone else's generosity I do everything I can to thank them and use the gift they have given and if possible have "paid it forward," shared their generosity with others. Have you ever been extravagantly generous?

In January 2008 while attending an interfaith council of churches meeting in Mount Laurel N.J., Methodist minister Karen Onesti became aware of Rabbi Bossov's progressive kidney failure and his recent placement on the waiting list for a kidney transplant. Rev. Onesti offered him one of her kidneys.

Describing the experience, Onesti cited Romans 8:28: In all things God works for the good of those who love him, who have been called according to his purpose. "Both Andy and I love the Lord and we are called to do God's purpose," she explained "This is not just our story," Bossov said. "This is the story for all those people who have been giving before us and for those who gave the day after us and those who will give in the future."

The transplant was a success!

What is so cool about the kingdom of God is it is a gift. It is a gift freely given for anyone to accept and use. It is also a gift that came at a price. When you think about it, the man who freely gave the money so my friend could buy the plane ticket had to work to earn that money, so also did the person paying for the student's education and my uncle who gave me the generous down payment. And there is no question that Rev.

Onesti's gift came at a price to her own body and health. All of these gifts were given freely, but they came at a price. There is a saying in the United States: "freedom isn't free," reminding us of our brothers and sisters who risk their lives serving in the armed forces so that we can have the freedom of democracy.

Jesus paid the price so that we might freely enjoy the kingdom of God. It is a gift we do not deserve and one we have not earned. It is an act of extravagant generosity of God. It is an act of love. It is a gift that once we accept it and begin to focus living it out every day in our own lives, we naturally begin to store up treasures through the relationships we begin to make as we share the love of God. No thief can steal that, and instead of dreading when the world as we know it comes to an end, instead we look forward to the day we can all be together, when every knee will bow and tongue confess that Jesus Christ is Lord and Savior.

Where is your treasure in life? Take a moment and look at your bank account and personal calendar. Where is it you spend most of your money? What do you spend most of your time on, or who do you spend most of your time with? What does your money and time tell you your treasure is? What is it you are focusing your money and time on? Wherever your treasure is, that is where your focus will be. How much of your money and time do you give to those in need? Are you ready to become an extravagant giver in the name and the love of Jesus? Amen.

– Deborah Spink Winters

Hymns
Opening Hymn
My Hope Is Built on Nothing Less
Jesu, Jesu, Fill Us with Your Love
Sermon Hymn
Take My Life, God, Let It Be
Take My Gifts
Closing Hymn
How Firm a Foundation
Creating God, Your Fingers Trace

August 15, 2010

12th Sunday after Pentecost (Proper 15 [20])
Pres: 20th Sunday in Ordinary Time

Lessons (See p. 10 for guidelines)

Semi-continuous (SC)	Complementary (C)	Roman Catholic (RC)
Isa 5:1-7	Jer 23:23-29	Rev 11:19, 12:1-6, 10
Ps 80:1-2, 8-19	Ps 82	Ps 45:10, 11, 12, 16
Heb 11:29—12:2	Heb 11:29—12:2	1 Cor 15:20-26
Lk 12:49-56	Lk 12:49-56	Lk 1:39-56

Speaker's Introduction for the Lessons
Lesson 1
Isaiah 5:1-7 (SC)
Isaiah uses poetic imagery to describe the actions of the Southern Kingdom of Judah toward God and how God will deal with them and all who do not follow God's law of love.

Jeremiah 23:23-29 (C)
Although the lyrics of a popular song claim "from a distance, God is watching us," Jeremiah reminds us that it is God who seeks us out and wants to be in relationship with us.

Revelation 11:19, 12:1-6, 10 (RC)
The book of Revelation uses apocalyptic language, symbolic language based on Jewish traditions to describe the coming of Messiah.

Lesson 2
Psalm 80:1-2, 8-19 (SC)
The psalmist uses the same poetic imagery and language used in Isaiah to acknowledge what God has done to the Northern Kingdom of Israel and what will now happen to the Southern Kingdom of Judah.

Psalm 82 (C)
God instructed his righteous council to provide for the disadvantage in society. Since they are judging unjustly, God will now judge the earth.

Lesson 3
Hebrews 11:29—12:2 (SC/C)
Hebrews reminds us of the kind of faith our ancestors had and how God provided in each situation. That is the kind of faith we strive to have.
1 Corinthians 15:20-26 (RC)
Paul reminds us that Jesus Christ conquered death once and for all; we need only have faith in the work of Jesus.

Gospel
Luke 12:49-56 (SC/C)
Jesus warns his audience to look at the signs of the times to realize the destruction that is soon to come. In this scripture text, are any of these signs true for us today?
Luke 1:39-56 (RC)
Mary believed by faith that she was going to bear the son of the most high God. Her faith was confirmed when she visited her cousin Elizabeth, and Mary then magnified the Lord.

Theme
God gives us the greatest gift of all: Love.

Thought for the Day
Why do we spend our lives running away from the One who loves us most?

Sermon Summary
Blockbuster movies are making millions on our fears that one day computers will revolt and take over the world. What would we do if that happens? How do we handle it when we have trouble controlling a new puppy or kitten? How do we handle it when our children head into the teen years and begin to rebel? How did God handle it when the southern kingdom of Judah revolted? We have the choice to revolt against God or to follow Jesus as our Lord and Savior. The choice is ours.

Call to Worship

We have come today to give our thanks and adoration to the One who called us before the world was made, who knew the abilities and talents we would have while we were still being knit together in our mother's womb, and who knows every hair on our head. Come let us worship the God who loves us and sent his son Jesus, the Christ.

Pastoral Prayer

God of Love, we praise your name for all the ways you have been there for us, the times we clearly see your hand working in our lives and for the times we have no idea, as the footprint poem reminds us that you carry us. Today we come before you asking you to be a part of our lives. We bring our joys and our sorrows before you knowing that no matter what happens in life you are always there for us, loving us and guiding us in the right path. You do not promise that life will be easy or even fair, but you do promise that you will always be there and that we will be abundantly blessed so that our cup will overflow with your love. Open our hearts, our minds, our souls, our spirit, our lives to be blessed by you. We give our relationships, our finances, our dreams, our hopes, our failures, our disappointments, our hurts, our loves, our expectations, our careers, our future to you. Teach us to love in Jesus' name. Amen.

Prayer of Confession

One: God has taken God's place in the divine council.
All: God judges how well we share God's love.
One: God requires us to give justice to the weak and to the orphan.
All: God wants us to rescue the weak and the needy.
One: And to deliver them from the hand of the wicked.
All: Forgive us, God, when we do not share your love, when we do not love others as ourselves. Forgive us and empower us to share your love with all we meet. Amen.

Prayer of Dedication of Gifts and Self

God of Love, thank you for the many ways you show your love to us. Thank you for the way you provide for us. Thank you for the many bless-

ings you have given us, and now help us to bless others in your name.
Take these gifts we now give back to you in love, our gifts of time, talent,
and treasures, and use them to your glory. In Jesus' name we pray. Amen.

Hymn of the Day
Faith of Our Fathers

The text of this well-loved hymn is written by Frederick William Faber and
first appears in his collection *Jesus and Mary* (1849). It was written shortly
after Faber's conversion to the Roman Catholic faith. Due to the distinctly
male language of the original text, subsequent hymnals worked to make it
more inclusive. Some change the word "father" to "mother" in additional
verses. In the *New Century Hymnal* (1995) there is a complete reworking
of the text to "Faith of the Martyrs." In *Voices United* (1997) the reworked
text includes mothers, sisters, and brothers in a revision that is closer to
the original. There are sufficient choices for this great text to satisfy all
understandings of inclusivity. The unifying feature for all translations is the
tune St. Catherine, written by Roman Catholic organist Henri Friedrich
Hemy. This is a strong tune that is an ideal companion to the text.

Children's Time: An Angry Prophet

Ask the children if they ever get angry. What might be some situations?
Do they always mean it? Are they able to apologize afterward? What does
that feel like?

The Bible tells a story about the prophet Isaiah. He had noticed that
people did not do what God wanted, even though God had always taken
care of them. He was angry!

So Isaiah made up a story. He said, "There was a vineyard that the
owner cared for. He cleared it and weeded it and watered it. And do you
know what the vineyard did? It produced sour grapes. So, do you know
what I'm going to do? I'm going to break the hedge and the fence, let the
thing get trampled down. I don't care about it anymore. I'll let the weeds
take it over. God deserves better."

Do you think the prophet meant it? Probably not. But it was a way of
expressing how angry he felt. I wonder what the people did in response?

Prayer: Forgiving God, there are times when we get angry. When we
do, help us find ways to deal with it. Help us become more loving
again. Amen.

33

The Sermon: The Gift of Love
Scripture: Isaiah 5:1-7
(For sermon materials on Hebrews 11:29—12:2, see the March/April 2010 issue of *The Clergy Journal*; for sermon materials on Luke 12:49-56, see the May/June 2010 planning issue of *The Clergy Journal*.)

Computers are wonderful machines that aid humans in so many areas it is hard to keep up with how fast they are developing. One rule of thumb that is generally true is that computers are only following the commands and data that the human programmer puts in; data in, data out. Parents have sometimes kidded that they wish they could program their children as well as some computers can be programmed. Just think: parents wouldn't have to fight to get the children out of bed, or to clean their rooms, or to go to school, or to do their homework, or to brush their teeth, or to go to bed on time. They would have everything programmed in so the children would just do it.

Of course one of the main fears about computers is that someday they will go beyond "data in, data out" and become sentient and begin to think for themselves and maybe think they could run the earth a whole lot better than we humans can. The movie industry has been making a lot of money off of movies like *The Matrix, The Terminator, Battlestar Galactica, Eagle Eye,* and *I, Robot* where rogue robots become sentient and try to take over the world! What would you do if your computer suddenly decided to take over your house? Your bank account? Your car? Your calendar? Your life? Or maybe to put this a little more realistically (at least for now), what do you do when your computer has a virus? Do you destroy it or do you try and save it first? Do you try and remove the virus, clean up the hard drive, and save as many good programs as you can? At what point do you make the decision that it is at the point of no return and it is better to ditch the computer rather than save it?

Let's take this to a more personal level. What if you were given a puppy or a kitten who you had trained to follow your every command and who, until a little while ago, had done just that. All of the sudden you come home and your pet has strewn the trash all over you house, left its mark in various rooms, ripped your furniture and put holes in your screen door, and has even tried to bite you. What now? What do you do? Do you try to save your pet? Do you try to retrain your pet? At what point do you make the decision that there is nothing more you can do, so you try to give your pet away or think about putting your pet to sleep?

Or what if it were your children? I love the story in the Bible about the father who asked his son to go work in the vineyard and the son answered ala Bart Simpson, "Not!" But later he went and worked in the vineyard just like his father asked (Matthew 21:28-31). Since his first son told him "not," the father went to his second son and asked him to go work in the vineyard and he said, "sure Dad," but he never went. So which one did the will of the father?

What do you do when your kids do not want to get up when you call them, or refuse to clean their room or do their homework? What do you do when they specifically disobey you? Do you let them get away with it? At what point do you begin to discipline them to teach them the responsibilities they have to begin to take for their own lives? What do you do to get their attention that they are on the wrong track in life and need to change their behavior? Does there come a point where you need to ask your children to leave? Do you call in *SuperNanny*? What if you are *SuperNanny* and it is your kids?

God has sent the prophets over and over again to the southern kingdom of Judah to warn the people that their behavior is unacceptable, but they refuse to listen. God chose Abraham, raised up Moses, led them through the wilderness, and provided judges and kings to show them the right way, but still they refuse to follow. Instead of loving their neighbor as themselves they are taking advantage of their neighbor every chance they get. They don't care for the widow, the orphan, the foreigner; instead they exploit them for all they're worth. What's a parent to do?

God has been clear from the very beginning that humans will be held responsible for their behavior. Adam and Eve could stay in the Garden of Eden forever IF they followed God's wishes. The 12 tribes of Israel could stay in the Promised Land forever IF they followed God's way. The southern kingdom of Judah would be fine and not have to worry about its enemies IF they followed God's will.

The choice is ours today. There is a way that brings life and a way that brings death. Jesus has given us the opportunity to choose life, to choose to love God, to choose to love our neighbor as ourselves, to choose to live God's law of love. The consequences are severe. To live without love is a lonely heart hardening way to go. To live a life of love is to be open to the Spirit of God and an adventure that is beyond description. The choice is yours. Are you ready to give your life to Christ? All of it and learn to love? If so, pray this prayer with me:

35

Dear God, I am tired of trying to live life on my own. I am tired of being angry and lonely and not knowing who I can trust with my life. Lord, I open my heart to you. Come into my heart, Lord Jesus. Forgive me of my sins, of all that I have done wrong, of all the things that I have done that have hurt others, hurt God, and hurt myself. Wash me clean, Lord, and put your Spirit in my heart. Today with your help I make the commitment to follow you for the rest of my life. Guide me, teach me how to love. All this I pray in Jesus' name. Amen.

– Deborah Spink Winters

Hymns
Opening Hymn
Christ Is Made the Sure Foundation
Lord, I Want to Be a Christian
Sermon Hymn
As Man and Woman We Were Made
We Plant a Grain of Mustard Seed
Closing Hymn
Bind Us Together
I Was There to Hear Your Borning Cry

August 22, 2010

13th Sunday after Pentecost (Proper 16 [21])
RC/Pres: 21st Sunday in Ordinary Time

Lessons (See p. 10 for guidelines)

Semi-continuous (SC)	Complementary (C)	Roman Catholic (RC)
Jer 1:4-10	Isa 58:9b-14	Isa 66:18-21
Ps 71:1-6	Ps 103:1-8	Ps 117:1-2
Heb 12:18-29	Heb 12:18-29	Heb 12:5-7, 11-13
Lk 13:10-17	Lk 13:10-17	Lk 13:22-30

Speaker's Introduction for the Lessons
Lesson 1
Jeremiah 1:4-10 (SC)

Jeremiah is called by God at a young age to minister to the southern kingdom of Judah. Jeremiah's ministry will start with destruction and uprooting before rebuilding and planting can take place.

Isaiah 58:9b-14 (C)

Isaiah reminds his congregation that if they honor the Sabbath, God will honor them.

Isaiah 66:18-21 (RC)

God tells Isaiah the time is coming when God will gather all nations and tongues. As a sign that this will take place, the nations will see all the tribes of Israel returning to Jerusalem.

Lesson 2
Psalm 71:1-6 (SC)

The psalmist, while facing troubles in life, remembers how God has always been the psalmist's rock and fortress and asks God once again to help with present-day trials and tribulations.

Psalm 103:1-8 (C)

The psalmist praises God for the ways God has forgiven, healed, redeemed, satisfied, and renewed the psalmist. God can do the same for each of us.

Lesson 3
Hebrews 12:18-29 (SC/C)
The writer contrasts God's appearance at Mount Sinai to Moses and the celebration at Mount Zion, the city of the living God.

Hebrews 12:5-7, 11-13 (RC)
Just as parents discipline their children to teach them the difference between right and wrong, so God disciplines all who follow so they might yield the fruit of peaceful righteousness to the glory of God.

Gospel
Luke 13:10-17 (SC/C)
Jesus uses the Sabbath to glorify God and heal the woman with the crippled spirit, much to the chagrin of the religious leaders of Jesus' day.

Luke 13:22-30 (RC)
Jesus warns that not everyone will enter into the household of God, and for those who do, it is probably not in the order you expect!

Theme
Stop giving God excuses and just say YES!

Thought for the Day
I attribute my success to this – I never gave or took any excuse.

– Florence Nightingale

Sermon Summary
We all give excuses in life. Our ancestors in faith had excuses too. Moses, Gideon, and Jonah tried to give excuses to God, yet, when each said "yes" to God, their lives would never be the same. The same is true when we say "YES!" to God.

Call to Worship
All: Praise the LORD, all you nations!
One: Extol him, all you peoples!
All: For great is his steadfast love toward us,
One: And the faithfulness of the LORD endures forever.
All: Come let us praise the LORD!

– Adapted from Psalm 117

Pastoral Prayer

God of our Ancestors who first doubted and questioned your existence, who wondered if you would keep your word while they found excuse after excuse not to keep theirs, thank you for always being there for them and for us. We bring you today our corporate concerns and ask your guidance for our world leaders, our president and our nation, our community and neighborhoods, and our church. We also bring before you our personal concerns for our families, our careers, our health and well-being, our homes, our finances, and our futures. Thank you for being there yesterday, today, and tomorrow. You are the rock, the foundation upon which we build our faith in this world and in the next. Amen.

Prayer of Confession

Great Omnipotent God, we are a people of excuses! We are too tired or too busy or too poor or too lazy to take your Word seriously in our life. Like Moses, Gideon, and Jonah we have our excuses as to why we cannot follow your will in our lives or just spend some time with you in prayer. Forgive us God. Help us to understand that all our excuses just keep us from your love and the greatest adventure of our life – following you. Amen.

Prayer of Dedication of Gifts and Self

Omniscient God, you know we tend to be people of excuses. Help us this day to take responsibility for sharing your love with all we meet. Bless these gifts as a symbol of the love we share with you and with the world. Amen.

Hymn of the Day
Lead On, O King Eternal/Lead On, O Cloud of Presence

First sung in 1888 by the graduating class of Andover Theological Seminary, this text by Ernest Shurtleff appears to be a song of battle. This was not the intent. Military imagery is used to parallel the everyday struggles found in all our lives. Contemporary hymn writer and theologian Ruth Duck reworked the original text into a remarkable hymn emphasizing God's presence rather than God's military might. There is a strong use of imagery, which connects to the biblical references in Numbers 9. LANCASHIRE was composed by Henry Smart in 1835 in celebration of the 300th anniversary of the Protestant Reformation. It is a strong tune that matches either text.

Children's Time: Any Age Will Do

Ask the children if they can define a prophet. If they need prompting, you can suggest that often people think of old men with beards. Do you think those are the only people who are prophets? No – the Bible tells us that women were prophets too. There are also young prophets.

What does a prophet do? *(They speak for God. If children mention something such as "predict the future" you might move them toward understanding that prophets really tell how they think things will go if the people do not change.)*

Once a young boy named Jeremiah heard God calling him to be a prophet. He wasn't very excited about the idea. Jeremiah knew that some people got very angry with prophets. They didn't like it when a prophet told them how they needed to change their lives. So Jeremiah said, "But God, I'm too young. I can't do it."

"Don't be silly," God said. "I'll be right there with you, every step of the way. I'll help you find the right words to say and – when people are mean to you – I'll help you stand tall."

So Jeremiah said "Yes." What would you say if God asked you to be a prophet?

Prayer: Loving God, you have words that people need to hear. Help us to be your prophets, and tell your message to others. Amen.

The Sermon: No Excuse Sunday
Scripture: Jeremiah 1:4-10

(For sermon materials on Hebrews 12:18-29, see the March/April 2010 issue of *The Clergy Journal*; for sermon materials on Luke 13:10-17, see the May/June 2010 planning issue of *The Clergy Journal*.)

I was wondering if you had heard about the "No Excuse Sundays" some churches are having? They send a letter to their congregation that reads something like this:

- To make it possible for everyone to attend church next Sunday, we are going to have a special "No Excuse Sunday."
- Cots will be placed in the foyer for those who say, "Sunday is my only day to sleep in."
- There will be a special section with lounge chairs for those who feel that our pews are too hard.

- Eye drops will be available for those with tired eyes from watching T.V. late Saturday night.
- We will have steel helmets for those who say, "The roof would cave in if I ever came to church."
- Blankets will be furnished for those who think the church is too cold, and fans will be running for those who say it is too hot.
- Score cards will be available for those who wish to list the hypocrites present.
- Relatives and friends will be in attendance for those who can't go to church and cook dinner too.
- We will distribute "Stamp Out Stewardship" buttons for those who feel that church is always asking for money.
- One section will be devoted to trees and grass for those who like to seek God in nature.
- Doctors and nurses will be in attendance for those who plan to be sick on Sunday.
- The sanctuary will be decorated with both Christmas poinsettias and Easter lilies for those who never have seen the church without them.
- We will provide hearing aids for those who can't hear the preacher and cotton for those who say the preacher is too loud.

(Author Unknown)

What's your excuse? Everyone has at least one. Even our ancestors in the faith had their excuses. Moses kept coming up with excuse after excuse why he couldn't follow what God was asking him to do. First he asked God, "Who am I that I should go to Pharaoh?" (Exodus 3:11). Then Moses wanted to know what to say when the Israelites asked him what the name of the God who sent him was (Exodus 3:13). Then Moses raised the concern, "But suppose they do not believe me or listen to me?" (Exodus 4:1). Then Moses protested that he was the wrong man for the job because he was slow of speech (Exodus 4:10). Lastly in exasperation Moses blurts out, "O my Lord, please send someone else!" (Exodus 4:13).

When the angel of the Lord visited Gideon to commission him to deliver Israel from the hand of the Midianites, Gideon protested, "But sir, how can I deliver Israel? My clan is the weakest in Manasseh, and I am the least in my family" (Judges 6:13). Gideon not only asked for a sign to make sure what he is hearing was from God, but he actually put God to the test to see if God was going to keep God's word. Gideon did what has come to be called the "fleece test." He placed a fleece of wool on the ground and told God if in the morning there was dew on the fleece but not on the floor, he would know God would come through. The next day the fleece was wet and the floor was dry, but that wasn't enough for Gideon. Gideon put God to the test one more time (maybe as a move to try and get out of it altogether?) and asked this time for God to have the fleece be dry and the floor to be covered in dew, and of course God did just that (Judges 6:36-40).

And then there is Jonah who, when God asked Jonah to go preach to Nineveh, Jonah ran in the opposite direction to try and get out of it. He ended up getting swallowed by a big fish before realizing it was just plain easier to do God's will.

Here Jeremiah is trying to tell God he is too young to do God's bidding, and I really can't blame him. After all, look at the ministry God is calling him to, a ministry that will start with destruction, plucking up and pulling down long before Jeremiah will get the chance to build and to plant.

What's your excuse? What excuse do you give instead of following God with your life: Too old? Too tired? Too poor? Too busy? Too weak? Too scared? Too bashful? Too depressed? Too angry? Too overwhelmed? Too (fill in the blank)? *(If possible show the Nike excuses commercial video at http://www.youtube.com/watch?v=obdd31Q9PqA.)*

Ephesians 1:4 tells us that God chose us in Christ before the foundation of the world. Jeremiah knew he was called before he was even formed in the womb. So are you and I. God has a purpose and a plan for each of us. It is a plan that when we say "yes" to God, Jesus promises he will give us an abundant life here and now and into all eternity. It is the premise for the bestselling book *The Purpose Driven Life: What on Earth Am I Here For?* by Rick Warren. Rick asserts that unless you understand you were made by God and for God, life will never make sense.

When Moses finally said "yes" to God, Moses helped to form the 12 disorganized tribes into the nation of Israel. Gideon said "yes" to God and defeated the Midianites. Jonah, after a ride in the belly of a large fish, was so effective in his preaching that the whole city of Nineveh repented. Jeremiah helped guide the southern kingdom of Judah through their exile in Babylon and gave them the vision of a new covenant God would write on their hearts and ours.

What is God calling you to do? What is the excuse you are letting stop you from saying "yes" to God? Do you not trust God? Do you need to have a sign like Gideon, or for your brother to walk along with you like Moses, or a ride in a belly of a large fish like Jonah, or can you take that first step and begin to follow God's word in your life? As Proverbs teaches us, "Trust in the Lord with all your heart, and do not rely on your own insight. In all your ways acknowledge him, and he will make straight your paths" (Proverbs 3:5-6).

Take God at God's word and see what happens. No more excuses; just say "yes" to God and the life God has called you to from before you were born. You will be saying "yes" to what will prove to be the greatest adventure of your life! Amen.

– Deborah Spink Winters

Hymns
Opening Hymn
I Heard the Voice of Jesus Say
Awake, O Sleeper
Sermon Hymn
Come, O Fount of Every Blessing
Day By Day (Godspell)
Closing Hymn
I Am Yours, O Lord
More Love to You, O Christ

August 29, 2010

14th Sunday after Pentecost (Proper 17 [22])
RC/Pres: 22nd Sunday in Ordinary Time

Lessons (See p. 10 for guidelines)

Semi-continuous (SC)	Complementary (C)	Roman Catholic (RC)
Jer 2:4-13	Sir 10:12-18 or Prov 25:6-7	Sir 3:17-18, 20, 28-29
Ps 81:1, 10-16	Ps 112	Ps 68:4-5, 6-7, 10-11
Heb 13:1-8, 15-16	Heb 13:1-8, 15-16	Heb 12:18-19, 22-24
Lk 14:1, 7-14	Lk 14:1, 7-14	Lk 14:1, 7-14

Speaker's Introduction for the Lessons
Lesson 1
Jeremiah 2:4-13 (SC)
God through Jeremiah wonders aloud why the children of Israel have rejected God. After all God has done for them, why did they choose to follow other gods that have no power? Why do we?

Sirach 10:12-18 (C)
Proverbs reminds us that pride goes before a fall and Sirach teaches that pride was not created for human beings, but it starts when we forsake God.

Sirach 3:17-18, 20, 28-29 (RC)
Sirach weighs the need for human beings to humble themselves rather than let the root of pride take hold.

Lesson 2
Psalm 81:1, 10-16 (SC)
God honors our choices in life, whether it is to follow God and seek God's blessings or to reject God and take life as it comes.

Psalm 112 (C)
The psalmist shows that the real key to happiness is found in following God's commandments.

Lesson 3
Hebrews 13:1-8, 15-16 (SC/C)
Hebrews outlines what a community who follows Jesus Christ and lives the law of love looks like.
Hebrews 12:18-19, 22-24 (RC)
Hebrews describes what Mount Zion, the heavenly city of Jerusalem, is like.

Gospel
Luke 14:1, 7-14 (SC/C/RC)
Jesus teaches a story about the difference between someone who is willing to humble themselves and someone who is full of pride. Which are you in this story?

Theme
We are to grow beyond the "honeymoon stage" into a mature relationship of love.

Thought for the Day
Love is a choice you make from moment to moment.

– Barbara DeAngelis

Sermon Summary
All relationships go through the "honeymoon stage," even our relationship with God. Are we willing to allow our relationships to mature and work on the problem areas of our lives, or will we just become a "fat little baby"?

Call to Worship
One: Sing to God, sing praises to God's holy name;
All: Lift up a song to God who rides upon the clouds.
One: A parent to orphans and protector of widows.
All: A provider for the homeless and an advocate for the afflicted.
One: A refuge for those in need.
All: Let us tell the world of the mighty deeds our God has done and continues in us today!

– Adapted from Psalm 68

Pastoral Prayer

Lover of my soul, it is you who first loved us. You reached out through your son, Jesus. You invited us to come into a relationship with you. Help us to trust you with who we are and who we can become, to be willing to take you at your word. We ask your guidance and healing in our relationships with others and in our spiritual lives with you. Hear our personal prayers that we now raise to you in silence *(a time of silent prayer)*. Thank you for hearing our prayers and for answering them. Give us the courage to live the answers we hear, and help us to continue to grow in love with you far beyond the "honeymoon stage." Amen.

Prayer of Confession

Jesus summed up the whole law into two, reminding us that we should love God and love our neighbor as we love ourselves. Forgive us, God, when we love ourselves more than others and more than you. Forgive us when we only look out for ourselves or for our loved ones and neglect to see the need around us. Help us to be willing to get involved, to be willing to share your love with every person you place in our path. Amen.

Prayer of Dedication of Gifts and Self

Creator God, thank you for the gift of life and for the gift of love you so freely give us. Please accept these gifts of love we give back to you. Use us and these gifts to make our church, our community, our nation, and our world a place that reflects your love and your kingdom here on earth. Amen.

Hymn of the Day
What Does the Lord Require of You?

This simple canon was written by contemporary singer and songwriter Jim Strathdee. This song is based upon Micah 6:6-8; the first stanza asks the question and stanzas two and three provide the answers. There are two ways of presenting this song, each requiring that you divide your singers into three groups. The first way is the simplest to organize – teach the whole song to everyone and then sing it as a round. The second needs a bit more organization; however, it is often simpler for untrained singers to learn. Assign each stanza to one group and get them to sing only their stanza, not the whole song. With this method start with the group singing stanza 1 and let them sing their part alone. The second time through add stanza 2 and then stanza 3 the third time through. Once you have everyone singing, continue for a number of times allowing people to experience the joy of singing in harmony.

Children's Time: Living Water

(Preparation: Bring a basin, a pitcher of water, and some small paper cups – enough for all the children. Also, bring three glasses: one clean, one obviously dirty, and a plastic or paper one that has a leak.)

Talk to the children about being thirsty. Invite them to imagine they are really thirsty. Pour some water into each of the three cups – do it over the basin so the water does not drip on the floor.

Ask the children which one they might like to drink from. Allow all responses, and invite them to express why they made their choices.

Talk a bit about how the prophet Jeremiah used things like this to show how different it is when we live the way God wants, and when we don't. It's kind of like the difference between dirty water and clean water. *(Pour some clean water into the extra cups and distribute to the children.)*

Prayer: Thank you, God, for the wonderful water we have to drink, and wash with, and bathe in. Thank you, too, for prophets who help tell your word. Amen.

The Sermon: Beyond the Honeymoon Stage
Scripture: Jeremiah 2:4-13

(For sermon materials on Hebrews 13:1-8, 15-16, see the March/April 2010 issue of *The Clergy Journal*; for sermon materials on Luke 14:1, 7-14, see the May/June 2010 planning issue of *The Clergy Journal*.)

When couples get married and after they come home from their honeymoon, if they are affectionate with each other in public, you will often hear people kid them that they are still in their "honeymoon stage." I was curious as to what the definition of a "honeymoon stage" was and exactly how long it lasted. This is what I found out at marriagefriendlytherapists.com:

> The 'honeymoon' stage of newlyweds or in early courtship is a wonderful time during the relationship when we try to present our best selves to new lovers whom we tend to idealize and who idealize us. Serious relational conflict is avoided. This phase is not always present in every relationship 100% of the time, but it is present often.

This is an important developmental time for relationships and it typically lasts around 6 months. During the first stages of marriage, we often see it last 6 months – two years, seven years is a long honeymoon phase.

This honeymoon stage occurs in most relationships, between a married couple, a new class and its teacher, an employee and a new job, new friendships, a church and its new pastor, etc. We idealize each other and try to be perfectly what that other person idealizes, but we can only do it for so long, six months to two years being the norm and for some they can idealize each other as long as seven years. After that, as hard as we try we begin to let our hair down and who we really are begins to shine through and is experienced sometimes with shock and hurt by the other person in the relationship. It is how any relationship handles this adjustment, this realization that the other is not the idealized "perfect" person we thought they were, that is the test of whether the relationship will grow and mature so real intimacy can take place.

This "honeymoon stage" can even take place in our relationship with God.

In our scripture lesson today God is wondering aloud through Jeremiah why the children of Israel have left him and gone after other gods. Is the honeymoon stage over in their relationship? God reminds the southern kingdom of Judah and the northern kingdom of Israel all they have gone through together: how God led them out of the land of Egypt where they were slaves, through the wilderness where they learned to trust and rely on God for everything from their safety to the water they drank and their daily meals of manna and quail, until they were finally ready to enter into the Promised Land. It was while in this land of plenty, in this Promised Land full of good things, that the people of Israel stopped following God and started following other gods who had no power whatsoever.

Maybe that was what they were drawn to, gods who would not require anything of them, gods who would let them behave however they wanted, who didn't care if they took advantage of the disadvantaged in their society, the widow, the orphan, the foreigner, the poor and needy for their own greed, to line their own pockets. They did not want to be in relationship with a God who was going to challenge them to grow and mature in their faith. They'd prefer a wood puppet made out of their own hands which they could control and tell what to do, rather than a healthy mature loving relationship.

And it was not just the people who left God; it was also the priests and the rulers and the prophets who transgressed. Can you think of priests, rulers, or politicians of our day who have transgressed and not followed God in their public or private lives? People who are supposed to be leaders in our society who, rather than following God with their lives and reaching out to help others, would rather do only what is best for themselves? Why do we sometimes turn away from God? Why would we not want to go beyond that "honeymoon stage" to begin to really address the issues in our lives that need to be worked on, that need to be in-line with the love God wants so badly for us and for all of our relationships?

Amy Grant sings about a person who really does not want to grow in Christ. This is someone who is a baby in the faith, who does not want to grow out of the honeymoon stage and really face the things in his life that will enable him to grow into mature adulthood and a full relationship with his Lord and Savior. Maybe you are familiar with the words:

Amy Grant, *Fat Baby*

I know a man,	His spiritual tummy,
Maybe you know him, too.	It can't take too much.
You never can tell,	One day a week,
He might even be you.	He gets his spiritual lunch…
He knelt at the altar	*Chorus:*
And that was the end.	He's just a fat little baby.
He's saved and that's all	He wants his bottle
That matters to him.	And he don't mean maybe…

The song goes on to say, among other things, that the fat baby's daily devotions are stuck in the mud. And while his Bible is the "biggest King James you've ever seen," he will never grow in his faith.

We can be a fat little baby in our faith and try for as long as possible to stay in the "honeymoon stage" in our relationship with God and in our faith walk. Or we can begin to be honest about who we are in our walk with Jesus and the things we need to begin to work on to be in a closer walk with Jesus, in a more intimate and mature relationship that knows now bounds throughout all eternity. The choice is yours. Amen.

– Deborah Spink Winters

Hymns
Opening Hymn
How Firm a Foundation
By Gracious Powers
Sermon Hymn
O Jesus, I Have Promised
I Would Be True
Closing Hymn
Lord, Make Me More Holy
If You But Trust in God to Guide You

September 5, 2010

15th Sunday after Pentecost (Proper 18 [23])
RC/Pres: 23rd Sunday in Ordinary Time

Lessons (See p. 10 for guidelines)

Semi-continuous (SC)	Complementary (C)	Roman Catholic (RC)
Jer 18:1-11	Deut 30:15-20	Wis 9:13-18
Ps 139:1-6, 13-18	Ps 1	Ps 90:3-6, 12-17
Philem 1-21	Philem 1-21	Philem 9-10, 12-17
Lk 14:25-33	Lk 14:25-33	Lk 14:25-33

Speaker's Introduction for the Lessons
Lesson 1
Jeremiah 18:1-11 (SC)
It's just clay. A lump of clay. But when a prophet walks down the potter's alley it suddenly becomes clear what it means for a lump of clay – and for us – to be transformed!

Deuteronomy 30:15-20 (C)
Robert Frost talked about a road that converged in a wood, and how the road less traveled made all the difference. Moses talks about a road less traveled too.

Wisdom 9:13-18 (RC)
The more we know about this universe, each other, and ourselves, the more we know we don't know. That was ancient wisdom. It's modern wisdom too.

Lesson 2
Psalm 139:1-6, 13-18 (SC)
The psalmist is awed by the depth of God's knowledge about us. This is nothing new to God, but it's great when we figure it out.

Psalm 1 (C)
Jewish sages spoke of The Two Ways – the way of life and the way of death. In the very first song in the Psalter these two ways are graphically illustrated.

Lesson 3
Philemon 1-21 (SC/C); 9-10, 12-17 (RC)
Slavery was an economic, not a racial, proposition in the Roman Empire – but it was still vile. The escaped slave Onesimus could be executed when he returns to his master Philemon, yet Paul insists he go back.

Gospel
Luke 14:25-33 (SC/C/RC)
Jesus says we'd be foolish to build a house or go to war without first counting the cost. We'd be just as foolish if we become disciples without first knowing about the cross.

Theme
Christian discipleship includes the whole package – including mutual accountability and servanthood.

Thought for the Day
Praise God. We don't *have* to serve each other. We *get* to.

Sermon Summary
When his slave Onesimus escaped, Philemon discovered he may not have fully counted the cost of what it would take to be a Christian disciple. He was the head of a household, and the head of a house church. He must exchange lordship over that household for servant ministry.

Call to Worship
One: O God, you have searched me and known me.
All: God, I praise you, for I am fearfully and wonderfully made.
One: You know when I sit down and when I rise up; you discern my thoughts from far away.
All: Even before a word is on my tongue, O Lord, you know it completely.
One: How weighty to me are your thoughts, O God! How vast is the sum of them! I try to count them – they are more than the sand; I come to the end – I am still with you.
All: God, I praise you, for I am fearfully and wonderfully made.
– Based on Psalm 139:1-6, 13-18

51

Pastoral Prayer

Caring God, who knows us better than we know ourselves, whose steadfast love is eternal and abiding, we lift up upon your altar the concerns, the joys, our requests for our daily bread, and petitions for forgiveness, as we seek your wisdom in ministry towards each other and to your suffering world. Abide with us, guide us, side with us against the adversity that afflicts us. May our daily bread include a portion for the entire world, so that we will not be satisfied until all experience your care and love. Our prayer for healing is that all might share in it. We praise you, God, because you are God. Bless us this day. Amen.

Prayer of Confession

God of gifts, God of giving, you have granted us a home within your congregation, a refuge, a shelter against the storms of life. There are no words to describe the wonder, the majesty of this gift. We sit in the company of saints. Yet we often ignore the opportunities for service, for prayer, for fellowship with each other. We create hierarchies. We insist on our rights, instead of bending a knee to wash the feet of the saints in our midst. Forgive us, heal us, inspire us, that we may receive each other with the same grace and love which you have extended to us. These things we pray in the name of the suffering servant, Jesus Christ our Savior. Amen.

Prayer of Dedication of Gifts and Self

Creating God, you are the potter, we are the clay. May our entire lives, from our rising to our sleeping, all that we do, and all that we give, be worthy enough that you might throw the clay of our days onto your wheel and craft a thing of beauty for the work of your kingdom. Amen.

– Adapted from Jeremiah 18:1-11

Hymn of the Day
The Servant Song

This hymn, composed by Richard Gillard, was first published in *Songs of the Kingdom* (1977). It was arranged by American arranger, composer, and editor Betty Pulkingham. The number and order of stanzas of this song vary according to the hymnal source; however, the intent and meaning are very clear. Do not sing this song too quickly; a walking pace is best, thinking two beats per measure, not four. Use of soloists on some stanzas will enhance the presentation. Simple dance movements, expressing the text, can make a worshipful addition to the singing of this hymn. It was originally composed for unison singing with guitar accompaniment, so care should be given when using organ or piano. Do not re-articulate the repeated notes; rather, make the accompaniment more singing.

Children's Time: Friends

Ask the children questions about their friends. What do they like about their friends? Are there things that their friends do that they don't like? What makes someone a friend? You might talk about some of your own friends and what you like about them.

Wonder with the children about the experience of meeting someone and not liking them at first, but later becoming good friends. Perhaps you have a specific experience you can share, or you might invite the children to share something.

Talk about how one of our Bible readings today is from a man named Paul, and he's writing about his friend Onesimus. Onesimus used to be a slave, and he belonged to a man called Philemon. Paul is writing to Philemon and asking him to treat Onesimus not as a slave, but as a friend. Wonder with the children about how Philemon might have thought about Paul's suggestion. It may have been hard for him at first, but Paul reminds him that this is what a follower of Jesus should do.

Jesus invites us to see people in new ways; as followers of Jesus, we try to see everyone as a friend.

Prayer: Loving God, Jesus said that we were his friends. Help us to love others – to reach out and make other people our friends. Amen.

The Sermon: Do I Gotta?
Scripture: Philemon 1-21

(For sermon materials on Luke 14:25-33, see the March/April 2010 issue of *The Clergy Journal*; for sermon materials on Jeremiah 18:1-11, see the May/June 2010 planning issue of *The Clergy Journal*.)

Tossing and turning, struggling to get comfortable, how many of us know what it is to have a sleepless night? The harder we try to sleep, the less likely it becomes. One thing seems certain: We can't force sleep.

Sleep experts often suggest certain strategies. Don't fight it. Don't look at a clock. Get up and read a book. Quit trying so hard: after all, you don't *have* to sleep, but you do *get* to rest.

I wonder how much sleep Philemon lost after hearing what Paul had to say in today's scripture text. The details aren't clear how this escaped slave, perhaps having heard Paul preach at Philemon's house church, had escaped his life of slavery and had sought out and ministered to Paul in prison.

In Paul's time, prison was not a place of punishment, but where you waited for trial. Your punishment, if you were convicted, was no incarceration, but physical – a beating, torture, or death in any number of awful ways. Prisoners depended on family or friends for food and medical care. Paul, a traveler, had few options – until an escaped slave came to take care of him.

In the Roman Empire slavery was not based on race. There was no assumption that certain groups of people were inferior and therefore meant to be slaves. It was an economic condition. People became slaves because they were born into the condition or were captured in war or mired in debt. Slaves might engage in backbreaking drudgery, or they might be the powerful managers of their owners' fortunes – but that didn't change the fact that they were slaves and did not control their lives. No matter how well-treated, slaves wanted more for their lives.

But Paul, recognizing there is nothing he could do to change the social fabric of the Roman Empire, seems to try a risky gambit. Based on the assumption that Onesimus is private property, Paul sends him back to his owner, who has the right to torture or kill him. Paul is fulfilling the letter of the law. But he makes it clear to Philemon, who he describes in flattering fashion as "our dear friend and co-worker" (Philemon 1), that his appeal on behalf of Onesimus will be on the basis of love, and not as a command – though he hints that he could easily give such a command.

This Onesimus, Paul tells him, has become his son. His name meant 'useful' but as an escaped slave he is useless. He could become useful again. Indeed, he could become, if Philemon allows, a brother in Christ.

But – and here one can almost hear the soundtrack of violins playing "Hearts and Flowers" – if the loss is too much for Philemon to bear, Paul is willing, despite the fact that he is imprisoned, to pay him for what he lost.

And if that weren't enough to make Philemon lose sleep, what made it worse is that everyone knows what Paul said.

There's nothing private about this letter. It's addressed not only to Philemon but also "to Apphia our sister, to Archippus our fellow soldier, and to the church in your house . . . " Timothy is co-author. And greetings come from Epaphras, also imprisoned for the gospel, as well as Mark, Aristarchus, Demas, and Luke (cf. Philemon 1, 2, 23, 24). For those of you keeping score, that includes two of the four evangelists.

Philemon was the head of a Roman household that was part of the Ephesian church. That household was not just a family structure. It was an economic island. The *paterfamilias*, in this case Philemon, was the head of a group of what could be a hundred people or more, including family, friends, artisans, poets, philosophers, servants, and slaves. The *materfamilias*, usually the wife, ran much of the household, especially the economic portion. Everyone was interconnected and was accountable and responsible for the welfare of all.

Christian congregations in the first century seem to have consisted of several households (there were at least four in Corinth), each independent, but together forming a larger body. In many ways the household of God resembled the structure of the household of Rome. Paul couldn't change the household structure. But in the name of Jesus Christ he was attempting to change the way it worked. Onesimus might have been a slave – but he is also now a brother.

We have to count the cost when we set out to be a disciple. There may be consequences. Jesus himself said that becoming a disciple might mean taking up your cross.

Philemon may not have fully counted the cost of what it would take to be a Christian disciple. Even though he was the *paterfamilias* of a Roman household, he was also a part of the household of God. That meant he must exchange lordship over that household for servant ministry. So what happened? We can't be sure, but the fact that this letter made it into scripture means it is likely that Philemon did the right thing. There is a tradition that comes down from the historian Eusebius, writing four centuries after the fact, that Onesimus became an overseer (the word is sometimes translated bishop) of the Ephesian congregation.

What is certain is that the early church had many slaves among its members, and that because of the gospel, relationships were transformed. In a third century letter Askleopios, who is a Christian, writes to master Hierakammos, "chief to the Strategus" but also a fellow believer. Askleopios, "helper of the overseer," if he is not actually a slave, can only be a step above as a hired hand. Nevertheless, he seems to be in charge of his fields and a trusted partner. In this personal letter that reports on the price their wine is fetching in the marketplace, he greets Hierakammos as "Lord brother" and recalls a conversation they had when they had eaten breakfast together. The legal structure of the Roman Empire may have seemed impervious to change, but the new relationships that follow when we have been transformed in Christ make all that irrelevant.

We live in a society that *can* be changed. And our lives are even more transparent than Philemon's, who discovered that thanks to Paul everyone knows his business. In that light it's important to remember that we don't *have* to treat everyone differently because of the presence of Christ in our lives.

We *get* to.

– Frank Ramirez

Hymns
Opening Hymn
What Is This Place?
Lift Every Voice and Sing
Sermon Hymn
Will You Let Me Be Your Servant?
For Christ and the Church
Closing Hymn
Go, My Children
God Be with You Till We Meet Again

September 12, 2010

16th Sunday after Pentecost (Proper 19 [24])
RC/Pres: 24th Sunday in Ordinary Time

Lessons (See p. 10 for guidelines)

Semi-continuous (SC)	Complementary (C)	Roman Catholic (RC)
Jer 4:11-12, 22-28	Exo 32:7-14	Exo 32:7-11, 13-14
Ps 14	Ps 51:1-10	Ps 51:3-4, 12-13, 17, 19
1 Tim 1:12-17	1 Tim 1:12-17	1 Tim 1:12-17
Lk 15:1-10	Lk 15:1-10	Lk 15:1-32 or 15:1-10

Speaker's Introduction for the Lessons
Lesson 1
Jeremiah 4:11-12, 22-28 (SC)

Following a divine wind, the folly of God's people is laid bare, as is the landscape in an ecological disaster.

Exodus 32:7-14 (C); 32:7-11, 13-14 (RC)

The folly of God's people is laid bare when they created a golden idol, but so is Moses' love for them as he pleads on their behalf with God.

Lesson 2
Psalm 14 (SC)

The psalmist warns those who would oppress the poor, dear to the heart of God, that there are consequences to their folly.

Psalm 51:1-10 (C); 51:3-4, 12-13, 17, 19 (RC)

Self-knowledge, even if it reveals folly, can lead to deliverance if we turn back to God in confession.

Lesson 3
1 Timothy 1:12-17 (SC/C/RC)

Paul is quick to name his folly as one who persecuted believers, because it makes him exhibit A when it comes to the saving grace of Jesus Christ.

Gospel
Luke 15:1-10 (SC/C); 15:1-32 (RC)

Jesus compares the joy in heaven over the recovery of a lost sinner in terms we can understand and likens it to the celebration over a lost sheep and a lost coin.

Theme

God does not require defenders so much as new disciples with repentant hearts.

Thought for the Day

God's Word is not a museum where we gaze at the exhibits. It is a mirror where we recognize ourselves.

Sermon Summary

The Apostle Paul presents himself as exhibit A: the one who was lost who now is found, not because his testimony makes him a trophy but so we might see ourselves in his story – and then praise God, immortal, invisible, who is the source of all good things.

Call to Worship

Come forward, people of God, to turn back. Advance in discipleship to retreat from sin. Empty your hands and heart of worldly distractions that they may be filled with the good things of God. The Creator desires no less than this – that we lose ourselves as we have been shaped by the world, that we might be found, reborn, as God's children!

Pastoral Prayer

God of heaven, God whose will shall be done on earth as it is in heaven, we praise your name because it is not your will that one should be lost, but that all be gathered together in one body in Jesus Christ. As we have rejoiced when we have found what is lost, after searching in every corner and under every obstacle, so you have told us there is joy in heaven when we return again to you. We return to you. Receive us as your children; remold, remake us so that your image, reflected in our lives, might shine the brighter as a beacon so that others might find you as well. These things we pray in your name. Amen.

Prayer of Confession (based on Psalm 14)

One: In our folly we act as if there is no God. It sometimes seems as if no one believes in you, God of history, God of hope. It is as if there is no one who believes.

All: Look down from heaven on humankind. We still seek your wisdom. We seek you.

One: We have gone astray, lost all knowledge of you. Why do we not call on you when we need you, God?

All: Look down from heaven on humankind. We still seek your wisdom. We seek you.

One: Is the terror we feel because we have lost our way? Where are you, God?

All: Look down from heaven on humankind. We still seek your wisdom. We seek you.

One: You are in plain sight, God. Restore our fortunes! Amen.

Prayer of Dedication of Gifts and Self

Your place is with the poor, with the lost, with the searching. Our gifts this day include not only our wealth which has its source in your goodness, but also our actions and our intent, to stand by the side of the forgotten, the oppressed, the lost, the poor. Receive these gifts in the spirit with which they are given, and guide their use in your world. These things we pray in your name, giver of all that is good. Amen.

Hymn of the Day
Immortal, Invisible, God Only Wise

The text of this hymn was written by Walter C. Smith and first appeared in *Hymns of Christ and the Christian Life* (1867). There were six stanzas. A slightly revised version was published in *Congregational Hymns* (1884) by W. Garrett Horder. This version is the basis for the text found in *The Hymnal 1982* of the Episcopal Church. Based on 1 Timothy 1:17, this text should be sung with conviction. Reading the text in unison before singing it often allows for renewed understanding of overly familiar texts. St. Denio is a traditional Welsh melody adapted into a hymn during the revivals of the 10th century. It was arranged by John Roberts and published in *Caniadau y Cyssegr* (1839).

Children's Time: Letters

(Preparation: Bring a Bible and open it on your lap; also bring a letter as described below.)

Talk with the children about letters. Who likes to get letters? There are several letters in our Bible. A lot of them were written by a man named Paul. *(If some of the same children are present who were here last week, you might recall with them that you talked about one of his letters last week.)*

Paul wrote letters to other churches and to his friends, telling them about Jesus. He wanted people to know about Jesus' love, and how to live as followers of Jesus. We are glad that Paul wrote these letters and that we have them in our Bible. They help us learn how to be Christians and how to do things in church.

I have a letter here – let's see what Paul might have said: *(Read letter:)* "Dear friends: Jesus has taught me that God loves me no matter what. God loves you, no matter what, too. Share that love with others! Your friend, Paul."

Prayer: God, thank you for people like Paul who remind us of your love. Help us to share that love with others we meet. Amen.

The Sermon: Your Name Here
Scripture: 1 Timothy 1:12-17

(For sermon materials on Luke 15:1-10, see the March/April 2010 issue of *The Clergy Journal*; for sermon materials on Jeremiah 4:11-12, 22-28, see the May/June 2010 planning issue of *The Clergy Journal*.)

Originality is highly prized by our society. There's the old saying, "If you build a better mousetrap the world will beat a path to your door." But the classic mousetrap works just fine! Skip the cheese – mice don't really like cheese – and put a little peanut butter on the trap, carefully set the hair trigger, and hide it in a spot you won't step on in the middle of the night and the job is done!

There is a real need for new drugs to combat illnesses for which there is no treatment – but some of the drugs that are being developed combat conditions for which there are already perfectly good drugs that are available as inexpensive generics. What's the need of something new in those cases?

Our forebears did not prize originality. They thought it was more important to be derivative. Virgil wrote his *Aeneid* because he wanted to match Homer's *Iliad* and *Odyssey*. Shakespeare borrowed plots shamelessly. And the King James translators had no intention of starting over from scratch when they sat down to render the Bible in English. Confessing their reliance on the translations that had been published before, and which were pretty good themselves, they wrote in their essay "The Translators to the Reader": *Truly (good Christian Reader) wee neuer thought from the beginning, that we should neede to make a new Translation, nor yet to make of a bad one a good one, . . . but to make a good one better, or out of many good ones, one principall good one . . .*

In today's passage Paul is at pains to explain that all our best ideas have their source in God – and maybe to admit as well that we resisted God's great ideas for a good deal longer than necessary.

Paul wrote the first letter to Timothy (who was in Ephesus at the time) while traveling on the road from Macedonia and Nicopolis in Northwest Greece. Timothy was a well-known associate of Paul. Paul referred to him as his child, because he had been involved in his conversion (Acts 16:1-3, Phil 2:22). He had been listed as a co-writer of more than one of Paul's letters. He had been Paul's envoy to Thessalonica (1 Thes 3:2, 6) and Corinth (1 Cor 4:17, 16:10), and he is presented in these letters as representing Paul in Ephesus. He may have had a Gentile father and a Jewish mother. As was typical in the Roman Empire, his mother was the one who was responsible for his upbringing and education.

The apostle wants to remind Timothy of a little bit of his history. All Paul's initiative and creativity were going into defending the faith by the sword. Paul's own plan for his life made him "a blasphemer, a persecutor, and a man of violence" (1:13) It wasn't enough to engage the new Christians in debate, a debate in which Paul could more than have held his own. His zeal meant he had the need to obliterate, to crush those he considered heretics. Much like those in modern society who believe they are always, always right, and that others are always, always wrong.

But God had another plan for Paul's life, a plan that was merciful and sure. Paul learned that God does not require defenders so much as repentant hearts and new disciples. While Paul had intended to destroy on behalf of God, he learned that God's story meant that " . . . the grace of our Lord overflowed for me with the faith and love that are in Christ Jesus."

We hear sometimes from those zealous for the gospel that they want learn "new arguments" to defend the faith, as if somehow their cleverness would finally put those who oppose the gospel to rout. There's a fire in their eyes and a sneer in their voice. These modern inquisitors are always right. Their opponents, whether fellow Christians, or others who believe in God but do not know Christ, are wrong, wrong, wrong, in everything.

Oddly, Paul's zeal would be transformed. He would be just as zealous for the gospel of Jesus Christ, but he would be able to see what is good in the faith of others. He would be able to quote from pagan poets, secular playwrights, and other sources of ancient wisdom to make his point that everything points to love and mercy, and that love and mercy finds its best expression in Jesus.

It begins with self examination. God's word is not a museum where we gaze at the exhibits. It is a mirror where we recognize ourselves. That's why in his letter to a younger disciple Paul does not try to present himself as one who was always right, but as exhibit A: the one who was lost who now is found, not because his testimony makes him a trophy but so we might see ourselves in his story – and then praise God, immortal, invisible, who is the source of all good things.

Paul attempts to give encouragement to Timothy by reminding him that he was the first sinner, the persecutor of the faith, but "Christ Jesus came into the world to save sinners – of whom I am the foremost" (1 Tim 1:15).

This is God's creativity. It is God who has taken the initiative in reaching out to us, instructing us, and sharing his grace with us. This passage speaks to the essentials of faith and the saving action of God. This is something so glorious it ought to be song. Indeed, the doxology "To the King of the ages, immortal, invisible, the only God, be honor and glory forever and ever. Amen" (1 Tim 1:17) is the inspiration for a favorite hymn, "Immortal, Invisible."

God's creativity continues into the present age. It is God who has taken the initiative to establish and maintain a relationship with humanity. God's love has resulted in mercy, even to Paul, who calls himself the worst of sinners, and he uses himself as an example for others. God is reaching out to all humanity so that all may become heirs of the promise made to Abraham.

The parables of Jesus speak of God's intense, loving search for the lost. And our own testimony is most powerful when we cease to try to use creative, persuasive argument and instead testify to our own lost state, the miracle that we were found, and our own brokenness that God has healed. This is the message that is spoken through all of scripture. It is the good treasure that is dwelling with us. We are saved by the grace, the gift, of God.

All of us. Amen.

– Frank Ramirez

Hymns
Opening Hymn
Lord, Our Lord, How Majestic Is Your Name in All the Earth
Come Thou Font of Every Blessing
Sermon Hymn
Immortal, Invisible
Amazing Grace
Closing Hymn
There Is Joy
Hark the Voice Eternal

September 19, 2010

17th Sunday after Pentecost (Proper 20 [25])
RC/Pres: 25th Sunday in Ordinary Time

Lessons (See p. 10 for guidelines)

Semi-continuous (SC)	Complementary (C)	Roman Catholic (RC)
Jer 8:18—9:1	Amos 8:4-7	Amos 8:4-7
Ps 79:1-9	Ps 113	Ps 113:1-2, 4-6, 7-8
1 Tim 2:1-7	1 Tim 2:1-7	1 Tim 2:1-8
Lk 16:1-13	Lk 16:1-13	Lk 16:1-13 or 16:10-13

Speaker's Introduction for the Lessons
Lesson 1
Jeremiah 8:18—9:1 (SC)

Jeremiah, the weeping prophet, shares the pain of the people as they ask "Where is God?"

Amos 8:4-7 (C/RC)

Amos warns those who can't wait for worship to end so they can go back to stealing from the poor that God has a long memory.

Lesson 2
Psalm 79:1-9 (SC)

The psalmist calls aloud to God, cataloging the pains of the people, and asks, "How long?"

Psalm 113 (C); 113:1-2, 4-6, 7-8 (RC)

God is to be praised, says the psalmist, from sunrise to sunset, because the poor and suffering are never forgotten.

Lesson 3
1 Timothy 2:1-7 (SC/C); 2:1-8 (RC)

The apostle Paul writes to Timothy urging prayers for all, even leaders, while never forgetting God is God over all.

Gospel
Luke 16:1-13 (SC/C/RC); 16:10-13 (RC)

Jesus tells a parable about an ancient "hacker" who, with poverty looming, makes friends by helping others cheat his master. If only, Jesus says, the children of light looked out for each other so well.

Theme

Christians are obliged to pray for leaders, but not always to obey them.

Thought for the Day

Always pray for leaders when you pray for everyone, but don't confuse worldly government with our eternal allegiance to God through Jesus.

Sermon Summary

The apostle Paul advised Timothy to pray for leaders, but also to pray for everyone. It is better to live in harmony with the society at large when it is possible, but a Christian must never lose sight of our first obligation to one God, and one mediator, Jesus Christ.

Call to Worship

One: Praise God, all who have come to worship. Praise that holy name!
All: Blessed be God's from this time on and forevermore.
One: From the rising of the sun to its setting, the name of the LORD is to be praised.
All: The glory of God is high above the heavens.
One: Who is like God, who is seated on high, who looks far down on the heavens and the earth?
All: God raises us all, poor and rich, and seats us at the same table.
One: God gives us all a home, making us part of one family. Praise God!
– Adapted from Psalm 113

Pastoral Prayer

One: For the opportunity to sacrifice for others, to go without so others without can receive the bounty you have blessed us with,
All: We give you thanks and praise.

One: For the words of scripture that guard us and guide us, for the priorities that are made clear through our shared walk in your word,

All: We give you thanks and praise.

One: These things we pray in the name of Jesus Christ. Amen.

Prayer of Confession

We are too quick, God of patience and forbearance, to take up the ways of the world, to speak harshly and in judgment, raising economic walls, creating nations while you embrace all of humanity, drawing lines between political parties, and hiding from those we imagine are "others." But we are one people. You, who truly are wholly other than us, created us in love that we might in one voice proclaim your glory to the universe. Write your will on our hearts. Let your word become a balm of healing. Find us! Receive us! Forgive us! In your holy name we come before you, a confessing people, confessing our sins, but also confessing the love of Christ to a sorrowful world. Hear our prayer. Amen.

Prayer of Dedication of Gifts and Self

We raise our voices to you today, who are mindful before we spoke not only for what we desire, but what we need. Hear us, God of this season and all seasons, as we seek your wisdom this day. Our offerings are no sacrifice, but represent welcome freedom from the ties that bind us too closely to this world. Accept our gifts as we approach with awe, wonder, respect, and joy. Draw near, Lord Jesus. Let this present world pass away. Amen.

Hymn of the Day
Dear God, Who Loves All Humankind

The original text for this hymn, "Dear Lord and Father of Mankind," is the closing stanzas of a longer poem by John G. Whittier. The text, originally a contrast between the poet's Quaker upbringing and a possible more active form of worship, reminds us of the need for quiet, contemplative worship. Problematic language has caused numerous hymnal committees to alter the opening line or to re-write the entire text. REST, one of many tunes by this name, was composed for the Whittier text by Frederick C. Maker, an organist and choral director in Bristol. Its quiet melody and simple harmonies are a fitting support for the text. Singing in harmony will greatly enhance the presentation of this hymn.

Children's Time: Being Forgiven

Talk with the children about how they feel when they have done something wrong. Paul *(you might mention you spoke of him last week)* wrote many letters in the Bible. He wanted other people to know about God's love, and about the wonderful things Jesus had done.

But Paul wasn't always doing good things for the church. In fact, for a long time he was very mean. He did not believe that Jesus was sent by God. He wanted to stop people from telling others about Jesus and God's love. Then Jesus spoke to him, and Paul was changed.

Paul was so excited he wanted to tell everyone! His letters went all over the Mediterranean area, and people kept them. Paul would often tell people not to waste any time – spread the good news that God loves us all!

Prayer: God of grace, help us to spread the good news of your love all around the world, just like Paul did. Amen.

The Sermon: Choose Your Moment
Scripture: 1 Timothy 2:1-7

(For sermon materials on Luke 16:1-13, see the July/August 2010 issue of *The Clergy Journal*; for sermon materials on Jeremiah 8:18—9:1, see the May/June 2010 planning issue of *The Clergy Journal*.)

During the reign of King James I the most popular translation of the Bible wasn't the King James Bible. It was the Geneva Bible, translated in that city while Protestant Bible experts were exiled during the reign of Mary, Queen of Scots. First published in 1560, it never had any official standing, but it was the most popular Bible translation in England throughout the reigns of both Elizabeth and James.

King James, however, objected to the marginal notes printed in the Geneva Bible. To his way of thinking kings were appointed by God, and should never be questioned. But the Geneva translators, who were Calvinists, didn't share his view. Their marginal notes made it clear there were times when Christians should obey God rather than kings. The Geneva translators, for instance, applauded the midwives who disobeyed Pharaoh's order to kill Hebrew babies.

Some have interpreted Paul's admonition in today's passage to pray for those in authority as upholding, as it were, the Divine Right of Kings. However, the Geneva translators pointed out there could even be exceptions to this rule about praying. Referring to Julian the Apostate, a Roman emperor who rescinded Constantine's ruling making Christianity the official church of the empire, they noted in the margin: *"Although they persecute the church so it be of ignorance, else if they do it maliciously, as Julianus Apostata, they may not be prayed for"* (spelling updated).

Even so, there are some who will point to this passage and others to make their case that the New Testament authors insist that we must always support whatever government is in power. This point is only made when the party they support is in office, and it is conveniently forgotten when another administration takes over.

The fact is, governments can be wrong. It's a forgotten fact that into the 20th century the German language was spoken in many American cities. In cities like Cincinnati German flags, German culture, and German festivals were commonplace. That all changed when the United States entered into the European War in 1917. Suddenly all Germans-Americans were portrayed as the enemy of humankind. Persecution, attacks, and arrests led to the loss of German culture.

It is easy to shake our heads at another generation, but we need only remember the hysteria that followed 9/11 to recall that people branded dissent as treasonous. Churches fell over each other to line up behind any breach of civil rights. It is in this light that we must look at scriptures like this passage from 1 Timothy.

Two thousand years ago most people tolerated the brutal excesses of the *Pax Romana*, the Peace of Rome, because it eliminated the many small wars that would have erupted between rival little kingdoms. The uniformity of Roman law insured justice on a scale previously unknown.

Then as now we live in a larger world, and we are not to retreat from it. Prayer is to be offered for all rulers in the hope that we may live peaceably in society at large – especially because we are reminded by Paul that Jesus "gave himself a ransom for all" (1 Tim 2:1-7).

Still there was a basic disconnect for Christians in an empire where everyone had to prove they believed the Emperor was a god.

An anonymous second-century Christian put it best in a letter he wrote to an official named Diognetus defending believers as good citizens, countering rumors that Christians participated in strange rituals when actually we try to be good neighbors.

For Christians don't come from other countries, speak a different language, or act differently. They don't have their own economies, or dialect, nor do they have bizarre lifestyles . . . They live according to chance in both Greek speaking and foreign cities, and dress the same, eat the same foods, act the same in all the rest of life's ways – except that they also paradoxically differently because of their citizenship. They live in the same countries, but they are foreigners. They take part in the political life of their land, but they endure the hardships of aliens . . . They live on the earth but they are citizens of heaven . . . They are put to death, but they are brought to life. They are made poor, but they make many rich . . . People curse them but they bless in return. They honor those who insult them . . . Simply put, Christians are to the world what the soul is to the body. (Translation from *The Letter to Diognetes* appears in *The Household of God*, Frank Ramirez. Elgin: Brethren Press, 2009, p. 34.)

However, the anonymous author then lists several contemporary customs, such as disposing of unwanted children or sharing spouses, which Christians do NOT take part in, but adds that *"They are poor, yet they make many rich; they are in need of everything, yet they abound in everything."*

Nevertheless, despite the desire of Christians to find their place in the larger society, they were labeled a "mischievous superstition" by the Roman historian Tacitas. Fellow historian Suetonius claimed they were a radical cult that sought to rule the world.

This led the Roman governor Pliny the Younger to write to the Emperor Trajan around the year 115 for instructions on how to treat Christians. He tortured two slave women who he described as deacons, but found nothing damning beyond the fact that they rose before dawn to share a meal and to sing to Christ as to a god, and that they would not worship the Emperor. Otherwise they cooperated with society.

In our own day there are times we must stand up to authority and speak the truth to powers. The only question is when. Choose your moments. No one pays attention if you're always an adversary. It's like the Letter to the Editor column in the local paper. After a while we get to recognize the people who always have something to say, and mostly we tune it out. But the names you don't recognize, those are the ones you pay attention to.

Remember what Paul taught here. There is one God – and by implication Caesar is not a god and neither is any dictator, or any president, prime minister, or premier, for that matter. There is one mediator between humanity and God, and that is Jesus Christ. Jesus is Lord. Everyone else needs prayer, even – especially – those in power who we distrust or even despise.

– Frank Ramirez

Hymns
Opening Hymn
> Holy Holy Holy
> Praise, I Will Praise You, Lord

Sermon Hymn
> My Life Flows on in Endless Song
> In Christ There Is No East or West

Closing Hymn
> Oh Where Are Kings and Empires Now
> There Is a Balm in Gilead

September 26, 2010

18th Sunday after Pentecost (Proper 21 [26])
RC/Pres: 26th Sunday in Ordinary Time

Lessons (See p. 10 for guidelines)

Semi-continuous (SC)	Complementary (C)	Roman Catholic (RC)
Jer 32:1-3a, 6-15	Amos 6:1a, 4-7	Amos 6:1, 4-7
Ps 91:1-6, 14-16	Ps 146	Ps 146:7-10
1 Tim 6:6-19	1 Tim 6:6-19	1 Tim 6:11-16
Lk 16:19-31	Lk 16:19-31	Lk 16:19-31

Speaker's Introduction for the Lessons
Lesson 1
Jeremiah 32:1-3a, 6-15 (SC)
Jeremiah lives a parable to warn a faithless king who imprisoned him that you can't imprison God's plan of hope for the people.
Amos 6:1a, 4-7 (C/RC)
Amos warns the scoffers that appearances can be deceiving: the scales will be balanced, and God's justice will fall heavily on those who oppress the poor.

Lesson 2
Psalm 91:1-6, 14-16 (SC)
The psalm reminds us that calling on the name of God will find our trust in God is not misplaced.
Psalm 146 (C); 146:7-10 (RC)
You can put your trust in princes, or stake your claim with the God who abides with the poor. Your choice.

Lesson 3
1 Timothy 6:6-19 (SC/C); 6:11-16 (RC)
As he concludes his letter of instruction to Timothy, the Apostle Paul suggests we content ourselves with what we have so we might take hold of the life that matters.

Gospel
Luke 16:19-31 (SC/C/RC)

Jesus pleads with us to choose what is lasting by telling the parable of Lazarus and the beggar, which has left a lasting impression.

Theme

You can't take it with you so use it all wisely.

Thought for the Day

The things of this world don't last, but our choices live on long after us, and bring us fame or calumny.

Sermon Summary

Real living consists not just in the accumulation of things, but in choices consistent with our calling. It's not money that's evil, but the love of anything that is not at its heart God.

Call to Worship

(to the tune O Waly Waly)

> One: A voice is raised, a call is heard,
>   When God is praised in song and word.
>   Through centuries was forged this chain.
>   This moment seize. This treasure gain.
> **All: This call we hear to praise the Lord.**
>   **No chain we fear, nor threat of sword,**
>   **Delays our cause. We come, though awed,**
>   **One Christ, one cross, one Lord, one God.**

Pastoral Prayer

Almighty and Most High, we seek to abide in the shadow of your love. We trust you to be our refuge and our sanctuary. Deliver us from the snares of this world. Cover us like the wings of a mother bird providing refuge to her brood. We need no armor but your faithfulness. With you we will not fear the terrors of darkness, the arrows of misfortune, the destruction that can strike at any time. We who love you count on your deliverance. We call upon you by the name we have known from of old. Abide with us in trouble and trial; rescue us. Our satisfaction is complete with your salvation. Receive our prayers this day. Amen.

Prayer of Confession

Out of sight, out of mind. We pretend there are no problems by hiding them. We bury them on the back pages of the newspaper while elevating the trite and the trivial. We focus on trivial annoyances instead of staring life and death in the face. The world is offered salvation and chooses celebrity. We assent to injustice through our silence. God, hear our confession. Confront us with our sins of neglect. May your fire burn away our illusions. We pledge as individuals and a community of faith to be your witnessing people, speaking the truth to powers, standing like a tree planted in the waters against the changes of fad and fashion. Thank you for your forgiveness. In your name we pray. Amen.

Prayer of Dedication of Gifts and Self

We bring nothing into this world, and we take nothing out of it. What matters is what we do with all this stuff, all these things, all those possessions, while we're here. It is amazing, Creator God, the trouble we go through to make sure the world knows what's ours and what ought to be ours, when all along it's all yours. Today, in our offering, may we recognize once more our part as stewards and not owners of your good earth. Accept these gifts as we reorient ourselves toward radical discipleship. In this time of offering we praise you. Amen.

Hymn of the Day
Fight the Good Fight

The text, based on 1 Timothy 6:12, is first found in J.S.B. Monsell's collection, *Hymns of Love and Praise for the Church* (1863). The language of the time presents a very strong picture of striving for the good life or straight path with Christ as your guide. There are two tunes, PENTECOST composed by William Boyd and DUKE STREET composed by John Hatton, usually associated with this text. Both are fine tunes; however DUKE STREET tends to give stronger, more energetic support. The use of additional instruments, especially brass, will give a definite lift to the presentation of this hymn.

73

Children's Time: Prayer
(Bring a flipchart or whiteboard and marker.)

Talk about prayer. You might refer to the variety of prayers used in your worship service or at other times. When do the children pray? Do they have special prayers they use at mealtimes or at bedtime?

In one of our Bible readings today, the author talks about how we should pray for everyone.

Invite the children to join you in making a list of people for whom to pray. Focus on categories rather than individual names. For example, pray for leaders (as the scripture passage specifically mentions). Pray for those who are sick and for those who are hungry. Encourage the children to name categories and be respectful of all of them. You might wish to involve the whole congregation in making suggestions or limit it to the children. Be sure to include a category such as "people we don't get along with" or some other way of including praying for "enemies."

Prayer suggestion: Join in a simple prayer, thanking God that we can gather to worship and to pray, and trusting God to hear all our prayers. Pray for the people on the list.

The Sermon: Last Things First
Scripture: 1 Timothy 6:6-19
(For sermon materials on Luke 16:19-31, see the July/August 2010 issue of *The Clergy Journal*; for sermon materials on Jeremiah 32:1-3a, 6-15, see the May/June 2010 planning issue of *The Clergy Journal*.)

Abraham Harley Cassel (1820-1908) of Harleysville, Pennsylvania, was born into the culture of the Plain People of Pennsylvania. He was a member of the Dunkers, otherwise known as the German Baptist Brethren. His father did not believe in schooling. The more you knew, the feeling went, the more potential for sin. You couldn't very well extort money if you didn't know higher math.

The result was that though Cassel had only six weeks of formal education in his entire life, his passion for learning and books never abated. Largely self-taught, he grew to prize books with a passion. He collected books, haunting estate sales, hunting through attics, searching old bee boxes, and traveling great distances to purchase lots. He amassed over 10,000 volumes. His collection, especially when it came to German language books and documents, was unparalleled, and people traveled from around the world to examine his collection. Fortunately, he married a Quaker woman who tolerated his eccentricity.

Cassel was not only a farmer who managed a large property and many employees, and a scholar and writer of historical articles (although he always insisted he was uneducated because of his lack of schooling), he was also a minister among his people. Not only had he collected books, but he had preserved church records, ledgers, and letters, which helped him interpret the history of the German-speaking religious separatists of Colonial America. All of this important history would have been lost without him. However, in his last years as he went blind and his health began to fail, he worried about what would happen to his collection. He wanted it to benefit others, but he also hoped it would be kept together as a legacy. But as his death approached that seemed less and less likely.

No doubt he had to take to heart what Paul told Timothy – we bring nothing into this world, and we take nothing out of it. Regardless of how much time we have or think we have, it passes very quickly. As the Japanese poet Arakida Moritake (1473-1549) wrote on his deathbed: "My span of years today appears a morning glory's hour." Or as Shakespeare put it in the play *Cymbeline*: "Golden lads and girls all must, as chimney-sweepers, come to dust" (*Cymbeline*, IV, ii, 262-263).

Paul was warning Timothy that every time we put down roots, every time we get too comfortable, we are in danger of falling prey to the illusion that what we have is lasting. The things themselves, of course, are not the problem. Today's text is often misquoted. It's not money, but the love of money, that is the root of all evil. And oddly enough, it is the fellowship of Christ that must constantly guard against falling too much in love with this world.

A beautiful church can fool us into thinking that our aim as a fellowship is to care for the building. Certainly maintenance and upkeep are important, for safety's sake if nothing else. But the grand cathedral can become a monument, not to Christ, the savior who made it clear that he had no place to lay his head, but to ourselves.

Our homes, whatever form they take, matter to us. Home provides security for children, and a base for our mission and ministry. But home can become an idol.

How much better to always consider that what we say is ours belongs to God, and to make plans, as stewards, for the disposition of what we own, making sure that in what we do we honor God by our choices.

Maybe it was easy for someone like Paul, who seems to have loved travel, and whose hat was his home, to say, "If we have food and clothing, we will be content with these" (1 Tim 6:8). When we consider the beauty that surrounds us, whether in city or country, the landscape of nature or populace, it's easy to desire to put down roots and establish as much earthly security as possible. But there's such a thing as having too much. That's why Paul adds: "But those who want to be rich fall into temptation and are trapped by many senseless and harmful desires that plunge people into ruin and destruction" (6:9). That's why his advice to Timothy is to ". . . shun all this; pursue righteousness, godliness, faith, love, endurance, gentleness. Fight the good fight of the faith" (6:11-12).

We often say first things first, but we might better say last things first. Reflect on your passing and the legacy you will leave behind, make choices and changes, and take hold of the life that matters, the eternal life to which we are called.

This is not an easy message for us in our consumer society. Or rather, it's a subtle one. Our poverty need not be one of want. If we are good stewards, the wealth we accumulate, manage, and grow will provide not only for future generations, but for the work of the kingdom. But that cannot be an excuse for unbridled avarice at the expense of discipleship. Do not forget that when Paul took up a collection for the hungry in Jerusalem, the poor believers in Macedonia gave beyond all measure, while the rich Corinthians were slow in fulfilling their pledge.

So what happened to the Cassel collection? Before his death it was divided in three directions. However, decades later most of it was brought together again in the Cassel collection of Juniata College in Huntingdon, Pennsylvania. It remains a blessing for many who study this important period in American history. And in that collection is a letter written by Alexander Mack, Jr. (1712-1803), which underscores the lessons of today's passage. Shortly before his death at the age of 92 the German-born Mack wrote to his Germantown congregation with some last words of his own, which sounded much like the Apostle Paul's advice.

Mack did not choose to sum up his life or to give spiritual advice. He took his fellow believers to task for not taking care of a widow who needed their aid. Identifying himself as "an aged stranger and pilgrim on this earth" he admitted that the woman was very difficult and unstable, and though they could not readmit her to the flock, they could care for her. Too weak to go to visit them personally, he wrote, "I could not assume then that I would live to see New Year's Day, about four months hence. I did, however, have every right to assume that when the mortal shell of mine is buried, the New Testament is not buried with it. And it is there that the Lord speaks and says: 'It is more blessed to give than to receive!'"

– Frank Ramirez

Hymns
Opening Hymn
> Praise, I Will Praise You, Lord
> Praise to the Lord, the Almighty
Sermon Hymn
> Praise God from Whom All Blessings Flow
> A Charge to Keep I Have
Closing Hymn
> Have Thine Own Way, Lord
> The Care the Eagle Gives Her Young

October 3, 2010

19th Sunday after Pentecost (Proper 22 [27])
RC/Pres: 27th Sunday in Ordinary Time

Lessons (See p. 10 for guidelines)

Semi-continuous (SC)	Complementary (C)	Roman Catholic (RC)
Lam 1:1-6	Hab 1:1-4, 2:1-4	Hab 1:2-3, 2:2-4
Lam 3:19-26 or Ps 137	Ps 37:1-9	Ps 95:1-2, 6-9
2 Tim 1:1-14	2 Tim 1:1-14	2 Tim 1:6-8, 13-14
Lk 17:5-10	Lk 17:5-10	Lk 17:5-10

Speaker's Introduction for the Lessons
Lesson 1
Lamentations 1:1-6 (SC)

> The poet laments the desolation of Judea in sharp detail, yet retains the presence of mind to do so within the complex poetic form of the acrostic.

Habakkuk 1:1-4, 2:1-4 (C); 1:2-3, 2:2-4 (RC)

> Habakkuk believes in a listening God, and challenges God to act on the destruction and violence taking place. God responds: Make my message "plain" so all can understand. Justice will come at the "appointed time."

Lesson 2
Lamentations 3:19-26 (SC)

> We interrupt this heartfelt lament with this message from our sponsor: The steadfast love of the Lord never ceases. God's mercies never come to an end.

Psalm 37:1-9 (C)

> The psalmist laments the ferocity of his opponents, but is thankful for the blessings to be found in God's sanctuary.

Lesson 3
2 Timothy 1:1-14 (SC/C); 1:6-8, 13-14 (RC)

> Writing from prison, the Apostle Paul still finds a way to give thanks for Timothy's faith, grounded in mother and grandmother, providing a strong foundation for the testimony they share on both sides of imprisonment.

Gospel
Luke 17:5-10 (SC/C/RC)
Most of us think we've built up a pretty good credit account with God, but Jesus suggests our attitude about our station as disciples could use a little redefining.

Theme
God exalts the humble – so a little humility certainly wouldn't hurt us.

Thought for the Day
Mustard seed faith might just work a little better if we plant our prayers on our knees.

Sermon Summary
This message is not for the meek, the humble, the poor in Spirit, who are already blessed and will see God. Jesus berates the rest of us for not having the mustard seed faith that makes all things possible. Instead of congratulating ourselves we might try treating Jesus as Lord.

Call to Worship
One: People of God, when the thought of our afflictions becomes wormwood and gall, when our souls are bowed down with the thought of it all, call this to mind – and hope!

All: God's steadfast love never ceases, God's mercies never come to an end; they are new every morning; great is God's faithfulness.

One: The Lord is my portion, says my soul, therefore I will hope in God.

All: Our hope in God will be expressed in prayer and praise today!

– Adapted from Lamentations 3:19-26

Pastoral Prayer
God of all things, great and small, our joys and our concerns, our prayer requests spoken and unspoken, the triumphs and tragedies of our lives are stitched like a quilt into a thing of beauty and utility, but the larger

79

perspective is hidden from our eyes. Reveal your will for our lives in all the events, planned and accidental, that we share. Open our hearts to those circumstances we can change. Write words of comfort in the deep places of our souls for those we cannot change. And in everything we praise you, praying that we may see the world through the eyes of faith. Amen.

Prayer of Confession

God of history, abiding with your people through all generations, we have inherited a faith so strong that we ought to be able to move mountains. Yet we struggle to move our hearts. We are without compassion. We do not seek to know, nor desire to move, beyond our comfort level. Forgive us, and in forgiving, guide us to places of wisdom that we might see at last that all people are our brothers and sisters, all suffering is our own, and all struggles bring opportunities to become the hands, the heart, the presence of Christ. May we move mountains in your name, may the valleys be filled, and may every path made straight that your glory should be known the world over. In Jesus' name. Amen.

Prayer of Dedication of Gifts and Self

One: Let us rekindle the gift of God that is within us, a sincere faith lived in our forebears, mothers, fathers, grandparents, and others. Let us allow that faith to live in us now as we dedicate our gifts.

All: God, you did not give us a spirit of cowardice, but rather a spirit of power and of love and of self-discipline. Rekindle the flame that has burned brightly in our midst as we dedicate ourselves, our gifts, and the ministry we share with you. Amen.

– Based on 2 Timothy 1:5-7

Hymn of the Day
Great Is Thy Faithfulness

The text and tune were written by Methodist ministers, Thomas O. Chisholm and William M Runyan, respectively. The hymn became an instant favorite, especially with Will Houghton, president of the Moody Bible Society. The gospel-style harmonies provide great support for the text. One possible alternative for presentation is the use of soloist or small ensemble for one or more stanzas and the whole assembly for the refrain. This may be easier to say than do, as most congregations love to sing the entire hymn with great energy and conviction. Repeating the refrain for a second time at the close or using a descant (found in numerous hymnals) will give a splendid close to one of the church's favorite hymns.

Children's Time: A Mustard Seed Faith

(Bring a large plant or fruit – such as a watermelon – and a single seed from the same kind of plant or fruit.)

Show the plant or fruit to the children and talk about its size, shape, and so forth. Depending on what you brought, discuss things such as whether it will grow bigger, what it will taste like, and if it will produce leaves, flowers, or fruit.

Show the seed. Can you imagine that this plant or fruit was once this size? It was one of these little seeds. *(Wonder together how the seed knew how to grow up to be the right plant.)*

Do you ever have times when you feel like you don't matter much, when you feel like you may not be worth much, or that there is much you could not do? Maybe you felt kind of small, like this little seed.

One day some of the disciples said to Jesus that they didn't feel very important. They said to Jesus, "Give us more faith."

Jesus said to them, "If you had as much faith as a little mustard seed, you could do great things." *(Wonder how the disciples might have responded.)*

We all have within us lots of possibility for growing more and for doing big things – just like this seed. *(Wonder with the children about some great things they can do.)*

Prayer: Loving God, you have filled us with faith. Help us to remember that, and to know we can do great things with you. Amen.

The Sermon:
If You Can Read This Sermon Title You're Too Close
Scripture: Luke 17:5-10

(For sermon materials on Lamentations 1:1-6, see the July/August 2010 issue of *The Clergy Journal*; for sermon materials on 2 Timothy 1:1-14, see the May/June 2010 planning issue of *The Clergy Journal*.)

There's the old story about a woman who was tired of her husband falling asleep in church. On the way home from worship she started to scold him but he insisted he'd been awake. "Very well," she said triumphantly. "What did the minister preach about?"

"He preached against sin," her husband answered.

"What did he say about sin?" she continued.

"He was against it," he harrumphed.

I'm not sure if his answer proved whether he was awake or not, but generally a minister who has spent some time preparing for Sunday's worship would, all things considered, prefer you stay awake and pay attention. However, this week, some of you are getting a free pass. Some of you need to let your mind wander during this message. It is not about you. If you are humble, if you are meek, if you are a confessing Christian who is already aware of your sins and have asked Jesus for forgiveness, you have permission to close your eyes, lean back, and relax.

As for the rest of us, and I include myself in this category, please pay attention without letting on this is hitting us right in the heart. This message is directed to us.

The Bible speaks some uncomfortable truths. Sometimes people don't like the way the Bible speaks. In 1833 Noah Webster, whose influential dictionary shaped the American dialect, published his own version of the King James Bible because biblical writers insisted on using indelicate words to describe human things. He found biblical language "offensive," "distasteful," and "unseemly."

Now there's a place in Revelation where we are warned not to change a single word. All the same, if we could, who wouldn't do just a little pruning? Especially in today's passage where Jesus talks about slavery, acts as if slavery were normal, and then tells us we need to consider ourselves slaves in relationship to God.

Slavery is a real problem in the world today. Any reference to slavery that might suggest approval can be painful, or at least distracting. No one should suggest in any way that scripture approves of slavery. Even in the ancient world, where slavery was an economic, not a racial, condition, and slaves could earn money and buy their freedom, it was still an instrument of power and it was wrong, wrong, wrong.

So when we find a reference in Luke that sounds as if Jesus takes slavery for granted, we might consider what Jesus was actually saying in this text. He upbraids his disciples, who were his closer followers and should have been stronger in the faith, for their lack of faith, their inability to match the faith of a mustard seed. He calls them to stop acting as if they were entitled to a place in the kingdom, and to work a little harder to make it happen.

In the same way we should consider how this scripture might be directed toward us who are a little too fat and sassy in our faith. Especially in our era, when our hymns and our testimonies lead us to talk about "my Jesus" and "my God" and "my Bible." We can get to feeling pretty tight with the divine. "Just you and me, Lord, just you and me."

Now you sleepers who are not paying attention, this is why you're not in on today's sermon. You're the ones who sit in the last place, to whom Jesus says, come forward and take your place at the table of honor. You identify too much with the preachers of Colonial America who refer to us as worms and describe what it's like to be sinners in the hand of an angry God, when you're safe from God's wrath! You're really the ones to whom Jesus says, "Come unto me all you who are heavy laden, and I will give you rest."

The rest of us have to ask if we are really all that heavy laden? Are we pulling our fair share? Or have we pretty much had a free ride until now? We who are proud, too self-assured, lacking in humility, who put ourselves in the first place, and look down on others as unworthy of salvation, we're the ones to whom Jesus says, "Whoa!"

Yes, come to the table, but for once come to serve the master. Come expecting nothing but a full helping of discipleship. Tend God's sheep, then feed the poor. Maybe we've had it just a little too easy. The grace of God is free. Maybe because we've paid nothing for it we have no real idea of its worth.

The apostles said to Jesus "Increase our faith!" as if it were something to be done with a magic wand, with no effort. The tabloids keep assuring us that we don't need to sweat, that we can lose 40 pounds without dieting, that we can build up muscles without any effort.

Mustard seed faith might just work a little better if we plant our prayers on our knees. This is not a scripture for the poor in spirit. They are blessed already. It is for us.

And now take heart – because someone is on your side. Someone wise and good! Jesus, our master, and not only Jesus, but our sisters and brothers. The ones who are sleeping through this service. Who among you, Jesus asks, would just seat yourself, slave with master, poor with rich? In the Roman Empire such boundaries were honored as a matter of course. But we know from church history that this was ignored by the people of God. All came to the table, despite the restrictions of Roman society. The rich became poor. The poor were lifted up. Slaves were free. Masters bent to wash the feet of slaves.

Pray with me: Increase our faith, God Almighty. We come before you, humbled by the sacrifice of Jesus. As we break the bread and drink the cup let us call to mind the cross of Jesus until his return. Let us serve each other as slaves, not bound by laws or chained by the powerful, but freely pouring out our lives in service to each other and to God's kingdom, following your example. May we renounce the sins of selfishness and pride. One Christ, one cross, one table, one people, serving one God. Slaves to each other, freed with each other. In your great name we pray. Amen.

Okay. The rest of you. Wake up. We're through. And if someone asks you on the way home if you were awake just show them your bulletin. And if they want to know what was preached about, just say sin. If they want to know more details, say, we're against it. Especially our own sins of pride. Once more – Amen!

– Frank Ramirez

Hymns
Opening Hymn
 All Things Bright and Beautiful
 'Tis So Sweet to Trust in Jesus
Sermon Hymn
 Will You Let Me Be Your Servant?
 I Know Not Why God's Wondrous Grace
Closing Hymn
 Great Is Your Faithfulness
 Lord, I Want to Be a Christian

October 10, 2010

20th Sunday after Pentecost (Proper 23 [28])
RC/Pres: 28th Sunday in Ordinary Time

Lessons (See p. 10 for guidelines)

Semi-continuous (SC)	Complementary (C)	Roman Catholic (RC)
Jer 29:1, 4-7	2 Kings 5:1-3, 7-15c	2 Kings 5:14-17
Ps 66:1-12	Ps 111	Ps 98:1-4
2 Tim 2:8-15	2 Tim 2:8-15	2 Tim 2:8-13
Lk 17:11-19	Lk 17:11-19	Lk 17:11-19

Speaker's Introduction for the Lessons
Lesson 1
Jeremiah 29:1, 4-7 (SC)
The Old Testament lesson today is a letter from God to the exiles, to those who have lost their homeland and are wondering what to do now.
2 Kings 5:1-3, 7-15c (C); 5:14-17 (RC)
Today we hear about Naaman, a man who was strong in battle but plagued by leprosy. We hear about the way God heals, sometimes in ways that seem too simple to be true. Listen now for the word of the Lord.

Lesson 2
Psalm 66:1-12 (SC)
Our psalm for today is full of rejoicing about God's goodness to the people of Israel. It reads almost like a Call to Worship, for, in fact, it is.
Psalm 111 (C)
The psalmist today celebrates God's incredible works. Pay attention to all of the different blessings that are sent to God's people. Listen now for the word of the Lord.

Lesson 3
2 Timothy 2:8-15 (SC/C); 2:8-13 (RC)
We turn now to 2nd Timothy, a letter in what we call the "Pastoral Epistles." This letter was written to early pastors, congregational leaders, and lay people, teaching them what it meant to live a Christian life.

85

Gospel
Luke 17:11-19 (SC/C/RC)
Our New Testament lesson today follows a series of stories Jesus shares with his disciples about the difference between doing what we were ordered to do and going above and beyond.

Theme
Gratitude is a path to healing and wholeness.

Thought for the Day
In relation to others, gratitude is good manners; in relation to ourselves, it is a habit of the heart and a spiritual discipline.
> – Daphne Rose Kingma, *A Grateful Heart* (Berkeley, CA: Conari, 1994), 1

Sermon Summary
The Luke story can, at first pass, cast Jesus into the passive-aggressive, whiney figure who notices more those who didn't return in gratitude than the one who did. However, upon further study, the story opens a wealth of insight into gratitude as a path to wholeness.

Call to Worship
> One: This is the day the Lord has made, let us rejoice and be glad in it.
> **All: Happy are those who give thanks to God.**
> One: I was glad when they said to me "Let us go into the house of the Lord!"
> **All: Happy are those who give praise to God.**
> One: With joyful hearts who know how gracious God has been to us,
> **All: Let us worship God!**

Pastoral Prayer
Almighty God, for those who wait on healing, send your Spirit. For those whose healing waits on a change of heart, send your wisdom. For those who walk the long road with friends or loved ones who yearn to be well, send your grace. For those who grieve the ones who are basking now in your

glory, but whose absence leaves a dark hole, send your strength. For those who struggle to find something for which to give thanks, because there is simply no time for gratitude, no space for gratitude, and perhaps in their view no reason for gratitude, send your amazing love to startle their hearts again. All this we pray in the name of Jesus Christ. Amen.

Prayer of Confession

Gracious God, we are here again, reading about the wholeness you give, and yet focusing on our brokenness; hearing of your incredible provision, and dwelling on what we lack; and talking about your healing without believing that it applies to our lives, our pain, and our needs. And with our vision fixed on what we don't have, we are empty of gratitude. Incite our hearts with your grace again, O Lord, and send us out rejoicing in you. Amen.

Prayer of Dedication of Gifts and Self

God, giver of every good gift, we say thank you – with our lives, dedicated to your service. We say thank you – with our financial gifts, surrendered to your purposes. We say thank you – with the work of our hands, anointed for doing your will. May these gifts bring about healing for our community and our world. May these gifts bring you glory and honor, through Jesus Christ our Lord. Amen.

Hymn of the Day
An Outcast among Outcasts

This relatively new and possibly unfamiliar hymn is a wonderful retelling of Luke 17:11-19. The text was written by Richard D. Leach, a well-respected minister and hymn writer. Leach has served churches since 1978 after graduating from Princeton Theological Seminary. He has a number of single author hymn collections published, all which contain remarkable contemporary writing. The text can be sung to the well-known Welsh tune, LLANGLOFFAN; however, United Methodist pastor, composer, and author Dan Damon has written a remarkable tune, POST STREET, that is well worth learning. Damon is fast becoming one of American's foremost creators of hymns where he is the creator of both timely, meaningful texts and strong, singable tunes – a talent not shared by many. His hymns can be found in most hymnals published after the mid 1990s.

Children's Time: Being Healed

Have you ever had a time when you felt all alone, cut off from everyone? Maybe someone has called you a bad name, or you just felt bad.

That's what happened to some people in Jesus' time. They had a skin disease – we don't know exactly what it was like. They were called "lepers" and they could not be around other people. They felt alone and unloved.

One day some of them went to see Jesus and asked him to help them. Jesus told them to go and see the priests, who were the only ones who could tell them they were clean. Perhaps they had gotten over their skin disease, but people did not trust them. Or maybe Jesus healed them – we don't know. What we do know is that they no longer had the skin disease, and they felt healed and made whole.

One of them came back to say thank you. This person was a foreigner, someone who was even more disliked than the others. This person felt healed even more than the others, because now this person would be loved and accepted.

Prayer: God of grace, you love each one of us and you accept each one of us. May we also love and accept one another. Amen.

The Sermon: A Ray of Wholeness
Scripture: Luke 17:11-19

(For sermon materials on Jeremiah 29:1, 4-7, see the July/August 2010 issue of *The Clergy Journal*; for sermon materials on 2 Timothy 2:8-15, see the May/June 2010 planning issue of *The Clergy Journal*.)

The other nine, where are they? We've asked this question before. The other clients we helped by working nights and weekends? Where are they? The other customers in the restaurant we served with a smile, even when our feet hurt. Where are they? The church members we made meals for, the neighbors *we* helped move? Where are they? And when the birthday or baby shower or wedding comes along, those people *we* lavished with gifts and time, where are they?

A minister may receive a handwritten note, expressing how much that sermon meant to them in their time of need, but after a while, after a few difficult conversations in the narthex, she may start to wonder who is grateful, who appreciates her, and she may wonder why she's even doing this. A teacher may see that glow in a child's eyes, that light-bulb moment, and even hear a joyful compliment, but one angry parent or critical supervisor can nearly erase the joy of that one moment of praise.

At first pass, I believed this story was about Jesus sharing in that pathos, that disappointment we all know, when only 1 in 10 people express their gratitude for what we have done. The more frenetic the pace of life becomes, the more rushed our thank-you's can be. So perhaps this story is about Jesus understanding what it feels like to be slighted, to work hard with little recognition, to acknowledge the sad fact that 90% of us are ungrateful for blessings when they happen. Or perhaps we are grateful only 10% of the time. I have known many church members who have been heartbroken after they have given and given of themselves only to receive "constructive feedback" or outright slams. They hadn't yearned for a giant trophy that said, "Best Church Person Ever!!!!" but rather a simple thank you. Perhaps that is part of the story for today.

But, I believe there is more. I can't picture Jesus, who gave himself freely that all may receive grace, would also be found whining, "You never call. You never write." I can't picture Jesus, who called himself 'the servant of all,' seemingly begging for payment in the form of momentary praise. And, I can't see Jesus lamenting that the lepers actually *did* do what he asked of them, which was to present themselves to the priests. Such a portrayal seems passive-aggressive for Jesus, who confronted religious and political leaders head-on. When Jesus made rebukes, he would either say it plain: "Get behind me, Satan!" even to his best friends. Or, he would tell a story, so that people would be able to hear the truth he was sharing, even when the truth stung and implicated them. So, there must be more here than the first read.

This is a perplexing story, virtually the same as another story from Mark's Gospel, except that Luke highlights the actual number of lepers who Jesus healed and that the returning leper was – of all people – a Samaritan. Some of the other facts, like where and why the lepers were to go to the priests, if they were healed then or upon returning to Jesus, are just not resolved. But what we do know is that one did return, and that one who returned with "thank you" on his lips was both the unlikely one and the one Jesus said "had been made well."

So this story, just like the healing of the leper, goes beneath the surface. Notice that Jesus doesn't slander the others for not returning to give thanks to him. He blesses the one who did return and sends him out healed and whole.

Barbara Brown Taylor says that the question among us is not, "Where are the nine?" but "Where is the tenth?" "Where is the one who followed his heart instead of his instructions?" Doesn't the church resemble a dutiful procession of cleansed lepers who are "doing the right thing by the temple"? Where is the one who wheels round to return the wildness of love? (Barbara Brown Taylor, as quoted in Paul Duke's sermon "Down the Road and Back," *Christian Century,* September 27, 1995.)

My drive home from college was via a sunny, almost timeless road tucked into the tree-covered foothills of Southern Virginia. It was not uncommon to pass an abandoned pick-up truck that had evolved over time into God's newest flowerbed. There were roadside vegetable stands. There were many churches with preachy signs like "Feeling distant from God? Well, who moved?" or "Message from God: 'Don't make me come down there!'" Occasionally a cow or a deer would gaze at me from the side of the road as I drove past, but I often had the road to myself.

There was one intersection, however, that is memorable, and not just to me, but to nearly everyone who has used this road. An older African American man in overalls with a broad smile would stand in the median at a particular place and wave at passing cars. He'd shout out "Thank you! God bless you! Thanks for coming through." It would have been quite a sight had he done that only for a day, but the man was there every day, rain or shine, cold or blistering hot, for years. It was amazing to me how contagious his gratitude was. I'd find myself unable to dwell on whatever problem I'd been dwelling upon because, oh, there he was again, waving and saying thank you. I don't know if or how this man made a living, but I know he made many lives different in that few seconds it took to speed past him, most of us waving back at him. He seemed to be living the practice of gratitude day in and day out, and it seemed to make him whole and cast a ray of wholeness on the rest of us.

The healing that Christ offers comes not only in the act of salvation but in the life of gratitude it enables us to live, that, in fact "makes us whole." We live to cast rays of wholeness upon others, radiating our gratitude to a world speeding past in search of fulfillment. As we live into gratitude, practicing it with what we say, how we move, and how we live, it is contagious. It preaches more brightly than any roadside church sign. It shines into hearts starved for affirmation. May your life cast a ray of wholeness onto others this week as you strive to *practice* gratitude. And may God bless you with wholeness as you return, like the healed leper, to offer your thanks and praise to God.

– Rebecca Messman

Hymns
Opening Hymn
We Gather Together

Let All Things Now Living
Sermon Hymn
Shout to the Lord

In the Lord I'll Be Ever Thankful
Closing Hymn
Now Thank We All Our God

Give to Me, Lord, a Thankful Heart

October 17, 2010

21st Sunday after Pentecost (Proper 24 [29])
RC/Pres: 29th Sunday in Ordinary Time

Lessons (See p. 10 for guidelines)

Semi-continuous (SC)	Complementary (C)	Roman Catholic (RC)
Jer 31:27-34	Gen 32:22-31	Exo 17:8-13
Ps 119:97-104	Ps 121	Ps 121:1-8
2 Tim 3:14—4:5	2 Tim 3:14—4:5	2 Tim 3:14—4:2
Lk 18:1-8	Lk 18:1-8	Lk 18:1-8

Speaker's Introduction for the Lessons
Lesson 1
Jeremiah 31:27-34 (SC)

The Old Testament lesson today comes from the prophet Jeremiah. It refers to a famous proverb about "sour grapes." However, notice how these verses dismiss the idea that suffering can be passed from parent to child.

Genesis 32:22-31 (C)

Today's lesson from Genesis takes place after Jacob's attempt to appease his brother Esau by sending him hundreds of livestock, hoping that Esau will accept him again when they meet, which will occur immediately after today's lesson.

Exodus 17:8-13 (RC)

The people of Israel are with Moses in the wilderness, being fed by manna from heaven and water poured forth from a rock. Now, the people prepare for battle.

Lesson 2
Psalm 119:97-104 (SC)

Today's psalm is reminiscent of the 1st psalm, "their delight is on the law of the Lord, and on his law they meditate day and night." Let us now delight in the word of the Lord.

Psalm 121 (C); 121:1-8 (RC)

We hear now a psalm about the protection of God. Every time you see a mountain, or "lift up my eyes to the hills," recall this psalm and God's faithfulness to us.

Lesson 3
2 Timothy 3:14—4:5 (SC/C/RC)

Today's lesson from Timothy is a famous text in discussions about what the Bible means and how it is to be used. Let us now, too, be inspired by the inspired word of God.

Gospel
Luke 18:1-8 (SC/C/RC)

The Gospel of Luke has a special place for widows, orphans, and those who are typically at the margins. Today's lesson is about being persistent in our prayer. Listen now for a word from the Lord.

Theme

Our posture before God matters. There will be seasons of crawling to God.

Thought for the Day

If you await answer to prayer, examine your posture. What you hear striding through life might be worlds different from what you hear on your knees.

Sermon Summary

Persistence in prayer may require seasons of crawling on your hands and knees to God. There are things to be gained in these "low" times, conversations with God that pass us by when we rush, when we don't bend, when we don't kneel. Our posture before God in prayer matters.

Call to Worship

One: Jesus says, "Come to me, all who are weary and carrying heavy burdens."

All: "And I will give you rest."

One: Jesus says, "Let anyone who is thirsty, come to me."

All: "And let the one who believes in me drink."

One: Come into God's presence and be renewed, in body and spirit.
Come with hearts ready to find their kneeling place before God.
And wherever two or more are gathered, God is there.

All: Let us worship God!

Pastoral Prayer

Loving God, we pray to you in all seasons. In our seasons of rejoicing, praising you for the joys and blessings we know in our lives. In our seasons of mourning, crawling to you, begging for comfort and understanding. In our seasons of strength, seeking your wisdom to guide our energies. In our seasons of weakness, coveting your grace and acceptance. In our seasons of waiting, holding out our hands for answers and needing of patience. And in our seasons of rest, settling into true Sabbath, living at a sacred pace with your love enveloping us. Be with those we hold in our hearts this day. Answer their prayers and grant them your peace as they wait. May it be so. Amen.

Prayer of Confession

Pray with me, now, coming to the cross to truly lay our burdens down. Pray with me, asking for forgiveness from the Lord and trusting in God's amazing grace and love. Pray with me, as any of the words that are said touch upon your brokenness . . . doubt . . . fear . . . anger . . . grief . . . boredom . . . loneliness . . . exhaustion . . . hopelessness . . . anxiety . . . resentment . . . being stuck . . . hurt that won't go away . . . prayer that has yet to be answered . . . faith that seems half-hearted and shallow . . . words that have hurt others . . . forgiveness yet to be given . . . forgiveness yet to be accepted. In your mercy, Lord, hear our prayer. Amen.

Prayer of Dedication of Gifts and Self

We praise you, Lord of all generosity, for the chance to give. How freeing it is to release the hold that money would like to have on our hearts. How joyful it is to participate in the coming of your commonwealth of love. How excellent it is that you hear our prayers and multiply the workings of our hands into the movement of your Spirit. Bless this, our church, our community, and our world, that we might be agents of your healing. In Christ's name we pray. Amen.

Hymn of the Day
There's a Wideness in God's Mercy

This text is from a longer hymn, "Souls of Men, Why Will Ye Scatter?" first published in *Oratory Hymns* (1854). Frederick Faber was born into a Calvinist home, strongly influenced by John Henry Newman and ordained a priest in

1839. Like many others in the Oxford Movement, Faber converted to Roman Catholicism in 1846. He wrote over 150 hymns. There are as many tunes associated with this hymn text as there are hymnals. Some of the more common are IN BABILONE, a Dutch 18th century melody; GOTT WILL'S MACHEN, an 18th century Swiss melody by Johann Steiner; BEECHER, by John Zundel; and WELLESLEY, by Lizzie Tourjée. Each bring a special support to the text and the choice is probably best picked by which is most familiar to the singers.

Children's Time: God Listens

Talk with the children about how Jesus told a lot of stories to teach people. We call these stories "parables." Sometimes these stories are kind of funny. One time Jesus told a parable about a widow and a judge to teach people about praying. *(In telling the following story, invite the children to join you in making exaggerated facial expressions and sound effects.)*

Someone had done something wrong to the widow and she went to the judge for help. He was supposed to decide what was fair. She knocked on his door *(knock on floor to simulate knocking on door)* and said, "Help me." The judge just ignored her and said, "Go away!" This happened many times. *(Repeat the lines and the actions as appropriate.)*

Finally, the judge gave in. "I can't stand it," he said. "This woman is driving me crazy! I'll give her what she wants so she'll go away and not bother me."

Do you think God is like that mean judge? Of course not! Jesus wanted people to realize that God is much kinder than that. We can talk to God in prayer, and know that God – who is much nicer than that judge – listens to what we ask for, and cares for us.

Prayer suggestion: Invite the children to suggest justice concerns and use these in your prayer.

The Sermon: On Hands and Knees
Scripture: Luke 18:1-8

(For sermon materials on Jeremiah 31:27-34, see the July/August 2010 issue of *The Clergy Journal*; for sermon materials on 2 Timothy 3:14—4:5, see the May/June 2010 planning issue of *The Clergy Journal*.)

Crawling on hands and knees to God is usually not what we "upright" people enjoy doing. But I imagine each of us has had some time in our lives when we were like the woman in today's Gospel story, "continually coming," begging for justice, pleading to God with urgency, banging on the doors of heaven, over and over and over again.

Today's lesson, as Luke flat-out says, is "about our need to pray always and not to lose heart." It is about crawling, begging, and pleading to God, and trusting that God will not delay in responding.

The image of "crawling" was given new life for me when I read about Gary Snyder, a man who describes his adventure of crawling on his hands and knees through the mid-elevation Sierra forests *(The Gary Snyder Reader: Prose, Poetry, and Translations,* Gary Snyder, New York: Counterpoint, 1999). He acknowledges that we usually imagine ourselves striding through the open terrain of alpine expanses, but there are places where that won't work. The forests were often so burned or logged that the undergrowth becomes so dense that it would be virtually impassable . . . unless you crawl through it. If we insist on strolling or sauntering, the under-story parts of the forest are left in wild peace. But this terrain, he said, was only experienced if "you dive in – down on your hands and knees on the crunchy Manzanita leaf cover and crawl around between the trunks."

As he snaked along, he sniffed out prized Boletus mushrooms and encountered whole worlds of insects. I can picture the muddy clothes, the brambles in his hair, the birds he startled, the rattlesnakes that startled him, the fearful and beautiful encounters that took place when crawling, seeing life so close that you can't come away clean. There are places in life that we just can't get to standing upright.

This week I was tromping on my hands and knees through this sermon, sniffing around all over it to point to you where there is good food in the Christian story. Most people, even ministers, try to stick to the wider roads where they can walk upright, but there are some places in life that you just can't fit through if you can't bend, if you aren't willing to travel through the mud on your knees awhile. There are conversations to be had with God that are etched on the mossy underside of logs, rarely typed onto well-marked trail signs.

Luke's Gospel says that prayer, especially our prayers for justice, should be that persistent. Even an unjust judge can be worn down, so God, who is loving and just, wouldn't turn us away, although we may have to spend some time on our hands and knees praying persistently. This effort is not because God enjoys making us wait, but because there are some messages we can't receive any other way. And, as persistent as the woman was, timing was certainly not under her control. Crying out "day and night" may not mean just *one day and one night*. Persistence can mean crawling through a week or a month or sometimes years. We may be called to slip and slide over rough patches on the calendar in our season of crawling.

In Luke's Gospel, the parable of the persistent woman comes in a series of stories teaching us how to communicate with God. Immediately before this story, Jesus is talking about the way God's kingdom is not coming with things that can be easily observed, pointed at, nailed down. Then after this story Jesus tells the story of the Pharisee and the tax collector, calling people to trust God and be open with their frailties, rather than simply relying on their individual righteousness. Then after that Jesus tells us to receive the Kingdom of God as a little child. If there is one thing children know well, it is how to crawl, how to be persistent in asking for what they want, and how timing is not under their control.

Persistence in prayer can take you from crawling on your hands and knees into a powerful moment of rising up. At Princeton Seminary, each seminarian senior is given the privilege of preaching once during their final year. I remember a woman named Kim who said, "For my sermon today, we are gonna do our testimonies!" People gasped. It was sort of awkward. "We don't really do that here," most of us worried. "Maybe she wasn't prepared, it is a busy time of year," someone whispered. But in fact what happened was the most memorable worship service I could remember during my entire career there.

One after the other, people began to stand up and share how God had healed them. One well-dressed man confessed he had been homeless earlier that year, but through prayer and the community, he was now in a home. One woman had battled cancer that year, but she was, thank the Lord, in remission. All around us people began to stand up and testify to the ways that God had healed them until those who remained in their seats were the ones who felt stooped, crooking our heads around to behold the stories and hearing our own stories tapping on our brains to be freed.

I was called to examine my own posture in prayer in an unexpected way this week. I saw a sculpture by Jean Antoine Houdan called "Jesus Healing." His arm is outstretched, which did not surprise me. What did surprise me was the angle of his hand. This hand was clearly facing down, as if it was cupping the head of a person on their knees. The stone fingers and broad palm low, the eye downturned. I noticed that there was not room under there for a superwoman posturing herself for perfection in all

97

things. There was not room under there for a man convinced his world will shatter if he falls to his knees. There was not room under there for a church that is rigid with the way things have always been done and stuffed full with guilt for what it has not done. Our posture before God matters. If you have spent this week on your knees, your trousers wearing thin in persistent prayer, take heart. Will God delay long in helping you? I tell you, God will quickly grant justice to you. Do not lose heart, God's hand is reaching out for you. Be encouraged; you may find yourself hearing from God in unexpected ways, and you may find yourself rising up with powerful testimony on your lips.

Thanks be to God.

– Rebecca Messman

Hymns
Opening Hymn
My Shepherd Will Supply My Need
Come and Fill Our Hearts
Sermon Hymn
O Jesus, I Have Promised
O Savior, in This Quiet Place
Closing Hymn
Precious Lord, Take My Hand
Out of the Depths

October 24, 2010

22nd Sunday after Pentecost (Proper 25 [30])
RC/Pres: 30th Sunday in Ordinary Time

Lessons (See p. 10 for guidelines)

Semi-continuous (SC)	Complementary (C)	Roman Catholic (RC)
Joel 2:23-32	Sir 35:12-17	Sir 35:12-14, 16-18
	or Jer 14:7-10,19-22	
Ps 65	Ps 84:1-7	Ps 34:2-3, 17-23
2 Tim 4:6-8, 16-18	2 Tim 4:6-8, 16-18	2 Tim 4:6-8, 16-18
Lk 18:9-14	Lk 18:9-14	Lk 18:9-14

Speaker's Introduction for the Lessons
Lesson 1
Joel 2:23-32 (SC)

We hear now from the prophet Joel of plague turned to prosperity, of locusts one day and luxury the next, as God recognizes the faithfulness of the people.

Sirach 35:12-17 (C); 35:12-14, 16-18 (RC)

The writings of Sirach, like the book of Proverbs, contain instructions for living. Today's lesson is about divine justice. Listen now for a word from the Lord.

Lesson 2
Psalm 65 (SC)

Today's psalm is an overwhelming thank you for the beauty and the abundance of the earth. As we shuffle through fall leaves, this psalm is also our song of thanksgiving to God.

Psalm 84:1-7 (C)

Home, God's house, the place where everyone belongs and where the glory of the Almighty God fills us. As we listen to the song of the psalm writer today, we too long to be in God's dwelling place.

Lesson 3
2 Timothy 4:6-8, 16-18 (SC/C/RC)

We turn to Paul's second letter to his assistant Timothy. Paul was writing from prison, encouraging Timothy to remain faithful to the gospel even if it leads to suffering, like what Paul was experiencing.

Gospel
Luke 18:9-14 (SC/C/RC)

The Pharisees had been asking many questions of Jesus about the nature of God, how to be saved, and who might be saved. Today's lesson deals with how we should and should not pray.

Theme

We are – each one of us – both the Pharisee and the tax collector.

Thought for the Day

God condemns the good person that I want to be – but am not – and accepts the bad person that I don't want to be – but am.

– Jurgen Moltmann, *A Chorus of Witnesses*
(Grand Rapids, MI: Eerdmans Publishing Company, 1994), 32

Sermon Summary

Jesus' parable is about the good person and the bad person, prayer, and God's radical response to the two extremes that dwell in our communities, in our souls. This parable is above and beyond the notion of redemption for the evil in us. It is also a rejection of the false pretense of goodness we all put on.

Call to Worship

One: We come to worship.

All: We drop our masks at the door.

One: The mask of self-sufficiency and sainthood,

All: The mask of perfectionism.

One: We come to worship God just as we are.

All: God, who loves us just as we are. God, who alone makes us into what we were meant to be.

One: Let us worship God!

Pastoral Prayer

Almighty God, when we consider how radical you are compared to our puny standards, when we take on the enormity of your grace compared to our worst failings, we are lost in gratitude and wonder. Lord, pour out your mercy and love upon us, when we are trapped in perfectionism and the wild goose-chase of pleasing everyone. Lavish your grace upon those whose bodies are in pain, whose hearts are broken, and whose expectations have been dashed. Restore your church to a place where sinners are loved and accepted, rather than a haven for the self-satisfied. Lead our world into such generosity of Spirit, so that our divisions would fade away and our wars come to an end. We pray this in your radical name, Jesus the Christ. Amen.

Prayer of Confession

God of radical grace, we confess that we are the ones who see ourselves as noble, generous, law-abiding, and kind. We claim to be better than "those other people." Our prayers ask that you would echo our egos and bless us for how good we are. However, this is a façade. We dwell in self-doubt, insecurity, and selfishness. We fear letting anyone, especially you, know how we really are, when we are alone with our souls. Forgive us, God, and accept us as we are, sinners who rely on your grace, who are frantic and desperate for your joy, who long for your wisdom and are thirsty for your love. Amen.

Prayer of Dedication of Gifts and Self

Holy One, we pray that you would receive these, our gifts, as an offering of our love and worship. May they bring you joy and glory! May we offer not just our gifts but our very selves as an offering to you, that you would transform our offerings and ourselves into vessels, carrying into this world the commonwealth of your love. That with them, the hungry might be fed, the lonely might be comforted, the grieving might know your consolation. In Jesus' name. Amen.

Hymn of the Day
Just as I Am, without One Plea

The well-loved hymn text was written by Charlotte Elliott. It was first published in her *Invalid's Hymn Book* (1836). Though an invalid at the age of 30, she continued to write and edit. After her death her brother, Henry Venn Elliott, found a file containing well over 1000 letters of thanks for this hymn. He commented that this text alone ministered to more people than he had during his whole ministry. WOODWORTH, a tune by William Batchelder Bradbury, was first published in the *Third Book of Psalmody* (1849), where it was set to "The God of Love Will Sure Indulge." It was subsequently paired to the Elliott text and appeared in Bradbury's *Eclectic Tune Book* (1860), the source used by Dwight L. Moody and Ira D. Sankey.

Children's Time: Being Honest

Jesus told a story about two people who prayed very differently. They both went to the temple, which was like a big church. But once they got there, they did different things.

One of them stood up straight and tall. *(Demonstrate this as you talk, using exaggerated motions such as puffing out your chest and sticking your nose in the air; invite the children to join you in the actions.)* This person said something like this: "Hey God, it's me. You know how good I am. I'm just a little bit better than everyone else. I just wanted to remind you of that."

The other one didn't stand up tall, but bowed his head *(demonstrate, and invite the children to join you)* and said quietly, "God, it's me. You know who I am. I've done some things I don't feel good about, and I want to talk to you about them."

Then Jesus said, "Which one do you think felt closer to God?" Ask the children what they think. While affirming their answers, explain that you think the second person probably felt closer to God. Point out how good it can feel to be totally honest with God in our prayers. We can tell God exactly how we're feeling and know that God understands us and loves us, no matter what.

Prayer: Merciful God, help us to be honest with you in our prayers and our living. Amen.

The Sermon: The Best of the Worst
Scripture: Luke 18:9-14

(For sermon materials on Psalm 65, see the July/August 2010 issue of *The Clergy Journal*; for sermon materials on 2 Timothy 4:6-8, 16-18, see the May/June 2010 planning issue of *The Clergy Journal*.)

"I am glad that I am not like that Pharisee: judgmental, arrogant, hypocritical. Though I could probably name a few people who are just like him."

As we crane our necks to identify the Pharisees near us at church, we participate in an exercise of missing the point of this parable. Every one of us is the Pharisee. And, though we feel relieved that we don't cheat on our taxes, don't steal people's identities online, and don't hold up banks, in some way, every one of us is the tax collector. But before we can truly connect with this story, we have to pull it away from some cultural litter that has surrounded it.

Growing up in church, we've learned to see Pharisees as "those perennially pious hypocrites," the bad guys of most stories. I even remember a Vacation Bible School song that went, "I don't want to be a Pharisee, 'cuz a Pharisee ain't fair, you see." But, in today's story they were initially to be seen as the *best* characters. They followed the law of Moses and tried to live a life devoted to God.

Theologian Jurgen Moltmann has said that it would be best simply to call the Pharisee the "good man" (*A Chorus of Witnesses,* Grand Rapids, MI: Eerdmans Publishing Company, 1994, 32). Likewise, the tax collector, who we've been trained to see as a sympathetic figure with a bum rap, was actually a man whose whole business was corruption, complicit with the Roman Empire and skimming money off the top as he went. He might better be called "the bad man," the Bernie Madoff of his day. The people listening to Jesus would have heard this story as "the good man and the bad man," like we'd imagine an old Western movie, the man in the white hat and the man with the black hat.

The good man. He prays. He tithes. He fasts twice a week. He goes to church. What could be wrong with that? Why would he not be justified too? The bad man. He stands "far off." His eyes avoid any eye contact with God. Then he beats his chest, like the mourning crowds would do later in Luke after Jesus had been crucified. He doesn't ask for anything but mercy. Why should *he* be justified? Wouldn't it be enough if he was given mercy? Given another chance to live a good life, to try again? But this story holds a striking reversal: the worst character walks away with the best scenario, justification, the biblical word for being "right" in the eyes of God, while the good man walks away with nothing. How is this fair? After all, we live in a world where you reap what you sow, you get out what you put in, and hard work and virtuous living lead to the good life. Is this just a divine version of "nice guys finish last"?

If you are here this morning, you are in church rather than "those who go to Starbucks." You try to put your fair share into the collection plate, unlike those who have attended for years but never give a dime. Last time you checked, you're weren't on America's Most Wanted list. And sometimes, you get frustrated with those long prayers of confession, which list out many vague sins that you don't think you've been up to lately. After all, church isn't supposed to make us feel badly about ourselves is it?

It is in this moment when each of us comes to terms with the Pharisee living inside us. We all define ourselves by what we are not to God, "not an addict, not a spouse abuser, not a crooked CEO." Sometimes our conversations with God can sound like fall political ads, highlighting more what we are not than what we truly are. "Thank God I am not a drinker, but I pray for my uncle who is." "I am not nearly the gossip she is." "Lord, help him with all his shortcomings, help him to get on the right path!" Today's story is about being who we truly are with God. It is about realizing how broken and bent we truly are, so that we can acknowledge how much we are truly in need of God. It is only then that we quit relying on ourselves, quit wearing the mask that causes us to live a divided life between our true selves and the selves we show the world, quit using our works and our money to buy us satisfaction, and finally rely on God to accept us and love us as we are.

An odd thing happens to me when I go to the doctor. I find myself trying to tell them how strong I am. How, despite my condition, I truly have been getting along well and making the best of things. I even saw an "A+" written on my file and was so proud of myself, that I must have made a great impression on this doctor. Later, I realized that A+ was actually my blood type. After I finished laughing at myself, it was as if I had seen my own inner Pharisee on the X-ray machine. Doctors do best when we let them know what is not working. The very act of trying to impress, of minimizing our brokenness, can get in the way of our healing.

That's when we embrace the tax collector within us, that part of us that has hidden in the shadows, "far off" from our family and friends who expect us to be fine all the time. That part of us that has been broken by relationships, broken by temptations, broken by self-loathing, broken by our past, broken by our fear of the future, broken by the choices we made and the ones we didn't make. The shadow side of our soul finally steps into the light and hears Jesus say, "You have been justified." Not for what you aren't, but for what you are.

What Jesus wants is ourselves. The worst part of our lives finally aired out, no longer weighing us down with perfectionism, but thrown off at the foot of the cross. Jesus is seeking tax collectors, who dwell within every person, ready to be made whole again by his amazing grace, ready to receive his radical love that gives us what we do *not* deserve in the radical commonwealth of Christ's love where the last shall be first, the sick will be healed, the blind shall see, and the poor shall be rich, and you and I will be called children of God. Amen.

– Rebecca Messman

Hymns
Opening Hymn
Lord, You Have Come to the Lakeshore (*Tu Has Venid a la Orilla*)
Let Us with a Gladsome Mind
Sermon Hymn
Humble Thyself in the Sight of the Lord
Kyrie
Closing Hymn
O Love That Will Not Let Me Go
Create in Me a Clean Heart

October 31, 2010

23rd Sunday after Pentecost (Proper 26 [31])
RC/Pres: 31st Sunday in Ordinary Time

Lessons (See p. 10 for guidelines)

Semi-continuous (SC)	Complementary (C)	Roman Catholic (RC)
Hab 1:1-4, 2:1-4	Isa 1:10-18	Wis 11:22—12:1
Ps 119:137-144	Ps 32:1-7	Ps 145:1-2, 8-11, 13-14
2 Thess 1:1-4, 11-12	2 Thess 1:1-4, 11-12	2 Thess 1:11—2:2
Lk 19:1-10	Lk 19:1-10	Lk 19:1-10

Speaker's Introduction for the Lessons
Lesson 1
Habakkuk 1:1-4, 2:1-4 (SC)

Habakkuk, the prophet, lived during a time of sword-rattling and fear that his homeland, Israel, would be conquered, and we know that it was. But to Habakkuk, we hear God's word: Write the vision.

Isaiah 1:10-18 (C)

Isaiah, the 7th century BC prophet, refers to the destruction of Sodom and Gomorrah. But even more so, he shares a word from God about how we should and shouldn't relate to God. Less festivals, more justice.

Wisdom 11:22—12:1 (RC)

We hear now from the Wisdom of Solomon. These chapters recall the wisdom that led the Israelites through their desert wanderings.

Lesson 2
Psalm 119:137-144 (SC)

Listen now to the words of the psalmist, as he continues to alternate between praise and petition.

Psalm 32:1-7 (C)

This week's psalm speaks of happiness in forgiveness and the freedom that comes in confession. Listen for a word from the Lord.

Lesson 3
2 Thessalonians 1:1-4, 11-12 (SC/C); 1:11—2:2 (RC)
Listen now for the word of the Lord as it comes to us from the Second Letter of Paul to the Christians who were living in Thessalonica, the capital of Macedonia. He sends his blessing.

Gospel
Luke 19:1-10 (SC/C/RC)
Luke's Gospel is a familiar story, with a character who may be known more for his short stature than for his great faith. Listen with new ears to the word of the Lord.

Theme
Our words are tools for blessing.

Thought for the Day
When we bless others, we encourage them, literally placing courage, that comes from God, into them.

Sermon Summary
Words are God's gift that we might bless others and bless God. Granting your blessing doesn't have to be administered only by ministers, nor are blessings only right for life's red-letter days. We bless and support the little things, as Paul did for the struggling church in Thessalonica.

Call to Worship
One: Bless the Lord, O my soul;
All: And all that is within me, bless God's holy name.
One: Bless the Lord, O my soul;
All: And forget not all God's benefits.
One: With blessing on our lips and joy in our hearts, let us worship God!

– Adapted from Psalm 103

Pastoral Prayer

> One: Blessed Lord, author of all of our blessings, hear us now: as we lift up to you our quivering spirits, as we place before you our heavy burdens, as we open to you our deepest longings.
>
> One: For those in hospitals and nursing facilities this day.
>
> **All: Bless them, O Lord.**
>
> One: For the heartbroken and the lonely.
>
> **All: Bless them, O Lord.**
>
> One: For the penniless, for those tired of being patient, and for those who are simply tired.
>
> **All: Bless them, O Lord.**
>
> One: For leaders who shape the course of our lives.
>
> **All: Bless them, O Lord.**
>
> One: For servants who partner with you in sculpting our churches.
>
> **All: Bless them, O Lord.**
>
> One: And for all the saints who from their labors rest.
>
> **All: Bless them, O Lord.**
>
> One: In the name of the Father, and of the Son, and of the Holy Spirit. Amen.

Prayer of Confession

Holy God, we bless you with our lips. And the same lips can stir up conflict. The same lips speak judgments against other people. The same lips spread gossip. The same lips twist the truth so it justifies our lives. The same lips are silent when someone else is being wronged. We use our voices now to pray for forgiveness. Guide all of our words that they might be full of love and truth. Amen.

Prayer of Dedication of Gifts and Self

We must always give thanks to you, O Lord, for our blessings: the simple and the profound, the material and the spiritual, the ordinary and the extraordinary. We offer our gifts to you, and our very lives, that we might live to be blessing to others, following the example of your son, Jesus Christ, in whose name we pray. Amen.

Hymn of the Day
O Day of God, Draw Nigh

R.B.Y. Scott, author of this text, was a theologian, scholar, social reformer, and minister of the United Church of Canada. He was professor of Old Testament at United Theological Seminary, Montreal, and later at Princeton University. This hymn was first published in 1937 by the Fellowship for a Christian Social Order, a group of scholars committed to issues of social justice and peace. The tune associated with this hymn comes from the *Genevan Psalter* (1551) and was later arranged by English organist William Crotch. Crotch included it in his publication *Psalm Tunes* (1836) and gave it the name ST. MICHAEL. This hymn is a prayer and should be sung with great expressiveness and concern for the text. Use organ for accompaniment or try singing it without accompaniment as a "breath prayer."

Children's Time: A Letter to Your Church

(As preparation for this story, think about what kind of letter Paul might write to your church. Try to include a few words of praise and thanksgiving as well as a word of hope for something yet undone. Remember to keep this at a level appropriate for the children with whom you will be speaking. Write this brief letter on a sheet of paper and roll it up to resemble a scroll.)

Talk with the children about St. Paul. Remind them you spoke about Paul a few weeks ago; that he was an important person who, amongst other things, wrote many letters that are now in our Bible.

Paul often wrote to churches. He would praise them for what they were doing, and gently make suggestions of other things they might do. What if Paul wrote a letter to our church? This is what I thought he might write *(read the letter)*. Can you think of other things Paul might want to say about us?

Prayer suggestion: Make up a prayer that incorporates the praise and concern you mention in your letter.

The Sermon: School of Blessing
Scripture: 2 Thessalonians 1:1-4, 11-12

(For sermon materials on 2 Thessalonians 1:1-4, 11-12, see the July/August 2010 issue of *The Clergy Journal*; for sermon materials on Luke 19:1-10, see the May/June 2010 planning issue of *The Clergy Journal*.)

My soon-to-be fiancé and I rolled suitcases outside, loaded them in the trunk, and received the many extra gifts my mother usually sent along with us when we headed back to Northern Virginia: some famous "Danville chicken salad," a few Frescas for the road, and the Pepperidge Farm cookies that my dad seems to love more than anyone else does.

They seemed to be loading us up even more than usual this time, an extra round of goodbye hugs, extra warnings of State Troopers on Highway 29, and special handshakes of formality appropriate only because this was Dave's first trip to their home. Though I had left home many times before, this time had the pageantry and ritual of the changing of the guard in London. Attempting to honor their graciousness, Dave shook their hands, each one firmly, then spoke these immortal words: **"Thanks for all the hostility."**

Seconds ticked by without a giggle, so I thought my ears were playing tricks on me. I finally said, "What?" His eyes bulged and he shouted, **"Hospitality! Thanks for all the hospitality!"** The car was strangely quiet as we pulled away. My parents waved for a long time. And that exchange was burned into all of our memories. It would be shared numerous times, even at our rehearsal dinner. Of course, that visit, with its clumsy ending, had been the weekend Dave had asked my family for their blessing. Blessing upon his plans to propose to me, blessing upon the family we'd become, blessing that can only be given, never taken. Blessing, calling God into ordinary moments that they become sacred.

Paul's words to the Thessalonians are a blessing. His words bless what the Christians in Thessalonica probably felt were ordinary, possibly even disappointing, seasons of their life together. He blessed them for loving each other, for enduring persecution, and for keeping their faith. He blessed them, reminding them that God was at work in them and that only through God's power can anything prosper. This entire letter serves as a sacred huddle in the midst of a difficult moment: "stand firm, work hard, great job." For anyone who has ever gone through tough times, we know the importance of words of blessing.

Ministers are asked to bless all sorts of things, from newborn babies to bag lunches. When I was in Guatemala, I attended the blessing of a new cow or a car that began working again. All the elders and ministers would arrive and pray over the humming engine, giving thanks to God for the gift of mobility and livelihood. But it is a falsehood to believe only ministers can bless things. If I were to sneeze, many of you would utter blessings right now. So speaking words of blessing is not meant just to be holy-sounding words spoken by professionals, but what we all do all the time: recognizing God's beauty and calling God's presence into our daily lives. The book of James tells us that our words are to serve the purpose of blessing, and that our tongue is like a bridle or a rudder that can steer the direction of our entire body. The words we say to each other matter to God.

The centrality of words was at the heart of Greco-Roman thinking. Words were what made us human, different from sparrows and oak trees and stones. Words. And from there we see how Jesus, who was God and human at the same time, was called "the Word" made flesh, the only teacher whose words were truly connected to the heart of God.

And because all of us need constant help in taming our tongue, in not saying that one thing that we can't unsay, the Bible is full of tools that train us in loving language, in compassionate speech, or simply in silence. There are prayers. There are moments of blessing from parent to child. There are dreams. There are people being still, listening to God. There is the Holy Spirit who appears in tongues of fire and helps people understand one another when before they have talked past each other.

And there are hymns. Hymns are God's way of training our tongues to bless. Have you ever noticed how easy it is to get a tune stuck in your head? Music may be the only thing that lasts longer than the sting of critical words. Music may be the only thing that fills our minds more than our grief and fears. That's why when we are most in need of God, most in need of the right words, a change of heart, we find ourselves caught up in a song. How many of you have told everyone you were doing just fine, thought that the grief or anger was gone, and during the hymn, found your eyes flooding with tears? That was the truth of God flowing through you. It is holy speech, blessing that fills us up, becoming like the rudder for our quivering spirits. And music seems to connect us again with nature: the rustle of fall leaves, the duets of frogs and crickets, the driving cadence of cicadas, as birds and rivers and animals join in with their rhythm and roll and roar.

The world blurred out, unable to focus on any eyes but Dave's, I remember standing in front of a church, hearing my tongue speak these words, "To have and to hold . . . for richer . . . for poorer . . . in sickness and in health." "I do." Though my wedding day was the grandest of days, I hope to be able to pronounce those words of blessing on days when my emotions are all over the place, when I feel like falling asleep at 7 p.m., or some day long in the future, when his hands are veiny and bony and move slowly. And also, I hope to pronounce blessing upon the lady who cuts me off in traffic, the person who fights against what I believe in, and the dog who wakes me up at 3 a.m.

If you feel like your words may not sound as positive as Paul's, or like you aren't as excited about your job or your family or your church as Paul sounded, you don't have to start from scratch. If you aren't sure how to proceed, bless with a hymn lyric: Blessed Are You, Great Is Thy Faithfulness. Or, Your Grace Is Amazing. If you aren't sure where to start, begin as Paul did with your friends, "I give thanks for my friend Mary." If you need a reason, look at our world that cries out for even one person to stop the cycle of critique and defense with a word of blessing.

May it be so, for you and for me, this day.

– Rebecca Messman

Hymns
Opening Hymn
Though I May Speak
Rejoice, Ye Pure in Heart
Sermon Hymn
Bless the Lord, O My Soul
When We Are Called to Sing Your Praise
Closing Hymn
When in Our Music God Is Glorified
For All the Saints

October 31, 2010

Reformation

Lessons
Lutheran   Jer 31:31-34   Ps 46   Rom 3:19-28   Jn 8:31-36

Speaker's Introduction for the Lessons
Lesson 1
Jeremiah 31:31-34

God speaks to the prophet Jeremiah in today's lesson of a new covenant. While we hear "new covenant" of Jesus Christ, today's lesson speaks to the restoration of relationship between Israel and God.

Lesson 2
Psalm 46

Today's psalm inspired Martin Luther's hymn, "A Mighty Fortress Is Our God, a bulwark never failing." Seeking refuge may seem weak to us, but when God is our refuge, it is our strength.

Lesson 3
Romans 3:19-28

Romans is Paul's lengthiest and most theological letter. Though Paul never visited the church in Rome, we hear his most powerful exposition of the gospel of salvation by grace through faith in this letter.

Gospel
John 8:31-36

Our lesson today from John's Gospel focuses on truth – not some vague understanding of truth, but God's truth that is revealed in Jesus Christ. Listen now for the word of God.

Theme
The truth of God still sets us free.

Thought for the Day

May Christ give us this liberty both to understand and to preserve. Amen.

– Prayer of Martin Luther, "The Freedom of a Christian,"
Martin Luther: Selections from his Writings, (New York: Doubleday, 1962), 42

Sermon Summary

It's hard to get excited about the Reformation because of competing priorities, the escalation of biblical illiteracy, and the dark history of Protestant/Catholic relations. But, amid a maelstrom of relativism, there is a need for the truth of Christ and the essentials of the Reformed tradition, now more than ever.

Call to Worship

Leader: Be still and know that I am God, says the Lord.
People: Be still and know that I am God.
Leader: Be still and know that I am.
People: Be still and know.
Leader: Be still.
People: Be.
All: **Let us worship God.**

– Adapted from Psalm 46

Pastoral Prayer

Holy One, gather us into your truth. Open our eyes and our ears that we can hear your voice over our own frantic spirits. Hide us in your refuge. Free us from all of those chains that we bear. We pray for freedom from grief and loss. We pray that the grip of violence and fear would loosen from our world and that the wardens of apathy, anxiety, and "anything goes" would finally release us. Protect us from illness that would trap our bodies and plague our minds. We praise you for you are, indeed, our truth, our refuge, our strength, and a very present help in times of trouble. We bless your name, Lord Christ. Amen.

Prayer of Confession

Gracious God, we know that apart from you, we can do nothing. Our promises are broken. Our faith is shaken. Our hopes are shallow. Our conversations about the meaning and purpose of life are wilderness wanderings. Startle us again with your truth. Forgive us for our drifting commitment and our lethargic reading of your word. Breathe into us your truth that we might be set free again in You, Lord Jesus. Amen.

Prayer of Dedication of Gifts and Self

We give as the reformers taught us: Not to earn love from you, Lord, not to buy anything from you, but as our response to your amazing grace in Jesus Christ. We give all that we have and all that we are, that you might renew us and send us to be the vessels of your love and the messengers of your truth in this world. We pray that these, our gifts, bring you joy, honor, and glory. Amen.

Hymn of the Day
We Shall Overcome

One of the foremost anthems from the 1960s civil rights movement, this song was often sung at rallies and other gatherings where social justice was the theme. Its actual origins are not certain, however African American preacher and hymn-writer Charles A. Tindley wrote a gospel hymn "I'll overcome some day" in 1901. An earlier slave song "We Shall Overcome" was already part of the African American history and the two songs merged into its current form in the early 1940s. The song speaks both to and from the heart. It is a song of faith in a better future. Though God is never mentioned in the text, the presence of God as the giver of that faith is obvious. We will overcome because God has already overcome!

Children's Time: Adopted as God's Children

(Note: When using this story, be sensitive to issues of adoption. If you have children in your church who are adopted, be certain to focus on the "normalcy" of families with adopted children – they are not unusual aberrations, but are an important part of the fabric of our community.)

Talk with the children about legal documents. You might bring a contract, license, or other item. These kinds of papers tell us that things are official. Long ago, Jesus talked about something that was kind of like a legal document, only even better.

Some people came to believe in Jesus, and he reminded them it was one thing to say they believed, but another to do the things Jesus taught. When they don't do as Jesus taught they slide away from God and God's love; but when they do try to obey Jesus, they get closer to God and feel God's love all that much more strongly.

"It's like being adopted," Jesus said. "You will receive from God all that God has to offer – it's like being one of God's own children. God will love you and care for you as being very special."

We don't need a legal document to know we belong to God. When we listen to Jesus and try to do what he wants – even if we don't succeed – God loves us and cares about us. No matter what.

Prayer: God, Mother and Father of us all, we are so glad you have adopted all of us to be your children. Never stop loving us, we pray. Amen.

The Sermon: Truth in a Truthy World
Scripture: John 8:31-36
(For sermon materials on Romans 3:19-28, see the July/August 2010 issue of *The Clergy Journal*; for sermon materials on Psalm 46, see the May/June 2010 planning issue of *The Clergy Journal*.)

It's hard to get excited about the Reformation. It's not what we see on the front page of the newspaper. Very few people post their thoughts on the Reformation on their Facebook updates. And aside from some chuckle-generating comments on *Prairie Home Companion* about life in Minnesota, few people talk with pride about their connection to Martin Luther. Even reverends have a hard time getting revved up to talk about the Reformation, when there are so many other issues bearing on our lives.

After all, most people are barely literate in basic biblical knowledge, so to break out your doctrinal preferences and how you are "reformed and always reforming" can leave one way out on a limb in conversation. When many people around us don't know the biblical narrative that well, it's difficult to engage them on the importance of the Reformed tradition. It is not their tradition.

Then, some people avoid speaking of the Reformation, recalling the days when Protestants and Catholics were like the Hatfields and the McCoys, in a duel that spanned centuries, evoked major wars, and only in recent decades cooled into underlying mutual suspicion. It hasn't been too long since people feared electing someone who was Catholic as president, fearing that the Pope would govern our country from afar. Or that Protestants wouldn't do things simply because "they were too Catholic."

Protestant churches would bristle at the sight of a large cross in the sanctuary or too many candles, because "that's what the Catholics do." And still, beneath the surface, Catholic families struggle when their son or daughter marries a Protestant, and Protestant families struggle when their child marries a Catholic. Those old divisions, which scholars agree Martin Luther never intended to create, still are with us.

Then, after Vatican II reformed much within the Catholic Church, there has been a flurry of reconnecting going on, like neighbors happy to chat over the fence or swap things they don't consider essential, but not about to move in together.

So, how do we get excited about the Reformation? Because, even though the language our society uses has changed, the core questions about who we are, why we exist, how we know anything, especially someone or something as essential as the divine, are still being asked.

Stephen Colbert's first episode of "The Colbert Report" on cable television introduced to America a new word: *Truthiness.* Something is "truthy" if it is like the truth, if no one can prove it isn't the truth, and mostly if people want it to be the truth. And it's hard to get excited about that. I have been involved in many conversations that spiral into the ether as people begin saying, "Well, it may be truth to *you,* but my truth is different." "We all believe the same things, but we also can never truly know anything for sure."

The relativism that has become part of the air we breathe can have a stifling effect on our souls. What do you mean nothing can be truly known, besides what I think I know? How do I live if everything I've ever been told has a giant asterisk next to it: "Might not be true"? Our souls long for that anchor that they believe exists, the truth that created them. All the while, cultural winds would try to convince them that no such thing is possible for thinking persons. And far from getting excited, *this* thinking often can lead to anxiety and depression. Such thinking is certainly not freeing.

"Reformed and always reforming" in our world can be more than a catchy phrase. It can be water for parched souls. The Reformed tradition responds: We know what we know because the Bible reveals Jesus Christ to us, and Jesus is the revelation of God to the world. We reject the idea that humans are fine on their own, self-sufficient and capable to be moral leaders and even speak for God on their own. We reject the premise that a person or ideology can stand between us and a relationship with God in Jesus Christ, who came into this world to make known the living God. We reject the idea that any of us by ourselves can earn a relationship with God: not with an advanced degree, not by volunteering for a year in an impoverished country, not by creating a wealthy foundation, not by deep breathing and graceful stretching.

It is not what we do that connects us to God. It is God who is connecting, who is reaching out to us. It is not how friendly and balanced we are that evokes God's love, it is how loving God is, made known to us in Jesus, who steps into our anxiety and selfishness, who steps into our spiraling conversations about truth, who steps into our bewilderment and wandering from one illusion to the next, and says:

Read the scripture passage.

Seminary leaves no stone unturned in one's heart, mind, and soul. One fall day, questions were swirling around my mind like leaves. Every time I'd get close to an answer, another wind would swirl them in a different direction. I set up a meeting with my professor, and joined her for tea in her office, hoping that somewhere in her massive library was certainty and answers that I could "check out" and take with me.

A Reformation scholar who had read and written more books than I could imagine, she gave me a gentle smile when I asked her this question: "So how do you know it's true?" She took off her glasses. She took a deep breath. She didn't evoke Luther. She didn't quote Calvin. She said, "I guess I know like I know my mother. I've spent lots of time with her. After all these years, I begin to understand her, to see things like she sees things, and after awhile, I realize that I'm becoming more and more like her, and then, it's liberating to realize that she made me. That I came from her. Sure we have our moments. But, I could never believe that I came from nowhere. I could never imagine life without her. I believe in Christ with a community. So, I'm not alone in my journey. I spend lots of time with him, and we've had our moments too, but I could never imagine life without him. Not the scholar's answer, but my heart's answer, I suppose." I trusted that somewhere nearby the Holy Spirit hovered low. I trusted that the Word made flesh still whispered truth through broken vessels. I felt free indeed.

Thanks be to God.

– Rebecca Messman

Hymns
Opening Hymn
Holy Holy Holy
A Mighty Fortress Is Our God
Sermon Hymn
Thy Mercy and Thy Truth, O Lord
Jesu, Tawa Pano (Sing the Faith)
Closing Hymn
My Hope Is Built on Nothing Less
All Glory Laud and Honor

November 1, 2010

All Saints' Day

Lessons (See p. 10 for guidelines)

Semi-continuous (SC)	Complementary (C)	Roman Catholic (RC)
Dan 7:1-3, 15-18	Dan 7:1-3, 15-18	Rev 7:2-4, 9-14
Ps 149	Ps 149	Ps 24:1-2, 3-4, 5-6
Eph 1:11-23	Eph 1:11-23	1 Jn 3:1-3
Lk 6:20-31	Lk 6:20-31	Mt 5:1-12

Speaker's Introduction for the Lessons
Lesson 1
Daniel 7:1-3, 15-18 (SC/C)

Rather than predict things for the future, Daniel addresses his current situation. Four unjust rulers will rise up – something that probably happened in his time – and he is reassured that God's justice will win out.

Revelation 7:2-4, 9-14 (RC)

People of every race, tribe, nation, and language gather to praise God. Who are they? They are the ones who have been claimed by God.

Lesson 2
Psalm 149 (SC/C)

The psalm declares that the high praises of God be "two-edged swords" in the hands of the faithful to execute on the nations the judgment decreed.

Lesson 3
Ephesians 1:11-23 (SC/C)

Recalling the faith of the church in Ephesus the author praises them and emphasizes the high standing of Christ.

1 John 3:1-3 (RC)

God has lavished great love on us and calls us God's children.

Gospel
Luke 6:20-31 (SC/C)
Luke's beatitudes, shorter and blunter than Matthew's, tell us that we are blessed when we are poor and hungry. When we think we have it all, however, there is nowhere to go but down.

Matthew 5:1-12 (RC)
In these familiar beatitudes Jesus points out that, even when persecuted and mistreated, Christians are still blessed.

Theme
Even when we have nothing, we are blessed.

Thought for the Day
When we feel small or insignificant, Jesus reminds us we are blessed. Yet when we think we have it all, we close ourselves to God.

Sermon Summary
We may feel we are nothing, insignificant, or pointless. However, in just those times we are told we are blessed by God. Yet when we think we have everything, we realize there is nothing more to gain. Live different values, and notice the rewards.

Call to Worship
One: Come, saints of God: you are blessed.
All: We come to worship the one who made us.
One: Come, children of God: you are loved.
All: We come to worship the one who loves us.
One: Come, people of God: you are welcome.
All: We come to worship God.

Pastoral Prayer
Gracious God, Creator of all: on this All Saints' Day we are in awe of those who have gone before us. We think of your people – those of great name and those unknown – who have sought to open themselves to your love and compassion, and to share that with others. Help us, set apart

121

from the world by our love for Christ, to live the ideals to which we are called. Help us to love our enemies. Help us to celebrate the simple blessedness of being your people. Help us to continue being saints. Amen.

Prayer of Confession

God of compassion, we hear the call to recognize our blessedness. Forgive us those times we fail to celebrate who we are and what we receive from you. Forgive us when we deny our own blessedness and that of others. We also hear the call to resist a sense of believing we have made it. Forgive us when we close ourselves off to your blessings. Forgive us when we think we do not need you in our lives. Help us to recognize that without you, we are nothing. Amen.

Prayer of Dedication of Gifts and Self

Called by you to be saints, O God, we offer now ourselves and our gifts to you. Use what we offer to share love with friend and enemy, to alleviate hunger, and to share blessedness. We pray in Christ's name. Amen.

Hymn of the Day
Open My Eyes, That I May See

Clara H. Scott, author and composer of this hymn, taught music for many years at the Ladies' Seminary in Lyons, Iowa. This hymn was first published in *Best Hymns No. 2* (Chicago, 1895), edited by E.A. Hoffman and H.G. Sayles. This gospel-style hymn can be used in many ways: as a hymn, a prayer response, or a choral offering sung unaccompanied or by a vocal quartet. The refrain can also be used as an invitation to prayer. Organ and piano work equally well as accompaniment; however, if using the piano add some of the quieter elaborations or embellishments found in gospel music.

Children's Time: God's Saints among Us

(Preparation: Bring some newsprint on an easel, or a whiteboard or a chalkboard, and an appropriate writing implement.)

Talk with the children about All Saints' Day as a day when we think about people who have done, or are doing, God's will. This includes people who have died, and those who are with us even now. Today we are going to think about people in our own church who have been, or are, saints.

Talk about the things that people do in the church. Make a list of various ministries in the congregation: preaching, singing in the choir, teaching church school, making refreshments, mowing the lawn, handing out programs, taking the offering, and so on. Try to make the list as extensive as possible, including all kinds of ministries.

Rejoice at the great list of people who do the work of the church. Point out how important all of these ministries are – they allow us to worship and praise God, to learn about God and the Bible, to help others with food programs and providing meeting space, and so forth. Adapt the conversation to suit the ministries of your congregation.

In the Bible it says that the church is the body of Christ. That means all of us in the church – the saints – do the things that Jesus would do. Jesus' Spirit is in our hearts; when we come together as the church we try to think of what Jesus wants us to do, and we do that work together.

Prayer suggestion: Thank God for the people and ministries that you wrote down.

The Sermon: Space Dust
Scripture: Luke 6:20-31
(For sermon materials on Ephesians 1:11-23, see the July/August 2010 issue of *The Clergy Journal*; for sermon materials on Luke 6:20-31, see the May/June 2010 planning issue of *The Clergy Journal*.)

Several years ago some friends were watching Carl Sagan's *The Cosmos* DVD series. One of them – who had a rather limited view of the creation of the world and his place in it – was rather disturbed by the film.

"This guy seems to be saying that I'm just space dust," he exclaimed.

"Yes," said one of the others. But think of it – we all are!"

What does it feel like to be told you are nothing more than space dust? Possibly not a great feeling. Yet at the same time there is some comfort in realizing that, as the friend pointed out, we all are in the same boat. There is something reassuring about realizing that, as human beings, we are never alone. Ever. Similarly, we share a lot in common with one another, and that is encouraging.

"You are blessed," Luke records Jesus saying.

"You who are poor are blessed. You who are hungry are blessed. You who are crying are blessed. You who are hated are blessed."

123

Not "will be some day . . . " but "you *are.*"

These are Luke's beatitudes, and they differ somewhat from those of Matthew.

Most scholars – including the well-known Jesus Seminar – believe that these pieces recorded by Luke are much closer to what Jesus would have spoken than are the pieces by Matthew. One of the reasons is the overall belief that over the years people tend to add things to earlier texts rather than take away.

Matthew's beatitudes are far more familiar and popular. He has more of them. He makes the language rather flowery. There is a certain resonance, after all, to "poor in spirit" and "those who hunger and thirst for justice (or righteousness)."

There is also something quite pleasant about making these rather generic: "blessed are those who . . . " Matthew says; Luke has a blunter "blessed are you . . . "

Finally, Matthew conveniently leaves out the part that follows in Luke, who quotes Jesus as saying: you are blessed when you are poor, but you are cursed when you have it all.

It doesn't look quite so good embroidered on a wall hanging, does it? Luke cuts to the quick. Here Jesus shoots from the hip and hits us straight in the guts.

The Greek word that Luke uses – remember, Jesus would have been speaking Aramaic so even the original gospel itself is a translation – is *ouai* (oo-eye). It is often translated as "woe" or "alas." Some of the newer translations, however, seek to put a bit of a different emphasis on it.

An English paraphrase called *Good as New* says "go to the back of the queue" or line.

The Jesus Seminar, in their *Five Gospels*, go so far as to day "Damn you!"

Perhaps one that captures the sense best is the translation *The Voice* which says, "All you who are rich now, you are in danger, for you have received your comfort in full" and so on.

That seems to be what Jesus is getting at. It's not a condemnation, per se, but a simple statement of fact: if you think you have it all, what more can you receive? If you think you have got it, that may be well and good, but it puts you in a very different category than most others. Remember, Jesus is speaking here to people who live in abject poverty, and so the words "blessed are you who are poor" ring brutally true for them. Yet if someone amongst them has tried to put themselves above others, woe to them indeed. The higher you put yourself on a pedestal, the farther the fall.

You laugh today? You'll cry later. But if you cry today, you'll find reason to laugh later.

This is simple truth, isn't it? These are not telling us how to behave, but simply pointing out basic realities.

These beatitudes come in the sixth chapter of Luke, a text that includes a wide number of simple and basic quotations of Jesus, most dealing with the simple truths of life. Later on he will say (verse 43), "a good tree doesn't produce bad fruit any more than a bad tree produces good fruit." Simple truths.

Following the beatitudes, today's text continues with Jesus' well-known instruction to "love your enemies." Again, *The Voice* goes so far as to say "keep on loving your enemies," presumably suggesting that the earliest of disciples had already picked up this teaching from Jesus' earlier words and examples.

Numerous people have tried to explain away this phrase, finding it as harsh as the previous set of "woes." But Jesus is making a crucial point for the path of Christian living. The key principle here is that, as followers of Jesus, we are to function on a different plane. We do not reciprocate against others with the same kinds of behavior, but rather model a stronger – that is not to say higher – calling. Rather than merely copycat the not-so-good values of this world, we are invited to demonstrate a different way of living. When someone hurts you, do not seek there an excuse to hurt them back. Rather, find a way to diffuse it with love.

This is highly relevant advice to those who are powerless. When you have nothing left but your dignity, still you can use it as the strongest of weapons.

Martin Luther King Jr. once said, "If you stand and walk tall a man can't walk on your back." When you rise above the manner of living of today you will find yourself morally equipped to present a worthy challenge, and an invitation to try better values.

I once observed a parent spanking their child – not harshly, I'm relieved to say. However, the ostensible point of the exercise was to punish the child for nothing other than hitting a playmate. What was the point, I asked them, of hitting someone to punish them for hitting? It seemed at best to be contradictory.

What Jesus presents here is difficult stuff to those of us who think we've got it made, or who think that we know best how to live and serve. But for those of us who find ourselves woefully wanting in a world of mass confusion there is a wonderful hopefulness in this passage. "Try something different," Jesus seems to be saying.

We are space dust. In the grand scheme of things, we are mere fluff that can be blown away in the wind. Yet if we accept that, we will find ourselves blessed, for even the smallest bit of space dust is loved by God.

– Donald Schmidt

Hymns
Opening Hymn
> For All the Saints
> Maker, in Whom We Live
Sermon Hymn
> Blessed Are the Poor in Spirit
> Jesu, Jesu, Fill Us with Your Love
Closing Hymn
> We Are Marching/*Siyahamba*
> I Sing a Song of the Saints of God

November 7, 2010

24th Sunday after Pentecost (Proper 27 [32])
RC/Pres: 32nd Sunday in Ordinary Time

Lessons (See p. 10 for guidelines)

Semi-continuous (SC)	Complementary (C)	Roman Catholic (RC)
Hag 1:15b—2:9	Job 19:23-27a	2 Macc 7:1-2, 9-14
Ps 145:1-5, 17-21 or Ps 98	Ps 17:1-9	Ps 17:1, 5-6, 8, 15
2 Thess 2:1-5, 13-17	2 Thess 2:1-5, 13-17	2 Thess 2:16—3:5
Lk 20:27-38	Lk 20:27-38	Luke 20:27-38 or
		20:27, 34-38

Speaker's Introduction for the Lessons
Lesson 1
Haggai 1:15b—2:9 (SC)
Things may be tough now, but God reminds the people that God abides among them, and all is God's.

Job 19:23-27a (C)
Job cries out to God, but with the over-riding awareness that he knows God is there, and one day he shall see God with his own eyes.

2 Maccabees 7:1-2, 9-14 (RC)
Faced with fierce and horrible torture and death, people of God stand firm in the truth that God will be with them always.

Lesson 2
Psalm 145:1-5, 17-21 (SC)
Great is the Lord, and greatly to be praised, declares the psalmist, who also reminds us that the Lord is always near us.

Psalm 17:1-9 (C); 17:1, 5-6, 8, 15 (RC)
This prayer of David asks the Lord to guard and hide the psalmist from the enemies who surround.

Lesson 3
2 Thessalonians 2:1-5, 13-17 (SC/C); 2:16—3:5 (RC)
The author challenges the false belief that the "day of the Lord" has already arrived, and reminds the people of God's presence.

Gospel
Luke 20:27-38 (SC/C/RC)
Some Sadducees challenge Jesus regarding resurrection, and he explains that the things of God's world are different than this world.

Theme
Don't get caught up in details, but live to serve God.

Thought for the Day
It can be easy to get overwhelmed by a small focus. Recognizing God's presence in things makes them easier to take on.

Sermon Summary
We can get caught up in trying to predict the end of the world, or we can get overwhelmed by the huge problems in our world. When these things happen, it helps to remember that one step at a time – with God's help – we can do great things.

Call to Worship
One: We praise you, gracious God, for your presence among us.
All: We come to offer thankfulness and praise.
One: Our God is great, and greatly to be praised.
All: We come to worship in community.
One: God watches over us all, and is near to those who call.
All: We come with faith to celebrate God's presence.
One: Let us worship God.

Pastoral Prayer
God of questions and wonderings, we come before you uncertain of what is going on around us. We have questions: about the passages of time, about life and death, about physical things that happen in our world. When we are overwhelmed, remind us that you are with us, ever-present in our world, and challenge us to live in the moment. Concerns about the future can slip away in the gracious wonder of your embrace. May we transfer our wonderings about the end of the world to a commitment to live in your ways here and now, trusting in your compassion and guidance. Amen.

Prayer of Confession

It is difficult sometimes, O God, to focus where we should. Perhaps we get caught up in seeking details on the end of the world. Or we may neglect your presence among us and seek to forge ahead on our own. Sometimes we read the signs of calamity in our world as judgment on us or, worse still, on others. Forgive us, loving God. Help us to know that things happen which are beyond comprehension, that questions can live without answers, and that we need not know everything – indeed, we need know little but the wonders of your graceful presence. In Christ's name we pray. Amen.

Prayer of Dedication of Gifts and Self

We are here, giving God, ready to serve you. Take these gifts we offer; take the lives we live; take our dreams and hopes and spirit of adventure, and use these all to continue establishing your reign on earth. We pray in Jesus' name. Amen.

Hymn of the Day
O Master, Let Me Walk with Thee

Washington Gladden, author of this text, was a Congregational minister and leader in the social gospel movement. This text first appeared, under the title "Walking with God," in his periodical *The Sunday Afternoon* (1879). MARY-TON was first composed as to accompany the text "Sun of My Soul, Thou Savior Dear" in *Church Hymns with Tunes* (1874). Gladden chose this tune deliberately as a partner for his text and discouraged any other tunes from being paired with his text. Sing this devotional hymn at a moderately slow tempo, allowing the spirit to move through the words. One alternative way of presentation is to recite the text slowly as the music is played during the recitation.

Children's Time: The End of the World

Ask the children if they ever think about the end of the world. Have they perhaps ever seen any movies or read any books about the end of the world? What do they imagine it might be like?

A lot of people like to think about the world ending – some people get very excited and believe it will happen soon. However, according to the Bible, that's not the case.

Long ago some people in a place called Thessalonica were wondering about this, and the story got to St. Paul. He wrote them a letter and part of what he said was "don't let anyone tell you the wrong thing. The day of the Lord (which is another way of saying the end of the world) won't come for a long time." It seems that what Paul was really saying was that we shouldn't worry about it; instead we should concentrate on being God's people here and now.

The end of the world might be an interesting thing to think about now and then, but we shouldn't get too concerned about it. Rather, we should focus on doing the things God wants today.

Prayer: Thank you, God, for making this wonderful world and everything in it. Help us to live the way you would like, and not worry about the end. Amen.

The Sermon: Now, Not Then
Scripture: 2 Thessalonians 2:1-5, 13-17
(For sermon materials on 2 Thessalonians 2:1-5, 13-17, see the July/August 2010 issue of *The Clergy Journal*; for sermon materials on Luke 20:27-38, see the May/June 2010 planning issue of *The Clergy Journal*.)

Many years ago I was on the board of directors of a seminary, and we had just moved toward a new consolidated Master of Divinity program. The board was holding a meeting, and part of the point was to discuss the students who might be receiving the degree, and to determine their qualifications to receive the degree.

This conversation, however, got rather sidetracked by a discussion of the new academic hood that would accompany the degree. One of the board members went into a rather lengthy description of the hood, including expounding on the specific shade of the inside. Finally one of the other board members could not stand it.

"The darned thing is blue! Now, can we talk about the students?" That was the real issue, wasn't it? The students, not the hood they might be wearing. It is easy to get bogged down in details and forget the larger picture of what truly matters.

In today's Gospel a group of Sadducees approach Jesus with a strange, hypothetical question about a Jewish practice known as Levirate Marriage. If a woman married a man, and he died before they had a child, she was to marry his brother and have a child in the first man's name. "What would happen," the Sadducees asked, "if a woman married several brothers, one at a time? When she died, would she be married to them all?"

Their real question was to stump Jesus because they did not believe in resurrection. But Jesus goes a step beyond them. "You don't get it," he says. "Living beyond this world is, frankly, beyond this world. You cannot restrict your understanding to the way things are now. It will be different." Too readily we can get caught up in our current understanding of things, or in a small point of something trivial, and forget the bigger picture. I had a doctor's appointment once and ended up being late because of traffic. When I got there, I had to wait a further half hour before the doctor would see me. When I got home, my partner asked me, "How did you make out at the doctor's?" I proceeded to describe the traffic and the long wait, but was interrupted. "I meant, what did the doctor say to you?"

The Thessalonians have gotten distracted, and the author of this letter is trying to set them straight. The so-called "day of the Lord" has not yet occurred. In fact, what would make you think that? Certainly I didn't tell you, the author says.

Indeed, many things will happen before Christ returns, and the point is what we do in the meantime, not the energy we spend in trying to ascertain a date.

Such an important piece to hear and digest when there are those who love to pinpoint dates based on biblical passages. To think that the Bible is speaking about specific issues in 2010 is absurd at best. Beyond that, to get caught up in guessing dates and details takes us away from the reality that the Bible speaks *to* us in 2010, if not about us.

"Lots of things will happen before the day of the Lord," the author says. "The lawless one will come and try to knock your faith down."

Who is this lawless one? In those days people believed that for every force of good in the world there was a force with equal and opposing evil. It seems the author is trying to say that things will get worse before they get better. But ultimately, that does not matter if we recognize that God is in control. Rather than getting caught up worrying about the details, we need to look at the larger picture.

During the Second World War a Polish woman by the name of Irena Sendler was a nurse who worked in the concentration camps. The Nazis employed her to inspect children for typhus, for the Nazis had a grave fear of this disease spreading beyond the camps.

Sendler – who was not Jewish – donned a yellow star in solidarity with the Jews and began to work in the Warsaw Ghetto. She managed to smuggle Jewish babies and young children out of the ghetto, in ambulances, carriages, and even a toolbox. She cleverly brought noisy dogs in her vehicle when visiting the camps so the guards tended not to interfere with her.

It is believed that she rescued about 2500 children. Against the backdrop of some 6 million who were annihilated in the camps this is a tiny number – barely 4 one-hundredths of one percent. But to those children, and those descended from them, it was everything.

To focus solely on the "tiny" numbers Stendler rescued is to miss the fact that she was a lifesaver in a time of incomprehensible death. She could perhaps just as easily have thrown up her hands and said, "It's too big a situation, I can't do anything." But instead, she simply applied herself to what she could do.

We can become obsessed with worrying about the end of the world and what is going on around us. Or we can do something.

We can worry and wait, exasperated with the state of affairs in the world, with poverty and faithlessness, with death and destruction, with apathy and indifference. Or we can seek to live out the faith to which we have been called.

The author of Thessalonians urges the readers to remember the tradition of which they are a part, and which they have been taught. Over against huge obstacles they are invited – challenged – to rise above it all and do what they have been taught.

We are no different, really. We can get caught in the game of "coulda/shoulda/woulda" or we can work together to live out the call of Jesus Christ, trusting in the assurance that ultimately this is all in God's hands. And those are good hands.

– Donald Schmidt

Hymns
Opening Hymn
Praise to the Lord, the Almighty
All Creatures of Our God and King
Sermon Hymn
O Master, Let Me Walk with You
I Want Jesus to Walk with Me
Closing Hymn
Camina, Pueblo de Dios/Walk On, People of God
He Leadeth Me

November 14, 2010

25th Sunday after Pentecost (Proper 28 [33])
RC/Pres: 33rd Sunday in Ordinary Time

Lessons (See p. 10 for guidelines)

Semi-continuous (SC)	Complementary (C)	Roman Catholic (RC)
Isa 65:17-25	Mal 4:1-2a	Mal 3:19-20
Isa 12	Ps 98	Ps 98:5-9
2 Thess 3:6-13	2 Thess 3:6-13	2 Thess 3:7-12
Lk 21:5-19	Lk 21:5-19	Lk 21:5-19

Speaker's Introduction for the Lessons
Lesson 1
Isaiah 65:17-25 (SC)

God is going to bring in a new creation, turning the people to joy.
Former enemies will get along, and people will have a strong future.

Malachi 4:1-2a (C); 3:19-20 (RC)

This tiny reading reminds us that the Day of God is coming, and it
will be a joyous thing for all who revere God's name.

Lesson 2
Isaiah 12 (SC)

The author reminds us to give thanks and praise to God, for God is
our salvation.

Psalm 98 (C); 98:5-9 (RC)

The psalmist declares that every voice and horn and roaring sea will
rejoice, for the Lord is coming.

Lesson 3
2 Thessalonians 3:6-13 (SC/C); 3:7-12 (RC)

The letter writer admonishes the Thessalonians to be active in their
faith, never tiring from doing what is right.

Gospel
Luke 21:5-19 (SC/C/RC)
Jesus reminds the disciples that numerous things will happen before the world ends. Rather than worry about the time, we should be concerned with how to live now.

Theme
Never tire of doing right.

Thought for the Day
There can be a temptation to sit and wait for the world to end, but God calls us to be active and live our faith.

Sermon Summary
It can be easy to think we can rest on our laurels and celebrate what we have done and who we have become as people of faith. If we truly want to be people of faith, though, we need to live and share our faith each and every day.

Call to Worship
> One: God is creating a new world,
> **All: And invites us to be a part of it.**
> One: God is promising new and bright futures for those who follow God.
> **All: We rejoice in the goodness of God.**
> One: Before we can call, God answers our prayers.
> **All: Thanks be to God, who makes all things good.**
> One: Come, let us worship God.

Pastoral Prayer
Loving God of all space and time, your promises are real. You tell us that the future is good and we can trust you, for you have guided every moment of the past. You challenge us to live our faith truly and earnestly and we can trust you, for you lead us each step of the way. You invite us to live in the moment, rather than wait for tomorrow, and again we trust you, for you have always led us in the right ways. Fill us with your spirit now, that we might be your people in all we do. Amen.

Prayer of Confession

Loving guardian of the future, we come to you aware of the fact that we sometimes do crazy things with time. When we get caught up in worries about tomorrow, and forget the challenges of this day, forgive us, and remind us to take things more slowly and more gently. When we focus only on this day, and have no regard for how our actions might impact the future, bring us out of our narrow focus into a broader understanding of your views. When we get so caught up on the past that we ignore its meaning for today and tomorrow, bring us back to the awareness that we live in the here and now, in your presence. Amen.

Prayer of Dedication of Gifts and Self   11/14

Take the gifts we offer you, O God. Take the selves we are, O God. Take the hopes we have and the dreams we have, and use all of these things to make your reign a truth here in our world today. Amen.

Hymn of the Day
Forth in Thy Name, O Christ, We Go

This text, from Charles Wesley's *Hymns and Sacred Poems* (1749), is on a small list of hymns about work. Some hymnals have made small changes to make the language more contemporary ("thy" to "your," etc.). The number of tunes assigned to this text is as large as the hymnals that include it; Rockingham from Aaron Williams's *Supplement to Psalmody* (18th c.), Duke Street by John Hatton, and Canonbury by Robert Schumann are but three of the choices. Whichever tune you use, make sure that the music presentation has a straightforward directness that matches that of the text. This is an excellent choice as a final or sending forth hymn for a worship service with a theme of commitment or social justice.

Children's Time: Working Together for God

(Preparation: If doing the three-legged race demonstration, plan it with a volunteer, and bring a tie or strip of cloth to tie your legs together.)

Talk with the children about teams. Have any of them played games or sports where they are on teams? What's that like? One of the nice things about a team is that everyone gets to do what they can. When we're part of a team, it's important to do our part. We don't all have to do the same thing. What if you tried to play soccer or hockey, and everybody decided to be the goalie? It wouldn't work very well if everybody stayed in the net and no one went out to play.

Even in a small team it's important to do our part. Has anyone ever been in a three-legged race? *(You might demonstrate a three-legged race with one of the children. Choose a volunteer ahead of time and clue him or her in to your plan. Tie your ankles together and urge the child to go in a certain direction, but don't cooperate. Refuse to move; perhaps fold your arms and look around.)* It doesn't work very well if one person doesn't do their part, does it?

The Bible tells us that we must all do what we can to do God's work, and if we support one another and share our talents, we can accomplish much more.

Prayer: Thank you, God, for all the gifts and talents you give us. Help us to share them together. Amen.

The Sermon: Never Tire of Doing Good
Scripture: 2 Thessalonians 3:6-13

(For sermon materials on 2 Thessalonians 3:6-13, see the July/August 2010 issue of *The Clergy Journal*; for sermon materials on Luke 21:5-19, see the May/June 2010 planning issue of *The Clergy Journal*.)

The preacher stood in front of the congregation.

"I have an amazing secret to tell you," the preacher said. "It could change your life. It could certainly change your church's life." People got excited; they were leaning forward to hear the magic word.

"You've been telling me that your church cannot grow because there are not enough people. But I've found the answer. You see, there are thousands of people outside of this building yet within a mile or two of this church. Some of them are hungry for the gospel, starving for recognition, craving a message that tells them God loves them unconditionally and forever."

People looked a little surprised.

"Tell them the good news. Tell them the gospel you have in your midst. Don't be shy. Don't be lazy. Proclaim the message that a starving world is craving to hear and absorb. Proclaim it with every fiber of your being, with every ounce of oomph you've got. Proclaim it until you're tired, and then regain your strength and proclaim it again. Don't stop."

The people had been excited to bring in that guest speaker; however, they never invited the individual back.

November 14, 2010
25th Sunday after Pentecost (Proper 28 [33])
RC/Pres: 33rd Sunday in Ordinary Time

The apostle Paul began with a sense that Jesus Christ would soon return, and so the onus was on the church to proclaim the gospel as quickly and as widely as possible, in anticipation of that great event. As time progressed, however, Paul came to realize that perhaps he was wrong. Perhaps Christ was *not* returning as soon as he had thought.

The urgency to proclaim the gospel remained, though. In today's reading, Paul is emphasizing the need to proclaim the good news, not because we are running out of time (we're not) but because it's the right thing to do. So many in our world – especially those who may have been told that they do not belong or they do not matter – need to hear the message of God's love as proclaimed by Jesus Christ. Why should we make them wait?

Yet the church is lazy – then as now. We probably don't like to admit it, but it seems to be a reality.

People are busy. We work. Some people have two jobs. Kids have soccer and hockey and ballet practice. There are meetings to go to, and things to do, and so on, and so on. Yet the fact of it all remains that there is work to be done, and we are the ones to do it.

Paul says, in a phrase that can sound somewhat harsh, "Anyone not willing to work shouldn't get to eat" (2 Thess 3:10, *The Voice*). However, Paul is not making a blanket statement here. Such a thing would be absurd, suggesting that the disabled, children, and the elderly cannot eat if they cannot work. Such an idea clearly goes against the teachings of Jesus, and of Paul himself. Rather, Paul is fed up with those who claim to be active disciples, members of the church, and yet are not pulling their weight. As such, the passage stings a bit, doesn't it?

Paul goes on to explain what he means: "Never grow tired of doing good" (verse 13b). This is really what it is all about – do good, and never tire of it. That can be a challenge. Some people, quite frankly, drive us crazy. They can wear us down to the core. Yet, Paul says, do good. Love others. Treat them well.

These verses are not a call to labor for the achievement of salvation – Paul has been clear in other settings that not only is this not required but is in fact pointless. Instead, this is a frank recognition that Christians are called to live out their lives as faithful testimonies to the gospel. Don't sit around waiting for the rapture, Paul seems to be saying, but get on with doing good.

Churches often hold stewardship campaigns, often inviting people to examine their overall giving patterns as part of being a steward of God's creation. In many churches people are invited to make commitments of how they will give of time, talent, and treasure.

Years ago in a church's stewardship campaign a friend pointed out that you can give without loving, but you cannot love without giving. Similarly, you can do good without being a Christian, but you cannot be a Christian without doing good.

Consequently, if we are to be people of faith then we are to be people who *live* that faith. Laziness is no option, and not in the least a behavior to be modeled. The phrasing in verse 10 is seen by some as a turn of phrase that might best be understood as "if you're not going to earn a living you shouldn't expect a life." It does make sense.

Now, none of this is intended – by Paul or me – to make any of us feel guilty about how we live our lives. Not at all. Rather it is an invitation to turn our thinking around a little, and if not fully around at least to the point where we change our worldview. Giving, doing, loving are not options for us as followers of Christ and members of the church; they are an integral part of our faith. They are not pressures to make us do things, but opportunities to live our faith to the fullest.

Let us never tire of doing right. Ever. Let us reach out to others, and show them – in word and deed – the powerful message of this faith. When someone needs help because they do not know the point of going on, let us never tire of doing good. When an addict cries out for help, let us never tire of doing good. When a person says that they have been hurt and pushed aside, by the world or the church, let us never tire of doing good. Never tire of doing good. Ever.

– Donald Schmidt

Hymns
Opening Hymn
To God Compose a Song of Joy
This Is a Day of New Beginnings
Sermon Hymn
Be Not Dismayed
God Be with You Til We Meet Again
Closing Hymn
We Shall Overcome
Forth in Thy Name, O Christ, We Go

November 21, 2010

Reign of Christ/Christ the King (Proper 29 [34])

Lessons (See p. 10 for guidelines)

Semi-continuous (SC)	Complementary (C)	Roman Catholic (RC)
Jer 23:1-6	Jer 23:1-6	2 Sam 5:1-3
Lk 1:68-79	Ps 46	Ps 122:1-5
Col 1:11-20	Col 1:11-20	Col 1:12-20
Lk 23:33-43	Lk 23:33-43	Lk 23:35-43

Speaker's Introduction for the Lessons
Lesson 1
Jeremiah 23:1-16 (SC/C)

The prophet issues a stern warning to those "shepherds" who mislead God's people. God promises to bring in new leadership.

2 Samuel 5:1-3 (RC)

The people tell David that they are his own flesh and blood, and they anoint him shepherd/king of the people.

Lesson 2
Luke 1:68-79 (SC)

Zechariah's prophecy not only announces the birth of John the Baptist, but also proclaims God's faithfulness and salvation.

Psalm 46 (C)

God is our "very present help" in trouble, and in God we find our refuge.

Lesson 3
Colossians 1:11-20 (SC/C); 1:12-20 (RC)

Christ has rescued us from darkness and blesses us. Christ, the head of the body, has the first place in everything.

Gospel
Luke 23:33-43 (SC/C); 23:35-43 (RC)

When Jesus is crucified, the people mock and deride him – religious leaders, soldiers, and even one of the criminals crucified alongside. Yet Jesus promises paradise to the one who is faithful.

Theme

In a number of different ways we are reassured that God is our shepherd.

Thought for the Day

The image of God as shepherd runs through much of life. No matter who we are God seeks to provide us leadership and unconditional love and to guide us gently on the right path.

Sermon Summary

People often struggle with reasons for the death of Jesus. Today's Gospel clearly reminds us that Jesus died to show the world that God's love would prevail, no matter what. Whether we can deny it or ignore it, God's love is here to stay. Period.

Call to Worship

One: God – Shepherd, Ruler, Friend – calls us here.
All: We gather in the presence of God.
One: God – almighty, all-loving – calls us here.
All: We gather in the presence of God.
One: God – Creator, Lover, Parent, Child – calls us here.
All: We gather in the presence of God.
One: Come, let us worship the wondrous God.

Pastoral Prayer

God, your reign is all around us. When we feel distanced from you, still you come to us. When we feel we have disobeyed you, you offer forgiveness. When we become high and mighty, you remind us of the servant leadership you modeled for us and all people. Move through our world, giving assurance to all that you seek to lead us – not in pompous ways we might imagine, but in gentle and loving ways. Amen.

Prayer of Confession

There are times when we are confused in our understanding of who you are, loving God. We may imagine you as a ruler in a high palace, distanced from us and uncaring. At other times we may imagine you as a shepherd who is uncaring and ruthless, or as one who is powerless. Forgive us our misunderstandings, and help us to remember that the images the Bible presents to us are unending, and wonderful. You are beyond description, and always present, always loving and always caring. Amen.

Prayer of Dedication of Gifts and Self

Great ruler of all beings, we are your people. We bring what we have and what we are, and offer it all to you. Guide us, inspire us, fill us. Take our offerings and use them to do good throughout the world. Amen.

Hymn of the Day
Jesus, Remember Me

The music of Jacques Berthier and the religious community at Taizé has only become an integral part of North American worship repertoire in the past 15 to 20 years. The use of repetitive chant as an active and central part of worship is both powerful and sometimes threatening. What do we do with such a short piece? Why do we sing it with so many repetitions? Education is needed to help our worshipers understand the "breath prayer" and the power of simple repetition. Try singing this chant at the conclusion of the Luke 23 reading. Sing it a sufficient number of times, thus allowing the worshiper to feel the connection between the words of scripture and the words of the chant – the connection between scripture and self.

Children's Time: The End of the Story

One of the Bible stories we read today might seem a little strange. It's the story of Jesus dying on the cross, and usually we read it at Palm Sunday or Good Friday. But today is a day known as Christ the King Sunday/Reign of Christ Sunday *(use the title used in your church)*. It's a day to think about Jesus as a leader, and we read this strange story. It's a strange story because a lot of people didn't quite understand it at first.

Jesus came to tell us about God's love. More than anything, Jesus spent time telling and showing people that God loved them and wanted them to live in God's way. When people were doing things that were not good, Jesus would scold them – not to make them feel bad, but to encourage them to live in God's way instead.

Some people didn't like Jesus' message. They didn't want everyone to be told God loved them. So they decided to have Jesus killed.

What's interesting, though, is that it didn't stop Jesus. He kept right on, even to the very end – while he was on the cross – telling people about God's love. When one of the other people being crucified with him asked Jesus to remember him, Jesus told him they would be together in God's garden (paradise) that very day. Most people would probably only think about themselves at a time like that, but not Jesus.

On this day when we think about Jesus as a king or ruler, it helps to remember the style of ruler he modeled for us: one who would teach others about God's love, no matter what.

Prayer: God of eternal love, help us to receive your love, and to share it with others. Amen.

The Sermon: The Reign of a Real Leader
Scripture: Luke 23:33-43
(For sermon materials on Luke 1:68-79, see the July/August 2010 issue of *The Clergy Journal*; for sermon materials on Colossians 1:11-20, see the May/June 2010 planning issue of *The Clergy Journal*.)

At Dannemora State Prison in Dannemora, New York, a church stands. It is quite unique, being a free-standing house of worship on the grounds of a prison. It's no ordinary church, either. It has beautiful red oak pews donated by gangster inmate "Lucky" Luciano. There are two angelic figures near the altar that come from the flagship of Ferdinand Magellan, which sank off the coast of the Philippines in the early 1500s.

Something else that makes the church stand out is the name: St. Dismas. Tradition has assigned this name to the "good" thief crucified next to Jesus, and to whom Jesus makes the promise that they "will keep one another company today, in God's garden" to quote the *Good As New* translation of Luke 23:43.

This promise of Jesus is well-known, coming in response to the thief's statement that the other crucified thief (and, by extension, the others in the story) should stop mocking Jesus, for he has done nothing wrong. More than anything else, that simple fact tends to underscore some of the horror of the crucifixion: Jesus is innocent. A horrible enough death, to be sure, for someone who is guilty, but appalling and repugnant for one who is innocent.

So why does Jesus do it? Surely, as the religious leaders and others suggest, if he truly is/was the son of God, he could have saved himself. Or could he?

There is strength and value in reading this story today, the Sunday dedicated to the Reign of Christ, some five to six months away from Lent and Easter. Standing here, on the cusp of Advent, the story takes on a new flavor. It provides us the opportunity to reflect on the "kingship" of Jesus, rather than the whole piece of the crucifixion – and resurrection.

Accordingly, we can pause and reflect on some aspects of this small narrative, and see what it might tell us about Jesus as leader/ruler.

Perhaps first and foremost is verse 34a in which Jesus prays for forgiveness for those who "know not what they do." The phrase appears in double brackets in such Bibles as the *New Revised Standard Version* and the Greek New Testament published by the United Bible Societies. It does not appear in significant, ancient manuscripts; further, it makes no sense that someone would remove the verse, given its power, thus suggesting that it must be an addition. A great image of a leader, but probably not one of real value.

Other Gospels include the mockeries by others, yet Luke seems to want to make a point of them. They begin with the religious leaders, and then the soldiers, and finally one of the ones crucified with Jesus. Each time, the Greek verb gets a little stronger; clearly these people think that Jesus should have had the power to *do* something – anything. Yet he does not.

One of the more modern, and extremely popular, explanations of the death of Jesus here is that he "had to die" because of our sinful nature. It carries a sense that we are/were so bad Jesus had to take the place of a sacrificial lamb and make things right with God. There are, however, some major flaws in this argument.

Firstly, it ignores that God repeatedly through the prophets (such as in Isaiah 1:11-14, Hosea 6:6, and Amos 5:1-24, to name a few) condemns the sacrificial cult. If God has been so adamant, centuries before Jesus, that this system does not work, and God wants it rejected, it seems highly unlikely that God would suddenly bring it back.

Secondly, this stance implies that God is too weak to break rules of God's own making. Even if God had not rejected the sacrificial cult God could certainly have intervened here. To state otherwise suggests that God is not very powerful.

Lastly, this all suggests that we are more powerful than God: our sin can make Jesus do things. Seems preposterous, when you look at it that way.

So why did Jesus die?

To answer this, we go back even further: why did Jesus come to earth? To save us, yes, but to do this by speaking of God's love. Over and over – and over – Jesus proclaims in words and actions the unconditional and unwavering love of our Creator. Throughout history prior to Jesus the Bible tells us that God is constantly making covenants, each of which we tend to break or defy. So this time, God appears to try something new, sending Jesus to bring the message "home."

God loves you, Jesus essentially says, like a shepherd, and a woman with a lost coin, and a parent who cannot write off a child no matter how wayward. God will not leave us alone. God will love us when the world tells us otherwise. God will love us in the deep and difficult moments when we feel completely gutted and alone.

Perhaps most importantly, God loves us more than the power of evil demonstrated by the Roman government, seen by people in Jesus' day as perhaps the most evil and oppressive regime ever.

Jesus seems quite dedicated to showing that God's love is stronger than anything. In order to do that, Jesus has to stand up to everything. That includes folks such as the religious leaders of his own community, seemingly scared by his message and wanting to cut it short. That would also include the Roman government, which has been convinced that Jesus represents some kind of threat to them. (Kind of ironic, when you think of it, that they would be scared of a poor, itinerant preacher in a relatively obscure province.)

If Jesus is going to defy them, Jesus needs to stand up to whatever they want to throw. That means that, if they want to kill him, he has to submit.

Of course, the final word is not theirs, but Christ's own when he rises from the dead, stating emphatically and permanently that God's love is here to stay.

All this is powerful stuff, and important to note on this day. For surely, more than anything else, this bold statement Jesus makes by dying is the ultimate sign of a true leader, one who is called and challenged to reign over the world – then and now.

The church year is closing, and a new cycle begins next week. What better time than this to acknowledge and celebrate the ultimate act of leadership: by appearing to be a weak and suffering Messiah, Jesus ultimately trumps everything, and leads us back to God's garden.

– Donald Schmidt

Hymns
Opening Hymn
Crown with Your Richest Crowns

Crown Him with Many Crowns
Sermon Hymn
Eternal Christ, You Rule

O Love, How Deep
Closing Hymn
The Head That Once Was Crowned

A Mighty Fortress

November 25, 2010

Thanksgiving

Lessons (See p. 10 for guidelines)

RCL	Roman Catholic (RC)
Deut 26:1-11	Sir 50:22-24
Ps 100	Zeph 3:14-15
Phil 4:4-9	1 Cor 1:3-9
Jn 6:25-35	Lk 17:11-19

Speaker's Introduction for the Lessons
Lesson 1
Deuteronomy 26:1-11 (RCL)

When the people come into the promised land they are to celebrate thanksgiving, remembering God's goodness in rescuing them from slavery in Egypt.

Sirach 50:22-24 (RC)

This brief prayer invites the people to praise the God who works wonders and who – from the very beginning – sustains us and grants us mercy.

Lesson 2
Psalm 100 (RCL)

In five short verses, this psalm of thanksgiving makes it clear how we are to respond to the Lord who made us.

Zephaniah 3:14-15 (RC)

The Lord is in our midst and taken away all judgments against us.

Lesson 3
Philippians 4:4-9 (RCL)

In this familiar passage we are reminded to rejoice in God's presence, again and again.

1 Corinthians 1:3-9 (RC)

Paul reminds the Corinthians that their faith is strong, and the message they proclaim is gifted.

Gospel
John 6:25-35 (RCL)
When people track Jesus down, looking for bread to eat, Jesus challenges them instead to seek *real* bread – the word of God.
Luke 17:11-19 (RC)
Ten people with leprosy approach Jesus, looking for healing. Jesus offers healing to them all; interestingly, the only one to return to give thanks is a foreigner.

Theme
Seek new ways to give thanks to God, who is ever-present.

Thought for the Day
God has done more for us than we can possibly imagine. When we are giving thanks, it is important to pause and remember all that God has done.

Sermon Summary
When we are caught up in the eating and celebrating of Thanksgiving Day, take some time to reflect on God's overall goodness. For what do you have to give thanks? How can you do that in ways that will be pleasing to God, and transforming of the world?

Call to Worship
One: Come, give thanks to God with joy!
All: We will serve God with gladness.
One: Enter God's presence with a joyful song!
All: We shall enter God's gates with thanksgiving.
One: For God is good; God's love endures forever.
All: God's faithfulness continues through the ages.
One: Come, let us worship God.

Pastoral Prayer
Creator of all, giver of life, beloved parent of each and every person: we gather here at a time of thanksgiving to give our thanks to you. You did not just create, but you have been intimately involved in the well-being of your creation from that very first instant. When planets learned to spin

and microscopic creatures learned to crawl; when trees dared to stretch their branches and humans learned to laugh; when rivers stretched and sand began to dance – in all these things, Loving God, you were there. Lift our hearts now to give you thanks, not merely in words and thoughts, but in actions that make a difference and show to the world how much our lives are formed by you. Amen.

Prayer of Confession

Loving God, here at Thanksgiving our thoughts are on all you have done for us. Yet we know that, too, we need to think of things we have done. We know that at times our will is far from being aligned with yours. We have our own egos, our own agendas, our own desires – and too often we put all this above all else.

Forgive us. Help us to explore new ways of being your people, of living the lives you would have us live. Guide us on paths of peace and joy, and away from greed and anger. Give to all your people a renewed commitment to living as thanksgiving people. Always. Amen.

Prayer of Dedication of Gifts and Self

You have given so much to us and all your people, O God. Now we give of ourselves back to you. These gifts – a small token of what we have – are given to further your work. Our hearts and our hands – a small portion of what we are – are offered to you for your work as well. Amen.

Hymn of the Day
I Am the Bread of Life

This remarkable hymn by Suzanne Toolan, a member of the Sisters of Mercy, fast became a favorite in the Episcopal and Lutheran traditions in the 1970s. Since that time its popularity has spread to other denominations. Based on the John 6 scripture, it is a song of triumph and resurrection. Sing it during Holy Communion, if this is your tradition, or immediately following, if not. The effect it will have on the worshipers is spirit-filled. This is an excellent song to be accompanied by either guitar or keyboard instruments. The change from unison singing for stanzas to harmony for the refrain increases the energy felt. Adding brass during the refrain will add even more energy.

Children's Time: God's Bread

(Bring a loaf of bread and a Bible. You may choose to share the bread with the children or not.)

See the things I brought today? We have a loaf of bread, and we have a Bible.

Long ago, Jesus impressed some people when he turned a few tiny loaves of bread and a couple of fish into a big meal for thousands of people. They loved it so much, they wanted him to do it again. They went looking, and they found Jesus.

"Aha!" Jesus said. "You found me just because you wanted more bread. But why don't you seek God's bread?"

The people probably scratched their heads, but Jesus continued. "God's bread is me."

It seems that Jesus wanted the people to realize that having good food was important and wonderful, but learning about God was wonderful too.

Now, I can eat this bread. *(Break off a piece and eat it, and/or share it with the children.)* But, I can't eat this Bible, can I?

No, the way we "eat" the Bible is to learn about God, and Jesus, and God's love.

It's Thanksgiving, and you'll probably eat some wonderful food. When you do so, think as well about God's food – God's word about Jesus. And give thanks to God for all God gives.

Prayer: Thank you, gracious God, for all you give us and do for us. Especially thank you for Jesus, who teaches us about you. Amen.

The Sermon: Thanks. Giving.
Scripture: John 6:25-35

(For sermon materials on John 6:25-35, see the July/August 2010 issue of *The Clergy Journal*; for sermon materials on Deuteronomy 26:1-11, see the May/June 2010 planning issue of *The Clergy Journal*.)

The part of the scripture commonly called "The Ten Commandments" can be found twice in the Bible (Exo 20:2-17 and Deut 5:7-21). They are essentially the same with one important difference: in Exodus, the reason given for observing the Sabbath is that God worked for six days on creation, and rested on the seventh day. However, in Deuteronomy the Sabbath is set aside as a day to rest and remember God's mighty act in rescuing the people from slavery in Egypt.

This emphasis on deliverance from slavery is a key theme in the book of Deuteronomy, and it arises in today's reading. The people are commanded, upon entering the promised land, to bring the first fruits of their harvest and offer them to God as thanksgiving for being delivered from Egyptian slavery. Clearly, the people are not to forget God's great work in this seminal part of their history. This is the God who abhors slavery and oppression, and brings people out of it, even at great cost; let it never be forgotten.

This text forms a backdrop for today's focus – John 6:25-35 – and for the day itself.

Some people had been intrigued, maybe even overwhelmed, by Jesus' act of turning a few loaves and fishes into a meal for thousands. When they cannot find him the next morning they head off across the lake in search of him, and finally locate him.

The people probably think they are impressing Jesus by hunting him down, but he cuts them to the quick.

"You're not looking for me because you like what I'm doing," Jesus says. "No, you're looking for me because you like the food I gave you. You're hungry for bread; you need to hunger for something else. You need to hunger for the food I offer on God's behalf."

At best they begin to scratch their heads; at worst they are staring at each other going "huh?"

This sense of eating our fill has a familiar ring at Thanksgiving. More than any other day of the year this is the time for feasting, for making huge amounts of food, and then eating it until we all heave a huge sigh and declare, "Gee whiz, I wish I hadn't eaten so much."

Is that what it's really about?

Some years ago several of us were invited to have Thanksgiving at a friend's home. She was a nutritionist, and one of the most intriguing things about the meal was that it was healthier and leaner than most times. There were no potatoes and gravy, but rather a slightly flavored rice. There was a salad with minimal dressing. There were special things, too, such as an exquisite low-fat stuffing with bits of dried fruit in it, and a wonderful cocktail of cranberries, nuts, orange sections, and coconut in hollowed-out orange rinds. All in all, it was a wonderful feast.

Thus, it's a little embarrassing to say that we came away from there feeling cheated. Where was all the rich and fattening and gooey stuff we felt we deserved? Beyond that, what was it that made us feel we deserved it?

In these days when we are reminded that North Americans are some of the most obese people in the world, it seems a bit silly (at best) to want to pig out so heavily. And, beyond overeating and expanding our waistlines, what does it say about our theology?

Thanksgiving may include a turkey and pumpkin pie and sweet potatoes and numerous other treats, but is that really what it is all about? George Washington started American Thanksgiving as a day to give thanks for the American nation, and the end of the revolutionary war. Without in any way implying that there is an intrinsic link between American history and the biblical story, this nonetheless has echoes of the requirement for the Hebrew people to give thanks for being rescued by God from Egyptian slavery.

Thanksgiving Day has changed in its emphasis over the years, but surely it remains an opportunity to give great thanks to God for things other than food. It is a day to take stock of all God has done for us, to acknowledge them, and to find ways to express our appreciation. We may have found ourselves lifted from despair – can we find ways to express hope and promise to others? We may have found a job after a time of unemployment – can we help lobby for jobs? We may indeed have a comfortable life and plenty of food year 'round – can we find ways to share it with others year 'round? We may be grateful for the message of the gospel we receive in our church – can we share that with others in the community?

In short: can we show our thanksgiving in places other than our hips or waist?

The people told Jesus about the manna offered to their ancestors in the wilderness, probably in hopes that Jesus would offer them something similar. Remember, manna was something that provided sustenance day after day – never too much, but always enough. The people need not be admonished for wanting daily food.

But Jesus ups the ante. "You want *real* bread? Believe in me. I am the bread that God offers the world, that will give it life."

Even in giving the people manna, God pointed out that they need more than that. "One does not live by bread alone, but by every word that flows from the mouth of [God]" we read early in Deuteronomy (8:3). According to Matthew 4:4 Jesus quotes this same verse when tempted in the desert.

The word of God. That's the real bread of life.

151

If we could chew on that a little at Thanksgiving Day – and for the rest of the year as well – we would be much further ahead.

Go ahead and eat all you want on Thanksgiving Day; it only comes once a year after all! And watch some football if that's your pleasure, go for a walk, celebrate family – in other words, take a holiday and enjoy yourself.

But see if you can go a step further: reflect on all God has done for you, and look for concrete ways to show your appreciation.

God will thank you for it.

– Donald Schmidt

Hymns
Opening Hymn
Come, You Thankful People, Come
We Praise You, O God
Sermon Hymn
There's a Spirit in the Air
For the Fruit of All Creation
Closing Hymn
Now Thank We All Our God
Let All Things Now Living

November 28, 2010

1st Sunday of Advent

Lessons (See p. 10 for guidelines)

RCL	Roman Catholic
Isa 2:1-5	Isa 2:1-5
Ps 122	Ps 122
Rom 13:11-14	Rom 13:11-14
Mt 24:36-44	Mt 24:37-44

Speaker's Introduction for the Lessons
Lesson 1
Isaiah 2:1-5 (RCL/RC)

At the time of Isaiah, Jerusalem was highly vulnerable. It prospered or suffered at the hands of other more powerful nations. But God's presence alone, not the supremacy of Jerusalem, will ensure justice and peace.

Lesson 2
Psalm 122 (RCL/RC)

This is a song sung by pilgrims ascending the holy hill to Jerusalem for worship. The "thrones of judgment" refer to the justice Davidic kings were to ensure for their people.

Lesson 3
Romans 13:11-14 (RCL/RC)

Paul writes to a burgeoning community of Jesus followers in Rome during dangerous times. This chapter advises the community on how to live in the shadow of Roman imperial rule.

Gospel
Matthew 24:36-44 (RCL); 24:37-44 (RC)

An apocalyptic text which announces God's sovereignty over all the earth when contemporary signs point to the contrary, these words orient us during Advent to Jesus' coming again to establish God's reign of love.

Theme
We prepare for Christ's return by creating an international kinship of love.

Thought for the Day
The outcry and the birth-cry
Of new life at its term.

– Seamus Heaney

Sermon Summary
By reading Jesus' apocalyptic speech about not knowing the day and hour of his return in the context of his larger discussion with his disciples, we learn that "being ready" is not about the future but about how we are to treat "the least of these" in the present.

Call to Worship
One: We have come to God's house,

All: Gathered from our separate lives, reminded that we are one community.

One: In this place, may we learn how to beat our swords into plowshares,

All: And how to pray for peace without and within.

Pastoral Prayer
Sovereign God, it is hard to see your rule or even your will in the chaos that surrounds us. Help us to see you in the face of our friends and enemies. Help us to let go of calculating the "whys" and "whens" of life. Immerse us so fully in this present that we sense your presence with us, bringing to birth your new world of shalom, even here. We pray for victims of war, for all who struggle with illness, for the many among us seeking decent work, for all who are grieving, for our children that they may hope when hope seems hopeless, and for our church, that we may bear witness to your good news in troubled times. Amen.

Prayer of Confession
Nation rises up against nation and the peoples of earth weep and beg for release. The very land is wounded; the waters and skies are choked by our insatiable hunger for more. How can we be alert for you, Dear One, when we run from disaster to disaster or when we retreat into familiar routine at home and at work? We admit that we do not want to be surprised by your advent; we don't need

154

more uncertainty! So we have come to your house – confessing our weariness and seeking your strength. Have mercy on us. Show us the way forward. We pray in the name of the One who is the Way, the Truth, and the Life. Amen.

Prayer of Dedication of Gifts and Self

We offer these gifts that your kingdom may take shape here on earth, and that we may also be shaped in the giving, by the one whose very life is a gift to us, Jesus Christ. Amen.

Hymn of the Day
O Come, O Come Emmanuel

This is possibly the best-known hymn for the season of Advent. It was originally one of the seven medieval antiphons sung in conjunction with the Magnificat. There have been many revisions to the text and re-ordering of the stanzas. Whatever the order, the need for each stanza is important, as it gives a different name for the Messiah found in Hebrew scripture. The tune, VENI EMMANUEL, was first found in a 15th century French processional book. There are many arrangements and harmonizations of the tune, however possibly the best way is to sing it is to sing it unaccompanied, as chant, the way it was originally intended. As an alternate way of presentation, sing each stanza and then read the supporting Hebrew scripture, thus connecting the hymn and historical readings.

Children's Time: Getting Ready

(Bring a star – preferably one that you can hang on the church Christmas tree after the story, although any star decoration will do. The same star should be kept until January 6, when it will form a part of the Epiphany story.)

It's Advent. Do any of you know what the season of Advent is about? *(Affirm all answers; point out that Advent is the season where we get ready for Christmas.)*

This is a time when we think about Jesus being born, and we celebrate. What are some of the things you do to get ready for Christmas? *(Again, affirm all answers, adding things as necessary.)*

One of the things we do in this season is to think beyond Christmas. Even though our hearts and thoughts are really set on December 25, there's much more beyond that as well. Christmas isn't just one day. It's a whole season of its own, and even more than that, it's a way of living.

I brought a star this morning *(show it to the children)* to help us think about Christmas going longer than one day, or even one short season. We often put stars up at Christmastime. What are some kinds of stars you have seen? *(Accept all answers.)* Stars are special at Christmas, and yet they shine all through the year. Every night there are trillions of stars in the sky. Each of those stars can remind us of Jesus – his birth, and his being here with us each and every day. *(Hang the star on the Christmas tree where the children will be able to see it through the season.)*

Prayer: God of wonder, may every star we see remind us of Jesus and the love he brought to our world. Amen.

The Sermon: Ready for What?
Scripture: Matthew 24:36-44

(For sermon materials on Matthew 24:36-44, see the September/October 2010 issue of *The Clergy Journal*; for sermon materials on Isaiah 2:1-5, see the May/June 2010 planning issue of *The Clergy Journal*.)

The irony of our passage this morning is that the more narrowly we focus on it, the more we end up violating the express wishes of Jesus to not worry about the details of the day and hour of the Son of Man's coming, since that is the passage's precise subject matter! This dilemma can be avoided by recognizing that these verses are a larger conversation Jesus is having with his disciples in chapters 24 and 25. And that conversation concerns the establishment of an international community, living under the reign of Love.

Jesus' ministry and the writing of the Gospel of Matthew both took place during the violent, repressive rule of Rome over Judea and neighboring nations that Rome had conquered and incorporated into its empire. The entire conversation challenges the disciples to live as if they believe that God, and not earthly rulers or empires, is sovereign over the earth.

The political implications of such faithful living are underscored by where Jesus holds this conversation. According to Matthew, Jesus departs from the temple, where he had made various pronouncements about its immanent destruction, and has now seated himself upon the Mount of Olives (24:3a). The prophet Elijah is associated with the Mount of Olives. You will remember that Elijah mobilized stalwart national resistance against King Ahab, who had turned from covenant obedience to God to allegiance to the foreign gods of his foreign wife. And it is from this significant Mount that Jesus speaks privately to his closest followers.

By widening our lens from the lectionary passage to its context, we notice that it is the disciples, not Jesus, who initiate the conversation about when the temple will be destroyed and what the signs of the end of the age will be (24:3b). Perhaps after three years of following Jesus, they were looking for ways to evaluate their ministry's effectiveness and impact in light of the awaited coming. Maybe they were wondering how much longer they'd have to keep up this intensive ministry until massive social change came about. But it is they and not Jesus who initiates the discussion of timetables and signs.

Jesus, to the contrary, is focused on the present. He is more concerned with how the disciples will respond under threat, in the midst of chaos, and during national turmoil (24:4-8). He is principally concerned that they not forswear their allegiance to the *basilea* (empire/kingdom/kin-dom) of God that he has announced through his ministry. He warns them not to be led astray either by false messiahs or by war, or be diverted by personal assault.

In case they think time is a factor for them, Jesus goes so far as to promise them that if they remain faithful to him and God's empire, they will be tortured, put to death, and hated by all the nations (24:9). His resounding theme is that the empire will fall, "these times will end," but *that* is not to be a concern of the disciples. Their concern must be with how they live now; because how Jesus has taught them to live will challenge the very legitimacy of the Roman Empire.

In our passage for this morning, Jesus discusses "keeping awake" as a metaphor for faithful living. Notice, however, one does not keep awake in order to anticipate the coming of the Son of Man. Rather, such expectation should orient us not toward the heavens but toward our neighbors, particularly those who are imprisoned, strangers, the sick, and the poor. While our lectionary passage does not directly discuss this orientation, its warning and call to attention is the prelude to some of Jesus' most famous lines about the judgment of the nations and its peoples in the following chapter, which concludes his speech from the Mount of Olives to his disciples. Here we learn that "to be ready" is not a matter of predicting particular events but a matter of connecting to particular people (25:34-36, 40).

Now what's interesting in this very familiar passage is that the Son of Man comes to judge the nations, but he separates the people of these nations from one another according to whether they have extended uncommon and potentially seditious love toward "the least of these" (25:32). For those who were imprisoned under Roman rule were not run-of-the mill burglars. Some were peasants who could not meet their tax burden. Still others were men and women who had participated in unsuccessful popular movements to overthrow Rome; what today we would call political prisoners (Richard A.

Horsley, *Bandits, Prophets, and Messiahs: Popular Movements at the Time of Jesus,* San Francisco: HarperCollins, 1985, pp. 35-36).

Moreover to welcome the stranger, care for the sick, and ensure the survival needs of the poor (and Jesus and his followers were themselves poor), meant a veritable explosion of traditional boundaries of kin and an abrogation of religious laws concerning how the "unclean" could be incorporated in the social and worshipping community (see Mt 8 and 9).

While in our day these verses from Matthew have often been tamed to mean that individuals and the church should offer charity to "those in need," in the context of these two chapters of Matthew we realize that this kind of love challenges allegiances to kin and country. Jesus is about building an international fellowship of love that unites across and in spite of national and familial ties. The peoples are thus separated, not according to their national or familial affiliation but according to the love they have shown. Indeed in the Great Commission, which comprises the final verses of Matthew's Gospel, Jesus sends forth his followers saying, "Make disciples of all nations, baptizing them in the name of the Father and of the Son and of the Holy Spirit, and teaching them to obey everything that I have commanded you. And remember, I am with you always, to the end of the age" (28:19-20).

When the church talks about Christ coming again, we are referring to that time when all barriers to Love's full reign in our world will cease; a time when the world will embody the just-peace God has always and ever intended; a time when our world will be ordered by love. Let us live now, with anticipation toward that new world, undeterred by the reign of empire or the tests to reputation or even life that our faithfulness will entail, but with full trust in the One who has promised to be with us, no matter the day or the hour.

– Noelle Damico

Hymns
Opening Hymn
Keep Awake, Be Always Ready
Day of Peace
Sermon Hymn
Blest Be the God of Israel
Savior of the Nations, Come!
Closing Hymn
O How Shall We Receive You
Wake, Awake, for Night Is Flying

December 5, 2010

2nd Sunday of Advent

Lessons

RCL	Roman Catholic
Isa 11:1-10	Isa 11:1-10
Ps 72:1-7, 18-19	Ps 72:1-2, 7-8, 12-13, 17
Rom 15:4-13	Rom 15:4-9
Mt 3:1-12	Mt 3:1-12

Speaker's Introduction for the Lessons
Lesson 1
Isaiah 11:1-10 (RCL/RC)

Isaiah announces a king unsusceptible to bribes (what his eyes see) or to propaganda (what his ears hear), but one who lovingly and loyally intervenes on behalf of the poor and the meek, ending oppression.

Lesson 2
Psalm 72:1-7, 18-19 (RCL); 72:1-2, 7-8, 12-13, 17 (RC)

This psalm may have been a coronation anthem for Davidic kings. Righteousness, justice, and peace are the king's primary duties to his people. And these qualities likewise characterize the kingdom Christ Jesus proclaimed.

Lesson 3
Romans 15:4-13 (RCL); 15:4-9 (RC)

Paul emphasizes that Christ's promises are not only to the Jews but to the Gentiles. The Gentiles were not simply religiously "non-Jewish," they were culturally and linguistically diverse peoples also living under Roman imperial rule.

Gospel
Matthew 3:1-12 (RCL/RC)

Dressed like the prophet Elijah, John baptizes people in the wilderness. Like Elijah, John's call for repentance causes the people to confront hard political and spiritual choices.

Theme
Through repentance and baptism new possibilities are opened, defying and healing what has come before.

Thought for the Day
Life can only be understood backward; but it must be lived forward.
– Søren Kierkegaard

Sermon Summary
John calls the Jewish people to repentance without elaborating on the specifics of what is to come. His harsh words cause discomfort, because they make us aware of the anxiety (fear/attraction) that characterizes humanity's relation to God. But unveiling this anxiety and engaging it can provoke openness to God's new possibilities.

Call to Worship
One: Wilderness words pierce our complacency,
All: We long to be reoriented, reawakened to you, O God.
One: Your call to "turn around" is a call not only to others, but to us as well.
All: In this time of worship may we sense your judgment as surprising mercy.

Pastoral Prayer
It is hard, God, to think that we are the ones being judged. You turn the tables unexpectedly on us, causing us to reconsider the ways in which our decisions as individuals and as the church can help or hinder your promise yet to be born. Your judgment shines light on our shadowy world in which we make so many choices – enabling us to better see how we are interconnected with our sisters and brothers, how our actions and inactions affect not only us but others. Grant us the serenity to hear your word of judgment on us, that, confident in your mercy, we may chart a new course guided by love. Amen.

Prayer of Confession

God of mercy, we open ourselves to your judgment, that we might become more attuned to your will in our lives. We confess that we prefer to listen to those who say "all is well" and would be content to live within that echo chamber. Forgive us. But your word to us is a truthful word; for all is *not* well, within us or within our society. Allow your judgment to help us see more clearly and act with greater intention that we might live in harmony with you and within your creation. Amen.

Prayer of Dedication of Gifts and Self

We offer you these gifts as a sign of our commitment to you and our neighbors to live justly, to love faithfully, and to walk humbly together in your sight. Amen.

Hymn of the Day
Prepare the Way of the Lord

This chant from the community of Taizé makes a wonderful call to worship, entrance song, or response before or after scripture readings. A unison song, it is intended to be sung as in canon (as a round). Sing the chant all together many times to make sure worshipers are very familiar and then start using it in parts. Try it as a two-part round to start and slowly build it to its intended four-part presentation. This chant would make an excellent song to use for the whole season of Advent, bringing a sense of unity to the four Sundays.

Children's Time: Bearing Good Fruit

(Preparation: Bring a Christmas ornament that is a piece of fruit. If this is not possible, bring a piece of fruit – real or artificial.)

Note with the children that you have a piece of fruit. How does fruit grow? *(Accept all answers, adapting as necessary depending on the type of fruit you have brought.)* How many of you like fruit? It's one of the healthiest things for us.

There's an expression you may have heard, about a person "bearing good fruit." This refers to someone who does good work.

In one of today's Bible stories, John the Baptist is talking about how Jesus is coming. John points out that the messiah (Jesus) is looking for people who bear good fruit. In this Bible story, those trees that don't bear fruit will be cut down and tossed into the fire. Now, that does not mean they are being punished; being thrown on the fire means they are being put to use, but only as firewood. If a tree bears good fruit, it is usually kept and appreciated over and over. It is more valuable than firewood.

John is trying to say that he – and Jesus – hope that we will all be people who bear good fruit, that we will all be people who do good things. This piece of fruit can help us remember that. *(Hang the fruit on the Christmas tree.)*

Prayer: God, Creator, and Gardener, help us all to be those who bear good fruit, and do good things for the good of your realm. Amen.

The Sermon: From Anxiety, Possibility
Scripture: Matthew 3:1-12
(For sermon materials on Matthew 3:1-12, see the September/October 2010 issue of *The Clergy Journal*; for sermon materials on Isaiah 11:1-10, see the May/June 2010 planning issue of *The Clergy Journal*.)

John doesn't baptize in downtown Jerusalem, or even on a popular mountain, but out in the wilderness beyond Judea. Dressed from head to toe like the prophet Elijah, John's attire and food is ascetic. And his words are acerbic. Like Elijah, John is a confrontational figure – he's impolitic and, one might say, impolite.

But John cares nothing about such things. His chosen life is a harsh condemnation of much of what has gone wrong under Roman and religious rule in Judea. His charisma partly comes from his refusal to participate in the reigning religious and civic customs of the day, choosing instead to howl from the periphery his message of repentance.

And people flock to him. In a reversal of their ancestors' entry into the Promised Land, the people cross the Jordan River back into wilderness. There they meet John, confess their sin, and seek strength for living in dangerous times.

John is a sanguine man. When he sees the Jewish priests and teachers coming to also present themselves for baptism, John lashes out, "You brood of vipers! Who warned you to flee from the wrath to come? Bear fruit worthy of repentance." Then John explains that his baptism by water is simply preparation for the coming of one who is more powerful who will judge between the wheat and the chaff.

Interestingly, the text doesn't tell us if any of the Sadducees or Pharisees chose to receive baptism.

The Sadducees were priest-administrators within the temple in Jerusalem. The temple system was established during the Persian Empire's rule over Judea, and had been used by subsequent imperial administrations, including Rome, to control the populace and to receive revenues. And to those ends, the Sadducees collaborated with successive imperial administrations.

The Pharisees were interpreters of the Torah who lived among communities of Jews in Judea, Perea, and Galilee. They instructed the people in how to live faithfully. In the Gospels Jesus periodically accuses the Pharisees of interpreting the law to their own advantage, against the well-being of the common people.

The Sadducees and the Pharisees were more than strictly "religious" figures. By virtue of their positions they were also political and social leaders who sometimes shared the same fate as or spoke on behalf of the Jewish people.

The temple, where the Sadducees served, was a focus point for Jewish rebellion against Roman rule. A generation before John the Baptist's ministry, popular protests sprung up when the Romans appointed Archelaus, son of Herod the Great, ruler over Judea in 4 BCE. During the Passover celebration in Jerusalem, their cries grew louder so Archelaus sent in his troops as a show of force. When the Jewish people stoned his military, Archaleus responded brutally by ordering his entire army against them, slaughtering 3000 as they made sacrifices in the temple.

Around this same time, a delegation of Jewish elders and Pharisees journeyed to Rome to protest the rule of Archelaus and appeal for the independence of Jewish Palestine under their own, not Roman, administration. They were unsuccessful. A decade later, Jewish leaders again petitioned Caesar to remove Archelaus because of his cruelty and taxation, and this time Rome removed him. But the Imperial government appointed its own direct administrators to the provinces. The Governor Pontius Pilate was one of those administrators.

The Sadducees and Pharisees were forever deciding and re-deciding on their own and their people's behalf, when to capitulate, when to collaborate, when to challenge, when to sacrifice. So it is not surprising that these men make their way out with the crowds to the River Jordan. They most certainly would have wanted to investigate what John was saying and doing, at the very least because it could have direct bearing on their influence and position.

Was their presentation for baptism a cover? Was it genuine? Either way, John minces no words, "You brood of vipers . . . Bear fruit worthy of repentance."

The common people who were flocking to John in the wilderness, as well as the Sadducees and Pharisees, had been trying to figure out how to survive under Roman rule, and found themselves hurtling from protest to accommodation to resignation to revolt, with very little change being accomplished. Their promised land had turned into a nightmare. And John's wild call compelled them to journey out from the so-called security of occupation or certainty of revolt and into the wilderness where their ancestors once lived, contingently, sustained only by the hand of God. Charismatic and shocking, John calls for "repentance." What sort of turning around would be required? John does not spell it out. His role is to prepare people to receive the "one who is coming" who will provide a new way to live. John calls for a "halt" and insists the Jewish people reconsider who God is calling them to be and what God is calling them to do. Through baptism he opens a door for new possibilities that will defy and heal what has come before.

And we, with the Sadducees, Pharisees, and common people, stand before John, conscious of our shortcomings and our desire; both repelled and attracted, suspended, uncertain what to choose when the plan ahead is not clear. John exhorts us to dive into a baptism of repentance without knowing the outcome.

The great Danish theologian and public intellectual Søren Kierkegaard wrote on this anxiety, this encounter of fear and attraction that characterizes humanity's relation to God. This anxiety disrupts both our equanimity and our restlessness. But it is only by presenting ourselves to this condition of anxiety that we discover faith. The German theologian Dorothee Solle writes of the centrality of Kierkegaard's concept of anxiety in the context of a Christian re-visioning of a just life together within a nuclear world.

> For Kierkegaard, anxiety is on the side of freedom, not on that of necessity. But we are totally free only when we "renounce anxiety without anxiety," that is, when we believe. In anxiety we seek and flee our guilt; in faith we acknowledge it . . . Anxiety is a precondition of faith; those who are spiritless and without anxiety cannot believe, because nothing compels them to it. They stick with their bombs and

file cards. What is at stake is a passion for the infinite, for that which surpasses all the possibilities I can now recognize. (Dorothee Solle, *The Window of Vulnerability*, Minneapolis: Fortress Press, 1990, p. 120.)

This Advent, may we not retreat to bombs or file cards. Rather, allowing John's wild words to unveil the anxiety that characterizes our relationship to God may we open ourselves to God's coming possibility.

– Noelle Damico

Hymns
Opening Hymn
Isaiah the Prophet Has Written of Old
Wild and Lone the Prophet's Voice
Sermon Hymn
There's a Voice in the Wilderness Crying
Lo, How a Rose E'er Blooming
Closing Hymn
Hark! A Herald Voice Is Calling
Put Peace into Each Other's Hands

December 12, 2010

3rd Sunday of Advent

Lessons

RCL	Roman Catholic
Isa 35:1-10	Isa 35:1-6, 10
Ps 146:5-10 or Lk 1:47-55	Ps 146:6-10
James 5:7-10	James 5:7-10
Mt 11:2-11	Mt 11:2-11

Speaker's Introduction for the Lessons

Lesson 1
Isaiah 35:1-10 (RCL); 35:1-6, 10 (RC)

Humanity and creation are desperate, wounded, and incapable of saving themselves. This poem hinges on verse four where God saves and restores. This wildly impossible vision of wholeness is possible only because of God's initiative.

Lesson 2
Psalm 146:5-10 (RCL); 146:6-10 (RC)

The second of the closing quintet of psalms of praise in the Psalter, Psalm 146 extols the just nature of God who frees, heals, and reverses the fortunes of both the oppressed and the wicked.

Lesson 3
James 5:7-10 (RCL/RC)

In the first four chapters, James condemns the rich and urges that faith be demonstrated in concrete works of compassion and justice. Here James urges believers to trust in the reliability of God.

Gospel
Matthew 11:2-11 (RCL/RC)

Irenaeus first attributes this anonymous gospel to "Matthew" at the end of the second century. It was likely written to or from a city in Syria between 80-90 CE, following Rome's destruction of the temple.

Theme

The freedom and wholeness offered by Jesus defies our expectations and fulfills God's promise.

Thought for the Day

I believe in God who desires the counter-arguments of the living and the alteration of every condition through our work, through our politics.
– Dorothee Solle, *Against the Wind*, Minneapolis: Fortress Press, 1995, p. 39

Sermon Summary

The signs of Jesus' ministry testify to the impossible made possible, not as a condition of what we expect, but as an absolute gift of freedom and wholeness from God. When we understand the Messiah as continually enacting promise, we see and hear and become part of that promise.

Call to Worship

One: God who comes to save and restore,
All: We await your healing touch.
One: We are exhausted from trying to save ourselves!
All: We cry with one voice, Maranatha, come Christ Jesus, come.

Pastoral Prayer

The prophet Isaiah describes a way of life almost too fantastic for us to imagine: humanity, indeed all creation, whole and praising God. Help us imagine this possibility, dear Savior, because our limited vision is too caustic, too catastrophic, too constricted to revive our suffering world. We pray especially this morning for the animals, plants, and ecosystems of our planet, that as we humans search again the right measure of ourselves, that your Spirit might make possible that which seems impossible – abundant crocuses, gentle lions, and a clear-eyed, limber-kneed humanity, living in harmony and offering you praise. Amen.

Prayer of Confession

God of newness, we confess our comfort with the old order of things. We may pray for revolution, but in our hearts we hope there will be some reprieve. We extol your grand reversals, glibly imagining our fortunes will be bettered not worsened in their exercise. We are reluctant to name the power we have and so use it unwisely and irresponsibly. Help us this day to see ourselves and our world from the vantage point of your coming again, that we may rightly see and act for the well-being of the creation you so dearly love. Amen.

Prayer of Dedication of Gifts and Self
The gifts we have given are but a sign of our determination to live justly and to share generously. We ask that you would bless them, that in their distribution, the blind might see, the lame walk, and the poor receive good news. Amen.

Hymn of the Day
On Jordan's Bank, the Baptist's Cry
Charles Coffin wrote this hymn in Latin and published it in his collection *Hymni Sacri* (1736) while rector of the University of Paris. A century later, John Chandler translated it and included in his *Hymns of the Primitive Church* (1827). The editorial team of *The New Century Hymnal* (1993) created a new translation, "The Baptist Shouts on Jordan's Shore," for inclusion in their hymnal. Whichever translation used, it is a strong hymn that retells in versification much of the story of John the Baptist. WINCHESTER NEW is the usual tune associated with this text. It is a 17th century German melody brought to England by John Wesley and published in his *Foundery Tune Book* (1742) under the name SWIFT GERMAN TUNE. It appeared under its current name in W.H. Havergal's *Old Church Psalmody* (1864).

Children's Time: All the World
(Preparation: Bring a round Christmas ball that can be hung on the tree. You might bring a simple one, solid in color, or a decorative one. A ball that has an image of the world, or different people, or somehow represents a culture different than your own can be incorporated into the story nicely, although any ball will do.)

How many of you hang balls like this on your Christmas tree? *(If you have brought a special ball with some kinds of image or symbol, discuss that with the children.)*

There are several stories about why we hang balls on our Christmas trees. One concerns a little boy who went to see baby Jesus. He had no gift to bring, but he did have some balls in his pocket because he would sometimes juggle. When the baby began to cry, the boy brought out the balls and juggled them and the baby laughed. Some say we hang balls on our tree to remind us to bring joy to others.

Another reason is that round balls represent our planet Earth. They can remind us that God's love is for everyone, all around the world, and that Jesus came to show us that.

Today's reading from Matthew reminds us that Jesus helped all different kinds of people – it was like sharing love all around the world. *(Hang the ornament on the tree.)*

Prayer: God of all people, help us to spread your love and joy throughout the world. Amen.

The Sermon: What We Have Seen and Heard
Scripture: Matthew 11:2-11
(For sermon materials on Matthew 11:2-11, see the September/October 2010 issue of *The Clergy Journal*; for sermon materials on Isaiah 35:1-10, see the May/June 2010 planning issue of *The Clergy Journal*.)

Jesus has been teaching and proclaiming his message in the cities when he receives a query from John the Baptist who has been imprisoned. John's question, "Are you the one . . . or are we to wait for another," presumes Jesus' power and authority, power and authority he has established in his healing and teaching ministry in the opening chapters of Matthew's Gospel.

Jesus, alluding to the messianic signs indicated by the Prophet Malachi, sends word that John's disciples should report what they "hear and see." "The blind receive their sight, the lame walk, the lepers are cleansed, the deaf hear, the dead are raised, and the poor have good news brought to them" (Mt. 11:5). He adds, "And blessed is anyone who takes no offense at me," perhaps in recognition that there were different, and to some degree, competing visions of what the Messiah would do. The crowds gathered around Jesus to overhear this exchange.

Then Jesus turns to the crowds and begins to speak about John, challenging them, "What did you go out into the wilderness to look at?" and "What then did you go out to see?" Jesus exclaims that as great as John the Baptist is, "the least in the kingdom is greater than he."

There is a lot going on in these few verses. John has been jailed because he has publicly denounced Herod's decision to marry his brother Phillip's wife, something Matthew eventually tells us in chapter 14. This is not simply about adultery. When Herod the Great died and Herod Antipas, his son, was appointed over Judea, he was not given the title King. This marriage was about strengthening Herod's claim to Jewish kingship by wedding Herodias who was of the Hasmonean clan. John's condemnation is, we might say, personal and political. He publicly castigates Herod for marrying Herodias and he's jailed for it. Jesus lauds John, pointing to him as "more than" a prophet. Yet John's reward, like so many Jewish truth-tellers before him, is imprisonment, and soon, beheading.

For those in the crowd who think now that John has been jailed it might be safer to switch allegiances to Jesus who is healing and teaching, Jesus offers that ambivalent beatitude: blessed are those who take no offense at me. In other words, there will be some who take offense at the healing, welcome, and empowerment of the poor and the sick and the outcast. And those powerful people are the same people who've jailed John.

Jesus challenges the crowd who had flocked to see this man and now flock to see him, "What did you go out into the wilderness to look at?" John is not one who consorts with those who wear "soft robes." Jesus was baptized by this rabble-rousing man of judgment. And in linking his ministry with John's, he affirms John's call to repentance while simultaneously embodying a similarly dangerous ministry that is about also creating a new kinship based in covenant love. Such a kin-dom that unites the people who have been conquered and dominated by Rome and its collaborators will indeed be a threat to the powerful.

The question, "What then did you go out to see" and the imperative "tell John what you've seen and heard" challenge the crowd, the community to which Matthew wrote, and us about our expectations and our attestation. Why go out and see: curiosity? Idleness? Spiritual hunger? Suspicion? Revolutionary hope? Whether idle, sinister, or authentic, hearers of this passage both ancient and modern must also say what we have seen and heard, realizing that what we expect and what we witness may be quite different.

For whatever the positive content of our expectation, this passage clearly warns us that if we're looking for security in following Jesus, we need to let go of that. John is in jail and Jesus knows the powerful will take offense at his ministry. If we're looking for prestige, we would do well to remember that Jesus' ministry has been about healing and empowering the sick and the poor, and the least in the kingdom is greater than John, whom Jesus hyperbolically pronounced the "greatest" man "born of a woman." If we're looking for judgment that does not redeem, we can lay that aside too. Jesus' judgment is mercy, his actions heal; no one is expendable.

During the Advent season, the question "what do we expect" takes on an eschatological dimension. For we expect Christ's coming again and orient ourselves toward life together from the vantage point of the one, still to come, who will judge and set aright what has gone so horribly wrong in our world.

It is only from that ever-before-us-vision of God's promise that we are able to live rightly. We are not seduced by the priorities or benefits of the prevailing systems and structures of our world, nor are we defeated by their cruelty and injustice, for these are not the final word. We are not immobilized by pain or trapped in a cycle of recrimination in our families, for these are not the final word. We are not required to advocate a "winnable" vision or "realistic" goal, for we serve the one who is Alpha and Omega, the beginning and the end, who is not constrained by what exists, who lives as absolute promise, who always and ever is come and coming.

For once transfigured by God all things are made possible again, disclosing the eschatological potentials latently inscribed in the historically impossible. So that if we continue to look at the same event in the light of God's transfiguring power, we can now see . . . the hitherto impossible as possible. (Richard Kearney, *The God Who May Be: A Hermeneutics of Religion*, Bloomington and Indianapolis: Indiana University Press, 2001, p. 5.)

This eschatological orientation frees us up to understand that the Messiah is, at core, about promise – promise that concretely transforms our reality without being conditioned by it. We can allow the manacles of realism, cynicism, novelty, and romanticism that have imprisoned our faith to slip from our wrists. It is not about what we expect but about how we respond to what we "have seen and heard."

The signs of Jesus' ministry testify to the impossible made possible, not as a condition of what we expect, but as an absolute gift of freedom and wholeness from God. When we adopt an eschatological orientation that understands the Messiah as continually enacting promise, we become like blind people who suddenly see and deaf people who finally hear. And we become part of that promise.

– Noelle Damico

Hymns
Opening Hymn
Awake! Awake, and Greet the New Morn
Arise, Your Light Is Come!
Sermon Hymn
Comfort, Comfort Now My People
Lift Up Your Heads, O Mighty Gates
Closing Hymn
Praise the Lord Who Reigns Above
Love Divine, All Loves Excelling

December 19, 2010

4th Sunday of Advent

Lessons

RCL	Roman Catholic
Isa 7:10-16	Isa 7:10-14
Ps 80:1-7, 17-19	Ps 24:1-6
Rom 1:1-7	Rom 1:1-7
Mt 1:18-25	Mt 1:18-24

Speaker's Introduction for the Lessons

Lesson 1
Isaiah 7:10-16 (RCL); 7:10-14 (RC)

Isaiah asserts God's sovereignty in political crises. Against the will of the King, the child Emmanuel, God-with-us, shall be a sign of God's judgment and power. In this child-sign, Christian tradition has seen Jesus anticipated.

Lesson 2
Psalm 80:1-7, 17-19 (RCL)

Israel experiences God's anger as abandonment. Like a vine that the divine vinedresser has cultivated then allowed to be ravaged (vv. 8-16), the people cry for God's hand to be upon them, that they might be saved.

Psalm 24:1-6 (RC)

The earth is the Lord's, and those in the company of the Lord will receive blessings and salvation.

Lesson 3
Romans 1:1-7 (RCL/RC)

Paul composed this letter around 55 CE. Here, he introduces himself to Jews and non-Jews who have been conquered by the Romans and reside in the Imperial city, offering *God's Pax*, not the *Pax Romana*.

Gospel
Matthew 1:18-25 (RCL); 1:18-24 (RC)

While Christian tradition has promoted a virgin birth for Jesus pointing to Matthew's citation of the prophet Isaiah, interestingly the prophecy itself, from which we have read this morning, doesn't say, virgin, but "young woman."

Theme

God's sovereignty extends to public life, not only to personal decisions. Welcoming Immanuel means trusting God.

Thought for the Day

Well, I don't know what will happen now. We've got some difficult days ahead. But it really doesn't matter with me now, because I've been to the mountaintop.

– The Rev. Dr. Martin Luther King, Jr.,
final address at the Mason Temple, Memphis, Tennessee, 1968

Sermon Summary

Emmanuel's coming reminds us to trust God in personal and public affairs. The courage shown by Joseph invites us to welcome the baby by forsaking peace obtained by security to pursue God's true reign of peace; a perilous but promising call to seek justice in human and political relationships.

Call to Worship

One: Restore us, O God.
All: Like an ancient painting, we need cleaning, refurbishing.
One: Restore us, O God.
All: Like a neglected vineyard, we need weeding, pruning.
One: Restore us, O God.
All: Like an inheritance defrauded, we need restitution, reparation.
One: Restore us, O God.
All: Let your face shine that we might be saved.

Pastoral Prayer

God, we open ourselves to your dream for our world. We allow ourselves, this morning, to let go of expectations and cultivate, instead, a radical openness to where you would lead us. We are so used to this Christmas story – the plot bores us, the characters are predictable even in their surprising behavior, and we wonder what could possibly be said by you to us, through your Word, that we haven't heard a thousand times before. But today we shake off what we think we know, what we think we've heard, even what we think you want, so that we can listen anew, unprotected, like Joseph: asleep and yet aware. We are open, God; speak, that we might hear and respond. Amen.

Prayer of Confession

We confess, dear God, that we often pray without expectation of change. We form the words in our hearts or speak them aloud, but it is of little consequence. We satisfy ourselves with our sadness saying, it's hard to teach an old dog new tricks. We temper our hopes saying, that's just the way the world is. We claim we walk through life with eyes wide open, but our sophistication is in truth, sleepwalking; our "realism" the measure of our despair. Forgive us. May your mercy refresh us and reorient us. May your love astonish and alert us. May your promise unnerve and awaken us. Amen.

Prayer of Dedication of Gifts and Self

We present these gifts, and through them, ourselves and our lives, to you the source of all. Bless them and us that we may be a church alive and nimble, ready to live in your way. Amen.

Hymn of the Day
Toda la Tierra/All Earth Is Hopeful

This song, written by Catholic priest Alberto Taulé, comes from Catalonia, Spain. The English translation and music arrangement first appeared in the *United Methodist Hymnal* (1989). This song is also very popular in Latin America, where themes of a captive world awaiting liberation through the coming of the Savior are both familiar and loved. The rhythmic energy of this song invites a strong presentation with guitar and percussion accompaniment. Piano may be used, but the playing should be rhythmic and not too dense. Introduce this song by presenting it as an introit or gathering song sung by choir or a small group on one or more Sundays before you wish the congregation to sing it.

Children's Time: A Baby?

(Preparation: Bring a nativity that can be hung on the Christmas tree; or, bring a baby Jesus or other symbol of Christ's birth that can be hung on the tree; or, have a nativity scene that you can look at with the children; or, you may wish to bring the baby Jesus to be placed in the manger.

Look at the item you have brought, and invite the children to notice certain things. This will, of course, depend on the item you have brought. As you discuss the item, draw out the amazing fact that Jesus came as a baby in a stable.)

Jesus was the child/son of God, and so it would seem that such an important person would be born in a palace, and have lots of attendants. We might expect them to be rich, and be connected with the most important people.

But Jesus was different. He was born in a stable; his parents were poor; and he lived his life as a poor, wandering preacher.

This was God's way of showing us that Jesus was indeed different. He wanted us to realize that being poor and "insignificant" was not a problem. What matters to God is how we live: that we be people who show God's love and concern for others every chance we get. It doesn't matter if we are poor, or where we live, or what we look like. What matters is that we live the way God wants. When we think of Jesus in the manger, we can remember that. *(Hang the ornament, or place Jesus in the manger, as appropriate.)*

Prayer: God of love and light, thank you for sending Jesus to be our friend and savior. Amen.

The Sermon: The Courage of Joseph
Scripture: Matthew 1:18-25

(For sermon materials on Matthew 1:18-25, see the September/October 2010 issue of *The Clergy Journal*; for sermon materials on Isaiah 7:10-16, see the May/June 2010 planning issue of *The Clergy Journal*.)

Christian tradition often lauds Joseph as a good man because he did not divorce Mary upon finding out that his betrothed was pregnant. Our text, however, describes him as a "righteous" man. There's a dimension to the English word *righteous* that the word *good* does not convey: courage. And given the dream Joseph has had, he will need all the courage he can muster.

Matthew weaves a different birth story from that of Luke. It is full of danger, political intrigue, and massacre. No blessed annunciation to Mary. No discussion of laying Jesus in the manger. No heavenly host of angels singing, "Peace to all people." No sleepy shepherds hearing the "good news" and rejoicing. No. Matthew tells a much different story.

In two sentences Matthew recounts Joseph's discovery that Mary is pregnant and his unwillingness to disgrace her publicly. As soon as he had resolved to "dismiss her quietly," Joseph has a dream. And what a dream it was. Not only did the Angel say "do not be afraid to take Mary as your wife," he explains that the child is of the Holy Spirit. The child, who shall be called Jesus, will fulfill Isaiah's prophecy of Emmanuel. Amazingly, Joseph awakens and does what the Angel had commanded him.

I say amazingly because choosing this course was not only a personal matter of marrying a woman who, to all accounts, looked already to have been unfaithful, but it also was a dangerous decision, for the child Emmanuel was a political lightning rod, the one who would challenge and reorient the power of the nations.

Seven hundred years earlier as Syria and Israel threatened Judah, the prophet Isaiah confronted King Ahaz, commanding him to not put his trust in military security, but rather to trust in God. Isaiah proposes that Ahaz put God to the test. But the king refuses. Attempting to use piety as a cover for his faithlessness, Ahaz proclaims that he will not put the LORD to the test. King Ahaz will not trust in Yahweh; he will make his own political decisions.

The prophet responds, "Hear then, O house of David! Is it too little for you to weary mortals, that you weary my God also?" Walter Brueggemann notes that the use of "*my* God" by the prophet indicates that Yahweh has, as Ahaz requested, withdrawn the divine presence from Judah. Ahaz now stands alone. Isaiah explains that within two years the threats from Syria and Israel will count as nothing (Is 7:16) compared to what is coming: devastation at the hands of the merciless, massive empire of Assyria (v. 17).

The focus of Isaiah's prophesy is not on the "young woman" (NRSV), (who, in the Isaian prophesy is not a virgin), but on Emmanuel's coming as judgment upon the faithlessness of King Ahaz. This King trusted in his own power and his own armies. Walter Brueggemann writes, "The prophet seeks to gather the entire fearful drama of public life and reorganize it around this baby whose presence and whose name assert the cruciality of Yahweh in the public arena" (Walter Brueggemann, *Texts for Preaching,* Louisville: Westminster John Knox Press, 1995, p. 30).

But King Ahaz refuses to trust in Yahweh. So Isaiah prophesies the coming of Emmanuel, the child who will demand Judah reorient itself.

And Judah will bear the consequences of Ahaz's desire to direct public life and political challenges without the wisdom or companionship of Yahweh. This judgment however, is not the final word. A few chapters later Isaiah proclaims a powerful one from the stock of Jesse is coming and the spirit of the Lord will rest upon him. He will judge the poor with righteousness and faithfulness will be the "belt around his loins." Then "the wolf shall live with the lamb . . . the nursing child shall play over the hole of the asp . . . They will not hurt or destroy on all my holy mountain; for the earth will be full of the knowledge of the Lord as the waters cover the sea" (Is 11:1-9). The earth will cease its fighting and equity and justice will reign because of the coming of this "shoot from the stock of Jesse."

Hundreds of years later, this dream of a just and peaceful world where God is with us persisted in the hearts of the Jewish people.

When Joseph had this dream, King Herod the Great was the ruler of the provinces of Judea and Galilee. A despotic ruler, Herod's cruelty was surpassed only by his obsequiousness to the Emperor. He taxed the people harshly in order to erect temples and monuments glorifying the emperor, expanding his lavish royal palace, and supporting a sumptuous court life. After about 20 years of this, some Jewish people revolted.

But Herod quelled their antipathy through a masterful mix of messianic hope and imperial power. He got Rome to proclaim him, "King of the Jews" and rebuilt the Jewish temple on a scale and with opulence that was an architectural marvel. And though he placed the Imperial sign of the golden eagle atop the entrance to the main gate of the sanctuary, most people reveled that the *Pax Romana* could bring security which would lead to "peace."

It was at this precise moment that, according to Matthew, the Angel Gabriel appears to Joseph. Judea and Galilee are ruled by an opportunistic and violent "King of the Jews." Many had been co-opted into support, or at least passivity, by the temple's refurbishment. Into this nighttime of Jewish hope comes an angel promising that Mary's child is the long-awaited Emmanuel.

Walter Brueggemann contends, "Because of the baby, public history is not simply a matter of brute power. Public history is working on a different schedule toward a different purpose. The baby is a time bomb in the midst of the great powers, which they can neither stop nor deactivate . . . The Advent question for us is the same one faced by Ahaz. It is the same one faced by Herod and by Pilate. What would happen if life were so reorganized that the baby's presence became the central reality? Everything changes when 'God is with us.' The time of the baby is fast approaching, and that ticking sensation makes the nations nervous." (Brueggemann, *Texts for Preaching*.)

In his dream Joseph glimpsed God's vision for his world; a terrifying vision of hope that demanded and received his allegiance. May we have the courage of Joseph and welcome the baby by forsaking peace obtained through security for God's true reign of peace, that perilous but promising call to seek justice in personal and political relationships.

– Noelle Damico

Hymns
Opening Hymn
Isaiah the Prophet Has Written of Old
Like a Mother Who Has Borne Us
Sermon Hymn
My Soul Proclaims with Wonder
Come, Thou Long-expected Jesus
Closing Hymn
He Comes to Us as One Unknown
Put Peace in Each Other's Hands

December 24, 2010

Christmas Eve

Lessons

RCL	Roman Catholic
Isa 9:2-7	Isa 9:1-6
Ps 96	Ps 96:1-3, 11-13
Titus 2:11-14	Titus 2:11-14
Lk 2:1-14 (15-20)	Lk 2:1-14

Speaker's Introduction for the Lessons
Lesson 1
Isaiah 9:2-7 (RCL); 9:1-6 (RC)

This oracle is a public decree from the royal palace announcing the birth or coronation of a new king in Jerusalem, who will defeat enemies and establish justice for the people.

Lesson 2
Psalm 96 (RCL); 96:1-3, 11-13 (RC)

In this song of praise, the whole creation exults that God is king. God the King deserves praise from faithful people because God establishes justice and judges with righteousness and truth.

Lesson 3
Titus 2:11-14 (RCL/RC)

This epistle, addressed to Paul's trusted Gentile companion Titus in Crete, was likely authored by a disciple of Paul near the end of the first century. Awaiting Christ's return, followers are to live upright lives.

Gospel
Luke 2:1-14 (15-20) (RCL); 2:1-14 (RC)

Likely written by an anonymous author at the end of the first century, the Gospel of Luke and its "second volume" which we know as Acts recount Jesus' ministry and the birth of the church.

Theme

The Christmas story witnesses to God-with-us, a mystery which we are also called to articulate.

Thought for the Day

In life, in death, in life beyond death, God is with us. We are not alone. Thanks be to God.

– A New Creed, Uniting Church of Canada

Sermon Summary

Luke's birth story is historically inaccurate. Inaccuracies can raise concerns about the authenticity of God's coming in our material, lived world. But Luke, like others in Christian history, models what *we* are called to do: articulate, as best we can, the mystery of God-with-us, here and now.

Call to Worship

Children: Sing! Sing!
Adults: Good news takes wing!
Children: Sing! Sing!
Adults: Star glistening!
Children: Sing! Sing!
All: It's Christ the King!

Pastoral Prayer

In the darkness, your love comes! In times of anxiety, your love comes! In places of violence, your love comes! In the shadow of oppression, your love comes! It comes, seemingly wholly inadequate to the task; naked, crying, powerless. It comes, knitting together the dreams of heaven and earth, in flesh, in history, in our day; anticipated-unexpected, painful-healing, love; God-with-us. And we, in fear and amazement, hungry for glory and eager for security, are stopped in our tracks. Oh absurd love that rests our future on the tender breath of an infant, envelop our world this night. Soothe, provoke, judge, and inspire that all nations and all people may be healed! Good news! Good news! God is with us. We are not alone. Good news! Amen.

Prayer of Confession

Dear God, your angels promise us good news and urge peace among all. But we know that many people still suffer, in our own homes and around the world. We are sorry for those times when we have hurt others. We are sorry for keeping for ourselves that which we should share. This Christmas Eve, help us start over. May we live the peace you want for us. Amen.

Prayer of Dedication of Gifts and Self

For all who have given and for all who wanted to give, we thank you, God. For the gift of your child Jesus, born this night, we thank you, God. Through this offering, may love grow. Amen.

Hymn of the Day
Before the Marvel of This Night

This relatively unknown hymn is one of the gems for Christmas Eve. It was written by Jaroslav Vajda, poet, hymn writer, translator, and pastor. He was also senior editor with Concordia Publishing House until his retirement. He wrote this hymn for Christmas 1979. Carl Schalk wrote the tune, MARVEL. He has collaborated with Vajda on many new hymns. Together they make a remarkable team. For its first presentation in a worship service, it might be best to have it sung by choir, soloist, or small ensemble. Be careful to shape the phrases and dynamics, thus enhancing the text. Build to a crescendo (5th last measure) and then conclude in a softer, warmer manner. The organ's ability to sustain long notes makes it the preferred instrument to accompany.

Children's Time: The Candy Cane

(Preparation: Bring a red and white candy cane. You might also wish to bring canes for each of the children.)

How many of you like candy canes? Most people do. They're sweet and good – and they last a long time. They come in lots of sizes and colors these days. But the original ones were white and red. And, while we often see them with the round part up, they started out the other way around *(hold yours like the letter "J")*.

A candymaker in the American state of Indiana wanted to make a special candy at Christmas that would symbolize things about Jesus. He decided to make it sweet – representing God's love – and hard, reminding us that Jesus is the rock of God's love.

He made them in the shape of the letter "J," the first letter of Jesus' name. He made them white, as a symbol of Jesus being pure and good; and he put red stripes on them to remind us, even at Christmastime, that Jesus would suffer and die.

Over time, people forgot some of the symbolism, but they kept using canes at Christmas. *(Turn the cane the other way.)* Many people use them to symbolize the shepherd's crooks, reminding us of the ones who came to see baby Jesus, and then went out to tell everyone the good news. Whichever way we want to use them, they can remind us of Jesus. *(Hang the cane on the tree, and/or distribute candy canes to the children.)*

Prayer: God, you are sweet and good. Thank you for your love that you showed us in Jesus – as a baby and as an adult. Amen.

The Sermon: Speaking of Mystery
Scripture: Luke 2:1-14 (15-20)

(For sermon materials on Luke 2:1-14 (15-20), see the September/October 2010 issue of *The Clergy Journal* or the May/June 2010 planning issue of *The Clergy Journal*.)

The birth narrative from the Gospel of Luke may cause us to wonder, not in amazement but in skepticism. In Luke 1:5, the writer claims that "Herod the Great" was emperor when the Angel Gabriel got busy announcing pregnancies to Mary and her cousin Elizabeth. But now, in the beginning of chapter 2, he explains that Quirinius is governor of Syria. But Herod died in 4 BCE and Quirinius wasn't appointed governor until 6 CE. Luke leaves us with a worse conundrum than a virgin birth: a 10-year pregnancy! The second difficulty is that, according to extant historical sources, Augustus Caesar never called for a universal census!

For some of us, these kinds of inconsistencies and inaccuracies may be troubling but not fatal to the story. After all, Luke was constructing a birth narrative for Jesus that was like other birth stories of famous people at his time, and remarkably similar to that of Augustus Caesar who also was "born of a virgin" and at whose birth "good news" was proclaimed across the empire. The political figures and events are mentioned because Luke positions Jesus and the Empire (*basilea*) of God as a direct alternative to the Empire of Rome.

But for others of us, inconsistencies and inaccuracies like this about something seemingly as important, and perhaps as obvious, as in what year Jesus was born and whether Augustus ordered a census, can cause us to wonder whether God has really manifest in human history and whether God's coming can happen again, here and now in such a way as to change our material, lived reality. We wonder whether this all isn't just a fable designed to make us feel better, but one that is unable, ultimately, to truly affect the course of history or change humankind and our world for the better. The story becomes a kind of psychological fairytale, designed to help us cling to some hope of heaven as a way of enduring the world at our feet.

So first let me begin by saying that Luke has got it wrong, historically speaking. He's mashed up different political leaders and dates and actions, perhaps because he didn't know, perhaps in the interest of telling a good story, perhaps because he was genuinely confused. The second thing is that none of us, not even scholars, can say with certainty precisely when or, for that matter, where Jesus was born.

But wait, you say. Wasn't he born in Bethlehem? Maybe; that's Luke's story and Matthew's as well. Matthew, for the record, insists that Jesus was born during the reign of Herod the Great, not Augustus Caesar. But Mark, believed to be our earliest Gospel written around 70 CE, is silent. Jesus simply appears before John for baptism, as if out of nowhere. The Gospel of John takes a more philosophical approach proclaiming "the Word became flesh and dwelt among us," eschewing pregnancies, births, and historical specifics.

The apostle Paul, whose letters to Jesus' followers across the Middle East were written well before the Gospel accounts, highlight that God took human flesh – and that's about the end of it. No other historical records of that time mention Jesus' birth. Simply put, his birth was insignificant to the powerful of his day who were the writers of history.

So how do we end up with the manger scene with animals, not to mention wise men and a star (which you'll notice are wholly absent from Luke's story)? Well, we have St. Francis of Assisi to credit for the creation of the Christmas nativity reenacted year after year in children's pageants and Christmas carols.

Tonight we celebrate the birth of Jesus. And despite all evidence to the contrary in our traditions and liturgy, we know little to nothing about that occasion. And yet the story of Jesus' birth touches our hearts, describing one of the fundamental experiences of being human, the marvel of welcoming a new child. And since we do know that Jesus of Nazareth did in fact exist, he had to be born at some point. The idea of love coming as a newborn is appealing! Why not this way? Let's just get on with it, some of you may be thinking.

But to sidestep the creation of the story of Jesus' birth is to sidestep a core difficulty of human experience: how do we describe mystery? By this I don't mean how do we describe the biological mechanics of a possible virgin birth or the physics of "very God and very human" residing together in Jesus Christ. Nor do I mean to suggest we obfuscate empirical reality with simplistic theology to cover what we don't or don't *want* to understand. I mean, instead, that on Christmas, we are invited again to consider that through Jesus Christ, God keeps coming to us in our material, lived world and that we are challenged to declare our loyalty to this God who comes, literally, to save us. This mystery doesn't just present itself to us, but requires us to respond.

Luke's creation of this birth narrative signaled the significance of who Jesus was, and it called Judean followers of Jesus who were living in Syria under Roman occupation to a deeper allegiance. Luke used the storytelling conventions of his time and the ordinary Greek language of the ancient Mediterranean world to bear witness to the mystery of God-with-us in Jesus Christ. And like Luke, we are called to articulate the mystery of our experience of God-with-us in Jesus Christ for ourselves in our language and in our own time and place.

So tonight the provocative question is not whether Luke's story is historically accurate, but whether its telling helps us enter more fully into the new life that God offers. Does hearing Luke's story of Jesus' birth help us to name and pledge allegiance to God in Christ who is with us now? The God whom we have experienced here in this church, in our lives, reorienting us, calling us to recognize the full humanity of one another and the glory of creation, causing us to wonder and praise even in difficult times.

What *does* it mean for us to say that, because of Jesus Christ, we are not alone, God is with us? Where have you experienced God-with-you? What is your story of God's birth in your life? What new way of living has come from this experience? This Christmas Eve, may we find ways to express our own experience of God-with-us in Jesus Christ, that this fragile mystery might grow even in this dark night.

– Noelle Damico

Hymns
Opening Hymn
Jesus, Our Brother, Strong and Good
Manglakat na Kita sa Belen (Let Us Even Now Go to Bethlehem)
Sermon Hymn
There's a Song in the Air
Infant Holy, Infant Lowly
Closing Hymn
Hark! The Herald Angels Sing
Angels We Have Heard on High

December 25, 2010

Christmas Day

Lessons

RCL	Roman Catholic
Isa 52:7-10	Isa 52:7-10
Ps 98	Ps 98:1-6
Heb 1:1-4 (5-12)	Heb 1:1-6
Jn 1:1-14	Jn 1:1-18 or 1:1-5, 9-14

Speaker's Introduction for the Lessons
Lesson 1
Isaiah 52:7-10 (RCL/RC)

The sentinels are not shouting out warnings of approaching enemies. They are singing songs of joy! Listen!

Lesson 2
Psalm 98 (RCL); 98:1-6 (RC)

We with all parts of the created order are given reasons to join the sentinels in their songs of joy! We sing our hearts out and play all the beautiful instruments we can find as we come together as one great joyful chorus.

Lesson 3
Hebrews 1:1-4 (5-12) (RCL); 1:1-6 (RC)

Merry Christmas! One of our reasons for joy today is that God has made God known to us in an heir, one of us, who carries imprints of divinity in all he has said and done.

Gospel
John 1:1-14 (RCL); 1:1-18 or 1:1-5, 9-14 (RC)

John the Baptist saw the light of this heir shining in a world of much darkness. In the darkness so long, and content there, not many noticed the light Jesus brought, but those who did had an opportunity to find their way to life.

Theme

When a judge renders a judgment, one side or the other rejoices.

Thought for the Day

We have often forgotten that part of divine judgment is making right what was wrong. Therefore, if we are a part of God's good in the world, we have reason to be joyful, not fearful, in the face of judgment.

Sermon Summary

The old songs written and sung by those who misunderstood the divine determination to see that world eventually becomes what it was created to be fade away as a new song is sung. There is no containing the excitement as we see justice prompt joy. Creation unites to sing and play this new song.

Call to Worship

One: May our Christmas gifts this year enrich the poor rather than weigh down the wealthy.

All: Christmas justice!

Choir: Christmas justice!

All: May our hectic holiday have something to do with housing the homeless.

One: Christmas justice!

Choir: Christmas justice!

All: May our heavily ladened ladles not drown out the sounds of the growling stomachs of those who are hungry.

Choir: And may we not eat this day unless we share our bounty.

One: Christmas justice!

All: Christmas justice! In the words of the one whose birth we celebrate this day: Just as you have done it to the least of these you have done it unto me.

Pastoral Prayer

Gracious God, we are grateful today that your attentiveness to those who hurt far exceeds ours. We are grateful for your presence with all who are joyful today as well as all who cannot rejoice – even if attending Christmas

church services, even at family gatherings and feasts, even as friends toast
the holiday and all it's supposed to mean for those who are followers of Jesus. We are grateful for your relentless efforts to touch with your unconditional love those who are sad and lonely today, those who are afraid, those
who are confused, those who feel excluded, those who take themselves to
be unworthy of celebration. Because of Jesus we pray. Amen.

Prayer of Confession

Rather than getting lost in a long list of generalities today, O God, we
focus specifically on our failures to take more concrete steps to bring
justice where we can. We confess that for lack of energy from shopping
and otherwise self-imposed hectic holiday habits, we have either ignored
injustices close at hand or spoken empty words of protest accompanied
by no action at all. We will not wallow in shame, and we will do better. In
the meantime, we dare not seek forgiveness for our failures until we have
spoken with actions louder than words. Amen.

Prayer of Dedication of Gifts and Self

Gracious God, on this day of gift giving in our culture, we give all we can
give financially and all we can give of our time to make the world a better
place for those at the periphery who struggle and who, for whatever reason, cannot make life at this moment better for themselves. Amen.

Hymn of the Day
Oh, Sing to the Lord/*Cantad al Señor*

On a day when the service will be filled with well-loved carols, the use of
a new song might seem out of place. However, this delightful song, based
on the psalm for the day, might make a welcome change. It could be sung
as an introduction or response to the reading of the psalm. Use guitar
and/or percussion to enhance its lively nature. This Brazilian folk hymn
was translated into both Spanish and English by Gerhard Cartford who
worked on a Lutheran liturgy while living in South America. Cartford is a
pastor, professor, and musician.

Children's Time: Shout for Joy!
(Preparation: Bring a small bell, preferably one that can be hung on the Christmas tree.)

It's Christmas Day! Such a wonderful day of joy. *(Ask the children to tell you some of the wonderful things about Christmas. Accept all answers, and steer the conversation around to celebrating the fact that this is Jesus' birthday.)*

One of today's Bible readings is Psalm 98. It was written long before Jesus was born, but it is such a joyous psalm we read it today, and use it to help celebrate the wonders of Christmas.

This psalm talks about singing a new song, because God has done wonderful things. It calls on all of nature – the sea and everything in it, rivers and mountains – and all people to sing to God.

A hymn that we often sing at Christmastime is "Joy to the World." It is based on Psalm 98. The person who wrote the hymn wasn't even thinking about Christmas when he wrote it, he just wanted to praise God! Later, a tune was written at Christmastime by Lowell Mason; it is based on the sound of bells he heard one Christmas Eve.

Bells are a great symbol of Christmas – they ring out sounds of joy and help us celebrate. *(Hang the bell on the tree. As an option, you might also plan to sing "Joy to the World" after this story.)*

Prayer: God of wondrous joy, we celebrate this day with all of our hearts. Help us to share the good news of Christmas with everyone. Amen.

The Sermon: Joyful Judgment?
Scripture: Psalm 98
(For sermon materials on Hebrews 1:1-4 (5-12), see the September/October 2010 issue of *The Clergy Journal*; for sermon materials on John 1:1-14, see the May/June 2010 planning issue of *The Clergy Journal*.)

One of our country's preeminent professors of preaching, Dr. Thomas Long, has this to say about divine judgment in his commentary on the book of Hebrews:

> We must be careful not to hear [the language of judgment in scripture] through the mouthpiece of a thousand petulant hellfire and brimstone sermons. In the Scripture, the judgment of God is good news, a sign that God's love for the world will allow nothing to stand that will harm or destroy. The idea of judgment does not convey a

picture of a peevish God who gets mad at sinners and strikes out in retaliation; rather, God exercises "good judgment." God's judgment sets things right, repairs the broken creation (Thomas G. Long, *Hebrews*, Louisville: Westminster/John Knox, 1997, p. 109).

But those hellfire and damnation sermons have gotten the attention of all too many people, clergy included, and we have become caught up in fearing God's judgment and a violent, sudden upheaval to bring a so-called "final judgment" to the Earth and all its inhabitants.

Half-informed pastors, some preferring to stay half-informed and others ignorant of the whole truth, are to blame, and so are money-hungry doomsdayers who have made big bucks by trying to keep passive hearers of their sermons and readers of their books and viewers of their DVDs scared nearly to death. Those passive hearers have plenty of fault as well – at least in this country, where information is widely available. Martin Luther's foil, Johann Tetzel, hawking his indulgences, set a powerful precedent for those who, in any age, love to relish in a god (lower case g intentional!) whose greatest pleasure is damning as many people as possible to a burning eternal hell.

Psalm 98 is a corrective for that unfortunate and inaccurate under-standing of God and God's judgment, and this particular psalmist (there were several) didn't have the benefit of the teachings of Jesus that we have at our disposal today. Just as we have gotten away from the notion that God, like Zeus, is a weatherman, so also we have surely gotten away from the idea that God is spending God's days and nights figuring out whom to zap and how hard and when.

Divine judgment that causes pain is not a result of God's personal calculation for every wrong-doer; rather, judgment is the logical conse-quences that follow from bad choices, wrong choices, immoral choices. Judgment is not the dark side of karma, and judgment is not executed the second a wrong is done. Sadly, evil people often make all kinds of trouble and hurt untold numbers of people before an end comes to their influence and activity. We have no control whatsoever over when an evil person will be stopped, but eventually each one will.

Instead of fearing and fretting an angry God who is so enraged with humanity that good folks are hurt or destroyed by whatever God does to express God's wrath, including retaliation against evildoers, the psalmist here sees the joyful side of judgment. This is to say that every time judgment is determined by judge or jury, one side or the other has cause to celebrate – at least to some degree. Part of judgment is beyond the punitive aspect of it – if there is that (and with the God we learn about in the teachings of Jesus, we have reason to doubt it). Judgment often sets right what has been amiss.

Last year, a popular young performer was sentenced to five years of probation and 180 days/1400 hours of community service for a serious attack on his girlfriend. He cannot undo the trauma to her body and her spirit that he inflicted on her, but the judgment does fix a few things. He can't go near her, and the judge is determined that this entertainer will do some hard physical labor as his community service – making life better for people and places.

The psalmist was clued into this aspect of divine judgment. God isn't concerned about inflicting pain on anyone, even the evil and even the guilty. Their acts and deeds carry inherent consequences with them. Eventually those consequences will catch up to them. God is more concerned, from what we get here, with the constructive side of judgment, with making things right for the people who have been hurt, downtrodden, abused, excluded, overlooked.

Since the psalmist wrote what she or he wrote with communal worship in mind, it was easy to think of joyful judgment calling forth song. This is where the psalmist takes us in this worship piece of high praise. The old songs written and sung by those who misunderstood the divine determination to see that world eventually becomes what it was created to be fade away as a new song is sung. The sad songs, the songs of fear, the songs of angst are wasted melodies. They are songs from a time gone by for people who hadn't understood what the psalmist understood.

The reality of evil in the world is no cause for passively accepting it, which is tantamount to approving of it! We can speak out against evil, but judgment for wrongs will have to be taken care of in some other way. God's judgment condemns the wrong, but the divine energy is expended making things right – healing those who have been damaged by the forces that work against what God intended for this world. So let's stop singing the old songs; it's time to sing a new song about the restorative justice of God.

There is no containing the excitement as we see justice prompt joy. From one end of creation to the other, the expressions of joy are loud and unmistakable. The seas are roaring, the waters are clapping their hands, the hills get together and sing their deafening refrains!

Creation unites to sing and play this new song. Humanity and the created order rejoice. God's ways are winning out over evil – unevenly and little by little, but winning out nonetheless because God keeps on doing marvelous things. The loving Creator will not be outdone by any part of the created order, and most of the world in its joyful singing and celebration has already realized it. Amen.

– David Albert Farmer

Hymns
Opening Hymn
O Come, All Ye Faithful
Joy to the World
Sermon Hymn
O Sing a New Song to the Lord
Songs Anew of Honor Framing
Closing Hymn
I Heard the Bells on Christmas Day
Jesus Christ Is Born Today

December 26, 2010

1st Sunday after Christmas

Lessons

RCL	Roman Catholic
Isa 63:7-9	Sir 3:2-6, 12-14
Ps 148	Ps 128:1-5
Heb 2:10-18	Col 3:12-21
Mt 2:13-23	Mt 2:13-15, 19-23

Speaker's Introduction for the Lessons
Lesson 1
Isaiah 63:7-9 (RCL)

Praising God for God's direct presence in our struggles, we are reminded that God does not do God's most important work through any intermediaries.

Sirach 3:2-6, 12-14 (RC)

In the afterglow of Christmas, we celebrate the Holy Family, inviting the faithful to reflect on the gift and mystery of life, and the blessing of family.

Lesson 2
Psalm 148 (RCL)

As St. Francis of Assisi is said to have worded it: "Praised be you, my Lord, with all your creatures!"

Lesson 3
Hebrews 2:10-18 (RCL)

Our gracious God is the Creator of the skies and the earth, and all who inhabit them. Every created person and thing exists for our Creator and through our Creator.

Colossians 3:12-21 (RC)

Paul uses terms to describe how Christians should behave, showing compassion and kindness and acting in humility, gentleness, and patience. In order to call ourselves Christians we need to model Christ's behavior.

Gospel
Matthew 2:13-23 (RCL); 2:13-15, 19-23 (RC)

This gospel recounts Jesus' first road trip. But the circumstances were dire.

Theme

The Season of Christmastide calls on us to reflect on who Jesus was in relationship to God, the human family, and the world itself.

Thought for the Day

There's at best an oversight on our parts and at worst an arrogance to think that the way many of us do our praise as human beings matters the most to God, who created the *whole* world and everything and everyone in it.

Sermon Summary

Let us ponder the nature of praise and the call to the whole creation to praise the Creator.

Call to Worship

One: Most High, all-powerful, all-good Lord, all praise is yours, all glory, all honor, and all blessings.

All: To you alone, Most High, do they belong, and no mortal lips are worthy to pronounce your name.

One: Praised be you my Lord with all your creatures, especially Sir Brother Sun.

All: Praised be you, my Lord, through Sister Moon and the stars.

One: Praised be you, my Lord, through Brothers Wind and Air.

All: Praised be you, my Lord, through Sister Water.

One: Praised be you, my Lord, through Brother Fire.

All: Praised be you, my Lord, through our Sister, Mother Earth, who sustains and governs us.

– Attributed to St. Francis of Assisi

Pastoral Prayer

Praised be you, my Lord, through those who grant pardon
For love of you and bear sickness and trial.

Blessed are those who endure in peace,
By you, Most High, they will be crowned. Amen.

– Attributed to St. Francis of Assisi

Prayer of Confession

Gracious God, instead of groveling around in our prayers of confession about this or that, which we have done or failed to do, we ought to use the time to make amens where the actual harm has been done. We do confess to you our arrogance in thinking you love us more than you love the other beautiful parts of this astounding created order, but greater good will come if we honor all that you have created and if we see ourselves not as pinnacle but as part. Amen.

Prayer of Dedication of Gifts and Self

Gracious God, we give of our means and our energies so that neither human nor habitat will have to suffer. As we do, we pledge not to be a part of abuse or destruction through what we purchase or endorse. Amen.

Hymn of the Day

All Creatures of Our God and King/To You, O God, All Creatures Sing

W.H. Draper translated St. Francis of Assisi's "Canticle of the Sun" and prepared his translation specifically to fit the tune LASST UNS ERFREUEN. The tune was first published in *Geistliche Kirchengesänge* (1623) as an Easter hymn. The canticle was based on two psalms, 145 and 148, the psalm for the day. Sing it as a reflection on the psalm. Focusing on the connection between praise of God in creation and praise of God for the gift of the Messiah could make a refreshing addition to worship during Christmastime. There is a wonderful new translation by Miriam Therese Winter in *The New Century Hymnal* (1995), which could also give an interesting and fresh perspective during this time of traditional carols.

Children's Time: Let Everything Praise God!

(Preparation: Bring an ornament that can illustrate Psalm 148, such as an animal, bird, cloud, etc. Adjust the story accordingly.)

Yesterday was Christmas Day, and we will be celebrating the season of Christmas for 12 days – the 12 days of Christmas. It is a wonderful, joyous time.

On this first Sunday after Christmas each year we read Psalm 148. Like the other psalms, this was written long before Jesus was born. It was written to be a hymn the people would sing when they worshipped God. It is such a happy psalm we read it today.

In Psalm 148 they talk about everything praising God: sun, moon, stars, rain, clouds, all kinds of animals, storms, mountains, trees, and all kinds of people. Let everything praise God, the psalm says.

I've brought a *(show and refer to the ornament you brought)* to help us remember this joy. Whenever we see any of these great things God has made it can remind us of how great God is. We probably won't do that all the time, but it is a good thing to stop and say a word of praise to God. *(Hang the item on the tree.)* Let's do that now:

Prayer: God, you are great and wonderful. We love you. We thank you for all the love you bring, and for caring for us always. Amen.

The Sermon: Creature Praise
Scripture: Psalm 148
(For sermon materials on Matthew 2:13-23, see the September/October 2010 issue of *The Clergy Journal* or the May/June 2010 planning issue of *The Clergy Journal.*)

When I read or hear Psalm 148, this song in the deep recesses of my memory comes to the top of my brain. The title of the song is "Creature Praise." And for its time, the song had congregants who were used to sitting still and silent, tapping their toes and bobbing their heads. I recently found the song again on iTunes, and the rhythm still makes me move!

Large creatures, small creatures, short and tall creatures . . . young creatures, old creatures, hot and cold creatures . . . day creatures, night creatures, left and right creatures . . . near creatures, far creatures, any where you are creatures, come now and praise the Lord! (Mike Curb Congregation).

The psalm is about the whole of creation coming together to praise the Creator, and the writer of this portion of liturgy for the ancient temple worshipers is comprehensive in her or his perspective, constantly moving in this sweeping call of everything and everyone to praise God. The movement is from high to low, as it were, and low to high in all realms.

Notice the flow. In the created order, from heavens to heavenly bodies and then to the earth before calling out to the waters and the depths. The highest mountains and then hills that aren't as tall. Fruit trees before the call to the towering cedars. Earth creatures and then flying creatures above them. Kings

195

then commoners. Young men and then young women. (Sorry, ladies!) Young then old. It's a comprehensive call to praise God, the Creator.

This business of thinking of humans as the crown of creation in the sense that animals and objects are here purely for our use, our pleasure, our comfort regardless of any pain or abuse or destruction we heap upon them needs to be gone for good!

My older son was a first- or second-year high school student when he first became an animal rights advocate. He was a "latest cause" kind of guy, and while I respected all the causes he wanted to support, well most, I didn't get drawn into each one. This one really began to get to him, and when I caught on to how serious he was about the ways animals were being tortured for human well-being I began to learn myself – much to my dismay. I had no idea that certain cosmetics were tested on rabbits' eyes until the rabbits went blind or killed themselves first from the constant burning in their eyes.

It never occurred to me that monkeys were placed in machines that made them stand up and then sit again on "easy chairs" to see how many times it would take before the fabric began to wear; the monkeys sometimes died of exhaustion, or their bones or joints broke. Who could have imagined that cows were often fattened up to the point that they couldn't walk anymore and had to be held up in slings – all so there would be more cow to sell at market? I've never forgotten what I learned about these practices, and they changed my mind.

This is not what God's creatures were created for. There is no argument in favor of that stand. God's creatures are co-creatures with me and with you, and like us humans they have a function in praising God. William Ralph Inge made a permanent impression on me with this comment: "We have enslaved the rest of the animal creation, and have treated our distant cousins in fur and feathers so badly that beyond doubt, if they were able to formulate a religion, they would depict the Devil in human form" (Outspoken Essays, 1922).

Praise isn't limited to any one language – not any human language or human language all. Pure praise isn't logocentric, not primarily words and maybe not words at all. The primary basis of praise is in being the best we can be at what we were created to be. Animals, ironically, never have any problems with that. Neither do rocks and trees or skies and seas – if greedy and careless humans leave them be. This psalmist even has the sea monsters, generally the most frightening of all creatures for the ancient Hebrews, praising their Creator, who happens to be the same Creator who created us humans.

I don't get these people who make a sport out of cruelty to animals. Dog fighting and cock fighting. It's horrible. We all know the story of the rich and famous athlete who got caught funding dog fighting rings. He had to spend his time in jail, and then came out only to be picked up by a big time professional team that will make him filthy rich all over again. He was just one of many killing dogs by the dozen for bloodthirsty sick entertainment.

Today is the first Sunday in the briefest of all seasons in the Christian year, Christmastide. Some years, the season has only one Sunday in it, never more than two. It's the season of reflecting on the meaning of Emmanuel, God with us, incarnation, enfleshment. As much as Christians can find to argue about with each other, the precise relationship of Jesus to God probably has ranked second only to the great debates about sanctuary carpet color.

At the first ecumenical council, which Constantine called in Nicea in 325, Arius and his followers lost to Alexander and Athanasius and their followers, but really only in a formal way. This was the deal. Alexander and Athanasius believed, and got most of the bishops in attendance to sign their statement even though a good number of those signed more for reasons of expediency than conviction, that Jesus and God were of the same nature.

Arius said, "No way. No way someone who could be seen and touched and who tasted of physical death could be exactly the same as God the great Spirit." In Arius's view, Jesus shared creature-hood with us. I happen to agree with Arius, and that makes for an interesting Christmastide twist. When Jesus praised God, he did so as one of us; he did so as a true part of the created order. He wasn't play acting; he wasn't going through the motions to teach mere humans a lesson or two. He was the real thing. Amen.

– David Albert Farmer

Hymns
Opening Hymn
All Creatures of Our God and King
Creator of the Stars of Night
Sermon Hymn
Of the Father's Love Begotten
Let the Earth Now Praise the Lord
Closing Hymn
God of the Sparrow
Break Forth, O Beauteous Heav'nly Light

January 2, 2011

2nd Sunday after Christmas

Lessons

RCL
Jer 31:7-14 or Sir 24:1-12
Ps 147:12-20 or Wis 10:15-21
Eph 1:3-14
Jn 1:(1-9), 10-18

Roman Catholic
Sir 24:1-4, 8-12
Ps 147:12-15, 19-20
Eph 1:3-6, 15-18
Jn 1:1-18 or 1:1-5, 9-14

Speaker's Introduction for the Lessons
Lesson 1
Jeremiah 31:7-14 (RCL)

Shout for joy! God is gathering all God's people together, and in the gathered group are the marginalized and left-out people according to the standards and practices of this world. No one is left out!

Sirach 24:1-4, 8-12 (RC)

To followers of Judaism, the created world is God's, so faith and reason go hand in hand; learning about creation is learning about God; reasoning is done in the context of God.

Lesson 2
Psalm 147:12-20 (RCL); 147:12-15, 19-20 (RC)

Here God is still gathering people together and in particular the outcasts and emotionally wounded. Only the wicked, those who are causing pain to others, are cast aside and excluded from this particular round up.

Lesson 3
Ephesians 1:3-14 (RCL); 1:3-6, 15-18 (RC)

As God adopted Jesus as God's own child, so also God moves to adopt the rest of us who will respond to God's generosity and love by saying, "I too will own my place in your family, God."

Gospel
John 1:(1-9), 10-18 (RCL); 1:1-18 (RC)

Here's an uneasy juxtaposition. The God who gathers, the God who draws in, the God who goes the distance to make known to the world the fullness of God, the one who more than any other has been able to show as much of God as can be revealed in human form, is rejected by the very ones to whom God sent the light. (The NRSV translation of verse 18 is seriously in error. It's more of a paraphrase as you can see when compared to Young's literal translation of the verse: "God no one hath ever seen; the only begotten Son, who is on the bosom of the Father – he did declare.")

Theme

Many of us are determined not to see God at work regardless of how challenging that lifelong project is.

Thought for the Day

Not seeing the reality of God requires concerted effort by us, but it can be done; and it's a way of life many people choose.

Sermon Summary

God's light is a given. It is the proof of God's love and God's work. There are three ways those who know about God's light respond to it: 1) with eyes tightly shut; 2) squinting; and 3) with eyes wide open.

Call to Worship

If you feel lost, you are not lost to God. If you feel excluded, you are not excluded by God. If you feel that there is no hope for you, you are not hopeless in God's eyes. If you're stuck in the darkness and have forgotten how to recognize the reality of the light, you are welcome here today as we celebrate the God whose light is not only real, but also permanent. No darkness has ever been able to extinguish it, ever!

Pastoral Prayer

Gracious God, our world is filled with people who do not know your light; they do not know that you are the light. Their days are filled with darkness in every possible way. We seek ways to share the good news about your light with them. There are many, though, who know that you are the light, and they have seen your light for longer or shorter periods of time. But for hosts of reasons they have come to fear your light and so they intentionally embrace darkness so as not to be reminded of your unconditional love for them. May those of us who are focusing on the light encourage each one with whom we come into contact who is choosing darkness to risk wide-open eyes. Amen.

Prayer of Confession
Gracious God, many of us, some of the time at least, are precisely those people whom John challenged in his letters. We are people who love darkness more than we love light. We prefer to stumble and stub our toes as opposed to living in the light that both reminds of God's love and at the same time leaves us no excuses for choosing the wrong paths. Thank you for your untiring efforts to pull us toward the well-lighted pathways. Amen.

Prayer of Dedication of Gifts and Self
Searching God, relentless God of love, you lured us into the center of your love and changed our lives. We give of our means and of our time to help others see the rays of your light that will allow them to see the fuller light. Amen.

Hymn of the Day
Of the Father's Love Begotten
The original text is found in *Cathemerinon*, a collection of daily hymns written by Prudentius in the 5th century. It was translated by J.M. Neale and published in his *Hymnal Noted* (1851). The tune, DIVINUM MYSTERIUM, also known as CORDE NATUS, is based on a medieval liturgical chant for a Sanctus. Use a flexible tempo based on good recitation of the text. Organ is the preferred accompaniment; however, do not let the accompaniment dictate the natural rhythm of the text. Another possibility is to sing as free chant without accompaniment. Use a combination of soloist, small ensemble, and full congregation with everyone singing the final phrase "evermore and evermore." An alternate translation, "Of the Parent's Heart Begotten," is found in *The New Century Hymnal* (1995).

Children's Time: Shining in the Darkness
(Preparation: Bring some Christmas lights and/or plan to gather at the unlit Christmas tree and turn the lights on during the story. Alternatively, bring a candle you can light – safely – with the children.)

There are three versions of the Christmas story in our Bible – in the Gospels of Matthew, Luke, and John.

Matthew tells us about Jesus' father, Joseph, being worried when he learned Mary was to have a baby. God tells Joseph in a dream that it's okay, and he and Mary get married. Later, wise people come from the East to worship the baby Jesus.

Luke tells us about Mary and Joseph traveling to Bethlehem, and the two of them finding no place to stay except a stable. After Jesus is born, shepherds come and see him and then go out to spread the word.

John's story is very different. He doesn't tell us any of the details of Jesus' birth, but instead tries to talk about some of the symbolism of it. In the very beginning of his book he tells us three wonderful things about Jesus: John refers to Jesus as God's word, because at the very beginning of the world God spoke, and things were created. John then mentions that Jesus is life, for all people. Finally, he says that Jesus is like a light, shining in the darkness. No matter what the darkness tries to do, it cannot put out the light that Jesus brings.

In this season we remember this wonderful symbolism of Jesus. *(Hang the lights, and/or turn on the tree, or light the candle.)*

Prayer: Creator God, thank you for Jesus: your word, our life, and the light of the world. Amen.

The Sermon: Glimpse the Divine Light
Scripture: John 1:(1-9), 10-18

(For sermon materials on John 1:(1-9), 10-18, see the September/October 2010 issue of *The Clergy Journal*; for sermon materials on Ephesians 1:3-14, see the May/June 2010 planning issue of *The Clergy Journal*.)

The message for today is not for those who have never been able to "get" God or affirm in any way that there is a God, either because no one has helped them learn to focus or because intellectually or philosophically the idea of God doesn't take. Today's message is for those who have seen God, have had their souls brightened up by God's light, but who have shut themselves off from the light making a conscious decision, or a series of them, to dig into the darkness and try to block that light.

It's not a foreign impulse even for the most would-be devout. There was First Isaiah in the midst of the most profound moments of his early ministry, in temple seeking to honor God, when he all of a sudden got way more than he bargained for. In a vision, he saw God high and lifted up, and the first chance he had to speak in the dream, he said, "Woe is me! I am lost, for I am a person of unclean lips, and I live among a people of unclean lips" (Isa 6:5a NRSV, adapted for inclusive language).

The problem with too much light, God's light not excluded, is that we see more than we want to see. The lovable drag queens in "To Wong Foo Thanks for Everything, Julie Newmar," starring the late Patrick Swayze are moving into their new living quarters and immediately turn out the overhead lights! If we keep the draperies pulled and only low-wattage side lighting on in a room, we have no idea how dirty the floors are or how badly stained the sofa really is. My realtor, getting ready to put my house on the market, came in and pulled back the draperies in every room of my house. I was astonished and embarrassed. I thought my house was clean! I think it's an Irish proverb that says something like: Firelight will not let you read fine stories; but it's warm, and you won't see the dust on the floor!

Those of us who have had the privilege of getting a glimpse of divine light can respond to it three ways. We can try to deny it or neutralize it by shutting our eyes to what we already know is real whether we embrace it as real or not. We can keep our eyes wide open and deal with both resultant extremes: the revelation of God's love and areas in our lives we didn't really want to see again. The third option is a middle-of-the-road effort: squinting, eyes mostly closed but with some modest effort to stay reminded of the light without being overwhelmed by greater love than we think we can cope with or without having to worry too much about any more of a clean-up than we care to undertake.

No one can see God head on. It would be too intense if we could, sort of like trying to look at the sun with a naked eye. What we can see is light emanating from God, most clearly in the light that Jesus brought into the world as the preeminent catalyst of divine light. Light: "And the Word became flesh and lived among us, and we have seen his glory, the glory as of a parent's unique child, full of grace and truth" (Jn 1:14, preacher's paraphrase). Shutting our eyes to the light: "He came to what was his own, and his own people did not accept him" (Jn 1:11). Opening our eyes to the light: "But to all who received him, who believed in his name, he gave power to become children of God, who were born, not of blood or of the will of the flesh or of the will of humanity, but of God" (Jn 1:13-14, adapted for inclusive language). Squinting: "The light shines in the darkness, and the darkness did not overcome it" (Jn 1:5).

There is plenty of darkness in the world – evil and apathy, those powerful cousins, see to that. There are those who were so overcome with a sense of unworthiness or embarrassment at what needed to be cleaned up within them when they encountered the light of God as Jesus radiated it, that they ran into the darkness where, ever since, they have kept themselves, eyes tightly shut, for fear of ever seeing that much love and acceptance or need to clean up what has been let go spiritually or otherwise. Plenty of those who knew Jesus best realized God spoke and worked through him. It was essentially undeniable, but not able to cope with what they caught of the light of God in Jesus, they embraced and are still embracing the darkness.

Squinting isn't a worthless undertaking; it can do some good, some limited good. It keeps too much light (more than you want) out of your eyes, but it does let you confirm that the light is still there. Squinting works if you just want a reminder now and then there is still divine light in this world, though you are not letting it do all it can do for you.

The light is a reality. Darkness has never won out over the light, and even in the darkest nights of the soul, rays of light may still break through. Educational psychologist, specialist in gifted children's issues, and academician Maurice F. Freehill has been credited with asking this pointed question: "Who is more foolish, the child afraid of the dark or the man afraid of the light?"

The only option that changes our lives for the better, now and into the future, is to look with wide-eyed wonder into those amazing rays of light – lighting up the depths of the darkness within and helping me love myself even before I tidy up because the light lets me know at once that God does. As small as I could feel before the Creator, the light shows me that there's no need to run because in God's family no one is insignificant. "The Lord is my light and my salvation . . . The Lord is the strength of my life, of whom shall I be afraid" (Ps 27:1 KJV).

– David Albert Farmer

Hymns
Opening Hymn
Of the Father's Love Begotten
Thanks to God Whose Word Was Spoken
Sermon Hymn
The Light of the World Is Jesus
Jesus, Thou Joy of Loving Hearts
Closing Hymn
The Lord Is My Light
My Light and My Salvation

January 6, 2011

Epiphany

Lessons

RCL	Roman Catholic
Isa 60:1-6	Isa 60:1-6
Ps 72:1-7, 10-14	Ps 72:1-2, 7-8, 10-13
Eph 3:1-12	Eph 3:2-3, 5-6
Mt 2:1-12	Mt 2:1-12

Speaker's Introduction for the Lessons

Lesson 1
Isaiah 60:1-6 (RCL/RC)

A part of Epiphany is enlightenment! God's light is the basis of our enlightenment because with it our perspective is forever changed by light enough to see all of those whom God draws in.

Lesson 2
Psalm 72:1-7, 10-14 (RCL); 72:1-2, 7-8, 10-13 (RC)

What a different world it would be if all leaders were concerned, first, about honoring a benevolent God and, second, about all of those whom they lead who suffer and struggle.

Lesson 3
Ephesians 3:1-12 (RCL); 3:2-3, 5-6 (RC)

The Season of Epiphany is about the universality of God's love and the ministry of Jesus. The Apostle Paul was the key figure who began the spread of Jesus' message beyond the confines of Judaism.

Gospel
Mathew 2:1-12 (RCL/RC)

The coming of the wise ones from the East (farther east than Bethlehem is in relationship to the West – very possibly Iran) is the story of the early impact of Jesus' birth on the world beyond where most Jews were living near Jesus' second birthday.

Theme
Many of us on the "inside" of Christian community are shocked when we witness examples of faithfulness by those on the "outside."

Thought for the Day
It's amazing what anyone may find if she or he follows with determination the hints of God's leading and luring.

Sermon Summary
The Magi have been misunderstood for millennia. They made a journey that was as much a journey of the heart as it was a journey of terrain. The Magi were more attentive to the meaning of Jesus' presence in the world than were most who knew him best.

Call to Worship
One: Darkness is covering the earth,
All: And thick darkness the peoples.
One: But the glory of God continues to shine in the darkness.
All: People from all nations are drawn to that divine light.
One: Sovereigns and commoners.
**All: The old and the young. Look at all the people gathering
around the light!**

– Adapted from Isaiah 60:1-6

Pastoral Prayer
Gracious God, we pray today for all of those in our one human family who live under the cover of darkness, whether they have chosen and created their darkness or have had it thrust upon them. And we pray for them as people who have known darkness ourselves. Some of us who gather for worship today carry our darkness with us, and we are here today seeking God's light for ourselves as well as for others. If we are able, O God, we would be light, even tiny rays, for those who doubt that there is any light for them. Even as Jesus brought light, so might we. Amen.

Prayer of Confession
Gracious God, we own our tendency to think that our beliefs are the best, that our ways are the most wonderful, that our beliefs are the most believable!

Owning our arrogance, we dare to see your work in those people and places we have thought beyond the reach of your love and your leading. Amen.

Prayer of Dedication of Gifts and Self
Gracious God, we marvel at the lavish and sacrificial gifts given to make the world your kind of place by those who claim not to know you or your will. Can we offer less? Amen.

Hymn of the Day
'Twas in the Moon of Wintertime
This hymn gives an interesting interpretation of the story of the Nativity and the arrival of the Magi. It was written by Father Jean de Brébeuf, a French Jesuit priest and missionary, as a teaching story for the first nations' people living near Lake Huron in Canada. Written about 1642, it was translated from the Huron language into French approximately 100 years later. In 1926, Toronto historian and author Jesse Edgar Middleton paraphrased it in English. The use of first nations' imagery makes it an excellent example of how to be inclusive in our teachings and worship. Stanzas may be sung by soloists or the whole congregation with the refrain being sung by all.

Children's Time: Star of Wonder
(Preparation: Bring a star. If possible, bring the star you used on November 28, although any star will work fine. You might also wish to bring stars, perhaps cut from paper or felt, to give to all the children.)

I've brought a star this morning. You may recognize it – I first brought it six weeks ago, at the very beginning of Advent.

Do you recall any of the things we said way back then? *(Briefly recap that story with the children.)*

The star is also a very important part of today's story. Matthew tells us about some wise people who lived far away from Bethlehem where Jesus was born. They liked to study stars, and they were extra intrigued when a big star rose in the sky, over Bethlehem. They felt that it was a sign from God and was telling them something very important. So they prepared for a long journey, and headed off. The star led them all the way, and when they found Jesus they worshipped him, and gave him special gifts. They knew he was very special, that he was the son of God.

In a dream, God warned them to beware of King Herod, who did not like to think that another king – Jesus – had just been born, and so they went home by a different road.

This star can remind us of these ones who risked much to find Jesus. It can also remind us that sometimes when we encounter Jesus, it causes us to change the way we're going, and the way we're doing things. *(Hang the star on the tree, if it is still up, and/or give stars to the children.)*

The Sermon: All Things Wise and Wonderful
Scripture: Matthew 2:1-12
(For sermon materials on Matthew 2:1-12, see the September/October 2010 issue of *The Clergy Journal* or the May/June 2010 planning issue of *The Clergy Journal*.)

Let's get rid of some of the misunderstandings about the wise ones who came from the East to honor toddler Jesus. There's the first one. Jesus wasn't a baby in a barn's manger when the wise ones arrived. He was about two years old. The shepherds were at hand when Jesus was born and made it to the innkeeper's barn before Mary and Joseph and their baby born in transit left to get back to their home. The wise ones didn't. Crèches with wise ones bowing before the baby in a feed trough are non-biblical – if that matters.

The wise ones were following a star that shone intermittently – never in the daytime and not every night. This extended their arduous search for the one whom they believed the star was leading them to. We have to imagine that some days they made no progress at all toward their destination, and on other days they actually lost ground, traveling opposite where they needed to be going. If you don't believe in the historicity of the story, then you may have no problem with the details, but if you do believe the trip and the encounter took place it's important to pay attention to all the details contained in the story, which, by the way, is only told in the Gospel of Matthew.

The wise ones were not monotheists as far as we know; yet, they were open to divine leadership. They did not believe what the Jews believed and had no access to Jewish scripture that might have shown them how some Jews had long looked for a leader to come and help them become (again?) fully the people God wanted them to be. The wise ones were devoted first and foremost to the gods and goddesses they knew in their religious practices, probably in what we call today the country of Iran. The ongoing tension between Iran and Israel today makes the connection between the wise ones and Jesus all the more interesting!

The wise ones were stargazers in their home country; they were not kings. They probably were not rich. There is no indication whatsoever of how many of them made the trek. There might have been as few as two wise ones, and there might have been a whole crowd of them. The fact that three kinds of gifts were offered (gold, frankincense, and myrrh) is not proof of the fact that three men came, each presenting to a two-year old one gift type.

These extraneous (and incorrect!) details have dominated our understanding of the wise ones, who show up in most churches on Christmas Eve even though they did not make it to Jesus' manger and even though the lectionary clearly presents their story during the season of Epiphany. Honestly, if we don't look more deeply into the Matthew 2 story than we have, it's not worth the read. I say this as someone reared in the Beaver Dam Baptist Church in Halls Crossroads, Tennessee, taught to revere the wise men because those roles second in sacredity to plastic, Caucasian baby Jesus alone. The roles of the wise men went usually to the patriarchs in the church choir and were not shared; typically, only sickness or death saw the appointment of a "new" wise man. Those wise men stirred awe within as they processed down the center aisle wearing the capes accented with cotton puffs and their bejeweled cardboard crowns. We were not a lectionary people, and I knew nothing of a Christian season called Epiphany until I began my seminary studies. I haven't noticed much of a difference in pageants, though, in lectionary churches.

It seems fascinating at first that Matthew, often portrayed as the most "Jewish" of the Gospels, is the only one of the four Gospel writers to tell about the impact of Jesus' birth on a decidedly non-Jewish (and probably non-monotheistic) group. Yet, when all of the visions of an ideal world in Hebrew scripture are analyzed, it's not such a surprise. The Jews are not and never have been a proselytic religion; they do not and have not believed that people have to become one of them in order to get in good with God. Thus, anyone (or any group) who does justice and honors the ways of God (knowingly or not) is embraced as people of God.

The wise ones did not embrace Judaism and had no conversion experience before they began following the star that eventually would lead them to the home of Mary and Joseph and Jesus. They simply followed the light they had, and eventually they were rewarded for their risks. They saw the one whom God had appointed to set the tone for a renewal of Judaism, and they chose to honor him as they would have honored any leader into whose presence they came as "foreigners."

As a rule, we people of faith don't like it when those who aren't people of faith do a better job, and chances are those who first heard the story of the wise ones acting on a divinely planted impulse that got them to Jesus while most of the Jews right around him were oblivious to what his presence in the world might mean hated it. Luke's shepherds weren't exactly high class, but at least they were Jews! And the shepherds had angels singing songs of confirmation. The wise ones had only a star shining now and then to either encourage or discourage them; there is certainly no fanfare and no confirmation from anyone once they see little Jesus that he is to be someone great among the Jews and the peoples of the world.

The story of the wise ones teaches us that God is not limited by or obligated to work within the structures of anything human-made, religious institutions included. It also teaches us that when we feel drawn to follow some star, even a faintly flickering one, we might do well to follow it. That star might get us to a place where we can learn more about God than we will ever learn if we stay within our present theological framework, as if God has said everything that God will ever say. In the end, even Jesus himself didn't fit in very well to the way things were, and, though it cost him his life, he dared to follow God to places where his contemporaries said that God could not and would not go. Amen.

– David Albert Farmer

Hymns
Opening Hymn
Rise, Thou Light of Gentile Nations
How Vast the Benefits Divine
Sermon Hymn
We Three Kings
Together, Lord, We Come to Thee
Closing Hymn
Magi Came from Lands Afar
Star in the East

January 9, 2011

1st Sunday after Epiphany
The Baptism of Our Lord

Lessons

RCL	Roman Catholic
Isa 42:1-9	Isa 42:1-4, 6-7
Ps 29	Ps 29:1-2, 3-4, 3b, 9b-10
Acts 10:34-43	Acts 10:34-38
Mt 3:13-17	Lk 3:15-16, 21-22

Speaker's Introduction for the Lessons
Lesson 1
Isaiah 42:1-9 (RCL); 42:1-4, 6-7 (RC)

God's ideal servant – individual or group such as a faith community – tirelessly pursues justice. Listen for a word from the Lord in the teachings of Second Isaiah.

Lesson 2
Psalm 29 (RCL); 29:1-2, 3-4, 3b, 9b-10 (RC)

This ancient liturgical piece, sung or chanted in corporate temple worship, draws the heavenly beings, God's attendants as imagined in that day, into the challenge of hearing God in a frightful natural event, a serious storm. The voice of God in catastrophe may not be a voice of punishment at all, but rather a voice of encouragement to be strong and/or to take protective cover.

Lesson 3
Acts 10:34-43 (RCL); 10:34-38 (RC)

God appointed and God anointed Jesus to take up the ministry he dared to perform.

Gospel
Matthew 3:13-17 (RCL)

Speculations abound as to why Jesus, utterly devoted to God and already a morally upright person, asked John to baptize him since

John's baptism was usually associated with repentance. From Jesus'
point of view, however, the motivation was righteousness.
Luke 3:15-16, 21-22 (RC)
When Jesus had been baptized and was praying, heaven was opened.

Theme
Righteousness is both measure of and motivation for spiritual acts.

Thought for the Day
Righteousness should drive us as it drove Jesus.

Sermon Summary
Jesus was drawn to baptism because of John the Baptizer; Jesus' response
to his baptism took him, however, in his own direction.

Call to Worship
One: Words of the Apostle Paul:
**All: If anyone else has reason to be confident in the flesh, I have
more:**
One: . . . circumcised on the eighth day . . .
**All: . . . a member of the people of Israel, of the tribe of
Benjamin . . .**
One: . . . a Hebrew born of Hebrews . . .
All: . . . as to the law, a Pharisee . . .
One: . . . as to zeal, a persecutor of the church . . .
All: . . . as to righteousness under the law, blameless.
One: Yet whatever gains I had, these I have come to regard as loss
because of Christ.
**All: More than that, I regard everything as loss because of the
surpassing value of knowing Christ Jesus my Lord. For his
sake I have suffered the loss of all things, and I regard them
as rubbish, in order that I may gain Christ and be found in
him, not having a righteousness of my own that comes from
the law, but one that comes through faith in Christ, the
righteousness from God based on faith.**
– Adapted from Philippians 3:4b-9

Pastoral Prayer

Gracious God, we seek to be motivated by the desire to do acts of righteousness wherever we have opportunity. Many of those who need to be reminded of your love this very day are suffering because righteousness does not prevail in their lives. They have not been given fair trials. They have been denied adequate health care. They are hungry, and they must put their hungry children to bed with stomachs growling. As your instruments in the world, we desire to be driven by righteousness as Jesus was. Amen.

Prayer of Confession

Gracious God, we confess that righteousness often matters very little to us until its absence impinges on us. Without waiting to see what it feels like before we're willing to try to help others who are struggling because righteousness has been diverted from them, we, because of Jesus' example, would use our energies to trying to make righteousness a reality for all. Amen.

Prayer of Dedication of Gifts and Self

We give our gifts today, O God, and pledge our efforts in a very focused way: to try to fulfill all righteousness, following the example of Jesus. Amen.

Hymn of the Day
When Jesus Came to Jordan

This text was written by Fred Pratt Green in 1973 as the result of extensive correspondence with Dirk van Dissel, a theological student in Australia. Van Dissel was concerned that the proposed *Australian Hymnbook* would not have liturgical office hymns, especially on the Baptism of Jesus. The final version of this text was reviewed in The Hymn Society of Great Britain and Ireland's journal *Bulletin* and deemed "a triumph." There are numerous tunes associated with this text – as many as there are American hymnals that include it. Probably the best known tune is MUNICH from Neuvermehtres Gesangbuch (1693); however, the English folk tune, KING'S LYNN and a DE EERSTEN ZIJN DE LAATSTEN, composed in 1973 by Dutch-born organist August Mehrtens, are alternates. The text of this hymn is of significant importance and its use should be encouraged by using any familiar 7.6.7.6 D metered tune.

Children's Time: A Special Child of God

(Preparation: Plan to show children the methods and items used for baptism in your church. If convenient, gather at the font or baptistry. Plan your discussion with the children to reflect the practice of baptism in your church.

Talk about how a couple of weeks ago you celebrated Jesus' birthday, and last week you celebrated the wise people traveling a long, long way to tell the world that Jesus was special. Today one of our Bible stories tells of Jesus' baptism, when God spoke from heaven and said that Jesus was very special. In our baptism, God says that we are special, too.

Show the children the font or baptistry, and other items used in baptism, such as a shell, pitcher, napkin, towel, and so forth. Talk about how baptisms are performed.)

When we are born, we are God's children, and God loves us very much. No matter who we are, no matter where we are born, God loves us. When we are baptized, it's our way of saying, "We belong to God." *(If your church practices infant baptism, you might say something like "Parents bring children for baptism as a way of saying that they know their baby is a special child of God.")*

Whenever the church baptizes people, we believe that God says to the world, "This is one of my special children, and I love them."

Prayer: Thank you, loving God, for claiming us as your children. Bless us this day we pray. Amen.

The Sermon: Fulfilling Righteousness
Scripture: Matthew 3:13-17

(For sermon materials on Acts 10:34-43, see the September/October 2010 issue of *The Clergy Journal*; for sermon materials on Matthew 3:13-17, see the May/June 2010 planning issue of *The Clergy Journal*.)

John the Baptist may not have been as much of a solo act as most interpreters have originally thought. He may have been out in wilderness not living alone at all, but rather in a community that made its home in the wilderness – intentionally away from the distracting and corrupting influences of the crowded urban areas. If this is true, and I'm inclined to think it was, then John the Baptizer was likely a part of a religio-political party, one of the established parties in first-century Judaism – called "Essenes." You've heard much more about the two major parties, Pharisees and Sadducees, but there were others; and the Essenes Party was one of the others.

There were probably several branches of Essenes that existed rather independently of others. The simple fact that they lived in communal isolation from other groups virtually necessitated this lack of contact with others. Here are a few other quick facts about the Essenes.

They lived celibate lives. When individuals joined the community they gave all their property to the community and became voices in how what they owned collectively would be used. They promised not to take oaths, and they didn't eat meat; they further rejected the ritual of animal sacrifice practiced by mainstream Judaism. Slaves or servants were not allowed within the community as they all agreed to be servants to each other. They committed to be channels of peace in the world, and they were essentially pacifists who agreed to carry weapons ONLY to protect themselves from wild animals and robbers.

With the Pharisees, but unlike the Sadducees, the Essenes believed in life after earthly life. Initiates were confirmed as members of the community through a water ritual, which we could call baptism. If all of this sounds rather Jesus-ish, there's a very good reason for it.

In modern times, the most famous recollected Essenes are those who lived at the community of Qumran where, in 1945, the Dead Sea Scrolls were discovered. By almost all scholarly accounts, those scrolls, some dating all the way back to 300 BCE, were core documents in the library of the Essenes who lived at Qumran.

Some of the fears of being in the wilderness were dramatically minimized by living in community out there. In any case, that was John's place of ministry, and people from the safe cities were risking their lives to get out to the wilderness to hear John's sermons, which would have called hearers to a way of life based on the Essenes take on evolving Judaism. John would have called his sermon hearers to lives of righteousness, and to seal this commitment to righteousness he asked them to be baptized as the Essenes were baptized. We have to believe that a number of the people who went out to hear John preaching in the wilderness sought membership in the Essenes community and stayed.

John the Baptistizer and Jesus were cousins. John was a little older than Jesus, and John had committed himself to a ministerial career long before Jesus did. The relationship between the two was likely very strong, and Jesus for a time was John's disciple; John was Jesus' mentor.

Many of the emphases from John's Essenes community can be seen in Jesus' core teachings. Something else we can now work into the picture is that Jesus' spiritually exhausting 40 days in the wilderness where his own vision for ministry became painfully clear very well may have taken place literally out in the wilderness in the vicinity of the Essenes community with John his mentor nearby.

The principle earthly figure to whom the Essenes looked for guidance and hope they called "the Teacher of Righteousness." The French scholar, the late Andre Dupont-Sommer, believed that Jesus self-identified as this teacher of righteousness, a very logical outgrowth, he believed, of the suffering servant figure taught about in Third Isaiah (55-56): "Surely, he hath borne our griefs and carried our sorrows." This alone would have kept Jesus from having anything at all to do with the militaristic messianic expectations.

It's a fascinating proposal, and in our lesson from Matthew today, what does Matthew's Jesus say when John the Baptizer hesitates to baptize him? Jesus says he should be baptized by John "to fulfill all righteousness." On that basis, John consented to administer or preside over the baptism. God, then, in the first Gospel is entirely pleased with Jesus' baptism and his reason for having been baptized. Many scholars believe this is the point at which Jesus was adopted by God as God's unique child. It isn't proper to refer to Jesus as God's only child or as God's only son. That John 3:16 reference should, by the very language of the fourth Gospel, refer to Jesus as God's unique, one-of-a-kind child – certainly not God's only child. We are all children of God.

His baptism didn't make Jesus either a sinner or a saint. It didn't prove he needed to repent, and it didn't seal him as beyond the lure of self-centeredness. Baptism doesn't do anything exteriorly to the one who is baptized. It's an affirmation – yea, a celebration and potentially a risk – based on what has already happened within. Baptism generally is a public act; there have been exceptions, of course. And the public act identifies one with a specific movement and presumably that movement's foundational philosophies. "They will know we are Christians by our love . . . ," and so forth.

If I had the opportunity to ask Professor Dupont-Sommer a question about his theory, it would be this: If Jesus did so closely identify with the Essenes, why did he not buy into their separatist sensibilities? For John the Baptizer, righteousness meant separation from the evils of mainstream society, but for Jesus righteousness meant returning to the nitty-gritty of life. Even when his life was at risk, Jesus kept going back into the thick of things because for him righteousness had more to do with engagement and less to do with avoidance. John stayed in the wilderness for the most part, and those who wanted to hear him had to go to him. Jesus, clearly breaking that pattern, went directly to those who were the victims of injustice as well as to those who were hungering and thirsting after, you know: righteousness. Amen.

– David Albert Farmer

Hymns
Opening Hymn
>Down to the Sacred Wave
>The Son of Man from Jordan Rose

Sermon Hymn
>Down by the Jordan
>When Jesus Came from Galilee

Closing Hymn
>The Solid Rock
>Come Holy Spirit, Dove Divine

January 16, 2011

2nd Sunday after Epiphany
RC/Pres: 2nd Sunday in Ordinary Time

Lessons

RCL	Roman Catholic
Isa 49:1-7	Isa 49:3, 5-6
Ps 40:1-11	Ps 40:2, 4, 7-10
1 Cor 1:1-9	1 Cor 1:1-3
Jn 1:29-42	Jn 1:29-34

Speaker's Introduction for the Lessons
Lesson 1
Isaiah 49:1-7 (RCL); 49:3, 5-6 (RC)

As Israel awaits restoration to its homeland after exile in Babylon in this second Servant Song, Isaiah looks to a time when God will make the servant-nation a saving light to the nations.

Lesson 2
Psalm 40:1-11 (RCL); 40:2, 4, 7-10 (RC)

This deliverance psalm, attributed to David but probably dating to the Exile, is a prayer of thanksgiving to God for deliverance from unspecified trouble, promising faithfulness by those who trust in God.

Lesson 3
1 Corinthians 1:1-9 (RCL); 1:1-3 (RC)

To begin his extensive, complex letter to Christians in the Greek city of Corinth, Paul writes a confessional salutation, declaring the saving faith in Jesus Christ that Paul holds in common with the Corinthians.

Gospel
John 1:29-42 (RCL); 1:29-34 (RC)

The day after baptizing Jesus in the Jordan, John identifies him as the Lamb of God, sparking intense curiosity to know and learn more by inquiring minds among John's disciples.

Theme

Evangelism: coming and seeing.

Thought for the Day

Whatever we practice, not (save at rare intervals) what we preach, is usually our great contribution to the conversion of others.

> – C.S. Lewis, "Letter to a Lady, 2 February 1955," in W. H. Lewis, *Letters of C.S. Lewis* (New York: Harcourt Brace Jovanovich, 1966), p. 261

Sermon Summary

Just as Jesus' identity as "the Lamb of God who takes away the sin of the world" is embodied in his behavior, so our faith is manifested in deeds of justice, mercy, and peace in which we engage, as we invite others to "come and see."

Call to Worship

One: As we wait patiently for the Lord,

All: As we look for deliverance from what we suffer,

One: God hears; God draws us out; God makes our steps secure;

All: And God gives us new songs of praise to sing.

One: We come, with confidence and trust, to worship God,

All: And to declare God's faithfulness, steadfastness, and love in the great congregation.

> – Adapted from Psalm 40:1-11

Pastoral Prayer

We come to you with joyful hearts, O God, hearts filled with wonder and praise: for the magnificence of the cosmos you have created; for the constantly changing complexity of the life you have given us; but most of all for your Incarnation, your dwelling, among us. The knowledge that you have provided us with a savior is too big to keep to ourselves – as it was for John the Baptist and the Apostle Paul and countless others whose lives have been altered by knowing him who is the Lamb of God who takes away the sin of the world. Help us, in speaking and acting, to tell the Good News of forgiveness and love of him who is your Son, under whose Mercy we stand, even Jesus Christ our Lord. Amen.

Prayer of Confession

Our lives are filled with words, O God, words and words and words: on television, in books, on the Internet; words we hear and words we speak. Our culture of words lulls us into complacency. We say we believe in helping others; we even identify who those "others" might be: the homeless, the helpless, the hopeless; those who lack food, shelter, companionship; those who have been beaten down by life or left behind in our affluent society. Even so, we too often fail to follow our words with actions. Forgive us, we pray. Help us to connect what we say and what we do, that we may become ever-growing disciples of him who is your Mercy, our Savior, our deliverance. Amen.

Prayer of Dedication of Gifts and Self

Gracious God, you have multiplied your wondrous deeds and your love toward us in many ways. We give you thanks for your grace, given to us in Christ Jesus, and for your constant faithfulness toward us. In response, we offer you these our gifts, praying that you will use them to strengthen the work of your church in the world; through the merits and under the Mercy of your Son, Christ our Lord, we pray. Amen.

Hymn of the Day
Lift High the Cross

Originally written by George William Kitchen, this text was revised into its current stanza and refrain format by Michael R. Newbolt, principal of the Missionary College at Dorchester. It was included in this new format in *Hymns Ancient and Modern* (1916). Sydney H. Nicholson, music editor of that hymnal, composed the tune CRUCIFER specifically for the revised text. This hymn requires a vigorous, almost march-like pace. Think two beats per measure rather than four. Detaching the bass notes will help to energize its presentation. If this hymn is unfamiliar, teach your congregation the refrain and have soloists or the choir sing the stanzas. The refrain can also be used alone as a response before or after scripture or as a call to worship or gathering response.

Children's Time: Share the Good News

Ask the children about some things that they like. Maybe they have a favorite game, or a favorite TV show. Perhaps there is a snack they like a lot, or a song they like to sing.

If you really like something, do you keep it a big secret? Probably not. Usually, when we find something we really like, we want to tell people. We might run to tell our friends, "Hey, this game is lots of fun," or "Here, try some of this – it's really delicious." We like to share good news.

Well, that was how people found out about Jesus.

When Jesus was grown up, he started to travel around the countryside, teaching people about God's love. People liked the things he was teaching. Of course, there were no newspapers, no telephones, no TV, radio, or Internet. But people were so excited they ran to tell their friends. Soon lots and lots of people were following Jesus.

When people find something they like, they want to tell others. When people learn about Jesus and God's love, they want to tell others, too.

Prayer: Gracious God, it is a joy to learn of your love. Help us to celebrate it and share it every day. Amen.

The Sermon: Evangelism: Two Umbrellas
Scripture: John 1:29-42

(For sermon materials on 1 Corinthians 1:1-9, see the September/October 2010 issue of *The Clergy Journal*; for sermon materials on Isaiah 49:1-7, see the May/June 2010 planning issue of *The Clergy Journal*.)

Nathanael said to [Philip], "Can anything good come out of Nazareth?" Philip said to him, "Come and see." (John 1:39)

What does the word *evangelism* mean to you? Does it lead you to picture Billy Graham, or any one of dozens of preachers who appear on television, speaking and asking for donations? Do you see images of pairs of young male Mormon missionaries, making their rounds through town? Or perhaps your neighborhood Jehovah's Witnesses, with copies of *The Watchtower* in hand? Or maybe the saffron-robed Hari Krishnas who pass out flowers in airports? Regardless of the specific associations we may have, I suspect that for many of us *evangelism* is a word fraught with negative connotations, hinting at (we judge) unseemly zeal that demands an on-the-spot faith decision.

If we look to the root of the word, however, we find that it comes from the Greek word *evangelion,* meaning, "the good news of Jesus Christ." Thus, *evangelism* means "the bringing (or preaching) of the Good News."

All well and good. But what (we may ask) does this mean for us, here and now?

Nathanael said to [Philip], "Can anything Good come out of Nazareth?" Philip said to him, "Come and see."

In today's Gospel lesson, we find John the Baptist explaining that a man called Jesus is a person of some importance: *"the Lamb of God who takes away the sin of the world."* As is the case with many charismatic religious figures of the first century, John has followers, disciples surrounding him, people who have been impressed by what they have heard him say and what they have seen him do.

Two of these disciples, curious, decided to check Jesus out. When Jesus asks them what they are looking for, they evade his question by asking another: *"Rabbi, where are you staying?"* Perhaps as a challenge, but certainly as an invitation, Jesus replies, *"Come and see."* They are so impressed that they begin to look for their friends and relatives – in the case of Andrew, his brother Simon – to share their eager perception that this man Jesus is the Messiah whose coming has been foretold. The following day, when Jesus decides to migrate north to Galilee, he says to Philip, *"Follow me."* Then Philip finds Nathanael to offer the same invitation.

Let me suggest to you that the essence of Christian evangelism is this: One person's saying to another, "Come and see." This ripple effect takes place in the Gospel text: from John's disciples to Jesus' disciples, from Andrew to Simon, from Jesus to Philip, from Philip to Nathanael. At every turn, someone challenges another, "Come and see," and by doing so makes available the Good News of Jesus Christ. We don't need to make it complicated; all we have to do is to say, "Come and see."

Nathanael said to [Philip], "Can anything good come out of Nazareth?" Philip said to him, "Come and see."

When I was a sophomore in college, about halfway through the year, a woman named Vida came to live in the dorm room next door to mine. As I learned only much later, Vida's first weeks were a real struggle. The sum total of my knowledge of Vida was this: She came from Western Africa and was studying far from home. She knew very little English, either written or spoken. She was at least ten years older than the rest of us. She was one of only a handful of non-Caucasians on campus. She spent a lot of time by herself.

One day, I got a note from the Dean of Students: "I need to see you." Such summonses usually meant trouble. I had no idea what to expect.

When I got to her office, the Dean explained that Vida needed help. "You live right next to her," she said. "I want you to start taking Vida to some of your activities."

My initial internal response was, Good grief! How was I supposed to do that, when the poor woman could barely communicate in English? Aloud, and with some trepidation, I voiced my misgivings to the Dean.

"Oh, you'll find a way," she chuckled. "I have every confidence in you."

That meeting took place on a Friday afternoon. For a whole day, I fussed and sputtered to my friends. Vida came and went, her very presence in the dorm making me feel ashamed for not speaking to her.

Finally, late Saturday night, I knocked on her door. "Vida," I asked, "Are you a Christian?" When she looked at me quizzically, I pointed to the cross I wore around my neck, under my t-shirt (so as not to be offensive to others). Vida's head began to bob up and down excitedly. "Would you like to go to church?" I asked. Again, she nodded. Then, I explained to her – very slowly, as if the plodding cadence would make up for her limited English – how to get to the church I attended.

"The service is at 10:30," I said in parting, congratulating myself on having figured out a way to meet the Dean's assignment.

The next day, I went off to church as usual. I kept looking around for Vida during the service. She wasn't there.

Vida wasn't in her room that afternoon. She came in very late the next few nights, carrying piles of books. I wondered what I'd done wrong.

The following Sunday, I got up earlier than usual. I knocked on Vida's door. "Are you awake, Vida?"

"Yes," came the sleepy reply.

Suddenly, in that instant, everything became clear. "Will you come to church . . . with me?"

You see, telling her wasn't enough. I had to take her with me.

It was pouring rain as we were about to leave. Vida looked out the window, pointed to the rain, and began to shake her head no. I looked at her beautiful African dress. Then a lightbulb went on in my head. "Are you afraid you'll get wet?" I asked. "I have two umbrellas," I told her. "You'll be just fine."

So, every Sunday for the next two years, Vida walked to church with me. Not until I was in seminary did I realize what had happened. Dr. Bruce Metzger, highly respected professor of New Testament, remarked during a lecture: "Evangelism is one beggar, telling another beggar where to find bread." I could have added, "Evangelism is having two umbrellas, and offering one to someone else."

Nathanael said to [Philip], "Can anything good come out of Nazareth?"
Philip said to him, "Come and see."

You and I are called to pass on the faith we have received from someone else, not for the purpose of filling up the church with warm bodies; certainly not to bring in new people to pay our bills; but because every person we meet deserves the invitation: "Come – with me – and see." When we do so, we'll need to have a second umbrella ready, just in case.

This is our faith, under the Mercy.

– Nancy E. Topolewski

Hymns
Opening Hymn
Christ for the World We Sing
Christ, Whose Glory Fills the Skies
Sermon Hymn
On Jordan's Bank the Baptist's Cry
Behold the Lamb of God
Closing Hymn
Just as I Am, Without One Plea
O Lamb of God, Still Keep Me

January 23, 2011

3rd Sunday after Epiphany
RC/Pres: 3rd Sunday in Ordinary Time

Lessons

RCL	Roman Catholic
Isa 9:1-4	Isa 8:23—9:3
Ps 27:1, 4-9	Ps 27:1, 4, 13-14
1 Cor 1:10-18	1 Cor 1:10-13, 17
Mt 4:13-23	Mt 4:12-23 or 4:12-17

Speaker's Introduction for the Lessons
Lesson 1
Isaiah 9:1-4 (RCL); 8:23—9:3 (RC)

Writing sometime in the mid-eighth century BCE, amid dire upheaval and foreign conquest of Israel, Isaiah offers hope that a new age and a new ruler from Galilee will bring light to the nations.

Lesson 2
Psalm 27:1, 4-9 (RCL); 27:1, 4, 13-14 (RC)

This psalm of trust, attributed to David, speaks of the protection from enemies that the temple offers, where God can be experienced as an active presence.

Lesson 3
1 Corinthians 1:10-18 (RCL); 1:10-13, 17 (RC)

Paul addresses one of the primary issues that has led to his writing to the Corinthians: disunity created by attaching earthly allegiance to human teachers and not to the message of Christ.

Gospel
Matthew 4:13-23 (RCL); 4:12-23 (RC)

The arrest of John the Baptist motivates Jesus to begin his public ministry, proclaiming repentance and calling his first disciples from among the fishermen at the Sea of Galilee.

Theme
Discipleship: Going fishing for conversion.

Thought for the Day
Conversion requires an alteration of the will, and an alteration which, in the last resort, does not occur without the intervention of the supernatural.
– C.S. Lewis, "The Decline of Religion" (1946), published in *First and Second Things* (London: Fount Paperbacks, 1985), p. 74

Sermon Summary
The calling of the first disciples – rough, work-with-their-hands-down-and-dirty fishermen – who learn to go and "fish for people," offers the radical understanding that anyone can be called to a changed life as a disciple of Jesus Christ, even in our day, among us untimely born.

Call to Worship
One: The Lord is our light and our salvation;
All: We need not fear.
One: The Lord is the stronghold of our lives;
All: We need not be afraid.
One: The Lord provides strength and courage, as we wait for God's coming.
All: As we wait, we offer worship, and praise, and thanksgiving, here in God's house.
– Adapted from Psalm 27

Pastoral Prayer
We thank you, gracious God, for breaking in upon the times of our lives. In times of seeking and in times of finding; in times of holding and in times of losing; in times of war, in times of peace; in times of fear, in times of assurance; in times of light and in times of darkness; in times of prosperity and in times of impoverishment; in times of belief and in times of unbelief. When hearts are full and when they are empty, you remain steadfast, powerful, protective, enfolding, and present. Within all time, we stand, under the Mercy who is your gift to us, your Son, even Jesus Christ our Lord. Amen.

Prayer of Confession

We hear your Son calling us, O God, out of our everyday-ness into something more. His voice says, "Follow me," but we tell ourselves that his call is for later, for when we feel more sure of ourselves and of our ability to do as he asks. And so one day melts into another, and another, and another; and still we make no move. Forgive us, we pray, for the foolish inertia that says we can follow Jesus whenever and however it is convenient for us. Help us to recognize the urgency of discipleship, to go with joy where we need to go to fish for people; we pray under the Mercy of your Son, even Jesus Christ our Lord. Amen.

Prayer of Dedication of Gifts and Self

Here in these offerings, O God, we present to you the fruits of our labors, the gifts of our hearts, the commitment of our calling as disciples of your Son. Bless, we pray, what we offer. And help us, in new and ever-broadening ways, to follow where your Son may call and lead. For it is through his merits and under his Mercy that we pray. Amen.

Hymn of the Day
Tú has venido a la orilla/You Have Come Down to the Lakeshore

This song, based upon the Gospel for the day, is one of the most popular to have come from the post Vatican II spiritual revival in the 1970s. The text and tune were written by Spanish priest Cesáreo Gabaraín in 1979. The preferred accompanying instrument is the guitar. Use a broken chord style of playing with light percussion added. If piano is the only instrument available, keep the accompaniment light and flowing, with broken chords in the left hand and a singing right hand melody. Encourage singers to harmonize as they sing, primarily using the intervals of a third or sixth below the melody. This easily heard harmony is often found in keyboard arrangements of this charming hymn.

Children's Time: Shining a Light

(Preparation: Bring a flashlight.)

(*Show the flashlight to the children.*) When might you use one of these? *(Accept all answers.)* When it is dark, a light like this can help us find our way. It helps to keep us from getting lost.

Long ago, after his baptism, Jesus started his ministry. He lived in a place called Capernaum (cap-ER-nee-um). When he learned that John the Baptist had been put in prison, Jesus decided it was time for him to begin his ministry. You might remember that John the Baptist told people that Jesus was coming.

Jesus started to preach around the area where he lived, and he told people that God was giving them a chance to start again. He also told people that his ministry was like something one of the prophets had said long ago: it was as if a new light had come to the people. *(Turn the light on.)*

Jesus was saying that the things he was going to tell the people about God would help them find their way; his teachings would help them know how God wanted them to live.

Prayer: God of everlasting light, the teachings of Jesus help us know how to live, and we give you thanks. Amen.

The Sermon:
Discipleship: Fishing, Converting, Living a New Life
Scripture: Matthew 4:13-23

(For sermon materials on 1 Corinthians 1:10-18, see the September/October 2010 issue of *The Clergy Journal*; for sermon materials on Matthew 4:13-23, see the May/June 2010 planning issue of *The Clergy Journal*.)

"Follow me, and I will make you fish for people."

"What can you tell me about the disciples of Jesus?"

The question dropped out of the air, only seconds after the starting bell, landing with a loud splat among the members of the ninth grade New Testament class.

It was the second week of school, in a very warm and humid September. Many of the class were half-asleep; others sat in quivering fear that the teacher would single them out to respond to the question.

I knew that the answers had been in the homework for the day, homework I had been very careful to prepare, being new to the school and ballistic with anxiety. The fidgeting that rustled around me revealed that most of the class had not done the reading – and I wasn't the only one in the room who knew that.

Dead silence.

Edgar Brill, the teacher, looked around from one face to another, his gaze fixing on each student's eyes in a sort of optical half-Nelson. As the silence continued, now and then punctuated by a half-hearted cough, he became more and more animated.

"Think, now!" he admonished. "Think! What work do the disciples do, before they even become disciples?"

Tomb-like silence.

Finally, a hand rose in the back of the room. "They were fisherman," came a timid voice.

"Fishermen," Mr. Brill acknowledged, "is the correct response."

Again, the searchlight gaze. "Why does Jesus choose fishermen?"

Again, the heavy silence.

I gulped surreptitiously, hoping I would not be singled out to respond, because I had no clue about why and how Jesus might behave or act.

Then, a flash of insight: Fishermen. Men who make their living outdoors by hard physical labor. Men who are sturdy, muscular, perhaps even graceful in their movements. Men, in short, who look like Edgar Brill.

No one I had encountered as a teacher that semester seemed more oddly part of that profession as Edgar Brill. He was a tall man, burly, with large hands, confident of his physical prowess. Why was he in a classroom, instead of working on a farm or in a coal mine somewhere? And anyway, what would he know about disciples?

"You wouldn't think that Jesus would choose low-class laborers," he observed. "He's the Son of God, after all! He can have anyone he wants as disciples. But Jesus calls fishermen. Because they aren't rich or powerful, these fishermen have *credibility* and can talk to others like themselves – the people Jesus comes to and for in the first place."

The boy next to me raised his hand. "If Jesus lived here, in northeastern Pennsylvania, right now," he asked, "do you think he would have picked coal miners to be disciples?"

A broad smile from the teacher. "You get the idea," he beamed.

To me, whose very limited comprehension of the Bible was confined to Sunday school stories of the Old Testament patriarchs and a loose synopsis of Jesus' ministry, this explanation made perfect sense. "Remember this," Mr. Brill continued. "If the disciples are fishermen, then being disciples is going fishing for people. And if fishermen can be disciples, so can you."

I tell this story because it represents one of the most powerful "Aha!" moments of my life. Who of us, at some time or another, has not thought about the disciples as terribly exalted and blessed? Even though Jesus could call anyone, he chooses these particular people, finding in them potential that they do not recognize in themselves.

Matthew tells us that Jesus sees Simon, Andrew, James, and John and tells them, *"Follow me, and I will make you fish for people."* Matthew does not record their reactions; he simply reports: Jesus calls four men, goes around the region of Galilee, teaches in the synagogues, proclaims the Good News of the Kingdom, cures people of their sicknesses and diseases. No heavenly trumpets sound. No unearthly voice booms from the clouds. No thunder or lightning punctuates the scene. It's all so very deceptively simple: Jesus goes fishing and catches people, then tells them they will do the same.

"Follow me, and I will make you fish for people."

The British author J.R.R. Tolkien was a devout Roman Catholic who was fascinated with the mission and ministry of Jesus. One way he reflected on the call to discipleship was to write three remarkable books, known collectively as *The Lord of Rings* trilogy. The story line is superficially simple: there is a Ring of great power and great potential for evil – as a matter of fact, of the greatest power and the greatest evil that anyone could possibly imagine. Through a sequence of events, the Ring comes into the hands of Frodo Baggins, who is a hobbit, a half-sized human, small, shy, comfort-loving, unassuming, outwardly unremarkable. He finally realizes that he must destroy the Ring, but that he needs help to do so.

In the company of three fellow hobbits, Sam, Merry, and Pippin; Gimli the dwarf; Legolas the elf; Boromir and Aragon, both men; and Gandalf the wizard, Frodo leaves the safety of his home in the Shire of Middle-Earth and heads for the fires of Mount Doom to destroy the Ring. Along the way, each member of the Fellowship discovers that talking about destroying evil is one thing; actually *doing* it is quite another. But what not one of them could accomplish alone, is for all nine of them to attempt together – and their lives are forever changed in the process.

"Follow me, and I will make you fish for people."

I'm sure you have your own mental picture of the calling of the first disciples. The more I have learned about the life of Jesus over the years, the more cloaked in mystery that calling has come to exist in my mind. I can't approach this story without chills running up and down my spine. If Jesus can use uneducated laborers, smelling of fish and sweat, to be his disciples, then can he not use us as well? Does not the call of Jesus come to us, where we are, as we are, who we are, personally, by name, through baptism, in events that touch our hearts and challenge our minds? Do we not, at various times, feel the weight of that discipleship, like a net full of fish, tugging at us, compelling us to do certain things? And has not that discipleship involved us in a process of change, of conversion, of being made into new people, leading new lives?

Forty-four years later, I still remember the excitement that overcame me as Edgar Brill described discipleship as going fishing. His saying so signified that I could be a disciple too. And more than that, it made me *want* to be a disciple with all my heart. It made me want to be a disciple like Edgar Brill – and eventually led me to ordained ministry. And if I can be a disciple of Jesus Christ, fished for, caught, and given new life, so can you.

This is our faith, under the Mercy.

– Nancy E. Topolewski

Hymns
Opening Hymn
Christ for the World We Sing
God Himself Is with Us
Sermon Hymn
Lord, You Have Come to the Lakeshore
Our Faith Is in the Christ Who Walks
Closing Hymn
I Want to Walk as a Child of the Light
Jesus, Lead the Way

January 30, 2011

4th Sunday after Epiphany
RC/Pres: 4th Sunday in Ordinary Time

Lessons

RCL	Roman Catholic
Micah 6:1-8	Zeph 2:3, 3:12-13
Ps 15	Ps 146:6-10
1 Cor 1:18-31	1 Cor 1:26-31
Mt 5:1-12	Mt 5:1-12

Speaker's Introduction for the Lessons
Lesson 1
Micah 6:1-8 (RCL)

This dialogue between God and the prophet Micah, dating from the eighth century BCE, takes the form of a legal argument, culminating in a single-verse summary of God's expectation for ethical behavior.

Zephaniah 2:3, 3:12-13 (RC)

The seventh-century BCE prophet Zephaniah speaks to a time – the Day of the Lord – that should lead to a renewed search for righteous behavior among those who remain after God's punishing wrath against the nation.

Lesson 2
Psalm 15 (RCL)

The psalmist addresses ritualized expectations of those who want to enter the temple to worship God.

Psalm 146:6-10 (RC)

As the Psalter moves toward its close, the psalmist praises the all-powerful Lord God as Creator and Redeemer, whose reign is forever.

Lesson 3
1 Corinthians 1:18-31 (RCL); 1:26-31 (RC)

Paul addresses the significant divisions within the Corinthian church by contrasting the foolishness of the Cross as perceived by the world with the wisdom and power of God.

231

Gospel
Matthew 5:1-12 (RCL/RC)

Matthew begins the first of five major discourses in his Gospel with the Sermon on the Mount, placing Jesus beside the Sea of Galilee as he teaches about characteristics of Christian community life.

Theme
Discipleship as blessed poverty.

Thought for the Day
Absolute poverty is thine when thou canst not remember whether anybody has ever owed thee or been indebted to thee for anything.

> – Tauler, *Sermons,* quoted in Charles Williams (editor), *The New Christian Year* (London: Oxford University Press, 1941), p. 170

Sermon Summary
The Beatitudes, far from urging passive acquiescence to the status quo, focus on the call for justice for those on society's margins and the radical understanding that true riches consist in knowing, loving, and following the Lord Jesus Christ.

Call to Worship
One: Praise the Lord, O my soul!

All: Praise the Lord, the God of Jacob, who is our help and our hope.

One: The Lord our God has made heaven and earth, the cosmos round about us.

All: The Lord our God keeps faith forever, giving justice for the oppressed and food for the hungry.

One: Let us worship the Lord, who reigns forever,

All: And tell God's name to all generations.

> – Adapted from Psalm 146:6-10

Pastoral Prayer
You have shown us, O God, what is good, what is blessed: the poor, those who mourn, the meek, those who seek righteousness, the merciful, the pure in heart, the peace-makers, the persecuted. You require of us that we

do justice, love kindness, and walk humbly with you. For this legacy of right action based in faith, we offer you our thanks and praise. Help us, we pray, to remember that your blessings come to us now and are but part of your self-giving love, your abundant Mercy who is your Son, Jesus Christ our Lord. Amen.

Prayer of Confession

You have shown us, O God, what is good, what is blessed: yet we behave as if we have never seen either goodness or blessedness. The poor, those who mourn, the weak, the merciful, we read the list, then promptly forget the imperative to make all things new in you. Forgive us for our blindness, we pray. Forgive us for failing to see the glaring needs of those who surround us. Forgive us for our lack of kindness and humility. Help us to be better people, we ask under the Mercy of your Son, Jesus Christ our Lord. Amen.

Prayer of Dedication of Gifts and Self

God our Father, we are here. Jesus, Savior, we are here. Spirit, Comforter, we are here. We are here, and gifts we bring. Bless us, Father; bless us, Savior; bless us, Spirit; bless these our gifts. Use us, Father; use us, Savior; use us, Spirit, as we offer ourselves and our treasure to the honor and glory of your name. Amen.

Hymn of the Day
Blest Are They

This musical setting of The Beatitudes was composed by David Haas, one of America's most prolific and well-known singer/songwriters. It is one of the many wonderful pieces to come from the Roman Catholic music revival of the 1970s and 1980s. The traditional style of presentation is the use of a soloist on the stanzas and the whole congregation on the refrains. This method enhances the difference between the recitation of the Beatitudes and the response to that recitation. Allow the sweeping rhythm to propel the song forward. The preferred instrument for accompaniment is guitar with or without piano. Light hand percussion will enhance the singing.

Children's Time: If You're Happy…

What does it mean to be happy? What are some things that make you feel happy? *(Accept all answers.)* Sometimes we are happy when things go our way; at other times, when we hear good news; at other times, when something that was not going well changes and gets better. There are lots and lots of reasons to feel happy.

There's a very famous passage of the Bible where Jesus told some people things that would make them happy.

The passage is called "The Beatitudes" and often they are translated with Jesus saying "Blessed are . . . " But sometimes they are translated "Happy are . . . " because they talk about things that make us feel content and happy.

What's strange, though, is they are not necessarily the things we might think of.

"The ones who are poor in spirit are happy," Jesus says. He went on to say that those who were meek and lots of others are happy, too.

Some people thought these were a little strange, but I think Jesus was on to something. He wasn't saying "these kinds of people are laughing and smiling all the time" but he knew that, when we are humble, when we want righteousness and the things God wants, and when we keep life kind of simple, we have a happiness inside from knowing we are trying to walk in God's way.

Prayer: God of blessing and joy, we are glad when we know we are close to you. Help us to feel that way often. Amen.

The Sermon: Discipleship: Blessed Poverty
Scripture: Matthew 5:1-12

(For sermon materials on 1 Corinthians 1:18-31, see the September/October 2010 issue of *The Clergy Journal*; for sermon materials on Matthew 5:1-12, see the May/June 2010 planning issue of *The Clergy Journal*.)

> *Then [Jesus] began to speak, and taught them, saying:*
> *"Blessed are the poor in spirit, for theirs is the kingdom of heaven"*
> (Matthew 5:3).

In today's familiar Gospel text from the Sermon on the Mount, we hear again the Beatitude, *"Blessed are the poor . . . "* What the Bible says about poverty is often a source of controversy. This passage, and another found in Matthew 26:11, *"For you will always have the poor with you,"* are recalled and remembered.

One long-ago community Thanksgiving Eve service in which I participated, and of which I have vivid memories, featured the local Catholic priest preaching on the text about having the poor with us always. He admonished the assembled congregation, "Let us be thankful for our poor." I remember that his sermon made me very uncomfortable. Like a stomach full of undigested chili, this text comes back in our throats, and we taste it in our mouths again and again.

In biblical tradition, the poor and those outside, on the margins of society, receive God's special care. Nowhere does God tell God's people to let someone else watch out for the marginalized. Neither does God tell the poor to be patient, to endure, to be confident. Nowhere does God say, "Forget about your empty stomach at the end of the month. Forget about your lack of health insurance. Forget about your hungry kids and your homelessness. Are your unemployment benefits running out? Go get a job. In heaven, you'll get all you need, and more."

No. God's justice is entirely different, and the scriptures are unequivocal: God is with the poor. God is against those who keep the poor in poverty. God is against oppressors and in favor of the oppressed. God calls for justice for the poor *right here, right now.* And perhaps most significantly, God calls on us to offer that justice.

The Gospel narrative mirrors this call to justice and righteousness, in the person and work of Jesus: Jesus, who could have been born in a palace, is born in a stable. Jesus, who could have been birthed by a queen, is birthed by an unknown child-woman. Jesus, who could have hung out with the high and mighty, prefers the company of the downtrodden and the outcast. Jesus, who possesses all wisdom and power, allows himself to be emptied of wisdom and power and dies on the cross.

In Jesus, wealth and poverty, power and suffering clash – or maybe cross each other. I am convinced that the same themes clash or cross in us as well: Few of us comfortable middle-class folks need to go back very far into our own lives, or the lives of our parents and grandparents, to know what poverty really is.

We are accustomed to hearing the Beatitudes expressed passively: *"Blessed are those who mourn, for they shall be comforted. Blessed are the merciful, for they shall obtain mercy. Blessed are the peacemakers, for they shall be called children of God."* "Blessed" is the translation of a Greek word, that is itself a translation from Jesus' own language of Aramaic. The original Aramaic word is not passive at all. Instead, it means to set oneself on the right way for the right goal; to turn around, repent; to become straight or righteous.

When I understand Jesus' words in their Aramaic context, I read the Beatitudes in a new light. I can hear Jesus saying, "Get up, do something. Get your hands dirty to help build a human society for human beings. Imitate the extravagant grace of God in your relationships with all people." Christian faith is not passive, but active; it is energetic, alive, going beyond despair. Christian faith calls us out of ourselves – and no one promises it will be easy.

Blessed are the poor in spirit, for theirs is the kingdom of heaven.

The area of southwestern New Hampshire that is our adopted home is, in many ways, a throwback to an earlier time. As it has been for centuries, much of the land area remains forest-covered. Small and medium-sized towns punctuate the state highways and backroads. A by-product of the settlement patterns is that people tend to know more about one another than may at times be comfortable. Folks speak their minds and value the independence that the state's motto, "Live free or die," represents.

We are "not from 'round here"; in local parlance, we are and always will be "flat-landers." We have learned local history and lore primarily by listening and asking judicious (and never invasive) questions. As we have become part of the community, living here full-time and working within a congregation, we have gradually been admitted into family circles through rites of passage and times of crisis. We have heard some amazing stories and have come to know and to love some very remarkable people.

Contemporary hard times have elicited the telling of stories about other times when, "Things were lots worse 'round here than they are now." The Great Depression is part of most families' oral histories. A phrase that often comes up in relating those experiences is, "We never knew we were poor."

We have heard stories of kids sleeping three and four to a bed during the winter to keep warm, because there wasn't enough firewood to burn in the stove through the night, then waking up to find ice on the inside of the window panes. Truck gardening, home canning, small game and deer hunting, keeping chickens, cows, and pigs, and baking from scratch helped lots of families get by. Worn-out clothes were saved to make quilt squares. Neighbors kept track of neighbors. "Use it up, wear it out, make it do, or do without" was an adage to live by.

The church was the extension of families and neighbors. Everybody worked; everybody helped. When hard cash was needed to meet expenses or to pay for missions, creative fund-raising included public dinners, bake sales, auctions, and bazaars. "We tried to do what Jesus would want us to do. Nobody ever went hungry, and we never knew we were 'doing without,'" was the way one of our now-departed saints described the way things worked. Folks just did what needed to be done, and in that approach to ministry, everyone was valued, everyone was cared for, and no one knew they were poor. Not a bad way to be.

Blessed are the poor in spirit, for theirs is the kingdom of heaven.

Whether we speak of the rich or the poor, Jesus calls all of us to open ourselves, to empty ourselves, to free ourselves from whatever possessions or attitudes or identities may encumber us, in order that we might be open and empty for God. How happy are those who give up their trust in themselves and learn to trust God! If we allow ourselves to be remade by God, our attitudes, which often value distinctions between rich and poor, "haves" and "have-nots," might soften.

We can, indeed, become agents of God's love and justice, if only we will get up, go ahead, move beyond ourselves, and rejoice in the Savior who makes all of this possible.

This is our faith, under the Mercy.

– Nancy E. Topolewski

Hymns
Opening Hymn
Lift High the Cross
O Sing a Song of Bethlehem
Sermon Hymn
What Does the Lord Require for Praise and Offering?
Rise, Shine, You People
Closing Hymn
When I Survey the Wondrous Cross
Lord, I Want to Be a Christian

February 6, 2011

5th Sunday after Epiphany
RC/Pres: 5th Sunday in Ordinary Time

Lessons

RCL	Roman Catholic
Isa 58:1-9a (9b-12)	Isa 58:7-10
Ps 112:1-9 (10)	Ps 112:4-9
1 Cor 2:1-12 (13-16)	1 Cor 2:1-5
Mt 5:13-20	Mt 5:13-16

Speaker's Introduction for the Lessons

Lesson 1
Isaiah 58:1-9a (9b-12) (RCL); 58:7-10 (RC)

Speaking through the prophet, the Lord asserts that specific kinds of religious behavior must be practiced if God is to intervene in history on behalf of God's people.

Lesson 2
Psalm 112:1-9 (10) (RCL); 112:4-9 (RC)

The psalmist sets forth some pointed understandings of the ways in which God will bless the righteous in response to their just and generous actions.

Lesson 3
1 Corinthians 2:1-12 (13-16) (RCL); 2:1-5 (RC)

Enlarging upon his paradoxical identification of God's wise foolishness, Paul conflates his message to a radical summation: the crucified Christ, present through the power of the Spirit.

Gospel
Matthew 5:13-20 (RCL); 5:13-16 (RC)

Jesus uses specific images to impress upon the audience gathered for the Sermon on the Mount the part that each person can play in spreading the gospel into the world.

Theme
Discipleship: Building up, shining out.

Thought for the Day
We might think that God wanted simply obedience to a set of rules: whereas He really wants people of a particular sort.

– C.S. Lewis, *Mere Christianity*
(New York: The Macmillan Company, 1952), p. 63

Sermon Summary
Using specific images, Jesus continues to broaden the definition of blessedness worked out at the beginning of the chapter to include the integrity of those striving to follow Jesus' example as light, salt, and a city set upon a hill.

Call to Worship
One: Let us praise the Lord!
All: We know that following God's commandments leads to happiness.
One: Let us praise the Lord!
All: We know that the generation of the upright will be blessed.
One: Let us praise the Lord yet again!
All: The righteous, the faithful, shall never be moved!

– Adapted from Psalm 112:1-10

Pastoral Prayer
We give you thanks, gracious Lord, for sharing your Son with us. We thank you for his life and teaching, seeking to draw us closer to you. We thank you for his death, for all the blessings in this world that came about because of his willfully pursuing crucifixion. We thank you for faithful witnesses down the space of years who like Paul have been determined to know nothing among us "except Jesus Christ, and him crucified." Grant us grace, we pray, to follow in the example of his life, building up those who are downtrodden and in need of your healing presence. We stand, now and ever, under the Mercy who is your gift to us, even Jesus Christ our Lord. Amen.

Prayer of Confession

We come to you again, God of all Mercy, to confess the many sins that taint our lives and cause our souls to shrink in fear. We confess that we confuse outward religion with the new life you call us to in Jesus Christ. We confess that we neglect the needs of those around us, focusing instead on trivial and superficial piety. We confess that we would rather hide our efforts to be faithful than to have them scrutinized by others. Forgive us, we pray. Help us, as we continue to grow in discipleship, to grow as well in justice, honesty, and integrity. We pray under the Mercy of your Son, even Jesus Christ our Lord. Amen.

Prayer of Dedication of Gifts and Self

As we offer our gifts, the fruits of our labors, we also offer ourselves to you, O God, as living sacrifices, ready to be your hearts and hands and feet in the world. Bless these our gifts, and us as givers, to your honor and glory, discipleship and praise; through the merits and under the Mercy of Christ our Lord we pray. Amen.

Hymn of the Day
Renew Your Church

This strong text was written by American Kenneth L. Cober for the American Baptist Convention in May 1960. The theme of the convention was "The Renewal of the Church: Imperative to Evangelism." Cober, the son of missionaries, grew up in Puerto Rico and was involved in Christian education and writing many books and articles in that field. The tune ALL IS WELL is an American folk tune in the Sacred Harp tradition ascribed to J.T. White. This hymn is a sung prayer for guidance. It would be very effective as a hymn of dedication, a call to renewal, or a stewardship hymn. Each stanza could stand alone as a sung prayer supporting the specific themes of renewal, word, prayer, and love.

Children's Time: Being Salt

(Preparation: Bring a saltshaker filled with salt.)

Long ago, Jesus was walking with the disciples. "You are like salt," Jesus said.

What do we use salt for? *(Accept all answers; some things are to flavor food, to pickle things, to preserve things, as a leavening agent to help bread rise, and so on.)*

Too much salt can be harmful to us, but we all need some in order to survive. Pretty amazing stuff, this salt.

"You are like salt," Jesus said, "and I want you to flavor the world with God's love."

How might we do that? *(Accept all answers.)*

"But," Jesus said, "if salt loses its flavor, it's no good."

Now that's a curious thing to say because salt *cannot* lose its flavor, and Jesus quite probably knew that. Salt can only lose its flavor if it stops being salt. Salt isn't salt if it stops tasting salty.

We are called to spread God's love around, and to share the good news that Jesus brought to the world. To do that is to be who we are. If we're not going to share God's love, it's as if we've stopped being ourselves, and have become someone or something else. And that's sad. *(Offer the children a grain or two of salt if they'd like.)*

Prayer: God, you call us to spread your love and good news to everyone. Help us to do that, we pray in Jesus' name. Amen.

The Sermon: Discipleship: Building Up, Shining Out
Scripture: Matthew 5:13-20

(For sermon materials on 1 Corinthians 2:1-12 (13-16), see the November/December 2010 issue of *The Clergy Journal*; for sermon materials on Matthew 5:13-20, see the May/June 2010 planning issue of *The Clergy Journal*.)

> *You are the salt of the earth. You are the light of the world.*
> *You are a city set upon a hill.*

For a number of years, I have worked with various committees that are charged with the oversight of persons seeking to become ordained ministers, within both the Presbyterian and United Methodist Churches. I have followed almost 50 candidates through the various evaluative processes, yet I find that even after a number of years, I can recall details that made each candidate's examination unique. One final examination stands out in my memory: that of a man I'll call James.

James had been working in a large suburban parish in New Jersey while he completed his seminary education. Things had not always gone well for him. During his examination, when I asked him about some of his difficulties, James responded by talking about the negative response he had encountered when he preached a sermon about his opposition to the arms race and his commitment to the anti-nuclear weapons movement.

The chairperson of the church's governing board was a retired air force colonel. At a board meeting a week or so after James preached his infamous sermon, this man was ready to take him apart. It turned into quite a confrontation: people *versus* seminary student, seminarian *versus* people.

"What did you say at the meeting?" I asked.

"I told them," he responded, "You praise me and tell me what a good job I'm doing when I go to the hospital and visit the sick. You tell me how compassionate I am with those who suffer from long-term illnesses. But when I rise to speak about a sickness that has the potential to destroy every person, not only in this town, but in the whole world, you tell me it's none of my business. How can I care about one, and not about the other?"

As I listened to him, I found myself wondering, "Could I have been as firm in the statement of my own discipleship?" I heard myself saying to myself, "Here is a person of integrity. Here is a just man."

You are the salt of the earth. You are the light of the world.
You are a city set upon a hill.

We are wont to live with the assumption that the Christian values which we hold up are the type of attributes to which we might someday aspire – over time, but not just yet. We are wont to think that all of what Jesus spoke about is still to come in our lives; it still has to be worked out in the future. We are wont to think that we might one day become gentle, or that we might eventually be peacemakers. To speak in terms of today's Gospel text, we think we should *become* the salt, that we should *make* ourselves the light, that someday we *might* be a city on a hilltop.

But that is not what Jesus says: "*You are the salt. You are the light. You are the city.*" It is not a question of what we should become. It is a matter of what we already *are*. And more importantly still, when Jesus speaks to his disciples in this way, he speaks in the plural. It is not just a matter of who I am; it is a matter of who we are.

Think about it. As individuals, we cannot be a town or city on our own. We can only be a town or a city – or, for that matter, a church – when we are together, working and praying and singing. Goodness, righteousness are not just qualities to which we aspire, a kind of moral state that we may attain, way off in the future. Goodness, righteousness are our response together, right here, right now, to the unmeasured grace of God.

You are the salt of the earth. You are the light of the world.
You are a city set upon a hill.

The image of *a city set upon a hill* brings to mind a very clear picture. A number of years ago on a trip to the Holy Land, our bus was traveling along the western bank of the Jordan River in Israel, on our way to the Dead Sea and Qumran, looking off in the distance at the mountains of western Jordan. These mountains are much higher than anything around them. When I spotted a small village, far across the Jordan rift valley, I realized that there certainly would be no hiding the existence of that settlement; it could be seen for miles. The same is true for the city of Jerusalem, as it sits some 3000 feet above sea level, a commanding presence for the entire countryside. That is why, regardless of where one comes from, one always "goes up to Jerusalem."

The integrity we are called to show as disciples of Jesus Christ is rather like that little town across the Jordan, rather like Jerusalem itself: it can be seen from a long way off. It stands up and stands out, if need be. It makes no apology for itself.

Integrity: soundness of moral principle; the character of uncorrupted virtue, uprightness, honesty, sincerity.

Going beyond the simple image, the integrity of faith is founded upon consistency, the ability to link together and to treat as a piece those challenges which confront us. The integrity of the community of faith is founded upon our constant, caring response to the cries of the world around us. The integrity of the community of faith is in doing justice, and loving kindness, and walking humbly with God. The integrity of the community of faith lies in its wholehearted, engaged striving to follow the example of our Lord Jesus Christ.

Jesus summarizes the integrity of the community of faith in three images: *salt of the earth, light of the world, city set upon a hill.*

I have saved the reading of the Old Testament lesson until now, as a summary of discipleship. The prophet Isaiah writes words that were undoubtedly familiar to Jesus, and clearly affected his own understanding of the integrity of faith. When you hear the word "you," think of all of us, together:

"Is it not to share your bread with the hungry, and bring the homeless poor into your house; when you see the naked, to cover them, and not to hide yourself from your own kin? . . . If you remove the yoke from among you, the pointing of the finger, the speaking of evil, if you offer food to the hungry and satisfy the needs of the afflicted, then your light shall rise in the darkness and your gloom be like the noonday" (Isaiah 68:7, 9b-10).

I have wondered, on occasion, about what might have happened to James, whose outspoken opposition to the arms race so angered some of the people in his student parish. I hope that over the years he has been able to harness the steely resolve of his convictions in ways that are not only confrontational, but constructive. I hope that the people in the parishes he has served in these years have realized that his passion, his integrity, are gifts to be affirmed, to be instructed by. I hope that my own life and ministry have grown in some small ways in passion and integrity, because for a few brief moments years ago, I listened to him talk of discipleship as building up, and shining out.

This is our faith, under the Mercy.

– Nancy E. Topolewski

Hymns
Opening Hymn
Ask Ye What Great Thing I Know
Rise, Shine, You People
Sermon Hymn
Christ Is the World's Light
This Little Light of Mine
Closing Hymn
Forth in Thy Name, O Lord, I Go
Blest Be the Dear Uniting Love

February 13, 2011

6th Sunday after Epiphany
RC/Pres: 6th Sunday in Ordinary Time

Lessons

RCL	Roman Catholic
Deut 30:15-20 or Sir 15:15-20	Sir 15:15-20
Ps 119:1-8	Ps 119:1-2, 4-5, 17-18, 33-34
1 Cor 3:1-9	1 Cor 2:6-10
Mt 5:21-37	Mt 5:17-37 or 5:20-22, 27-28, 33-34, 37

Speaker's Introduction for the Lessons
Lesson 1
Deuteronomy 30:15-20 (RCL)

Attributing his words to Moses, who will not enter the promised land
with the people of Israel, the compiler of Deuteronomy reminds them
that their choices have life-and-death consequences, with respect to
their relationship with God.

Sirach 15:15-20 (RC)

The Wisdom writer Ben Sira, writing in Jerusalem sometime before
180 BCE, speaks directly to the matter of human choice in sinful
behavior, which comes as a result of how God creates human beings.

Lesson 2
Psalm 119:1-8 (RCL); 119:1-2, 4-5, 17-18, 33-34 (RC)

In this, the longest of all psalms, the psalmist meditates on the law of
God as the pathway to right living, and as such the law is not to be
set aside, ignored, or forgotten.

Lesson 3
1 Corinthians 3:1-9 (RCL)

In response to some implied spiritual knowledge on the part of the
Corinthians, Paul tells them that their "special knowledge" comes via
a human, flawed teacher named Apollos, not from God.

1 Corinthians 2:6-10 (RC)
Laying the groundwork for his position on spiritual teaching, Paul reminds the Corinthians that they have not yet indicated sufficient maturity to receive the eternal wisdom of God.

Gospel
Matthew 5:21-37 (RCL); 5:17-37, or 5:20-22, 27-28, 33-34, 37 (RC)
Jesus continues setting out characteristics needed among those seeking to be his disciples. Particularly for the Jewish community, Jesus asserts that the requirements of the law should lead to greater valuing of individual lives.

Theme
Discipleship: Valuing all persons.

Thought for the Day
There is no question of what we can make [of Christ], it is entirely a question of what he intends to make of us.
– C.S. Lewis, *God in the Dock* (London: William Collins/Fount, 1980), pp. 83-84

Sermon Summary
Human beings are not objects to be exploited or turned into commodities. Human beings are children of God, known, valued, beloved, as Jesus points out in this singular passage from the Sermon on the Mount.

Call to Worship
One: God has placed before us righteous commandments.
All: It is up to us to follow them.
One: God has given us options for life or death.
All: It is up to us to choose them.
One: God is great, all-seeing, wise, and powerful.
All: It is up to us to seek, to choose, and to worship.
– Adapted from Sirach 15:15-20

Pastoral Prayer

Your perfection, O God, is shown not only in the tangible things you create. Your perfection has also created laws for your human children, giving structure and form to order our lives. When we are honest, we recognize our need for structure, form, and order – and use that framework to grow in faith. As we grow in faith, we recognize the need to know more and more of you, as we move ever onward toward your love. Our hope is grounded in you and in the life you offer us in your Son, who is your abundant Mercy; for this, your greatest gift, we offer you our thanks and praise. Amen.

Prayer of Confession

In spite of the clear laws you have provided for us, O God, we do our best to avoid following them. Where you would have us be attentive to the needs of our brothers and sisters, we would much rather look out for ourselves, and in the process treat others as if they are things, commodities, somehow less-than-valued. Forgive us for our arrogance, we pray. Restore in us a sense of our dependence upon you, and of the magnitude of your gift of Mercy: Mercy who is your Son, who died that we might live, even Jesus Christ our Lord. Amen.

Prayer of Dedication of Gifts and Self

In offering you these gifts, gracious God, we are offering the best of ourselves. We ask you to add your blessing to these gifts, and to the work these gifts will do, as we seek to be your ever-more-faithful disciples, following the example of your Son, Jesus Christ our Lord. Amen.

Hymn of the Day
Si Fui Motivo de Dolor, Oh Dios/If I Have Been a Source of Pain, O God

This text has an interesting background. The original text by C.M. Battersby, "If I Have Wounded Any Soul Today," was translated into Spanish by Sara M. de Hall and set to a new tune, CAMACUA, by Pablo Sosa. The Spanish text was then translated back into English by Janet W. May in 1962. The re-translation takes on a very new and different understanding due to this process. Pablo Sosa is an international composer and facilitator of church music, particularly global music of developing countries. He is in constant demand as a lecturer, workshop leader, and worship facilitator. This song should be sung with a sense of freedom, allowing the text to dictate the flow of each musical phrase. It makes a fine sung response to the reading of the Gospel of the day or any meditation or homily presented on this text.

Children's Time: Forgiving and Loving

The Bible tells us that often when Jesus looked at how people were living he was sad or upset. It seems that people knew how God wanted them to live, but they didn't do it. What does that feel like to you when you want someone to do something, and they don't? It's frustrating, isn't it?

One day Jesus got kind of angry about this. "Listen," he said, "remember how you're not supposed to kill? Well, that's one thing. But when you get angry and pray 'I hope so-and-so falls off a cliff' or some other mean and hurtful thing, it's really just as bad."

That doesn't mean we need to feel guilty when we have thoughts about someone, but it *is* a good reminder that Jesus wants us to think better of others. Even when someone is doing something hurtful, or that we don't like, or we wish they wouldn't do, it's not good to wish they were dead. No, the best thing in fact we can do is to pray for them. And to love them.

In fact, Jesus even said that if we're on our way to church and we remember that we have a grudge with someone, we should stop what we're doing and go and make things right. That's how important it is.

Prayer: God of grace, sometimes it is hard to love others. But you call us to do that. Please help us to be loving and forgiving. Amen.

The Sermon: Discipleship: Lessons from the Coal Mines
Scripture: Matthew 5:21-37

(For sermon materials on 1 Corinthians 3:1-9, see the November/December 2010 issue of *The Clergy Journal*; for sermon materials on Matthew 5:21-37, see the May/June 2010 planning issue of *The Clergy Journal*.)

The Wyoming Valley of northeastern Pennsylvania, an area blessed with the rich deposits of 75 percent of the world's anthracite (hard) coal, is my home. I was born there in 1953, near the end of the Anthracite Era, and lived there into my early thirties. The Valley's history is part of my intellectual and social genealogy. Let me share with you a story that is crucial to forging my understanding of what is right and just.

Beginning in the early 19th century, after a method of burning anthracite in open grates was perfected, the Wyoming Valley underwent tremendous growth, as coal began to fuel America's unparalleled industrial expansion. Waves of immigrants came to the valley looking for opportunities for a better life that work in the mines seemed to promise. First came the English, Welsh, and Irish, followed by Italians, Poles, and Eastern Europeans. Very clear social stratification resulted, based on country of origin and when people arrived. Small communities of different ethnic groups grew up around and at the fringes of the city of Wilkes-Barre.

Mining brought great wealth for mine owners, who built large, ornate homes in the city – donating them, interestingly, in the 1930s and '40s to help create Wilkes College (now University). Churches, schools, and other public buildings followed. But the class distinctions between owners and workers seemed to be written in stone (or, more accurately, in coal). The people who actually went into the mines to wrest the coal from the earth did not get rich. They faced the possibility of death or serious injury each time they rode the elevators from the surface to the slopes. As numerous underground disasters in the valley would show, the safety of mines was not a management priority – not, that is, until dozens of immigrant miners were killed.

Lucrative as it was, anthracite mining went into steady decline after World War II, as petroleum replaced coal as the fuel of choice. It was only a matter of time before the industry, like so many local mine-shafts, collapsed completely.

For many years, mine owners had not only been mining coal; they had been "mining the miners." Quotas were established for each shift in each mine, based on numbers of hopper cars expected to be filled with coal. As the easily accessible coal was extracted from ever-widening shafts, management gradually increased the size of the hoppers. Miners were wont to chip away at the "easy" coal, which should have been left as supports for the shaft ceilings – a practice known as "robbing the pillars." On January 22, 1959, someone doing just that chipped right through the roof of the River Slope of the Knox Mine in Port Griffith, Pennsylvania, just north of Wilkes-Barre, into the Susquehanna River. The river, choked with ice, found the weak spot, flooding the Knox workings and killing 12 men.

I have vivid childhood memories of the community's rage spilling over – rage that had accumulated for decades among miners against the mine owners. Amid the acrimony and accusations and legal proceedings, one thing was made abundantly clear. Miners had been exploited, dehumanized, turned into commodities, not treated as human beings of dignity, as if they were valued only for the coal they extracted from the earth.

How often do we turn human beings into things, instead of treating them as children of God?

Jesus speaks to the devaluation of human life in today's Gospel passage from Matthew. In a variety of ways, Jesus is saying to his hearers, "Don't turn your brothers and sisters into *things*." As is so often the case with his gospel teaching, Jesus addresses practical situations in human relations. For example, in the context of Jewish law, everyone who is angry with his brother will be liable to judgment. Whoever insults his brother shall be liable to the council. So, Jesus says, if you're out of sorts with your brother, don't just go away angry or blow him off. Before you make an offering at the altar, go and set things straight between you. Then come back and make the offering.

When it comes to such matters as adultery, divorce, and swearing falsely, areas of common life directly treated in Jewish law, Jesus goes behind and beyond the law to point out God's intentions in giving the law: that people might live in ordered relationship with God and with one another.

Human beings are of great value to Jesus. Elsewhere, he points out that every hair on our heads is numbered, and God sees every sparrow that falls from the sky. God knows all about us. God cares about us. God values us as the unique creations we are. That being so, how can we *not* treat others with the same respect and dignity?

Yet the question still begs an answer. How often do we turn others – or ourselves – into things, instead of remembering that we are all children of God?

In the months following the Knox Mine disaster, official inquiries were undertaken by the Commonwealth of Pennsylvania, the Bureau of Mines, and the Federal Bureau of Investigation. While aimed at different parts of the power structure of the anthracite industry, all of the investigations had in common the desire to see justice done for those who died in the Knox Mine and their families. Illegal mining practices were exposed. Corrupt labor officials were indicted for taking bribes and ignoring mine safety regulations. In the long and complex history of anthracite mining in northeastern Pennsylvania, no official inquiries had ever focused as clearly upon conditions affecting miners. That these conditions were not exposed until the industry effectively collapsed remains, 52 years later, a scandal of community life. *But they were ultimately exposed.*

How often do we turn others, or even ourselves, into things, instead of remembering we are all children of God?

The lessons that I take from the Knox Mine disaster, as it intersects with Jesus' teaching, are these: Many people in our world will spend their days suffering in ways most of us will never know. These people are all around us, hidden in plain sight. When we treat them as abstractions, as, for example, "the poor" or "the homeless," we turn them into things – and thereby abrogate our responsibility toward them. Out of sight, out of mind, like the Knox miners.

While it is not possible for us as individuals to be of help to the many people who are fighting for survival in our society, it is possible to change our attitudes and to remember that no person is a thing. You are not a thing. I am not a thing. No one is a thing.

When we are faced with a life-and-death event, like a mining disaster; when we try to relate responsibly to those around us; when we seek to perceive and understand ourselves and our place in God's good world, are we prepared to join Jesus and say, "Don't make each other into a thing?" Are we? Are we really?

This is our faith, under the Mercy.

– Nancy E. Topolewski

Hymns
Opening Hymn
Rejoice, Ye Pure in Heart
A Mighty Fortress Is Our God
Sermon Hymn
Dear Jesus, in Whose Life I See
Let Us Plead for Faith Alone
Closing Hymn
Lord, Dismiss Us with Your Blessing
I Want a Principle Within

February 20, 2011

7th Sunday after Epiphany
RC/Pres: 7th Sunday in Ordinary Time

Lessons

RCL	Roman Catholic
Lev 19:1-2, 9-18	Lev 19:1-2, 17-18
Ps 119:33-40	Ps 103:1-4, 8, 10, 12-13
1 Cor 3:10-11, 16-23	1 Cor 3:16-23
Mt 5:38-48	Mt 5:38-48

Speaker's Introduction for the Lessons
Lesson 1
Leviticus 19:1-2, 9-18 (RCL); 19:1-2, 17-18 (RC)

This section of Leviticus, one of the "Five Books of Moses," consists of what is often called "The Holiness Code." Listen for portions of what we know as the 10 Commandments.

Lesson 2
Psalm 119:33-40 (RCL)

The longest of the 150 psalms, Psalm 119 is written in praise of God's gift of the law. Strange to our ears is the line "I delight in it – God's law" (v. 35).

Psalm 103:1-4, 8, 10, 12-13 (RC)

A psalm of absolution, listen for words of pure grace. "The Lord is merciful, gracious, slow to anger, and abounding in steadfast love" (v. 8).

Lesson 3
1 Corinthians 3:10-11, 16-23 (RCL); 3:16-23 (RC)

In his first letter to the church in Corinth, Paul expresses concern for the congregation's splintering factions. Listen for the three groups that have emerged.

Gospel
Matthew 5:38-48 (RCL/RC)

In this section from Jesus' Sermon on the Mount we hear the power of God's law intensified. Can any of us "turn the cheek, walk the second mile, love our enemies, be perfect"?

Theme

God's desire for the church is to be united on the foundation of Jesus Christ.

Thought for the Day

Unity in the church is a given, a gift from God. Trust the gift, and allow Christ to hold us together.

Sermon Summary

Unity in the church is a gift. Our divisions are almost always petty and our image of unity is too restrictive and implies coercion. The foundation of Jesus Christ is substantial enough to allow for diversity.

Call to Worship

One: Teach me, O Lord, the way of your statutes,
All: And I will observe it to the end.
One: Give me understanding, that I may keep your law,
All: And observe it with my whole heart.
One: Lead me in the path of your commandments,
All: For I delight in it.
One: Turn away the disgrace that I dread,
All: For your ordinances are good.
One: See, I have longed for your precepts;
All: In your righteousness give me life.
One: God's statutes, law, commandments, ordinances, and precepts
 are good.
All: Can we also find delight therein?

– Based on Psalm 119:33-40

Pastoral Prayer

Gracious and merciful God, abundant in steadfast love, we praise you for your goodness and compassion toward all of creation. We give you thanks today for expecting us to live responsibly and lovingly, for guiding us in your ways, for mercy when we have strayed, for a love that never fails. Grant healing to the many who are injured and ill, reconciliation for those who are separated, and peace to the nations at war. Grant us a desire to live peaceably with all who share the gift of this earth as our home, and give us a respect for the foundational law of love, which you revealed through your Son and our Savior, Jesus Christ. Amen.

Prayer of Confession

Our sins are too close to us, O God. Our pride blinds us to the wrongs we have done. Centered on ourselves, our world is too small. We run even from your grace fearing you know us too well. We have strayed from the path you would have us follow, and we don't dare ask for help. Hear our prayer, O God. Grant us the promise that you will indeed remove our transgressions from us as far as the east is from the west. You alone can free us from ourselves. In Jesus' name. Amen.

– Based on Psalm 103:12

Prayer of Dedication of Gifts and Self

Generous God, for the gifts of faith and family, food and shelter, our church and our mission, we give you thanks. We offer to you our money and our intentions this day, trusting that you can use our gifts to reveal your redemptive love. Multiply our gifts, increase our resolve, and enhance our desire to live as your servants in the world so that your love may be known, your grace revealed, and hope restored to the many in need. Renew our unity centered on the foundation of Jesus Christ, in whose name we pray. Amen.

Hymn of the Day
Christ Is Made the Sure Foundation

This text has its origins in an early medieval Latin hymn "*Urbs beata Hierusalem,*" which was used for the dedication of a church. The term "Holy Zion" refers to the church transcendent, built of living stones of which Christ is the cornerstone. It was first published in English in John Mason Neale's *Medieval Hymns* (1851). The tune, Westminster Abbey, comes from a verse anthem "O God, Thou Art My God" by Henry Purcell. It was adapted into a hymn tune by Ernest Hawkins. Sing this hymn with boldness and great conviction. The addition of brass and percussion will make it a very festive processional or recessional. Descants, found in various hymnals, will also add great joy and excitement to its presentation.

Children's Time: Where God Is

Where does God live? Where can we find God? *(Accept all answers.)* Talk about places where God might be present, and how. For example, God is present here in our worship service, as we worship and glorify God.

God is present in our city streets, amongst the people and the things going on. God is present in our farmlands, in the beauty of the earth and the good food we take from the land. God is present in beautiful mountains and oceans and lakes and rivers – whenever we look at something and go "wow" God is there. God is inside each one of us, too.

The Bible says we are God's temple.

In biblical times, people didn't worship in a church like we do, but they worshipped at a special place in Jerusalem called the temple. It was a huge and wonderful building, and they believed it was where God lived. Every year, no matter where people lived, they would go to Jerusalem so they could spend some time in God's "house."

St. Paul said, "Remember, you are God's temple." In other words, we are a place where God lives – inside our hearts, inside our minds, inside our bodies. Wherever we go, God goes with us. Whenever we are hurting, God is with us. Whenever we are happy, God is with us. Whenever and wherever we are . . . God is with us.

Prayer: Thank you, wonderful God, that you are with us always. It is a joy to be your temple. Amen.

The Sermon: Unity
Scripture: 1 Corinthians 3:10-11, 16-23

(For sermon materials on Matthew 5:38-48, see the November/December 2010 issue of *The Clergy Journal*; for sermon materials on 1 Corinthians 3:10-11, 16-23, see the May/June 2010 planning issue of *The Clergy Journal*.)

Imagine that you had the opportunity to go back in time to meet with the Apostle Paul, the author of today's second reading from a letter he wrote to a congregation in the Greek city of Corinth. Paul, the writer of nearly half of the New Testament, the wise interpreter of Jesus to the non-Jewish world, and the great example of Christian missionary strategy, knew a few things about churches. Imagine you could ask him on behalf of our church, "Paul, what advice do you have for us? What will make our congregation stronger and more effective in our witness to the world around us?"

I think I know what he would say. He introduced his letter a few chapters earlier with these words: "Now I appeal to you, brothers and sisters, by the name of our Lord Jesus Christ, that all of you should be in agreement and that there should be no divisions among you, but that you should be united in the same mind and the same purpose" (1 Cor 1:10). One word, people. Unity. Paul tells the church at Corinth to quit pulling apart from one another and to move toward each other in a spirit of unity. Do Paul's words of counsel speak to us today? What kind of unity do we need?

Paul knew the people at Corinth. He helped begin their congregation, and even though he no longer lived there, he stayed in touch with the people, and he was hearing sounds of division from their communications. The small group of believers in Corinth was fortunate to have been influenced by three significant leaders – Paul, Apollos, and Peter (here called Cephas). Paul helped them begin, and Apollos was a frequent visitor; Peter might never have been there, but the people knew of him and his teachings.

Paul was hearing from Chloe, a friend in the congregation, that some were saying, "I belong to Paul"; others said, "I belong to Apollos"; and still others were boasting, "I belong to Cephas." What did they mean?

Individuals or small groups in the church were asserting their uniqueness by naming their favorite teacher. That doesn't sound so bad if you are simply mentioning the name of someone who has helped encourage your faith, but anyone who pulls away from the others to say, "I belong solely to my mentor" is being divisive. And such a divisive spirit encourages others to claim their set apart-ness, and a community bears witness to a fracture in their unity.

The word *unity* might not be an altogether pleasing word in today's culture where we are beginning to appreciate diversity. Unity sounds like the word *uniformity*, but there are worlds of difference between the two. Uniformity implies a sameness that will not permit diversity. Uniformity implies a coercive force necessary to create the appearance of unity. But let us not disparage unity, as it is the spirit of harmony and accord that allows a group to experience belonging even with awareness of their many differences.

Does the call for unity in a congregation imply there is no possibility for the presence of varying opinions? Does unity imply the absence of conflict? If that were true, why would anyone become part of this church? Would we dare say we do not allow for differences in belief and practice? No. Perhaps we need to let go of earlier images of what unity looks like. I think of the reports from people who visit totalitarian countries, nations that do not allow outsiders to see the inside. Visitors cannot explore a totalitarian nation without a proper "minder" who will allow them to see only what is acceptable. I think of church disputes settled in a dogmatic fashion by autocratic leaders telling people what they must believe. Such heavy-handedness creates separation in order to promote the appearance of unity, and such unity is seldom gracious and long-lasting.

Paul understood unity in the language of a builder and said that unity is built on a strong foundation, and that foundation, he told the Corinthians, has already been laid. So it is in our congregation. The foundation of the church is the message of Jesus handed down generation to generation, the story of Jesus born, lived, suffered, died, risen, and coming again is the foundation of the church. Each foundation has its denominational peculiarities, but it is the central message of Jesus that is the foundation of every Christian church. And, Paul emphasizes, this foundation is a gift. It "belongs to you" (1 Cor 3:22). We do not create it. We live in it, point to it, and welcome others into it, but it is not ours to create.

Is our image of unity too small? Too restrictive? Is the call toward unity one of pulling away to become the smallest, purest thinking group we can imagine? Perhaps we can consider unity through the language of the arts. When we consider the science of unity, we too easily become prescriptive and limiting, but the language of the arts allows for flow.

The visual artist draws with lines. In the language of separation we speak of lines in the sand that divide us. We threaten with the words, "Don't cross that line." The artist of unity draws circles with ever-widening spheres that bring people together. Someone has commented that whenever we Christians draw lines of separation to indicate who is welcome and who is not, it is only after the lines are drawn that we realize Jesus has been left on the side with the one not welcomed.

A dancer's image of unity appreciates that all of life is in motion, and unity in motion is a dance where we move toward one another and not away from one another.

Unity in music is realized in harmony. Different notes are sung or played but gathered together to complement one another. Chords are struck and harmonies realized. Several differing rhythms can be played at the same time and be in harmony with each other. Beats fill in the empty spaces and rhythms are made whole.

Paul's admonition to our church: know the harmony of unity. Live firmly rooted on the foundation of Jesus Christ and be formed by his redemptive love. Allow for the grace of individuality in practice and belief, but place your feet on Christ's sure foundation. Welcome all of humankind to know the firm footing of Christ's saving work proclaimed in our midst. "All things are yours . . . and you belong to Christ, and Christ belongs to God" (1 Cor 3:23). United in our common belonging! Amen.

– Paul Lundborg

Hymns
Opening Hymn
Welcome to the Love of God
Holy, Holy, Holy
Sermon Hymn
Blessed Be the Tie That Binds
The Church's One Foundation
Closing Hymn
On Our Way Rejoicing
Lord, Dismiss Us with Your Blessing

February 27, 2011

8th Sunday after Epiphany
RC/Pres: 8th Sunday in Ordinary Time

Lessons

RCL	Roman Catholic
Isa 49:8-16a	Isa 49:14-15
Ps 131	Ps 62:2-3, 6-9
1 Cor 4:1-5	1 Cor 4:1-5
Mt 6:24-34	Mt 6:24-34

Speaker's Introduction for the Lessons
Lesson 1
Isaiah 49:8-16a (RCL); 49:14-15 (RC)

For those who feel forsaken, hear these words from the prophet Isaiah that describe God's motherly love: "Can a woman forget her nursing child? I will not forget you" (49:15).

Lesson 2
Psalm 131 (RCL)

Listen to more words of faith expressed in the language of a mother-child relationship: "I have calmed and quieted my soul, like a weaned child with its mother" (v. 2). The Bible offers many images of God.

Psalm 62:2-3, 6-9 (RC)

Here is a psalm declaring confident trust in God, clearly expressed in verse two: "God alone is my rock and my salvation, my fortress; I shall never be shaken."

Lesson 3
1 Corinthians 4:1-5 (RCL/RC)

Paul describes himself with two words, and these words can be helpful in describing the work of all who follow Jesus: servant and steward. Can you accept those titles?

Gospel
Matthew 6:24-34 (RCL/RC)

Are you a worrywart? Listen to Jesus tell us what not to worry about: your life, what you will eat or drink, your body, what you will wear, and tomorrow. Instead, "strive first for the kingdom of God" (6:33a).

Theme

We are not alone as we follow Jesus. We are accountable to a community of disciples.

Thought for the Day

The life of faith is far too difficult for a solitary follower of Jesus. God gives us the gift of a community and asks that we be accountable to one another.

Sermon Summary

Paul describes his work to the Corinthians as that of a servant or steward, words that imply accountability to an owner. In like manner, we are accountable to God and to one another in living as followers of Jesus. This calling to follow Jesus is too important and difficult to accomplish alone.

Call to Worship

One: Do not worry about your life, what you will eat or what you will drink.

All: Calm and quiet your soul, like a weaned child with its mother.

One: Do not worry about your body, what you will wear.

All: Look at the birds of the air; they neither sow nor reap.

One: Can you by worrying add a single hour to your span of life?

All: Consider the lilies of the field; they neither toil nor spin.

One: Do not worry about tomorrow.

All: Calm and quiet your soul, like a weaned child with its mother.

– From Psalm 131 and Matthew 6:24-34

Pastoral Prayer

We praise you, Triune God – Creator, Savior, Spirit – for the gift of your church on earth. We are but one congregation, a small portion of the many, set apart to bear witness to your redemptive love. We thank you for one another, for the way you have brought us together and provided us with gifts for serving you. Hear our prayers today for the special needs not only of our own community but also for the many throughout the world who suffer. (Silence.) Assure us again of your great love, equip us to be your servants and stewards, and soothe our worried hearts with new energy to seek after you and your way in this world. In Christ's name we pray. Amen.

Prayer of Confession

You know us, O God, far better than we know ourselves. You know us as a congregation, a community of believers, and you see the gifts you have provided us that we have failed to use. You see the ways we have hurt one another by our actions and our failure to act. But in your mercy you steadfastly claim us as your children. Yours is the love of a gracious parent continually calling forth our best efforts and steering us in the ways you would have us go. Hold us all in your forgiving embrace this day and renew us for the important work of reflecting your great grace to one another and a waiting world. In Jesus' name. Amen.

Prayer of Dedication of Gifts and Self

We know your desire for us, O God, that we be your faithful servants and stewards, trustworthy in every way. Fill our hearts with gratitude. Help us to lift our eyes from ourselves to see you as the source of the abundant grace we have known. Grant us a generous spirit to give as you have given. Renew our will to use the gifts you have provided to further your mission in our world, and bring us together as a community accountable to you and to one another to share our gifts for service in Jesus' name. Amen.

Hymn of the Day
Siyahamba/We Are Marching in the Light

This energetic song of freedom comes from South Africa. It was first recorded with 14 other songs and published by the Church of Sweden Mission in 1980. In 1984 it appeared in the collection *Freedom Is Coming,* which brought it a worldwide audience. There are numerous translations of the text. For the word *marching* you may substitute walking, singing, dancing, praying, or many other action words. Do not forget the original Zulu words. They are worth learning as they fit the song best. This song should be sung without accompaniment, preferably in harmony. Teach the melody first and then let more experienced singers experiment with the harmonies, which will become obvious the more you sing this great song.

Children's Time: Worrying

How many of you ever worry about things? What are some of the things you worry about? *(Accept all answers.)* It's hard not to worry sometimes.

It seems we worry a lot more as we get older. Do you know adults who worry a lot? Do you know some of the things they worry about? Sometimes as grown ups we worry about things such as: will I continue to have a job? Will I have enough money to pay for food and clothes? Will my children be safe? Will we get sick? Lots of worries like that.

Jesus spoke about worrying one time. He tried to make a bit of a joke of it, to show his friends how silly it really is to worry. "Can any of you add an hour to your life just by worrying?" That's a silly question – of course we can't!

Jesus then invited his friends to look around them. "Look at the flowers," Jesus said. Aren't they beautiful? You know, God made them – all the different colors, the different sizes, the different perfumes. They're some of the most beautiful things on earth. Do you honestly think that God would take care of the flowers, and not take care of you? Of course not!

It's an important lesson for all of us to learn. Worrying about things doesn't really get us anywhere at all. But when we *are* worrying, we can ask God to help us remember that things will be okay. Even when they turn out differently than we might expect or want, still everything – including each one of us – is in God's care.

Prayer: Thank you God, for always caring for us – no matter what. Help us not to worry, but to trust in you. Amen.

The Sermon: Accountable
Scripture: 1 Corinthians 4:1-5

(For sermon materials on Matthew 6:24-34, see the November/December 2010 issue of *The Clergy Journal*; for sermon materials on 1 Corinthians 4:1-5, see the May/June 2010 planning issue of *The Clergy Journal*.)

May I risk oversimplifying? Here is a second consecutive sermon based on a 1 Corinthians text with a one-word message. It's a sermon also based on the premise that the counsel offered by the Apostle Paul to his Christian friends in the congregation at Corinth can apply to us today. It's a sermon based on imagining the question to be, "Paul, what do we need in our church life to be an effective congregation?" Last Sunday's word was *unity*. Today? *Accountability*.

Our congregation, like all others, is made up of people who are not alike. Among us there are different jobs, different ages, different genders, different gifts, different experiences, and mostly – different opinions. About nearly everything. If we need a semblance of unity in order to allow our differences to bring us together, that unity is enhanced by our willingness to be accountable.

Accountable to whom? Obviously, to God. Paul cautions his friends to be slow in pronouncing their judgments upon him and each other. "It is the Lord who judges me," he says (1 Cor 4:4b). The judge is the one who has authority to command our accountability, and that is the prerogative of our Creator.

But Paul adds value to our accountability when he describes the work that he and his assistants have done with the Corinthian church. "Think of us in this way, as servants of Christ and stewards of God's mysteries" (1 Cor 4:1). These titles are neither lofty nor domineering. Some texts read "slave" instead of servant. Certainly slaves had little authority. The word *steward* is said to have its origins in being a "sty-warden." The only context in which I have ever heard the word *sty* used is in describing the farm building set aside for pigs.

Servants and stewards share a lowly place in any community's social status. They are accountable to a higher authority, namely an owner. The servant and steward are put in a position to do what the owner or boss tells them. What is the most important quality in a good steward or a good servant? They must be faithful and trustworthy (1 Cor 4:2). Those who are faithful and trustworthy put themselves in a position of accountability before the owner or boss.

Maybe it doesn't sound too exciting to be a servant or steward. With our inborn love for freedom and independence we long to be our own boss. And describing God as our boss or owner does not do justice to the relationship God offers – a relationship more fully realized with the titles "child of God" (1 Jn 3:1), "beloved" (1 Jn 3:2), "friend" (Jn 15:15).

But along with our call to follow Jesus comes the gift of a community to belong to, and this community will not be able to function without our willingness to not only be accountable to God but also to be accountable to each other.

Is that scary? We work hard to protect our independence, our privacy, even our need to appear that we have our life together and don't need anyone's help. Generally, that works until we meet our first earth-shaking crisis. Often that first crisis is so unmanageable that we are tempted to flee from those who care for us. We are so stunned by our need that we are unwilling to admit it. We are more easily prepared to suffer alone than we are able to ask for a listening ear, prayers, or help with daily needs. We would rather give help than receive it. For some it takes time to realize that our accountability to each other is a mutual thing. We give and we receive.

Prior to WWII, a Lutheran pastor in Germany wrote some powerful words about what it meant to be together in a Christian community. He was worried about the church as he sensed the difficult times to come, and he invited people to come together to work hard to make a vibrant community committed to following Jesus. The same struggle is still present in today's world, where some who acknowledge being very spiritual express disdain for belonging to a community where that Spirit is experienced and named. Others too desperately belong to the community because they are terrified of being alone.

Dietrich Bonhoeffer was that pastor who said, "Let (all) who cannot be alone beware of community . . . and let (all) who (are) not in community beware of being alone" (Dietrich Bonhoeffer, *Life Together*, New York: Harper & Row, Publishers, Incorporated, 1954, p. 77).

Accountability within the Body of Christ is a gift given us when we have heard Jesus' call. It is the gift of not being alone while following Jesus. Consider the near impossibility of being a solitary disciple of our Lord and Savior. If you are only minimally aware of your own imperfections, you know the difficulties of discipleship will weigh you down. Perhaps you have known obstinate personalities and stubborn characters in your congregation, but remember – they have had to put up with you. Jesus says, "For where two or three are gathered in my name, I am there among them" (Mt 18:20). The presence of two or three persons requires unity and accountability – two qualities essential to a relationship.

Accountability means far more than having an opinion about another. Notice how Paul tells his Corinthian friends "it is a very small thing that I should be judged by you" (4:4). As a public person Paul was subject to the judgments and opinions of all who knew his name, but he was gifted with the ability to let their opinions wash away like water from a duck's back. He was eager to engage them, speak to them, listen to them, help them, and seek to understand them. It is the nature of accountability to value relationships within the community, not just to offer opinions.

We are servants, stewards, seeking to be faithful to God and accountable to one another. Thanks be to God! Amen.

– Paul Lundborg

Hymns
Opening Hymn
Seek Ye First the Kingdom of God
Have No Fear, Little Flock
Sermon Hymn
Bind Us Together Lord
Will You Let Me Be Your Servant
Closing Hymn
Go My Children with My Blessing
You Servants of God

March 6, 2011

Last Sunday after Epiphany/Transfiguration
RC: 9th Sunday in Ordinary Time

Lessons

RCL	Roman Catholic
Exodus 24:12-18	Deut 11:18, 26-28
Ps 2 or Ps 99	Ps 31:2-4, 17, 25
2 Peter 1:16-21	Rom 3:21-25, 28
Mt 17:1-9	Mt 7:21-27

Speaker's Introduction for the Lessons

The readings from Deuteronomy 11, Psalm 31, Romans 3, and Matthew 7 are for those observing the Last Sunday after Epiphany. The readings from Exodus 24, Psalm 2, 2 Peter 1, and Matthew 17 are for those observing Transfiguration Sunday.

Lesson 1
Exodus 24:12-18 (RCL)

This passage sets the stage for Transfiguration Sunday by telling the story of an earlier experience of God's revelation of glory on top of a mountain, this first time with Moses.

Deuteronomy 11:18, 26-28 (RC)

Moses concludes and summarizes the story of how God gave him the tablets of the law and admonishes the people to obey these commands. "A blessing if you obey; a curse if you do not obey" (11:27-28).

Lesson 2
Psalm 2 (RCL)

The psalmist's words admonish the kings and rulers of the earth to "Serve the Lord with fear" (2:10-11). Listen for the words that will also be heard in other readings today: "You are my son" (2:7b).

Psalm 31:2-4, 17, 25 (RC)

Listen to these four verses from the psalm that model the life of prayer: three verses of a plea for help, and one verse of God's answer. God counsels, "Be strong" (31:24).

Lesson 3

2 Peter 1:16-21 (RCL)

Peter recalls being an eyewitness to the transfiguration of Jesus on the mountaintop, and this fact is important in giving credibility to his written witness. How can one doubt a witness?

Romans 3:21-25, 28 (RC)

Verses 21-25 establish the context: "all have sinned," and verse 27 is at the heart of the Christian message of salvation: "a person is justified by faith, apart from works . . . of the law" (3:27).

Gospel

Matthew 17:1-9 (RCL)

Matthew's account of Jesus' transfiguration echoes the words heard at Jesus' baptism, the voice of God confirming Jesus' identity as "God's beloved son" (17:5). Jesus was far more than a rabbi and healer.

Matthew 7:21-27 (RC)

These are Jesus' concluding and summarizing words from his Sermon on the Mount, and he tells his hearers what he wants them to do with his words – these two things: "hear them and act on them" (7:24).

Theme

Jesus was transfigured. His friends were transformed. God is changing us.

Thought for the Day

Repeated exposure to the gospel message of Jesus will change us. That can be a scary thought, but it can also be a welcome thought.

Sermon Summary

Jesus is a force for change. Hearing Jesus' message will change us, a change which can begin in a moment and will be brought to fulfillment in the long, slow process of formation. It is good to long for the change God can bring.

Call to Worship

One: Listen! God's power is revealed from the top of a mountain.

All: Tell us the stories!

One: The Lord said to Moses, "Come up to me on the mountain . . . and I will give you the tablets of stone."

All: The 10 Commandments!

One: The psalm writer says, "Worship at God's holy mountain."

All: They did.

One: Peter remembers, "We heard this voice come from heaven while we were with him on the holy mountain."

All: Peter was a witness.

One: Matthew says, "Jesus took with him Peter, James, and John and led them up a high mountain."

All: And they were all changed!

Pastoral Prayer

Gracious God, today we are reminded of the words of one of Jesus' earliest followers, the apostle Peter, who said, "Lord, it is good for us to be here" (Mt 17:4). It is good for us to be here, O God, with you and with one another. You have summoned us here to be taught, renewed, and strengthened for our life of faith. We give you thanks for this congregation and for the power of your grace that we experience in worship. Grant mercy and hope to the many with worries and special needs, comfort and console the lonely and broken-hearted, and grant guidance and power to those in need of a new beginning. Do your work among and within us through Jesus Christ. Amen.

Prayer of Confession

Forgive us, dear God, for the tall walls of self-defense we have built around us. It is far easier to criticize and blame others than to accept responsibility. Give us courage to stand in your presence, accept your knowing look into our hearts, and be examined by your probing grace. (Silence.) We pray confidently with the psalmist: "Create clean hearts within us, renew a right spirit, restore to us the joy of your salvation, and sustain in us a willing spirit" (Ps 51:10-12). And we give you our thanks for hearing our prayers, for standing beside us with abundant and steadfast love, and for blessing us with the gift of your forgiveness. In Jesus' name. Amen.

Prayer of Dedication of Gifts and Self

Great are your works, O God! Even greater is your love for all of creation! We offer our gifts to you this day in grateful thanksgiving for calling us to follow you. Renew our trust in you and our courage to follow. Keep us close to one another that we might help and be helped along the way. Grant us patience to take one step at a time, and create a hospitable spirit among us that we might welcome others along the way. We renew our desire today to walk where you lead us. In Jesus' name. Amen.

Hymn of the Day
We Have Come at Christ's Own Bidding

Based upon the Gospel reading of the day, this strong text was written by Carl P. Daw, Jr. An Episcopal priest and hymn writer, Daw was appointed executive director of The Hymn Society in the United States and Canada in 1996 and held that position until his retirement in 2009. This hymn on the transfiguration was published in his first single author collection, *A Year of Grace: Hymns for the Church Year* (1990). In a commentary on this text, Daw discusses the "implicit comparisons of the disciples on the Mount of Transfiguration and the expectations of present-day Christians as they gather for worship." There are two tunes commonly associated with this text: ABBOT'S LEIGH by Cyril Vincent Taylor and HYFRYDOL by Rowland H. Prichard. They are both good tunes; however the Taylor tune seems to match the intensity of the text more closely.

Children's Time: God's Son, Jesus

(Preparation: Bring the front section of a newspaper with headlines of various sizes, or a poster that has different sizes of type to emphasize different things. The content is not the issue here, only the method of presentation.)

Talk with the children about how we might emphasize a point. If we want to say something very important, we might shout it out. If we want people to read something in a newspaper, we put a big headline. We might emphasize something on a poster. *(Show the examples you brought.)* If the children are of reading age, you could talk about things such as exclamation points, boldface type, and so forth.

There are many different things we do when we really want other people to know something. One of our Bible stories today is kind of like that.

Even though lots of people had been following Jesus, God knew that some people might wonder about who Jesus really was. God wanted to make sure that the disciples knew for sure.

One day Jesus took some of the disciples up a mountain, and they saw a strange vision. Jesus looked somehow different than he had looked before, and they saw Moses and Elijah standing with him. Then something incredible happened – they heard a loud voice from a cloud and it said, "This is my own dear son and I am pleased with him. Listen to what he says."

Even though the disciples knew that Jesus was special, this was God's way of saying it loud and clear, making sure they knew it. Whatever might happen to Jesus and to them, they would know that Jesus was God's Son.

Prayer: Thank you, God, for sending Jesus to be our friend and savior. Amen.

The Sermon: Changed
Scripture: Matthew 17:1-9

(For sermon materials on Matthew 17:1-9, see the November/December 2010 issue of *The Clergy Journal*; for sermon materials on Exodus 24:12-18, see the May/June 2010 planning issue of *The Clergy Journal*.)

"Listen, I will tell you a mystery! We will not all die, but we will all be changed, in a moment, in the twinkling of an eye, at the last trumpet."

– 1 Corinthians 15:51-52

"Jesus Christ is the same yesterday and today and forever."

– Hebrews 13:8

One dimension of the human predicament can be noticed in our reaction to the word *change*. Some of us, not too many in my experience, love the word *change*. Obviously, the sick want to be well, and the addicted want to be liberated, the imaginative want to be stimulated. Perhaps many of us want small changes in our life – to be taller, slimmer, more muscular. But not many respond well to change in the organizations they belong to. Consider government, schools, our church. Change happens slowly. Even reluctantly.

When we see something wrong in ourselves, in our family, our school, or church, we might be drawn to change. But when we are at peace with ourselves and content with all around us, change is a disruption. So we might hear "we will be changed in a moment, in the twinkling of an eye" or "Jesus Christ is the same yesterday, today, and forever" in very differing ways, alternately drawn to one and repelled by the other and vice versa.

Jesus is a force for change. And the story told about Jesus on this Transfiguration Sunday reveals how Jesus and his friends were changed through an event they shared on the top of a mountain.

The story is couched in mystery: " . . . up a high mountain, face . . . like the sun, clothes . . . dazzling white, suddenly . . . Moses and Elijah, bright cloud overshadowed him, a voice" (from Mt 17:2, 3, 5). This story goes beyond the miracles, wise teachings, and healings Jesus' friends had previously witnessed.

"He was transfigured before them" (17:2a). Transfigured, transformed, changed – Jesus no longer looked the same to them. They were awestruck by what they saw. They heard a voice from a cloud commanding them to listen. This was beyond anything they had known and experienced, and in spite of the command to "tell no one about the vision" (17:9), it was impossible to imagine that Jesus' friends were not also changed. How could anyone remain the same after being in the presence of this event so charged with holiness?

Will hearing this story change us? I'm reminded of the words from John's Gospel – his summary statement of why he wrote his Gospel. "But these are written so that you may come to believe that Jesus is the Messiah, the Son of God, and that through believing you may have life in his name" (Jn 20:31). These are not empty, purposeless words. These words are written, and the stories of Jesus are told so that you will be changed!

There are moments in life when our self-satisfaction is shattered and we long to be changed. Hearing this story perhaps draws us to that mountaintop and we long to be filled with such awe in the presence of God. We would love to be outside of ourselves, beyond our worries and burdens, totally enveloped in God's comforting grace. Something like that took hold of Peter, James, and John, and even though we can't say "they were never the same" because we recall how they fled in fear when Jesus death came near, some newfound courage later led them all to die the death of martyrs because of their faith in him. Could that new faith have been born on the top of this mountain?

Perhaps our perspective on change has been shaped by Hollywood stories, fairy tales, and the world of make-believe. With memories of those stories in your mind, it is easy to believe that change is magically instantaneous. Snap your fingers, sprinkle the fairy dust, touch with the wand and presto, change-o! But if you've been on this earth long enough and known yourself and the human condition well enough, you most likely have realized that very seldom is a person changed instantly. Change is a process that can have many beginnings.

I've come to appreciate a particular word in church vocabulary that describes the process of how God works with us. The word is *formation*, and throughout the ages the church's teachers and theologians have reflected on how God is forming us. Whenever we gather, we listen repetitively to stories from the Bible, prayers prayed in worship, and hymns we sing or listen to, and the impact of those words chips away at the hard places in our hearts, rounds off the rough edges of our lives, and leads us in a particular direction. Slowly, ever so slowly, sometimes too slowly according to our impatience, we are being shaped in the likeness of Christ, drawn toward the love of God, molded by the Spirit. We slip and fall away and are picked up and returned to the path by loving friends moved by the grace of God, and the process goes on.

If you are honest with yourself, you may have realized that you don't always want to be here in church. You probably don't always appreciate the music, the readings from the Bible, the sermon, the prayers. Maybe you're hard pressed to recall specific teachings that really excite you. But that's probably also true of all the meals you've eaten in your life. They all blur together with time, but they all work together to keep you nourished, strengthened, and alive.

You and I are being changed. God is working with us, within us, through us. Certainly, God isn't done with us yet. We are far from finished products. But let us pray that we will be open to God's work, desire God's presence, and need God's guidance. Today's story of a mountaintop experience reminds us there are the high moments in our life of faith, but those moments are balanced out by long, dry spells on the plains and prairies of faith. In the midst of our journey we are being changed by the One who knows our name and has called us to follow. Thanks be to God! Amen.

– Paul Lundborg

Hymns
Opening Hymn
> Open the Eyes of My Heart, Lord
> I Want to Walk as a Child of the Light

Sermon Hymn
> How Good Lord to Be Here
> Jesus on the Mountain Peak

Closing Hymn
> Christ Be Our Light
> Shine, Jesus, Shine

March 9, 2011

Ash Wednesday

Lessons

RCL	Roman Catholic
Joel 2:1-2, 12-17 or Isa 58:1-12	Joel 2:12-18
Ps 51:1-17	Ps 51:3-6, 12-14, 17
2 Cor 5:20b—6:10	2 Cor 5:20—6:2
Mt 6:1-6, 16-21	Mt 6:1-6, 16-18

Speaker's Introduction for the Lessons
Lesson 1
Joel 2:1-2, 12-17 (RCL); 2:12-18 (RC)

After a plague of locusts destroyed the crops, the prophet Joel called the people to a fast. He wonders if the plague is a sign of worse things to come.

Lesson 2
Psalm 51:1-17 (RCL); 51:3-6, 12-14, 17 (RC)

Have you ever felt miserable because you have wronged someone by your actions, or done something you have sincerely regretted? David wrote this psalm after realizing his guilt for an adulterous affair.

Lesson 3
2 Corinthians 5:20b—6:10 (RCL); 5:20—6:2 (RC)

Paul's words to the Corinthians apply well to the entire Christian community beginning the penitential season of Lent. He says, "Now is the acceptable time; see, now is the day of salvation!"

Gospel
Matthew 6:1-6, 16-21 (RCL); 6:1-6, 16-18 (RC)

For many centuries Christians have used these words from Jesus as instructions for the specific work of Lent. Pay attention to Jesus' counsel about giving alms, praying, and fasting.

Theme

How shall we observe Lent, the time of preparation for Easter? With alms-giving, prayer, and fasting.

Thought for the Day

Jesus' words from his Sermon on the Mount provide instructions for the season of Lent. Lent's rigorous discipline can school the Christian in grace.

Sermon Summary

The church can borrow Jesus' teaching and apply it to Lent. Practice generosity, practice prayer, and practice fasting. The practice of spiritual disciplines will never cause God to love us more, but such practice can awaken us to grace.

Call to Worship

> One: Welcome to Ash Wednesday, the beginning of Lent, the time of preparation for Easter.
>
> **All: Is it not true that Christians are Easter people? Why bother with Lent?**
>
> One: Can we appreciate Jesus' resurrection without recalling the story of his journey to the cross? Can we bask in the joy of Easter's good news without knowing the story of suffering and dying?
>
> **All: God knows our reluctance to enter the story. May God go with us on the journey.**
>
> One: May God go with us through ashes, confession, almsgiving, prayer, and fasting.
>
> **All: May God take us toward Easter. Amen.**

Pastoral Prayer

Gracious God, we begin again this journey from ashes to Easter, a journey you walked toward your cross. We give you thanks that the cross in our midst is empty, a reminder that suffering is not the last word, that your resurrection victory is the ultimate gift. Be with us in this solemn season of Lent. Grant us courage to learn the disciplines of this season. Let us never be impressed with our own efforts, but help us to use the disciplines of

•

almsgiving, prayer, and fasting to struggle with the ways we have fallen in love with the world's values of greed, self-centeredness, and consumerism. Strengthen us for this journey we begin together in Jesus' name. Amen.

Prayer of Confession

Too easily, gracious God, our faith becomes our hobby. We dabble with the scriptures, neglect the gift of prayer, cave in to the ways of the world, and know little about how to follow Jesus. In moments like this we know we fall far short of your desires for us, and we ask for forgiveness. Grant us new resolve to value our calling to be your disciples. Thank you for this new season of Lent. Help us to use this time to grow in your grace and be better equipped for the life of service you call us to. Deepen our love for you and your people, and deepen our desire to use our gifts for your purpose. In Jesus' strong name we pray. Amen.

Prayer of Dedication of Gifts and Self

Loving God, our gifts seldom match your expectations. The psalm writer reminds us that "the sacrifice acceptable to God is a broken spirit" (Ps 51:17). We never desire such brokenness, but we know that in those moments we have needed you the most and have been most honest with you, you have never abandoned us. Be with us when we are strong and forgive us our pride. Grace us with remembered brokenness and a deep trust in you. And bless and multiply our offerings in Jesus' name. Amen.

Hymn of the Day
Throughout These Lenten Days and Nights

This text was written by James Gertmenian, a Congregational pastor in Connecticut. He submitted it as a hymn for Lent and Holy Week to *NewSong*, a periodical edited by Brian Wren and published by Hope Publishing Company. There are two tunes commonly associated with this text, both equally fine musical partners – WINCHESTER NEW and TALLIS CANON. Though this hymn is penitential, it is also a hymn of courage and faith and should be sung with conviction. The organ is the preferred instrument for accompaniment as it gives a sustained sound. If possible, try singing stanza three without accompaniment to better enhance the words.

Children's Time: Giving Quietly

(Preparation: Arrange in advance for someone to come and make a tiny offering, with great fuss. They might wish to dress in a way that looks pompous for your region, such as a fancy three-piece suit, etc. Make sure they have a coin, such as a quarter, and have the offering plate nearby. If the coin can make a sound when placed in the plate that's even better.)

I believe we have a special guest today who wants to give an offering to the church. Please welcome *Name*. *(The individual comes in and makes a big fuss about how important his or her offering is. Then hold up the offering plate, and the guest will make a great flourish of depositing their coin, and then exiting.)*

Hmm. What do you think? How does the gift make us feel?

Jesus said something in Matthew about how we give. Jesus said, "Don't make a big fuss. Just share your gift as if you're giving it to God. That will make God feel good."

Today is Ash Wednesday, and we're starting the season of Lent. It will last for 40 days – plus Sundays – and take us to Easter. This season can be a chance for us to think about our relationship with God, and how we can become even closer to God. One way is to be humble in our giving. It is important to make an offering to God – and usually we do this by giving to the church. But we don't need to make a big show of it.

Prayer: God, you have given us so much, we offer some back to you. Help us to give with humility. Amen.

The Sermon: Doing Lent
Scripture: Matthew 6:1-6, 16-21

(For sermon materials on 2 Corinthians 5:20b—6:10, see the November/December 2010 issue of *The Clergy Journal*; for sermon materials on Matthew 6:1-6, 16-21, see the May/June 2010 planning issue of *The Clergy Journal*.)

Imagine you are participating in a game made famous by a television quiz show and you are given the answer, "Christmas and Easter." Next, ask the right question to evoke that answer. Surely, you will have no trouble stating, "What are the two biggest festivals of the Christian community?" Easy, right? Lifelong church members understand that on Christmas and Easter Sunday they need to arrive early to make sure they have a place to sit, or they will be consigned to the overflow area and feel like an outsider. The celebration of Jesus' birth and his resurrection from the dead are indeed at the heart of our Christian life together.

A festival worthy of such celebration is also worthy of thoughtful preparation. A community needs time to prepare to celebrate a festival. Take Christmas, for instance. Even though the exact date of Jesus' birth is not known, there came a time when Christians realized it would be a good idea to celebrate that birth. So they named a date: December 25. And people celebrated. As time passed there developed a new season of preparation, named Advent. And the same is true for Easter. At first the early Christians declared every Sunday as an occasion to celebrate Easter since Jesus' resurrection was described in the Gospels as having happened on the first day of the week. Years passed, and there arose the desire to name a particular Sunday in the year as the day to observe Easter, and a time of preparation was set aside, and it was named Lent.

Today marks the beginning of Lent, a time set aside to live with the important question: "How shall we prepare for Easter?" What shall we do while we are pondering this question? The world outside of the Christian community has little familiarity with Ash Wednesday and what we do today, but let us note that this is the day for us to be reminded that Jesus' resurrection from the dead is so central to the faith revealed to us that we need to be mindful and intentional about our preparations to celebrate it.

The good news is that we have some guidance provided for our preparations from church history and from the Bible, so we are not inventing the wheel of Lenten practice. Consider our reading from Matthew 6, the traditional reading for this day. This section from Jesus' Sermon on the Mount is the source of the church's threefold admonition for how to do Lent. "So whenever you give alms . . . " (Mt 6:2) "And whenever you pray . . . " (Mt 6:5) "And whenever you fast . . . " (Mt 6:16) Jesus was offering instruction for "practicing your piety" (Mt 6:1).

Jesus assumed that God's people were piously practicing almsgiving, prayer, and fasting, so he instructed them to not perform such practices hypocritically. Such piety, he warned, is not meant for impressing the general public; these practices are to be done discreetly, in a quiet manner, as a loving response to our gracious God. Jesus does not condemn almsgiving, prayer, and fasting. He seems to encourage God's people to do them rightly. He condemns the excessive show of spiritual practice that too easily becomes hypocrisy. But these three practices – almsgiving, prayer, and fasting – have become the church's response to the question, "How shall we prepare for Easter?" and my pastoral response to "How shall we do Lent?"

Almsgiving is a dated word to describe acts of charity generously given to relieve the afflictions of the poor. The time before Easter is a wonderful opportunity for followers of Jesus to practice cultivating a spirit of generosity. Are you a reluctant giver, torn between your desires to hang on to whatever you have earned in fear that you might not have enough and your equally fervent desires to learn from Jesus' generous self-giving? The season of Lent offers you a specific timeframe to practice new habits. You are being given a 40-day season to begin a new way of living. It is said that we need to consistently practice a new behavior for three weeks for it to become ingrained. Consider Lent as a laboratory for you to practice and learn generosity.

We assume that every Christian knows how to pray and prays frequently, but in our hurried moments of life our prayers are often limited to desperate cries of "Help me, God!" Thank God, all of our prayers are heard, but the season of Lent gives us a season to practice prayer. Set aside these days to learn a mealtime prayer, to read a book about prayer, to read the psalms prayerfully. Maybe you can begin your renewed life of prayer by beginning each day with, "God, please give me a new desire to speak and listen to you." If you're a quiet person and don't know what to say, read a psalm and make it your prayer. If talking to God is easy for you, be quiet and listen for God.

We who live in abundance are not familiar with fasting, but Lent can offer us time to practice the discipline of deliberately abstaining from self-indulgent behavior. Do you eat too much? Watch too much TV? Spend too much time on the internet, the telephone, texting, shopping? Have you forgotten what it's like to be hungry, by yourself, without a schedule? Almsgiving leads us toward others; prayer leads us toward God; fasting leads us away from our self and our self-centered desires. Can you control your desires and not be driven by them? Fasting isn't something new, but we are mostly unaware of it. Try it.

These disciplines of Lent are gifts to awaken us to pay attention to God's great love. We don't need to impress God with acts of generosity, prayer, and fasting. We aren't in a contest with each other to see who can be the best. But we are recipients of a heritage from generations who have gone before us who learned that giving, praying, and fasting are not ends in themselves. They are worthy Lenten practices to awaken us to God's abundant grace, appropriate ways for us to respond to God's love, and reminders that following the crucified Christ leads us towards Easter. Thanks be to God! Amen.

– Paul Lundborg

Hymns
Opening Hymn
Softly and Tenderly Jesus Is Calling

Day by Day
Sermon Hymn
O Lord, throughout These Forty Days

Savior, When in Dust to You
Closing Hymn
Take, Oh, Take Me as I Am

As the Deer

March 13, 2011

1st Sunday in Lent

Lessons

RCL	Roman Catholic
Gen 2:15-17, 3:1-7	Gen 2:7-9, 3:1-7
Ps 32	Ps 51:3-6, 12-14, 17
Rom 5:12-19	Rom 5:12-19 or 5:12, 17-19
Mt 4:1-11	Mt 4:1-11

Speaker's Introduction for the Lessons

Lesson 1
Genesis 2:15-17, 3:1-7 (RCL); 2:7-9, 3:1-7 (RC)

This story from the garden reminds us how quick we are to blame others for our actions rather than accepting the responsibility of our own choices.

Lesson 2
Psalm 32 (RCL)

This psalm of confidence and hope in God our creator and redeemer reminds us that the universe is full of God's steadfast love and that we can trust in that love.

Psalm 51:3-6, 12-14, 17 (RC)

This excerpt reflects on our sin and on our hope in God's forgiveness and deliverance.

Lesson 3
Romans 5:12-19 or 5:12, 17-19

Paul compares the choice of Adam (and Eve) with the choice of Jesus, reminding us that our choices matter ultimately: obedience to the hope of God or narrow focus on our own agendas.

Gospel
Matthew 4:1-11

This passage tells us that it is not the forces of evil, but the Holy Spirit that leads Jesus (and us) to the confrontation with our deepest human wounds and places of vulnerability.

Theme

Jesus doesn't do it for us; Jesus shows us it is possible.

Thought for the Day

We've all of us got to meet the devil alone. Temptation is a lonely business.
— Margaret Deland, *Dr. Lavendar's People*

Sermon Summary

We do not live in a dualistic universe, but in the undivided wholeness that is the One God. God invites us into the wilderness of testing so that in naming both our wounds and our divine image we can grow into our full and mature humanity.

Call to Worship

One: We come together to ask for courage to suffer and to withstand:
Many: The temptation to believe we are above temptation,
One: The temptation to believe we will have time to follow Jesus . . . later,
Many: The temptation to blame others for our choices.
One: We come to ask for the courage to suffer temptation
Many: And endure with grace.
All: We come to be more faithful disciples right now, right here.

Pastoral Prayer

Loving God, when we prefer the dependency of childhood to the responsibility of adulthood, call us back to the vision of your realm, which requires our deepest love and our fullest commitment. Grant us the honesty to accept our responsibility when we ignore your presence in our lives and resist your hope for creation. Then grant us courage to take up the unique task to which you call each of us, that task which is our part in bringing your realm to full revelation here and now. Amen.

Prayer of Confession

God of grace, we confess that it is easier to worry about pointless minutiae than to grapple with issues of real importance. It is easier to live in the distracting chatter of poorly scheduled days than to find quiet time to focus on your life-giving presence. It is easier to complain about feeling out of control than to work to change what we are able to change. We confess that it is easier to be lazy and apathetic than to be attentive and engaged. We confess that we have become content with "easy." God of grace, prod us into awareness that our choices matter and give us the courage to be grateful for the prodding. Amen.

Prayer of Dedication of Gifts and Self

Sustaining God, we cannot turn stones into bread, so please bless these tithes to become food and drink for those in need. We cannot depend on angels to rescue us, so please bless us to be a safety net for those who are falling between the cracks. We do not have all the power in the world, so please bless us to love even our enemies. Sustaining God, receive our lives and the abundance you have entrusted to us and transform them into living blessings here and now. Amen.

Hymn of the Day
Forty Days and Forty Nights

The text by George Hunt Smyttan first appeared in the *Penny Post*, March 1856, with the title "Poetry for Lent: As Sorrowful, yet always rejoicing." It was revised and appeared in Francis Pott's *Hymns Fitted for the Order of Common Prayer* as well as *Hymns Ancient and Modern* (1861). The tune HEINLEIN (also known as AUS DER TIEFE RUFE ICH) comes from the *Nürmbergisches Gesangbuch* (1676). It is attributed to Marin Herbst but also to Paul Heinlein – hence the name. Present this hymn in a simple, straightforward manner. Allow the text to dictate phrasing, particularly in the choice of where to breathe or lift for a phrase. The use of brass will greatly enhance the presentation of this hymn.

Children's Time: Entering Lent

(Preparation: Bring some items that pertain to Lent in your church – for example, a purple stole, parament, banner, Lenten devotional booklet, etc. You could also plan to point out a Lenten banner.)

Welcome to the season of Lent. This is a very special time of year for the church; it's a time of year when we really spend a lot of time thinking about Jesus and how he is a part of our lives.

Lent is a season of saying we're sorry to God for things we do not feel good about, and of learning new ways we can be better Christians.

The color for Lent is purple. This is an ancient color that symbolizes saying "we're sorry, and we want to start over." That's a big part of what Lent is about. *(Point out the items with the children, and talk about them.)*

One of the stories we read today is about Jesus being tempted just before he started his ministry. He was tempted to make food from a rock, to jump off the temple and expect God to catch him, and to bow down and worship the evil one. In all of these, Jesus showed that he wasn't interested in temptation – he was interested in serving God. That's what we're called to do as well. When we're tempted to do things that are not what God wants, this season helps remind us to follow God's wishes.

Prayer: Patient God, we know sometimes we do things that are not quite right. In this special season help us to re-focus our living on you. Amen.

The Sermon: Suffering (Temptation)
Scripture: Matthew 4:1-11
(For sermon materials on Genesis 2:15-17; 3:1-7, see the November/ December 2010 issue of *The Clergy Journal*; for sermon materials on Matthew 4:1-11, see the May/June 2010 planning issue of *The Clergy Journal*.)

I am going to start this sermon with two assumptions. The first is that the temptations in the wilderness were real temptations and that Jesus really, truly, all the way, heart, mind, soul, and body, suffered these temptations because he is and was fully human. The temptations are not a trick or an illusion. We cannot have it both ways; we cannot say Jesus experienced everything we did, *except* sin and temptation. Either the temptations were real or the whole story is pointless and that the incarnation *wasn't* one. Either Jesus was fully human or he wasn't; and if he wasn't, I have nothing further to say on the subject, ever.

The second assumption is that the opening verse of the Gospel lesson means exactly what it says. I know you heard it a minute ago, but listen again: "Jesus was led by the Spirit into the wilderness." Jesus was led by the Spirit. Of God. Jesus was not led by the devil. Jesus, about whom a voice from heaven has just said, "This is the Beloved with whom I am well pleased," was promptly led by the Spirit (of God) into the wilderness to be tempted.

In other words, dear friends, God's universe is not dualistic. There are not two gods; there is only one. I see puzzled faces. You have known there is one God since Sunday school days. As our Jewish friends say every Shabbat: *Shema, Yisrael, adonai elohaynu, adonai echad.* (Hear, O Israel, the Lord our God is one God alone!)

Ah, but do you believe it?

Dualism is so much easier to believe: there is God who is all things good, holy, loving, joyful, gracious, creative, abundant, just, merciful and eternal. And then there is Satan (by whatever name we use) who embodies all those qualities we define as unholy, those things we call "bad" or "evil." This is the being (we would like to believe) who tempted Jesus and tempts us. This being might be called "Not God." Dualism is the marvelous illusion that lets us believe that *any* part of creation (any part, any part at all) can be separate from God – ever. But scripture is very clear about this: "Jesus was led by the Spirit into the wilderness." Jesus was led by the Spirit. Of God.

Let me cut to the chase. There is one God, only one, and God embraces, embodies, contains, enfolds everything. Everything. All of it. Those verbs aren't really adequate because there are no adequate words: all our words are finite and imply finitude. Maybe we can simply say, God *is* All. There is *nothing* found in creation that is not also found in God. There isn't anything that is separate, because to separate anything out would mean that God is limited, partial, incomplete.

Jesus comprehends this in a way that few of us are willing to accept. Jesus realizes that his temptations are within him as behaviors and character traits that, taken to an extreme, become dangerous. He says this later in Mark when he says it isn't what we put *into* ourselves that makes us unclean, but what we give out, what emerges from us, what we think or do or say. So Jesus, the model of at-one-ment with God, follows the Spirit (of God) out into the barren places where there is nothing else to distract him, to wrestle with the inner tendencies that are likely to undermine his coming ministry . . . like pride, like power, like over-confidence, like (you should forgive me) a savior complex.

Jesus willingly enters that inner wilderness to face the truth about his (full) humanity. He goes *out* to go *into* the lonely, brutally introspective state that was necessary to become a mature and differentiated person in relationship with his Creator-Redeemer-Sustainer. He doesn't flee from what tempts him; he faces it courageously and compassionately. He doesn't accept the illusion that there is anything separating him from God except his own partial understanding and the tendency in all of us to try to force the world to fit our personal agendas.

Just as Jesus knew that his wounds and sins and demons resided *within* him, so he knew that his salvation was also within, in the unique divine core image that was his real identity. Do you notice that he doesn't plead with God to send angels to save him from his temptations? He already knows what he needs to know about salvation because the universe is not dual, but one. He knows he needs to name that divine core identity that is already there, side by side with the temptations, and claim it in the face of his own fears, his own mortality, and (I suspect) his desire for the world's approval to define him and motivate him.

But the message in this lesson for us is not about the choice Jesus made; it is about the one we need to make. It is not about how Jesus saw the universe, but about how honestly we are willing to see it. There is no such thing as substitution discipleship. Jesus wrestling with his temptations in the desert does not substitute for us wrestling honestly with ours right here and now. This task is an essential component of becoming fully human, accepting that we are both light and shadow, work and rest, joy and sorrow. Only in our full humanity can we claim our unique, complex, nuanced, whole and holy divine imprint. Creation is not dual: we are not good or bad; we are not holy or evil; we are not clean or unclean. We are all those all the time because we are created in God's image and God *is* All.

When we choose a destructive path or choose to allow one of our temptations to define us, there is no one to blame. Not our parents, our spouses, our children; not God, not the devil, and not our evil twin Skippy. We chose that path, perhaps unwisely, perhaps carelessly, perhaps apathetically, but we chose. And we can choose intentionally and joyfully to behave differently. We call the power to choose the whole and holy, salvation. Salvation is God's gift of God's own imprint written on our souls.

Living out that divine identity is the deepest purpose and ultimate meaning and greatest joy of our existence here and now. We call Jesus Messiah because he lived that identity so fully that we could actually recognize the divine visibly in him. Every day is our chance to live so that everyone we meet recognizes the divine visibly in us.

May we so live.

– Andrea La Sonde Anastos

Hymns
Opening Hymn
Eternal Lord of Love, Behold Your Church
Gracious Spirit, Heed Our Pleading
Sermon Hymn
If You But Trust in God to Guide You
Abide with Me
Closing Hymn
Bless Now, O God, the Journey
Put Down Your Nets

March 20, 2011

2nd Sunday in Lent

Lessons

RCL	Roman Catholic
Gen 12:1-4a	Gen 12:1-4
Ps 121	Ps 33:4-5, 18-20, 22
Rom 4:1-5, 13-17	2 Tim 1:8-10
Jn 3:1-17 or Mt 17:1-9	Mt 17:1-9

Speaker's Introduction for the Lessons
Lesson 1
Genesis 12:1-4a (RCL); 12:1-4 (RC)

It is in leaving the familiar and the comfortable that we (like Abram, Sarai, and Lot) move into the creative space where we can become great. Are we willing to trust that and go forth?

Lesson 2
Psalm 121 (RCL)

This psalm reminds us that our help comes from God both now and forever. "The hills" were the places of baal-worship; the psalmist contrasts them with God's presence in all places and all times.

Psalm 33:4-5, 18-20, 22 (RC)

In this excerpt, the psalmist reminds us that God delivers us from fear, shame, and trouble. The psalm responds to the perilous journey of Abram and Sarai, but also foreshadows Paul's words to Timothy.

Lesson 3
Romans 4:1-5, 13-17 (RCL)

In this chapter of the epistle, Paul uses the lives of Abraham and Sarah to remind us that our lives depend on blessings outside our control, rather than on earning God's love or grace.

2 Timothy 1:8-10 (RC)

Paul raises the issue of being ashamed of the gospel. Do we often avoid faithful discipleship because the gospel is so at odds with the values of the world?

Gospel
John 3:1-17 (RCL)
Nicodemus and Jesus meet at night, traditionally a time of openness to new perspectives and dreams, to talk about how to live in the eternal "now" and the always "new" of the Spirit.
Matthew 17:1-9 (RC)
Jesus stands both within a tradition and outside it; he represents fulfillment and also something completely unexpected. How do we deal with his outsider status and his unexpected revelations?

Theme
Endurance is not unyielding rigidity but allowing the divine image to flower anew daily.

Thought for the Day
Endurance is one of the most difficult disciplines, but it is to the one who endures that the final victory comes.

– Gautama Siddharta, founder of Buddhism

Sermon Summary
The ability to endure the loss of worldly identity is not limited to Jesus, nor is the mandate to manifest the divine image. Those are tasks for all disciples. Jesus teaches Nicodemus and us what is necessary: submitting to creative chaos in order to be transformed.

Call to Worship
One: We come together to ask for courage to endure:
Many: To endure our fear and embrace love,
One: To endure our confusion and accept truth,
Many: To endure our despair and continue to hope.
One: We come to ask for the courage to endure new birth,
Many: And allow our character to become holy.
All: We come to be more faithful disciples right now, right here.

Pastoral Prayer

God of splendorous darkness, call us into the silent night of renewal, into the refreshing and startling stories born of dreams. Draw us out of certainty into curiosity. Draw us out of reason into whimsical nonsense. Play us into mythic symbolism; tilt us into new perspectives. Grant us upside-down visions of possibility shining with your humor and your hope. Out of the scraps and leftovers of shattered plans, build us into the brilliant mosaic of your now and not-yet realm. Make us, yes! Oh, make it so. Yes! Amen.

Prayer of Confession

We confess we would prefer to ask questions forever rather than live the visions right now. We confess we would rather wait forever to have every detail explained than to risk unknown possibility. We confess that we prefer familiar safety to chaotic transformation. We confess we would prefer to talk forever than to admit we know what you need from us, and to get busy doing it.

Impatient God, wake us up! Reveal all our stalling tactics for what they are and give us the courage to leave them behind in order to become your living presence in our world. Let it be so! Amen.

Prayer of Dedication of Gifts and Self

God of enduring hope, we offer ourselves back to you to become the new hope of those who have lived with no hope. We offer ourselves back to you to become a new vision in a world that is content with old behaviors, old violence, old injustice. We offer ourselves back to you to become the abundance you desire for all creation. Bless us to this work and bless the wealth we bring so that it may become the seed of your new creation. Amen.

Hymn of the Day
Blessed Jesus, at Your Word

This text written by Lutheran pastor Tobias Clausnitzer is intended to be sung immediately before the sermon. Stanza three is based upon parts of the Nicene Creed, which could be recited immediately before the singing of this hymn, if your denominational liturgy permits. A brief explanation of the allusion to the creed would help the congregation understand the connections. A newer translation, "We Have Gathered, Jesus Dear," by Madeleine

Forell Marshall, appears in *The New Century Hymnal* (1995). Liebster Jesu was composed by Johann Ahle, cantor and organist at St. Blasius's Church, Mühlhausen. It was first published in 1664 and then revised for publication with the Clausnitzer text in 1687. Do not sing this hymn too slowly. While organ is the preferred instrument for accompaniment, brass quartet (as with all chorales) will greatly enhance the presentation.

Children's Time: Nicodemus

*(Preparation: Before you begin to tell the story, invite participation. Invite everyone to scratch their head whenever you say the word **Nicodemus**; blow softly whenever you say **spirit**; and wriggle their fingers – to represent light – whenever you say **God**.)*

Long ago there was someone called **Nicodemus**. He was puzzled about **God** and he had heard about Jesus. One night, **Nicodemus** decided to go and see Jesus and ask some questions about **God** and the **spirit**.

"I know you are a man of **God**," **Nicodemus** said.

"Indeed I am," Jesus replied. "No one can see the realm of **God** unless they are born again."

"How can I be born again?" **Nicodemus** asked. "I'm too old!"

"I don't mean being born again in a physical sense," Jesus said. "No, you need to be born of **God**'s **spirit**."

Nicodemus wasn't sure what Jesus meant, but Jesus explained.

"The wind blows wherever it wants; same thing with the **spirit**. You have to open yourself to **God**'s **spirit**. When you do, you'll be born all over again, and find you are growing closer to **God**."

Prayer: God, loving Spirit, help us all to be born again, and to be always open to your love. Amen.

The Sermon: Endurance (and Disintegration)
Scripture: John 3:1-17

(For sermon materials on Genesis 12:1-4a, see the November/December 2010 issue of *The Clergy Journal*; for sermon materials on John 3:1-17, see the May/June 2010 planning issue of *The Clergy Journal*.)

If we think of the synoptic Gospels as short documentary movies, John's Gospel would be a totem pole, a series of symbols stacked one on top of the other: light, bread, life, truth, water. You suspect that the relationship between those images means something, but you aren't sure what – although you can bet it isn't logical or linear. John is one long series of metaphors and the only way into a metaphor is through your right brain, through puns, parables, aphorisms, pictures, and poetry. But, in case you haven't noticed, the world at large prefers sound bytes to parables. People get more than a little impatient when (for instance) halfway through the sermon they have not heard a single simple, declarative sentence.

Nonetheless, let's give it a shot and see what we can learn from this amazing, peculiar, mysterious story and even more peculiar conversation between Jesus and Nicodemus. If you want to close your eyes, go ahead; turn your imagination loose. If you fall asleep, the next hymn will wake you up.

One caveat: this passage is a familiar narrative. My guess is that everyone here today (including me) has a past history with it and, therefore, a whole series of suppositions and interpretations we bring with us. However, if our intent is to learn something fresh and startling, let's listen as if we are hearing for the first time, paying attention to what is actually there.

The story begins at night (which – in this Gospel – is not a specific time of day, but a state of being, a "moment" of mystery, of dreaming, of right-brain activity); we are in what the Celtic people call "a thin place," a crossing or intersection where an old way of being brushes against a new perspective. This story isn't about a stupid man meeting a smart man, or an unperceptive man meeting a perceptive one. The text tells us that this meeting is between two teachers: one highly experienced (Nicodemus) and one relatively new (Jesus). In other words, we are eavesdropping on two professionals speaking in the jargon of their profession. But remember: this is John's Gospel; this is not merely a story, it is a metaphor.

Metaphors, by their nature, hold two unlike things in relationship. I would suggest that what is being held here, in this metaphor, is traditional wisdom, a familiar "way of knowing," and new facts that grate against the traditional wisdom or that highlight a fault line running through it. We are privileged to be observing the precise moment when an old identity shatters, explodes, literally disintegrates, and a new identity, a new being, is born from the chaos, integrated from the pieces.

And the courageous, daring soul who is willing to fracture in the process is Nicodemus. Let us pause for one moment and honor him from the bottom of our hearts. Let's celebrate his willingness to die in complete and utter trust, not knowing whether there even *is* a new birth to experience.

(That is what he has come to ask, remember?) Without his courage in the face of primal fear and primal annihilation, we would not have this story. How many of us would be as willing to let everything we have held most dear and most true, including our own identity, disintegrate? How many of us?

I propose that Nicodemus comes to Jesus to ask Jesus to affirm what Nicodemus is beginning to know: that only in deep relationship with the ever-transforming God is it possible to live in a completely new way. He comes to ask Jesus to bear witness to Nicodemus's spiritual and psychological disintegration in submission to that power and presence. Nicodemus knows that new, larger truths cannot be held in old vessels (the biblical analogy is that new wine cannot be stored in old wineskins).

Nicodemus knows that if he wants to become more holy, he will need to shatter and be reassembled; everything he "knows" to be true, everything that orders his universe, everything on which he has built his life and its meaning, will need to be released. His mind, heart, and soul must be broken open and then reincorporated (which means re-embodied), re-integrated. What endures through such process will probably not be the temporal particulars of his current existence. What will endure is his onto-logical being, the deepest expression of the holy within, bubbling up as new wine, blossoming forth as flower and fruit, being born from above as spirit answering to Spirit. When it is over, he may not even recognize himself.

These days of Lent, lived with intention, offer *us* the opportunity to do what Nicodemus did and test our own courage and faith. Are we willing to submit to the disintegration of the old person whose habits may have become counterproductive? Really willing, without any guarantees? Because that is how Nicodemus did it. We have the opportunity to embrace new possibilities with enthusiasm and joy, but it will not come without loss. We must choose to participate *in,* not merely to consider or talk *about,* disintegration, transformation, and new birth.

Jesus came "into our humanity" for a reason: in order to show us that our human state does not need to stop us from being born from above, as he was; from being resurrected, as he was. As I said last week, we can't have it both ways; if Jesus is not fully human, what he models is ultimately meaningless. If Jesus *is* fully human, then we can do everything he did – everything. There are no excuses.

Let me say that again. We have no excuses for living in any other way than the way we chose when we chose to call ourselves disciples: the way of continual disintegration and reintegration, of death and resurrection. This is the salvation about which Jesus speaks at the end of the passage. When we believe (and act on the belief) that the Spirit is already at work empowering us to be all that Jesus was and is, God's shalom will flower into being.

Nicodemus goes at night, in the time of dreaming, and is given a dream-vision of hope and glory. We are offered the chance to make the dream a living reality, here, now. This Lent can be our personal disintegration, and the integration, the waking, into God's realm; we only need to choose. May we choose with courage and trust.

– Andrea La Sonde Anastos

Hymns
Opening Hymn
Mothering God, You Gave Me Birth
Now There Is No Male or Female
Sermon Hymn
Spirit of Gentleness
Says Jesus, "Come and Gather"
Closing Hymn
This Is the Spirit's Entry Now
Wash Us, God, Your Sons and Daughters

March 27, 2011

3rd Sunday in Lent

Lessons

RCL	Roman Catholic
Ex 17:1-7	Ex 17:3-7
Ps 95	Ps 95:1-2, 6-9
Rom 5:1-11	Rom 5:1-2, 5-8
Jn 4:5-42	Jn 4:5-42 or 4:5-15, 19-26, 39, 40-42

Speaker's Introduction for the Lessons

Lesson 1
Exodus 17:1-7 (RCL); 17:3-7 (RC)

When we are thirsty we have a choice: we can trust in the abundance of God or we can look for someone to blame. This passage challenges us to look at our own default position.

Lesson 2
Psalm 95 (RCL); 95:1-2, 6-9 (RC)

The psalmist invites us to sing our praise to our Creator-Rock who supplies us with everything we need, even in the apparent scarcity of the wilderness. Do we offer thanksgiving even when we are in need?

Lesson 3
Romans 5:1-11 (RCL); 5:1-2, 5-8 (RC)

Justification is the term Paul uses to describe being transformed by faithful discipleship. This profound transformation into right relationship brings us into reconciliation (at-one-ment) with our fellow creatures and with God.

Gospel
John 4:5-42 (RCL/RC)

The Samaritan woman becomes one of the very first evangelists in bringing word of Jesus into her town. We are invited to wonder, do we listen to the people like her in our own age?

Theme
Character is not genetic, it is a series of daily choices embodied.

Thought for the Day
Character cannot develop in ease and quiet. Only through experiences of trial and suffering can the soul be strengthened.

– Helen Keller, *Helen Keller's Journal*

Sermon Summary
Jesus incarnates the character of God and demonstrates to all disciples in all times that our humanity does not stand in the way of our living fully into our divine character. What Jesus did and continues to do is possible for us when we choose to live as he did.

Call to Worship
One: We come together to build a holy character:
Many: A character merciful enough to proclaim justice,
One: A character truthful enough to expose illusions,
Many: A character compassionate enough to love our enemies.
One: We come to reveal together the divine within us and between us,
Many: So that hope can blossom more abundantly in creation.
All: We come to be more faithful disciples right now, right here.

Pastoral Prayer
Holy Epiphany, in the life of Jesus, our Christ, in the lives of the faithful women and children and men, you reveal the character to which we are called. You reveal justice and mercy in witnesses who live and die for truth in the face of self-serving power. You reveal visions of peace in parents who have sacrificed that children might live. You reveal love in those who care for their enemies.

Holy Epiphany, reveal yourself in us. Reveal yourself not only in our yearning, but in our doing; not only in our desire, but in our words and deeds. Reveal yourself through us and between us and around us in the eyes and voices and suffering of those we have never noticed before. Amen.

Prayer of Confession

Suffering God, you chose to suffer with us to show us how deeply and broadly and fully you love the universe you created. We confess that far too often we have accepted your suffering as entitlement rather than invitation. We confess that we are far too content to be loved and far too lazy about living and loving in your image. We confess that we are far too eager to be soothed in our discomfort and far too resistant to feeling uneasy about the uncomfortable injustice that burdens our sisters and brothers. Teach us to suffer so profoundly from our own sins of apathy and privilege that we will choose the better way of service and compassion. Amen.

Prayer of Dedication of Gifts and Self

You create us to live and to love in your image, generous God. You pour out opportunity after opportunity for us to practice your generosity on behalf of those who have the least, and those who need the most. Receive all that we bring here: the abundance you have entrusted to us, the bodies and souls and spirits you have shaped and inspired, the word of promise and hope you have proclaimed. Receive our tithes and our selves and pour them out as blessing into your beloved world. Amen.

Hymn of the Day
My Song Is Love Unknown

Samuel Crossman, one of the first English poets to also write hymn texts that were other than scriptural, wrote this lyrical text. It first appeared in *The Young Man's Meditation* (1664) during a plague. Crossman identified with the Puritans and was ejected from the Anglican ministry; however, he later returned to a conformist nature and was appointed one of the king's chaplains. LOVE UNKNOWN was composed for this text by John Ireland in 1918 at the request of Geoffrey Shaw, who wanted a new tune for the Crossman poem. Be sensitive when presenting the text and tune. They are very well matched but need to be presented in an unhurried, gentle manner. Use of a solo instrument or organ stop on the melody of the last stanza could greatly enhance the meaning of the words.

Children's Time: Good News!

One of our Bible stories today talks about one of God's wonderful surprises.

Long ago, many years before Jesus, God helped Moses and Miriam lead the Hebrew people out of slavery in Egypt. They knew they were going to a wonderful land that God had promised, but it seemed to be taking a very long time. They got tired of wandering, and they started to get cranky, and they got thirsty. They complained to Moses that they were going to die of thirst.

The people complained and complained, and Moses didn't know what to do. But God told Moses to strike a rock with his stick, and water came out of it – wonderful, cool, refreshing water.

It must have been a great surprise. It was God's way of showing that God hadn't forgotten the people. God was still with them.

Many years later St. Paul wrote a letter to the church at Rome that celebrated kind of the same thing. Paul was excited about knowing Jesus, and he wanted to tell everyone about it.

One of the things that Paul was excited about was the fact that, even though we were not the best people, Jesus showed us God's love and brought us close to God. How much more, Paul thought, God will do for us now that we are friends again!

Both stories are kind of the same. Even when we are cranky and complaining, or not doing what God wants, still God loves us and cares for us. That's good news!

Prayer: Thank you, God, for always loving us. Teach us to be your people. Amen.

The Sermon: (A Holy) Character
Scripture: Romans 5:1-11

(For sermon materials on Exodus 17:1-7, see the January/February 2011 issue of *The Clergy Journal*; for sermon materials on John 4:5-42, see the May/June 2010 planning issue of *The Clergy Journal*.)

We could spend all day talking about Paul's theology and trying to unpack the terms he uses. We could speculate about what he really means by "faith" or "justification" or "grace" or "righteousness" or, even, "sin."

Paul was a Pharisee by birth and training, used to discussing spiritual things in particular ways, and I think it was a passion that he carried with him through his conversion, a particular style of philosophical argument and a love of precise words, precisely defined. It might be fun to wrestle with some theology together. However, I would like to propose a different approach because it is my profound conviction that it doesn't matter what Paul meant by those terms; what matters is what they mean to you when push comes to shove and you need to make a hard decision.

So, just for today, I propose that we ignore all the theological jargon and go for the bigger picture. All Paul's letters are, in some way, concerned with how to live daily, weekly, consistently as a disciple, so Paul writes a lot about the *character* of Jesus and, therefore, the *character* of those who follow Jesus. And that character comes down to one thing: love.

Jesus told us and showed us what his life was about: love. If we follow Jesus faithfully, our lives are about love too. Of course, being human, our lives manifest a lot of things besides love, but where the rubber meets the road, it's simple. The fruitfulness of our existence will be judged on just one thing: how fully we have loved. Jesus tells us that over and over and over and over and over and over. He preaches it steadily right through his ministry, his trial, his crucifixion, his last breath, and his resurrection.

Jesus is divine because he incarnates love with every atom of his being. His character *is* love, pure and simple. We exhibit divinity to the extent that we exhibit love, to the extent that it is *our* character, to the extent that we stand in the same place Jesus did. We have peace to the extent that we, too, live and die in solidarity with sinners ("sinners," of course, being everything that is caught in time and is, therefore, partial, incomplete, "broken away" from the totality of who and what we are in the unveiled presence of God).

So what? So what does that really mean for you sitting right here today? What wisdom does this letter to a church that long ago closed its doors have to offer you tomorrow when you pick up a hammer or a pencil, when you turn on the tractor or the computer, when you see your first patient, have to fire an employee, discover that your son or daughter has been using drugs, learn that your spouse wants a divorce, get back the results of those medical tests you took last week, pick up the phone to hear that a friend has gone bankrupt or that a parent has died?

The wisdom is all about that word *practice*. Do you remember the old joke about the young man who jumps into a taxi cab in New York City? He asks the driver, "How do I get to Carnegie Hall?" and the cab driver replies, "Practice, practice, practice."

I said it was simple; I didn't say it was easy.

Paul tells us that we don't need to worry; we need to act. We don't need to waste one erg of energy memorizing the seven deadly sins or the nine gifts of the Spirit; we don't even need to be able to define "justification"; we only need to put some legs under our faith. We don't ever need to be afraid; we simply need to love. But love, in case you haven't noticed, requires stamina; it is an endurance sport like running marathons. And, just as we may know all the muscle anatomy in the world, and understand everything there is to understand about pacing and rhythm and strategy, we can't run a marathon without practicing running on the road, day in, day out.

Equally, we grow in loving by practicing love minute by minute by minute. Paul tells us that our practice starts with suffering, suffering willingly, patiently, without counting the cost; not because suffering is good in and of itself, but because love pays attention and, therefore, suffers whenever it is in the presence of injustice or pain or abuse or prejudice or hunger or need. Love *suffers* when a child is in danger of addiction, when a spouse has reached the end of a rope, when a parent's mind or health is slipping away, when a colleague loses a job.

Love endures that suffering with eyes and heart wide open: it doesn't deny it, it doesn't ignore it, it doesn't anesthetize it with convenient lies or illusions or pretense. Love doesn't pretend that we don't have resources to share with a friend (or stranger or enemy) who is in need. Love doesn't ignore the often hard choice of living with integrity. It doesn't deny our own mortality and avoid the work that needs to be done to prepare others for our absence. With daily practice, love becomes our character through and through, and because we *are* love, there is hope.

I don't know what the practice of love means specifically right now to each of you individually. I do know that right now you have an opportunity to practice. I suspect that it will not be easy; the loving that needs doing right now will test you in some way. It will require you to stretch your mind or your muscles or your heart. I suspect it will require courage or endurance or both. Paul reminds us that Jesus showed us how to do this. I am willing to bet that Jesus learned it from his mother who was willing to love with all her heart, with all her mind, with all her body, and with all her strength.

And I know one more thing: just as there is someone who is offering me the opportunity to practice my love on his or her behalf, so I (in my brokenness and idiosyncrasy and fear and need) am offering someone else the opportunity to practice love on my behalf. I can only hope that each of us individually has the courage and the determination to do so.

– Andrea La Sonde Anastos

Hymns
Opening Hymn
    My Song Is Love Unknown
    Lord, Whose Love through Humble Service
Sermon Hymn
    Love Is the Touch
    Spirit, Open My Heart
Closing Hymn
    The Church Is Wherever
    Lord, Make Us Instruments

April 3, 2011

4th Sunday in Lent

Lessons

RCL	Roman Catholic
1 Sam 16:1-13	1 Sam 16:1, 6-7, 10-13
Ps 23	Ps 23
Eph 5:8-14	Eph 5:8-14
Jn 9:1-41	Jn 9:1-41 or 9:1, 6-9, 13-17, 34-38

Speaker's Introduction for the Lessons
Lesson 1
1 Samuel 16:1-13 (RCL); 1 Samuel 16:1, 6-7, 10-13 (RC)

We tend to cling (like Samuel) to familiar ways and past glories. God reminds us that the old must make way for the new; appropriate grief gives way to answering the divine call to new work.

Lesson 2
Psalm 23 (RCL/RC)

The metaphor of the shepherd describes both God and how faithful disciples are called to be in a needy world. We are to provide space where souls can be restored and enemies eat together in peace.

Lesson 3
Ephesians 5:8-14 (RCL/RC)

We are called to live in the light: manifesting obedience, truth, attentiveness, and fruitfulness. We are not to resort to secrecy or cover-ups, especially in communities of discipleship.

Gospel
John 9:1-41 (RCL/RC)

It is not enough to see what our traditions have taught us to see. We must learn to look with God's eyes and be open to the ever-changing paradigms God offers in an ever-changing world.

Theme

It is not enough to look; we need to see what is real.

Thought for the Day

The only thing worse than being blind is having sight but no vision.

– Helen Keller

Sermon Summary

Jesus teaches us that blindness is not a matter of body alone; true vision depends on our willingness to receive what we know without resorting to illusion, and then to incarnate God's vision. Clarity is about relinquishing our comfortable mirages and accepting our agency to reveal God's realm.

Call to Worship

One: We come together to be God's hope:
Many: To live hopeful truth in the presence of lies,
One: To live hopeful compassion in the presence of violence,
Many: To live hopeful love in the presence of prejudice.
One: We come to shine together with the light of grace
Many: So that peace can unfold among us, becoming God's realm.
All: **We come to be more faithful disciples right now, right here.**

Pastoral Prayer

Vision-Beyond-Sight, inspire us with the courage to let go of our narrow assumptions and simplistic explanations and self-important doctrines, and accept the infinite expansiveness of your wildly improbable desire for creation. Invite us to leave the safe cloud of not knowing, the comfortable cloud of ignorance, the familiar cloud of apathy, those clouds that protect us from reality, and to stand with hearts wide open, leaning into the brilliant epiphany of your truth. Dawn in us to become the living vision of shalom you desire. May it so be. Amen.

Prayer of Confession

Pure Sight, we confess that too often we do not see what we don't want to see. We ask you to give us the courage and the desire to open our eyes and our hearts and our minds. Then we ask that you will forgive us:

for witnessing the needs of a sister, and ignoring them;

for glancing away from injustice;

for winking at dishonesty, at prejudice, or at violence;

for regarding a brother as beneath our notice;

and for expecting others to be blind to our blindness.

Grant us the yearning to look until we really see what you need us to see. Amen.

Prayer of Dedication of Gifts and Self

Holy God, you have given us ears to hear, minds to understand, and hearts to feel the needs around us. You have entrusted us with a portion of your abundance to act abundantly to meet those needs. Receive these offerings we bring back to you. Receive the lives you have granted us. Receive our hope to be persons of grace, justice, and love. Bless all that we are and all that we bring that it may be enough to heal the wounds of this world. Amen.

Hymn of the Day
Be Thou My Vision

This well-loved hymn is based on an eighth-century Irish poem translated into English my Mary E. Byrne. It was published in *Eriú* (1905), a journal of the School of Irish Learning. The versification of this translation, by Eleanor H. Hull, was first published in *Poem Book of the Gael* (1912). SLANE is an Irish tune arranged by David Evans for the *Revised Church Hymnary* (1927). The tune was named in honor of the hill in County Meath where St. Patrick incurred the anger of the Irish king for igniting a fire on Easter Eve before the pagan king could light the "royal fires." A slight stress on the first beat of each measure will help give the presentation a Celtic lilt. The number of stanzas and their ordering varies in hymnals. Some hymnals also alter some of the archaic language.

Children's Time: Seeing in a New Way

Have you ever had an experience where something wonderful happened, and nobody wanted to believe it? Sometimes people just do not want to accept good news.

The Bible tells the story of someone who was born blind. Some people thought that his parents must have done something wrong for him to be born blind. But Jesus said, "No, that's not how God works."

Jesus helped the man get his sight. The man was thrilled! Can you imagine not being able to see, and then being able to? That would be great!

Some people were not happy about this, though. They didn't want people to know that Jesus was a person of God, and they got very angry.

Some of them said, "This can't really be the person who was born blind." Others said, "The person who did this cannot really be a person of God." Others said, "A sinner couldn't do this."

They kept pestering the man with questions, trying to prove that the story wasn't true. But it was! Jesus had given the man his sight.

Then Jesus turned to the people who were so upset and said, "You are really the ones who cannot see. But you think you can see, and so I cannot help you."

Prayer: Thank you, God, for letting us see you – with our eyes and our hearts. Amen.

The Sermon: (Blind) Hope
Scripture: John 9:1-41

(For sermon materials on John 9:1-41, see the January/February 2011 issue of *The Clergy Journal*; for sermon materials on 1 Samuel 16:1-13, see the May/June 2010 planning issue of *The Clergy Journal*.)

If you will indulge me, I would like to revisit the lessons of the last three weeks and observe that one of our most entrenched temptations is to look for cause and effect everywhere. This can be highly problematic. For instance, the task and discipline of disintegration requires a willingness to accept that the way we structure meaning in our life is not the only way to do so. In fact, the linear connections we routinely make between an event and the *meaning* or *purpose* we attribute to it frequently do not exist.

In the same way, because we believe that character is largely dependent on genetics, we may act as if it is completely inflexible. This is partly due to a highly inaccurate understanding of genetic predisposition, but it is also influenced by our belief that an effect we have noticed (we are stubborn, for instance) is inextricably tied to a cause we happened to notice at the same time (our father is also stubborn). This is the equivalent of looking out your kitchen window while you are washing dishes, noticing that the moon is full, and ever after believing that the moon will be full whenever you are washing dishes.

In the same way, we can often attribute suffering (effect) to God's will for us (cause) rather than to God's unwillingness to circumvent our freedom, the freedom to act individually and corporately in ways that are *not* loving and life-giving. The "problem of evil" is not that God permits it; it is that we (*we*) choose to act in deadly and destructive patterns. Evil (effect) is a consequence of *our* choices (cause). Saying there is no God (cause) because God won't turn me into a puppet by taking away all the consequences of my unhealthy choices (effect) is the equivalent of saying my mother doesn't exist (cause) because she won't continue to breastfeed me in my 40s or 50s or 60s (effect).

The lesson today contains one of these inaccurate attributions of cause and effect. The disciples assume that the man's blindness (effect) has been caused by a sinful action, either his own action or his parents' action. We already know that there is something wrong with this worldview because, carried to its logical conclusion, all humanity should be blind. We are all sinners, after-all. Jesus says to the disciples, to us, "You are looking in the wrong place for the cause."

In this passage, Jesus uses language that will make sense to his listeners in their time and place; let's sit lightly to the actual words in the same way that we sit lightly to the question of the disciples. He is not proclaiming that God is literally moving through the world striking people blind in order to create opportunities for Jesus to heal them. Jesus is trying to help us see that God permits all kinds of blindness – most of which is self-chosen – because our awareness of blindness is what alerts us to the possibility of sight and vision.

The event of physical blindness and physical healing in this lesson is a metaphor. (Please remember we are in the Gospel of John.) Jesus is alerting us that we are all blind in some way or other. For some (the blind man) it is a physical reality; for others (the disciples and the man's parents) it is an inaccurate worldview; for others (the religious authorities) it is a willful desire to maintain a status quo that serves them well. Our own blindness – and let me say it again: we are all blind in some manner –

may be caused by any of those or by pride, prejudice, jealousy, the lust for power or wealth, apathy, fear, or a desire for vengeance.

True vision comes when we accept God's healing, when we are willing to claim what we know, willing to notice what we see, willing to listen to what we hear. It comes when we accept that we are defined by the limitations of our particular, personal blindness only as long as we want to be. When we want, *really* want, to be defined by clarity, truth, and God's vision, we will live by that divine inner sight. The healing Jesus does in verse 6 puts us on notice that *physical* blindness is not a stopper to holy vision. And, indeed, as the story unfolds, it is not the man without sight, but some of those who have been born with adequate visual ability, who prove to be completely blind to God's presence.

As we have journeyed steadily along the path of Lent, we have been shown what the pilgrimage of discipleship demands. First, it demands that we accept responsibility for our own temptations, to accept that *we* choose – each of us – how to manifest the power within us. We choose to use our personality traits to act expansively for love, justice, and peace, or to abuse them on behalf of narrow self-service. Second, it demands that we be instantly ready to submit our current identity to God's transformation, disintegrating so that we can be re-formed as vessels for larger truth, channels for broader love. Third, it demands that we answer the call to incarnate a love that acts without counting the cost: suffering, enduring, and then embodying the character of the one whose disciples we are.

Today, we learn that it demands that we look beyond the structures and assumptions of the temporal world in which we live. It demands that we stop seeing things as we have always seen them; it demands that we stop slotting events, people, and ideas into convenient boxes without paying attention. It denies us the excuse of ignorance we use whenever we want to stay in our comfort zone (rather than disintegrating and reintegrating). It demands that we give up the illusion that there are a limited number of people we need to love.

I invite you to reread this story at least once a day every day this week. I invite you to begin to notice what you have not been seeing. I invite you to accept that this invitation to heal-into-discipleship is not only for the blind man, but for me and for you. And I invite you to consider with all due humility that God's realm is resting on God's blind hope that you and I will choose to see it and reveal it. May God not hope in vain.

– Andrea La Sonde Anastos

Hymns
Opening Hymn
Be Thou My Vision

Not with Naked Eye
Sermon Hymn
Healer of Our Every Ill

Longing for Light
Closing Hymn
I See a New Heaven

Hope Is a Candle

April 10, 2011

5th Sunday in Lent

Lessons

RCL	Roman Catholic
Ez 37:1-14	Ez 37:12-14
Ps 130	Ps 130
Rom 8:6-11	Rom 8:8-11
Jn 11:1-45	Jn 11:1-45 or 11:3-7, 17, 20-27, 33-45

Speaker's Introduction for the Lessons
Lesson 1
Ezekiel 37:1-14 (RCL); 37:12-14 (RC)

The people have been in exile for many years. Ezekiel's vision reminds them that the prophetic word is life-giving, raising what is dead and bringing hope. They (and we) are called to trust in God.

Lesson 2
Psalm 130 (RCL/RC)

The psalm calls us to respond to trouble, trials, and pain with hope. Our sins will be forgiven and our burdens lifted by God's steadfast love.

Lesson 3
Romans 8:6-11 (RCL); 8:8-11 (RC)

We are not only temporal beings, limited to this moment. We are also spiritual beings, looking beyond what is and living as citizens of God's realm so that it may be fulfilled right now.

Gospel
John 11:1-45 (RCL/RC)

Jesus called Lazarus out of the tomb into new opportunity and new life. Jesus calls us, as well, to leave the deadly choices we have made and accept a new call to live more fully.

Theme

Discipleship: choosing to live into our divine image, not simply praising Jesus for living into his.

Thought for the Day

Peace and love are always in us, existing and working, but we are not always in peace and love.

– Julian of Norwich, *Revelations of Divine Love*

Sermon Summary

Bringing our lives into alignment with God, into at-one-ment, is the lifelong vocation of every disciple. Jesus showed us that it is possible and showed us the path that leads to alignment, the path of radical, inclusive love. Jesus did not and cannot walk our path *for* us.

Call to Worship

One: We come together to be God's peace:
Many: To love confidently in times of anxiety,
One: To love generously in times of scarcity,
Many: To love trustingly even those we call enemies.
One: We come to suffer, to endure, to hope,
Many: To become the character of Christ, the love of God, incarnate.
All: We come to be more faithful disciples right now, right here.

Pastoral Prayer

In the places of dryness, let me [us] be fresh water.
In the places of barrenness, let me [us] be blossom and fruit.
In the places of need, let me [us] be food and drink [bread and wine].
In the places of alienation, let me [us] be welcome.
In the places of fear, let me [us] be love.
In the places of violence, let me [us] be healing.
Let me [us] be your Spirit, embodied in flesh and blood, revealing that you dwell here and now. Amen.

Prayer of Confession

Spirit of life and peace, we confess that it is easier to love possessions, acquired and hoarded, than to love giving. It is easier to choose a momentary pleasure that soothes our anxiety right now, than to sacrifice comfort to meet the need of a sister or brother. It is easier to believe in the illusion of worldly prosperity, than live dependent on the reality of abundance outside our control. We confess that the ways of this world are delightfully seductive, and living for a greater good we cannot fully comprehend seems dull by comparison.

Remind us that we are choosing between mortality and eternal life, between the values of this world and your realm of peace. Help us choose what we claim we want. Amen.

Prayer of Dedication of Gifts and Self

Generous God, you have invited us to set our minds on generosity and to live into the peace of abundant sharing. You have invited us to set our minds on love and to live into the peace of compassionate justice. You have invited us to set our minds on your Spirit within us and to live into the peace of profound relationship with others. Receive all that we are and all that we return for your use and make it all a blessing. Amen.

Hymn of the Day
Spirit of the Living God

Daniel Iverson, a Presbyterian minister, wrote the first stanza and music as a response to a sermon on the Holy Spirit. He was attending a revival led by George C. Stephans in Orlando, Florida. The hymn was published by Moody Press in 1935. A second stanza, not always included in hymnals, was written by Michael Baughen for *Hymns for Today's Church* (1982). Easily learned and memorized, this hymn (with one or two stanzas) makes an excellent response for services of baptism, profession of faith, confirmation, ordination, and commissioning. It also makes a wonderful response to a prayer of the people litany. Where possible, encourage people to sing in harmony.

Children's Time: Lazarus Is Alive!

Talk with the children about how Easter is coming soon. Recall with them what Easter is about – Jesus dying on the cross and rising again on Easter Sunday. Recall that we are in the season of Lent, a time to think about Easter and all that it means.

Today one of our Bible stories is about a man called Lazarus who died. He and his sisters, Mary and Martha, were very good friends of Jesus. When Lazarus died, Mary and Martha were very sad. Jesus wasn't with them when he died, and when Jesus came, Lazarus had already been buried.

When Jesus saw Mary and Martha, he cried with them. It was a sad time. But Jesus also knew it was a special time to show them that God was always with them.

He told the people to uncover the tomb. Then Jesus prayed a special prayer and told Lazarus to come out. Nobody could believe it, but Lazarus walked out of the tomb. The man who had been dead was alive again.

Mary and Martha were very happy – and Lazarus was, too. Jesus did this so that people would know that God is with us, even when we die. Jesus wanted to show us that God's love was stronger even than death.

All people die, and when they do it can be a very sad time for the people who loved them. But we know that when we die, our spirits go to be with God, forever and ever. That's what Jesus came to earth to tell us.

Prayer: We thank you, God, that nothing can keep us from your love – not even death. Amen.

The Sermon: (Life and) Peace
Scripture: Romans 8:6-11

(For sermon materials on John 11:1-45, see the January/February 2011 issue of *The Clergy Journal*; for sermon materials on Ezekiel 37:1-14, see the May/June 2010 planning issue of *The Clergy Journal*.)

Before we fall into any temptation to separate matter and spirit (a tendency we inherited from Plato and his followers), let's be clear that Paul uses *flesh* in the context of this letter to refer to anything temporal or partial, anything restricted by the limits of time and space, anything less than God's unfettered and eternal fullness. Flesh is not the same as *body*. *Spirit* refers to the spirit of God, the *ruach*, God's own breath of creation, animating the universe. Spirit is not the same as *soul*.

If we read too quickly, it can be confusing, but Paul is not saying that our bodies are at war with our souls. Quite the opposite, in fact. He says five times in six verses that the Spirit – God's Spirit – dwells in *us*, inhabits *us*, animates *us*. Our bodies are the temporal vessels for God's divine image. This distinction is important; it *matters*. It makes all the difference in the world whether we believe that we partake fully of God's spirit because we are living creatures, or whether we think we are broken beings occasionally visited by a sacred impulse that comes from outside us and is alien to us.

The lessons of this Lent have reminded us again and again that we are sisters and brothers of Jesus because we partake of the same DNA, because we are created in the same image. As Jesus was fully holy and fully human, so are we.

When trinitarians describe Jesus, the Christ, we speak of God taking on human flesh. We try to compress into human speech God's passion for at-one-ment with God's universe by describing the incarnation as the act of Creator-God choosing to embody Creator-self within creation. For trinitarians, the humanity of Jesus is always seen through the lens of his divinity.

Historically, our unitarian friends and neighbors would have described this mystery somewhat differently. They would have said that the fully human Jesus, grown to adulthood and obedient to the call of the One who created him, chose to live fully into the divine image in which he was (and we are) created. For unitarians, the divinity of Jesus is always perceived through the lens of his humanity. It is worth remembering that Paul was not a trinitarian. Therefore, human bodies and embodiment are essential to his theology; we cannot be like Jesus without bodies.

Paul is trying to convey to the followers of the way, that what Jesus taught and how Jesus lived is what they (and we) are supposed to teach and how they (and we) are supposed to live. It did not occur to him that they (that *we*, right here today) could not do this. After all, Jesus showed us the way to do it and Jesus himself tells us this more than once that this is how and who we are called to be.

The question isn't, Can we? The question is, Will we? Will we not only hear it, not only say it, not only believe it, but claim it and live it? *The* question of Christian faith is, When am I (personally) going to act on what I say I believe and become the living embodiment of Christ-God in the time and place in which I have been born? In other words, when will

I stop thinking that atonement means that because Jesus died on a cross two millennia ago, I need to do nothing more than attend church once a month or so, occasionally write a check to some charity, and maintain a comfortable life of self-fulfillment?

To put it bluntly, Paul is telling us that it is up to us to get with the program. And the sooner, the better. He is writing to people who have gotten the mistaken notion that discipleship is a vicarious activity. Let me be equally blunt: the belief in substitute discipleship seems to be an ongoing problem of those who have called themselves Christian since Jesus himself went to his death.

Atonement – at-one-ment – is not something Jesus did *for* us. What Jesus did for us is to show us that *we* (each and every created being) is already implanted with the divine image, always was so imprinted back through all the generations of created beings, and always will be. It is *our* task to choose how to live that at-one-ment.

Paul says exactly what Jesus told us: salvation already *is*. God's realm of shalom already exists here and now. God already spoke it as grace and glory. It *is* already: among us and around us, the rock on which we stand and the vision toward which we journey. It is our reconciled universe bathed in the peace in which Jesus, the Christ, chose to live. It is the hope that does not disappoint. It is the Spirit already dwelling within us breathing and being life and peace.

As St. Patrick once claimed, it is Incarnate Love behind me, before me, beside me, beneath me, above me, with me . . . and within me. God's commonwealth is already revealed to those who choose it and it will be revealed in all its fullness when we (when you and you and you and you and I) choose to live it, personally and corporately. It is that simple, my sisters and brothers. It is that simple.

Paul says our flesh is hostile to God, not because flesh is evil, but because when we define ourselves by what is temporal and material, we fill up the space in which God's spirit can breathe and dance and speak and blossom. Just as physics tells us that two objects cannot occupy the same space simultaneously, so Paul says that we cannot simultaneously be whole-heartedly committed to personal agendas of individual success *and* to God's agenda of attentive relationship. We cannot have as our primary impulse both storing up excess for our personal security *and* abundant out-pouring generosity. We cannot be both profoundly self-focused *and* radically welcoming.

Next Sunday, we commemorate the moment Jesus entered the center of political, social, and religious power in order to invite those structures into transformation. It is symbolically the moment Jesus enters the center of our personal structures and invites us to set our minds and hearts on the life and peace of the Spirit which dwells within. Two thousand years ago, the power structures chose their direction. Today (every day), *we* choose: death or life. It is that simple.

– Andrea La Sonde Anastos

Hymns
Opening Hymn
O Holy Spirit, Root of Life
O Holy Spirit, by Whose Breath
Sermon Hymn
I Bind Unto Myself Today
Spirit, Spirit of Gentleness
Closing Hymn
I Sing a Song of the Saints of God
Come, Holy Spirit, Come!

April 17, 2011

Passion/Palm Sunday

Lessons

RCL
Isa 50:4-9a
Ps 31:9-16
Phil 2:5-11
Mt 26:14—27:66 or 27:11-54

Roman Catholic
Isa 50:4-7
Ps 22:8-9, 17-20, 23-24
Phil 2:6-11
Mt 26:14—27:66 or 27:11-54

Speaker's Introduction for the Lessons
Lesson 1
Isaiah 50:4-9a (RCL); 50:4-7 (RC)

Aspects of Jesus' life and mission are foreshadowed in the songs of the suffering servant (Isaiah 40-55) who proclaims, "It is the Lord God who helps me."

Lesson 2
Psalm 31:9-16 (RCL)

In the midst of distress and surrounded by adversaries, the psalmist trusts that God's faithful and steadfast love will save God's suffering servant.

Psalm 22:8-9, 17-20, 23-24 (RC)

The psalmist has belonged to God since birth, and God hears the psalmist's cry when surrounded by adversaries.

Lesson 3
Philippians 2:5-11 (RCL); 2:6-11 (RC)

Paul adapts words of a hymn received from people who had come to Christ before him. This hymn gives an early Christian understanding of Jesus' ministry of offering forgiveness and salvation.

Gospel
Matthew 26:14—27:66 (RCL/RC)

This portrayal of the arrest, trial, and crucifixion of Jesus shows him open and vulnerable to the words and actions of those around him. How do our words and actions cause suffering?

Theme

Passion/Palm Sunday calls us to trust in God's purpose for the Messiah and for us.

Thought for the Day

Understanding the meaning of Christ's "Passion" gives understanding of the meaning and uniqueness of the Christian faith.

Sermon Summary

Passion/Palm Sunday calls us to be more than spectators. We are called to reflect on the understanding Jesus had of his mission and purpose, and apply that understanding to reflection on our own mission and purpose.

Call to Worship

One: On this special Sunday we come to worship, thanking God for the promise of a Messiah and the gift of a Savior.

All: Jesus calls us to demonstrate our faith in our daily living.

One: Like the people long ago, we also welcome Jesus.

All: We prepare ourselves to follow him to the cross and beyond.

One: Blessed is he who comes in the name of the Lord!

All: Hosanna in the highest!

Pastoral Prayer

Gracious God, the events of Holy Week show us how much we are like the people who spoke to Jesus, or about him, and whose actions affected him. Like Peter, some of us may be faltering in our discipleship; we pray for your strength and support. Like Barrabas and the unnamed thief, some of us may be living as prisoners to bad choices; we pray for your compassion and transforming love. We pray your wisdom for all those who like Pilate and the Pharisees bear the responsibility of social, political, or religious leadership. And for all those who like Mary mourn the loss of a child or a loved one, we pray the assurance of your eternal love. Grant us your mercy and peace. Amen.

Prayer of Confession

Loving God, today we remember the glad hosannas of those who welcomed Jesus into Jerusalem. Today and every day we want to be people who happily welcome and praise Jesus' presence with us. Help us to let go of whatever hinders us in learning to be humble, as Jesus was; to be obedient, as Jesus was; to be as passionate as Jesus was about ministering your grace to others. As people of faith may we be directed to bring the witness of Christ's love and compassion to our private and public activities. Help us to be anxious about nothing but in all things to trust in your faithfulness, that your peace will strengthen and sustain us, through Jesus Christ our Lord. Amen.

Prayer of Dedication of Gifts and Self

Because we have been blessed in our own lives, we want to be a blessing to others. May these gifts bring comfort and hope, in the name of Jesus, our Lord, our Savior, and our Friend. Amen.

Hymn of the Day
Go to Dark Gethsemane

This text was written by James Montgomery in 1820 and published in *The Christian Psalmist* (1825). Its original title was "Christ Our Example in Suffering." The author had three lessons in mind for the reader/singer: how to pray, how to bear the cross, and how to die. When it later appeared in *Original Hymns for Public, Private, and Social Devotion* (1853) a fourth stanza had been added. *The New Century Hymnal* (1995) has revised the text to "Journey to Gethsemane," which gives a more immediate, personal power to the singer's journey. Richard Redhead's tune REDHEAD No. 76 was first published in the collection *Church Hymn Tunes* (1853). The number assigned this tune was taken from its placement in the collection. Other names for this tune are PETRA, AJALON, and GETHSEMANE (due to its association with this text). One possible way to use this hymn is to divide the Passion Gospel into parts, placing this and other appropriate hymns throughout as sung meditations on the readings.

Children's Time: The Whole Story

(Preparation: Bring a book – preferably one the children might know, such as one of the Harry Potter *books, or perhaps a younger children's book; however, any storybook will do.)*

How many of you can read? How many of you like to have people read stories to you?

When we read a book, which end do we start at? *(The front.)* What about if you read a story from the ending, would it be as interesting? *(Pretend to start at the back of the book.)* Probably not – you'd know what was going to happen before you read it.

Sometimes, though, it can be good to know what the ending is like. If you're reading a book that's quite scary, it can help to read the end and learn that everyone lives happily ever after. Then you don't have to be so scared when you read.

Today we read a very important story in the Bible, and it's a very sad one. It tells about the things that happened to Jesus at the very end of his life. *(Adjust the way in which you tell the story depending on the age of the children.)* People lied about knowing Jesus, one of his friends turned him in to the police, they beat him, and finally they killed Jesus. They nailed him to a cross, which is a very horrible way to die.

It is a very sad story, and it might be hard to read. Except . . . we know the end of the story.

You see, this story has the happiest of happy endings. Jesus did not stay dead, but on Easter Sunday – which is next Sunday – he came back to life, and lives forever. So we can dare to read the sad story, and think about the things that happened, knowing that it is not the final word.

Prayer: God, help us to read the story of Jesus' death, and think about it – knowing that it does not end there, but continues with Jesus coming back to life. Amen.

The Sermon: Much Out of Little
Scripture: Matthew 26:14—27:66

(For sermon materials on Matthew 27:11-54, see the January/February 2011 issue of *The Clergy Journal*; for sermon materials on Matthew 26:14—27:66, see the May/June 2010 planning issue of *The Clergy Journal*.)

Today is known as Passion/Palm Sunday. The lengthy Gospel reading and the dual designation are ways of attempting to cover the wide range of events in what we know as Holy Week. It begins with the familiar story of Jesus' entry into Jerusalem with the people happily waving palm branches in welcome and continues with a retelling of the story of his "passion" or suffering. In some ways it is easier to celebrate today as Palm Sunday, recalling how the crowds joyfully welcomed Jesus into Jerusalem. We all love a parade!

It is more difficult to recognize this as Passion Sunday, because that designation evokes a different emotional response and calls us to be more than spectators. It calls to reflect on the understanding Jesus had of his mission and purpose. The name "Passion" comes from the Latin *passio* or *passum*, and it means to suffer, to endure suffering and pain. We hear the Passion story, the story of Jesus' suffering, and we recognize that the suffering of God, in Christ on our behalf, is as real as any suffering we experience.

The prophet Zechariah had written about the coming of the promised Messiah. Some 500 years before the story in today's Gospel reading, Zechariah called the people to "Rejoice, for your king comes to you, humble, and riding on a donkey." The mention of a donkey is significant and deliberate. It gives importance to a character in this drama that could otherwise be easily overlooked by those of us not familiar with the historical and cultural context in which the story takes place.

The Israel of Jesus' time was under occupation by forces of the Roman Empire. The county was far removed from the glory it had known in the days of David and Solomon. There was a deep-rooted hope within the Jewish people that the ancient prophecies of a mighty messiah, a new King David, would be fulfilled. The coming of the Messiah would restore Jerusalem to its position of prominence as the political and religious capital of the country and restore Israel to a position of respect from its neighbors. The general expectation was that the Messiah would be a powerful leader, and power meant wealth. There would be so much wealth that the people could afford to throw their fine cloaks on the ground to form a carpet on which the king could ride into the city seated upon a mighty warhorse, a symbol of power and might.

Matthew's description (in chapter 21) of Jesus' entry into Jerusalem hearkens back to Zechariah's prophecy and gives a sharp contrast to the popular understanding of who the Messiah would be and what the Messiah would do. Rather than seated on a mighty warhorse, the Messiah comes in humility, mounted on a donkey.

Anyone who has travelled in the Middle East will have seen donkeys. They are small animals – used and sometimes abused – as beasts of burden. If ridden, it would most likely be by children or women. Men would rather walk than be seen riding a donkey. That Jesus rode into Jerusalem on a humble donkey was an unmistakable declaration that rather than welcoming a warlord the people were welcoming a servant king, a man of peace.

In his specific instructions about finding a donkey for him to ride, Jesus was giving a deliberate and visual representation of what he had been teaching and demonstrating in all that he said and did. He had tried – and in gatherings with his disciples later this week he would continue to try – to have his disciples see in him a new understanding of the suffering servant spoken of by Isaiah and Zechariah.

Bruce Prewer is a retired minister of the Uniting Church in Australia who keeps himself very busy as a creative writer of prayers and liturgies that are shared on his website (home.alphalink.com.au). On the homepage his work is dedicated "to the Holy Other who can make much out of little and in our bankrupt time create wealth out of nothing." Prewer has written a creed that seems appropriate to quote on this Sunday with its dual designation as Passion/Palm Sunday, and when we are focusing on the definition and description Jesus gives of himself and his purpose and ministry.

In God we trust.
In the One who comes humbly among us,
taking on our humanity and breaking our idols,
in God we trust.
Riding a donkey and weeping over Jerusalem,
receiving shouts of praise from the common people,
gaining the enmity of the proud and the powerful,
in God we trust.
Riding to face a destiny foretold by prophets,
entering the holy city but with nowhere to lay his head,
coming to his own but his own not receiving him,
facing cruel death for the sake of those who love him not,
in God we trust.
This Palm Sunday Man,
this Passion Sunday God,
in God we trust.

For those who have eyes to see and ears to hear, the Gospels give clear indications of how Jesus understood himself and his purpose and ministry. His disciples had seen him reach out to those on the margins of society – tax collectors and lepers. They had heard him teach the rich to share their wealth and encourage religious leaders to come to new understanding of the scriptures. They were with him as he played with children, and they knew of the respect with which he spoke to women and Gentiles.

As we read this description of Jesus entering Jerusalem riding on a donkey, we have opportunity in our own time to consider who Jesus is for us and for our world. Passion/Palm Sunday calls us to consider what the life and ministry of Jesus mean for us. The One who came into the world in humble circumstances is the One who came into the city "humble, and mounted on a donkey." This is the One who comes to us and invites us to continue his ministry by loving as he did, by broadening boundaries of inclusion as he did, by being willing to suffer in service of others as he did. May people see the love of Christ in us, and may we see the love of Christ in them, and to God be the praise and glory. Amen.

– Gordon Timbers

Hymns
Opening Hymn
The King of Glory Comes
Hosanna, Loud Hosanna
Sermon Hymn
Jesus, Remember Me
My Song Is Love Unknown
Closing Hymn
The Flaming Banners of Our King
Ride on, Ride on in Majesty

April 21, 2011

Maundy Thursday

Lessons

RCL	Roman Catholic
Ex 12:1-4 (5-10), 11-14	Ex 12:1-8, 11-14
Ps 116:1-2, 12-19	Ps 116:12-13, 15-18
1 Cor 11:23-26	1 Cor 11:23-26
Jn 13:1-17, 31b-35	Jn 13:1-15

Speaker's Introduction for the Lessons

Lesson 1
Exodus 12:1-4 (5-10), 11-14 (RCL); 12:1-8, 11-14 (RC)

The annual Passover festival is a Jewish family observance recalling how God delivered the Jewish people from slavery in Egypt. It is also a reminder of the continuing need for deliverance from sin.

Lesson 2
Psalm 116:1-2, 12-19 (RCL); 116:12-13, 15-18 (RC)

What we give of ourselves in our offerings, service, and stewardship makes a testimony to God's love and mercy.

Lesson 3
1 Corinthians 11:23-26 (RCL/RC)

After they had completed the Passover celebration, Jesus invited his disciples to take, eat, and drink the bread and wine, recognizing in them his body and blood given and shed for the forgiveness of sins.

Gospel
John 13:1-17, 31b-35 (RCL); 13:1-15 (RC)

In the radical action of washing his disciples' feet, Jesus modeled "the new commandment" that his followers are to serve each other with the same kind of humility, willingness, and love.

Theme

Christians today receive and also continue Christ's servant ministry.

Thought for the Day

To willingly care for others, even and especially in menial tasks, is to show real love.

Sermon Summary

In what he said and did in the upper room, Jesus declared the same kind of new meaning and significance that he attached to his humble entry into Jerusalem, riding on a donkey. His actions then, and our actions now, declare God's unconditional love, forgiveness, acceptance, and inclusion.

Call to Worship

One: Our help is in the name of the Lord who made heaven and earth.

All: We bring to God our worship and praise.

One: Our trust is in the mercy and love of God.

All: We experience God's grace and goodness day by day.

One: Jesus said, "I give you a new commandment, that you love one another."

All: As Jesus loved us, we also should love one another.

Pastoral Prayer

Giving and forgiving God, our journey through Lent takes new shape and form as we move through Holy Week. We come to this Maundy Thursday worship to remember and learn from the life and ministry of Jesus. In washing the feet of his disciples, Jesus gave us the example of humility and service. The table fellowship he shared with his disciples reminds us to continue to celebrate and be thankful for your saving action on behalf of your people. In thanksgiving may we willingly serve one another and commit ourselves to freeing those who suffer oppression and injustice. As those who have been granted forgiveness, may we in turn be agents of your grace and mercy, through Jesus Christ our Lord. Amen.

Prayer of Confession

How quick we are, God, to claim your grace and forgiveness, but we just as quickly forget the call to continue Christ's ministries of caring and compassion. In this Holy Week open our hearts and minds to all that Jesus said and did. Remind us that Jesus took bread and wine and gave these common physical elements a new meaning and spiritual significance. Remind us that Jesus took basin and towel and demonstrated a humble service. Remind us that we are called and commanded to love one another as Jesus has loved us. Bless us, God, as we continue our journey with Jesus to the cross and beyond. Amen.

Prayer of Dedication of Gifts and Self

Lord Jesus, your life was given for us, a gift of love and grace and forgiveness. We are amazed and grateful, and in thanksgiving we bring this offering. Bless it to be used for ministry and mission that will show care and compassion and bring teaching and healing, in your holy name and to the glory of God. Amen.

Hymn of the Day
Jesu, Jesu, Fill Us with Your Love

This African folk melody was presented to the Church of Chereponi, Ghana, by musicologist A.A. Mensah. Tom Colvin, a missionary from Scotland, served in Malawi and Ghana. He wrote the words to match an adapted form of this indigenous song. It is a teaching song; one to help the people understand more fully the gospel story. It is easily learned and sung. Stanzas could be sung by soloists, a small ensemble, or sections of the total assembly, with the refrain being sung by all. As this is a song of the people, keep the tempo moving and be careful not to break the rhythm between stanzas and refrain – the beat should continue uninterrupted. Accompaniment is best with guitar and hand percussion, however piano or possibly organ may be used as long as the texture of the music remains light and clear.

323

Children's Time: Love One Another

(Preparation: If it is customary to have foot-washing in your church on this day, you could do this story just prior, and then wash the children's feet before the adults if they wish. Alternately, you could simply plan on washing the children's feet, or bring a basin and towel as symbols. You could also offer the children the opportunity to wash their hands in the water.)

Recall the Palm Sunday story with the children, how Jesus came in triumph into Jerusalem, and how excited the people were. Some of them called him a king. Now it was Passover time, and Jesus gathered with his disciples to celebrate a very special meal.

Jesus was their teacher, and they knew he was very special, so they were surprised when he did something rather unusual – he got up from the table and washed their feet! In those days, people walked around the dusty roads with sandals on, and it was a custom to wash people's feet when they came to visit. It was usually something that you would have your servants do. Instead, Jesus washed his disciples' feet. *(Show the basin and towel.)*

Jesus wanted the disciples to realize that none of us is better than anyone else. We should all serve one another, and care for one another, no matter what. In fact, Jesus said to his disciples something very special that night. He said, "I am giving you a new commandment. You must love one another, just as I have loved you. Then people will know you are my disciples."

(At this point, proceed with foot/handwashing as you wish.)

Prayer: God, help us love one another and care for one another, so other people might know we are followers of Jesus. Amen.

The Sermon: Love in Action
Scripture: John 13:1-17, 31b-35

(For sermon materials on 1 Corinthians 11:23-26, see the January/February 2011 issue of *The Clergy Journal*; for sermon materials on John 13:1-17, 31b-35, see the May/June 2010 planning issue of *The Clergy Journal*.)

We give a special name to the time span from Palm Sunday to Easter. We call it "Holy Week," and this special designation emphasizes the importance of many events that we now commemorate in the life of Jesus. In our Maundy Thursday worship we recall the night Jesus had a last meal with his disciples and instituted what we know now as the Lord's Supper. There is an added emotional dimension to this gathering when we remember that the one who would betray Jesus was there to share this last occasion of table fellowship with him. We also recall that while with the disciples that day Jesus gave a new commandment of love that comes to us in our own day and time.

It's interesting to note that the New Testament Gospels have different ways of retelling the events of this day. Matthew, Mark, and Luke speak of this last meal as a Passover meal, observing the exodus of the Israelites from Egypt when the angel of death "passed over" the Hebrew homes as the tenth – and worst – plague fell upon the Egyptians. In John's account the Passover would not be celebrated until the next day, and John is the one who tells us about Jesus' washing the disciples' feet as a sign of servanthood.

Taken together the Gospel accounts give us the story of the words and actions of Jesus as he washed the disciples' feet and shared a fellowship meal with them. In what he said and did that night Jesus declared the same kind of new meaning and significance that was attached to the way the week began as he entered Jerusalem, humbly riding on a donkey. With these words and actions, and in the face of fierce opposition from some and impossible expectations of others, Jesus proclaimed a new interpretation of the Kingdom of God.

This is what he had been doing throughout his ministry and this is what John's Gospel highlights in its particular way of telling about that last visit to Jerusalem. This Gospel throws its own spotlight on how the words and actions of Jesus declared God's unconditional love, forgiveness, acceptance, and inclusion.

We've read and heard these Holy Week stories so often that we may not appreciate how truly startling and counter-cultural Jesus was in what he said and did. Our Maundy Thursday worship gives us an opportunity to dig deeper and come to a fuller and broader understanding of who Jesus was and how he ministered. Maundy Thursday also gives us the opportunity to consider who we are as followers of Jesus and how we make our own testimony and offer our own ministry.

The word *Maundy* is derived from the Latin term *mandatwn novum*, the "new commandment" of love that we know from the familiar words of John 13:34: "I give you a new commandment, that you love one another." We're familiar with the verse, but we may not be as familiar with the context in which this commandment was given.

The focus on foot washing may take us out of our normal comfort zone. Jesus – on the night before his crucifixion – was determined to take on the humble role of a servant and wash his disciples' feet. "Unless I wash you, you have no share with me." In *The Message*, verse 8 is translated: "If I don't wash you, you can't be part of what I'm doing." It's as if Jesus is saying his disciples (then and now) must learn to serve one another with the same kind of humility and unselfishness in which he had served them. "I have set you an example, that you also should do as I have done to you" (v. 15).

We call today Maundy Thursday from the Latin *mandatum*, commandment. The commandment in question is that the disciples are to love one another as Jesus has loved them. The foot washing illustrates this in a very direct and dramatic way.

Foot washing was necessary. Tired and dirty feet would have been the norm after travelling in hot weather on rocky and dusty roads. Having your feet washed on arriving at a destination was an answer to a real need. Meeting that need would not be a pleasant task and was usually given to a servant. For Jesus to take on this humble task was a dramatic demonstration of humility and service. Peter strongly objected – as we might.

There is a degree of intimacy in having another person perform this service for us. To allow this service is to make ourselves somehow vulnerable. Recognizing this may make it easier to consider how Peter might have been feeling and why Peter objected so strongly. Was it a reluctance to see his teacher again humbling himself so publicly, as he had by entering Jerusalem riding on a donkey? Was it shyness on his part to be on the receiving end of such service from his master? Or was it an awareness that in this physical action Jesus was touching him spiritually in a deep and profound way? If we ask these questions of Peter we can ask them of ourselves.

Jesus said, "If I, your Lord and teacher, have washed your feet, you also ought to wash one another's feet." In his words and actions Jesus demonstrated that to willingly care for others, even and especially in menial tasks, is to show real love.

We can understand the washing of feet to include many ways of serving. There are times and situations when feet need care and attention. Anyone who has had a blister on heel or toe can identify with that need. People with mobility issues or other physical limitations know how important it is to have someone else tend to their feet. But we can also understand "the washing of feet" to mean providing preventive or restorative care and bringing healing and comfort on a much greater scale in situations of natural disasters, accidents, or war. There is a limitless number of ways in which we can fulfill this command to "wash one another's feet." Taken together, the Gospels point to the intimacy that is present in the two broad actions of Jesus associated with Maundy Thursday. In remembering and in re-enacting how Jesus shared bread and wine and how he washed the disciples' feet, we have meaningful points of contact and interaction with Jesus and with other people. We reach out to give and to receive from one another – plate and cup, towel and basin are offered as gifts of love and service from Christ himself. In gratitude we receive, and in love we give.

– Gordon Timbers

Hymns
Opening Hymn
    An Upper Room Did Our Lord Prepare
    Great God, Your Love Has Called Us Here
Sermon Hymn
    A New Commandment
    Jesu, Jesu, Fill Us with Your Love
Closing Hymn
    The Son of God Proclaim
    Where Charity and Love Prevail

April 22, 2011

Good Friday

Lessons

RCL	Roman Catholic
Isa 52:13—53:12	Isa 52:13—53:12
Ps 22	Ps 31:2, 6, 12-13, 15-17, 25
Heb 10:16-25 or 4:14-16; 5:7-9	Heb 4:14-16; 5:7-9
Jn 18:1—19:42	Jn 18:1—19:42

Speaker's Introduction for the Lessons

Lesson 1
Isaiah 52:13—53:12 (RCL/RC)

These words of prophecy were spoken initially to the Jewish people exiled in Babylon, urging them to return to rebuild Jerusalem. They also apply to God's suffering servant, the Messiah, in his work of redemption.

Lesson 2
Psalm 22 (RCL)

The psalmist asks the question Jesus cried out on the cross and the question we ourselves sometimes voice: "Why have you forsaken me?" With the psalmist and with Jesus we trust God's wisdom and mercy.

Psalm 31:2, 6, 12-13, 15-17, 25 (RC)

The psalmist pleas to God for refuge, for God is a strong fortress.

Lesson 3
Hebrews 10:16-25 (RCL)

This passage is an invitation to encourage one another to love and do good deeds, drawing strength in the awareness that Christ knows the hardships we encounter.

Hebrews 4:14-16; 5:7-9 (RC)

The author calls Jesus a great high priest, perhaps in order to emphasize Jesus' superiority over the Jewish high priest. Our access to God is made possible by the priestly work of Jesus.

Gospel
John 18:1—19:42 (RCL/RC)

John's account of Christ's suffering and crucifixion lifts up the images of the paschal Lamb, the good Shepherd, the obedient Son, and the King who will establish God's reign of justice and peace.

Theme

An instrument of torture is transformed into a means of salvation – and our lives are changed.

Thought for the Day

How a cross becomes our salvation is a divine mystery – a gift of God's love for which we offer God thanksgiving and praise.

Sermon Summary

Reversals and transformation are threaded throughout the story of God's interaction with humanity. Instead of deserved destruction, God time and again offers forgiveness and new beginnings. Good Friday is another amazing instance of reversal. In the death by crucifixion, God in Christ offers new life; forgiveness brings transformation.

Call to Worship

One: We do not have a high priest who is unable to sympathize with our weaknesses;

All: But we have one who in every respect has been tested as we are, yet without sin.

One: Let us therefore approach the throne of grace with boldness,

All: So that we may receive mercy and find grace to help in time of need.

One: Today we remember God's faithfulness, mercy, and love.

All: Today we recall God's saving action in Jesus Christ.

One: Today we renew our trust in God.

All: Today we recognize God's grace that makes this Friday good.

– Adapted from Hebrews 4:15-16

Pastoral Prayer

Open our hearts and minds, God, to all that Jesus said and did in his ministry and mission. Remind us that in taking up basin and towel he showed a humble service of caring and compassion. Remind us that in lifting up the plate and cup, Jesus gave new meaning to bread and wine as gifts of God, for the people of God. Open our hearts and minds, God, to realize how Jesus took up the cross and transformed an instrument of torture into an enduring symbol of your love and forgiveness. Transform us, God, to live in resurrection hope. Amen.

Prayer of Confession

God, today of all days, we remember your saving action in Jesus, the Son who is also the Christ. In him you declare that sins are forgiven. We trust this promise, God, because we know of your covenant promises from the time of Abraham and Sarah and their descendants, and in Christ Jesus we have the incarnation of your love and mercy for all people of all time. In our worship today we acknowledge the extent of our need and the extravagance of your grace and mercy. We come now to claim the transforming power of your love in and through Jesus Christ, our Lord and Savior. Amen.

Prayer of Dedication of Gifts and Self

God, the hymn speaks of our realizing that even if the whole realm of nature were ours, it would still be too small an offering to express our thanksgiving for your amazing love. As we present these gifts, we do so as an expression of our desire to give our soul, our life, our all. In response to Christ's gift of himself, may we give ourselves in service to others, in a ministry of care and compassion, and in a mission of sharing the good news of salvation. We pray in Christ's name. Amen.

Hymn of the Day
O Sacred Head, Now Wounded

The text is based on a Latin poem in seven sections, each addressing a part of the body of Christ on the cross. A translation, in German by Paul Gerhardt, was published in Johann Crüger's *Praxis Pietatis Melica* (1656). John Waddell Alexander translated the Crüger text into English, and it was published in *The Christian Lyre* (1830). This translation has since been revised numerous times, and several of these translations will be found in current hymnals. The tune PASSION CHORALE was originally a secular love song adapted by Hans Leo Hassler and used as a chorale tune in *Harmoniae Sacrae* (1613). Its association with the Gerhardt text was first established in *Praxis Pietatis Melica* (1656). When singing, set a moderate tempo and allow dynamics and breathing to enhance the presentation of the text.

Children's Time: Coming to Believe

(Preparation: Talk to the children about Nicodemus. If they were present on March 20 and you told the story of Nicodemus visiting Jesus, you might recall it now. Or, you could tell it very briefly in your own words.)

Nicodemus is a very interesting person. He was an important leader in the Jewish community. People would have looked up to him, and would probably have thought terrible things about him if they knew he was a follower of Jesus. That is why he came to see Jesus late at night, so he could talk to Jesus about his ministry without anyone finding out.

The Bible does not tell us what Nicodemus did right after that, but there is a very curious story about him at the end of Jesus' life.

In today's sad story of the death of Jesus, at the very end, Nicodemus appears again. When Jesus' followers took him down off the cross, they put him in the tomb of someone named Joseph. Nicodemus came and brought very expensive spices to anoint his body.

When he did this, all sorts of people would know that Nicodemus loved Jesus very much; no one else would have dared do such a thing after Jesus was crucified. It was as if Nicodemus wanted to say, "I don't care who knows it. I love Jesus, and I am not ashamed."

Even in the very sad story of Jesus' death, this piece shines out as something wonderful.

Prayer: Help us, gracious God, never to be ashamed of knowing Jesus. Amen.

The Sermon: Moniker for the Messiah
Scripture: John 18:1—19:42

(For sermon materials on John 18:1—19:42, see the January/February 2011 issue of *The Clergy Journal*; for sermon materials on Psalm 22, see the May/June 2010 planning issue of *The Clergy Journal*.)

There is so much about the Christian faith that has to do with reversals and transformation. The faith story is built around development of the relationship between God and God's people in which each covenants to be faithful to the other. As the story progresses, there is a recurring theme of God offering restoration rather than punishment when people fall away from their promise to live in God's way. Time and again the people wander into places of wilderness and experiences of captivity, and time and again God acts to set the people free and bring them back to right relationship. Each time this happens, the people experience a reversal of fortune as God transforms captivity into freedom and defeat into victory.

In one such time of exile and suffering the prophet Isaiah sets the stage for change with a voice crying out: "In the wilderness prepare the way of the Lord, make straight in the desert a highway for our God. Every valley shall be lifted up, and every mountain and hill be made low; the uneven ground shall become level, and the rough places a plain" (Isa 40:3-5). Speaking in terms of reversal and change in the physical environment, the prophet gives a vision of a new world in relationships as freedom replaces oppression.

The reversals continue as the prophet's promise is born into the world. Angel voices cry out to announce the birth, but the newborn king they welcome enters life in this world in a family of poor peasants. Instead of a life of princely privilege, Jesus takes up a servant ministry and calls those who follow him to do likewise. The kingdom he personifies and the reign he inaugurates is one in which the least and lowest are not only included but lifted up and made aware of how near they are to the heart of God. As with his birth and life, so with his death – reversals speak of dramatic change and powerful transformation. A day that brings death on a cross is a day of victory – a "good" Friday – because this day is a necessary prelude to the gift of new and eternal life celebrated on Easter.

Just as Christmas carols retell the nativity, there are hymns and spiritual songs that use music and poetry to tell this story of crucifixion and resurrection. Many Christians have a favorite hymn or song that tells of the reversals and transformations in the events of the week between Palm Sunday and Easter. Songs continue to be written that convey this story and that articulate a response of praise and thanksgiving for what God in Jesus has done for us. Many years ago the American evangelist and hymn writer Philip Bliss (1838-1876) wrote a song that is still meaningful for many people because of the way in which the tune and the lyrics highlight reversal and transformation.

The hymn begins with the seeming contradiction that "Man of sorrows" is a "wondrous name for the Son of God." None of us would likely want the designation of "Man of sorrows" for ourselves, and it seems an unlikely moniker for a messiah – but the witness of scripture and faith is that this is indeed a "wondrous name" to describe who Jesus is and what Jesus has done.

The version of the hymn published in *The Book of Praise* (The Presbyterian Church in Canada, 1997) portrays some very beautiful imagery as the words move forward from "Man of sorrows" to a resounding acclamation at the end of each verse. The "Man of sorrows" is the "Gracious Savior," the "Loving Savior," the "Blessed" and "Mighty Savior," and the "Wondrous Savior!" Each verse in cumulative succession speaks of change and transformation in the progression from crucifixion to resurrection. By the grace of God, something profoundly evil is transformed into something eternally good. And by the grace of God we ourselves are transformed into people who know ourselves to be no longer "ruined sinners" but people who have been "reclaimed" as God's own. Verse by verse the reversals roll on. The "guilty" and "lost" are made new, and the only fitting response is to sing "Hallelujah!"

Wonderful as it is to read or sing this or any hymn, other sensory experiences can heighten the connection with the scripture story of the events of the week between Palm Sunday and Easter. Worshipers are invited to see and taste the bread and wine of Communion and be connected to the experience of the disciples sharing a last supper with Jesus. We can hear the sound of a hammer striking wood and be connected to the experience of all those who watched and heard Jesus being nailed to the cross. In seeing and touching crossed pieces of wood we can be connected to the experience of suffering of the one who hung on Calvary. We can see and touch a nail and be connected to the physical cruelty of crucifixion as a necessary prelude to seeing the colors and smelling the fragrance of flowers on Easter Sunday that proclaim the joy of new life and resurrection.

Here today, on Good Friday, we can pause a while to reflect on what is possible by way of reversal and transformation in our own lives. One congregation found that a tangible way to facilitate this reflection was to distribute copies of a compilation of the verses from John 18:1—19:42 that relate the events of this day. Attached to each scripture pamphlet was a nail, a tangible reminder of how nails pierced the hands and feet of Jesus.

The nails are a physical and tangible expression of the human suffering Jesus experienced – a forceful connection to our own experience of suffering. And we can also recognize these nails transformed into an image of our own forgiveness and salvation, just as crucifixion is transformed into resurrection. The nails are in a variety of shapes and sizes; they have a variety of purposes, some specific and some more general. And in this way this collection of nails represents us, in all our diversity and with our various gifts and different needs, with our range of interests and diverse talents and varied opportunities for ministry.

Each person was invited to take a nail as a symbol and remembrance of the new life given in and through Jesus Christ. Each nail is a reminder to ask ourselves what we are doing with the new life God has given us in and through Jesus Christ.

– Gordon Timbers

Hymns
Opening Hymn
O Come and Mourn with Me Awhile

Were You There When They Crucified My Lord?

Sermon Hymn
Man of Sorrows, Wondrous Name

What Wondrous Love Is This?

Closing Hymn
When I Survey the Wondrous Cross

He Came Singing Love

April 24, 2011

Easter

Lessons

RCL	Roman Catholic
Acts 10:34-43 or Jer 31:1-6	Acts 10:34, 37-43
Ps 118:1-2, 14-24	Ps 118:1-2, 16-17, 22-23
Col 3:1-4 or Acts 10:34-43	Col 3:1-4 or 1 Cor 5:6-8
Jn 20:1-18 or Mt 28:1-10	Jn 20:1-9

Speaker's Introduction for the Lessons
Lesson 1
Acts 10:34-43 (RCL); 10:34, 37-43 (RC)

Peter's sermon is a summary of the meaning of Christ's life and ministry. The message is given in the home of the Roman centurion Cornelius, an indication of the universality of God's offer of salvation.

Lesson 2
Psalm 118:1-2, 14-24 (RCL); 118:1-2, 16-17, 22-23 (RC)

In one of the ancient "glad songs" of praise, we are given words to express our Easter joy: This is the day that the Lord has made; let us rejoice and be glad in it!

Lesson 3
Colossians 3:1-4 (RCL/RC)

In the early church, those baptized donned new clothes to symbolize the death of their old ways and their new "life" in Christ and the transformation of a person's thinking and way of living.

Gospel
John 20:1-18 (RCL); 20:1-9 (RC)

To John the evangelist, Jesus' crucifixion, resurrection, and ascension are integral and connect parts of the story of God's redeeming love.

Theme

In an amazing reversal the one lifted up on the cross is lifted up to God's glory.

Thought for the Day

Easter did not happen just once in the past. It happens every day.

Sermon Summary

A number of reversals of expectation in the life of Jesus precede the great reversal of death by crucifixion overcome in resurrection life. These kinds of reversals continue as the Risen Christ meets his disciples in every age.

Call to Worship

> One: Dawn breaks. Light out of darkness. Life out of death.
> **All: Christ is risen! Christ is risen indeed! Alleluia!**
> One: Hope replaces doubt. Faith overcomes fear. Love transforms hate.
> **All: Christ is risen! Christ is risen indeed! Alleluia!**
> One: The light shines in the darkness. The darkness has not, and will not, overcome it.
> **All: Christ is risen! Christ is risen indeed! Alleluia!**
> One: God has made this new day. We rejoice and are glad in it. God's love is always with us.
> **All: Christ is risen! Christ is risen indeed! Alleluia!**

Pastoral Prayer

On this Easter Sunday, far removed in time from that first day of resurrection, we come to the empty tomb with our own sense of wonder at what has happened to Jesus and what it means for us and for our world. God, may we, like the first disciples, be able to declare that Jesus is alive in a new and wonderful way. Like them, we want to tell what we have seen and heard and experienced of your grace and mercy. We praise you, God, that because Jesus lives we have hope and confidence that nothing past, present, or yet to come can ever separate us from your love made known in Jesus Christ. Amen.

Prayer of Confession

God, with praise and thanksgiving we celebrate the amazing truth that you bring forgiveness and new life. The resurrection of Jesus proclaims that nothing can separate us from your love. We need this assurance, God, because there are times when, like those first disciples, we are afraid, hiding behind locked doors, unwilling or unable to declare our allegiance to Christ. We ask you to change and transform us. Roll away the heavy stones of guilt or regret or disappointment. Remove whatever it is that keeps us from achieving our potential to be Easter people – people who love you, who are loved by you, and who share your love with all people. Amen.

Prayer of Dedication of Gifts and Self

Ever-living God, the resurrection of Jesus fills us with hope and joy. Because he lives we can live with a new sense of purpose and commitment. As we go about our ministry and mission we offer ourselves and our gifts to help bring new life to others, in Jesus' name. Amen.

Hymn of the Day
Thine (Yours) Is the Glory

Originally a French text, this hymn may possibly stem from an earlier German Advent carol set to the same tune. The French text was first published in *Chants Evangéliques* (1885), and the English translation, by Richard Birch Hoyle, was published in *Cantate Domino* (1924). The tune JUDAS MACCABAEUS is a revision of the chorus "See the Conquering Hero Comes" from Handel's oratorio of the same name. This makes an excellent processional for Easter Sunday. The use of brass and timpani will greatly enhance the presentation. Make sure that the accompaniment mirrors the text with appropriate dynamics – it is not just a loud hymn!

Children's Time: The Colors of Easter

(Preparation: Bring an assortment of candies, such as M & M's or Smarties, in various colors, or bring some ribbons in various colors. If bringing ribbons, you could give one to each of the children and invite them to wave them, or bunch them together to make a large tassel that you could hang in the worship area. Base the choice of colors on the items from this list that you would like to share with the children:

- *brown – earth, earthquake, rock at the tomb, or the tree from which the cross was made*
- *green – freshness of new life that comes with resurrection; garden of the tomb*
- *yellow – sun that rose on Easter morning*
- *red – color of blood, color of the wine of the new covenant*
- *blue – sadness of Jesus' followers at the crucifixion, and of the bright, clear sky on Easter morning*
- *orange – fire representing the work of the Holy Spirit which came to Jesus' followers at Pentecost)*

Prayer: God of new life, we thank you for bringing Jesus back to life. Alleluia! Christ is risen! Amen.

The Sermon: Amazing Reversals
Scripture: Matthew 28:1-10

(For sermon materials on John 20:1-18, see the January/February 2011 issue of *The Clergy Journal*; for sermon materials on Matthew 28:1-10, see the May/June 2010 planning issue of *The Clergy Journal*.)

As children, we know and appreciate all the excitement and anticipation associated with Christmas. As adults, we know that this wonder is sometimes diminished by all the fuss and bother that can also come with our Christmas celebrations. The day and the season loom very large in our consciousness, so it may be a surprise to learn that historically Easter was the greater and pre-eminent church festival.

This new awareness raises questions about why the change in popularity may have come about. Part of the reason may be that Christmas has all the familiar associations with the romantic story of the birth of a special baby. A story about birth is more readily accessible than a story about death and resurrection – death being a familiar but not attractive concept, and resurrection being not only unfamiliar but also otherworldly. Even so, each hearing of the Easter story can bring some helpful new insight or observation about this event that we may think is so strange and awesome.

The story gives us the classic conflict of good versus evil, with the surprising declaration that death is defeated in the return to life of the good man, Jesus. And it is important to note that this is not resuscitation but resurrection. Resuscitation has become more common with our 21st century advances in medical science. There have been an increased number of situations in which people who would otherwise be left with the determination of "dead" are able to continue their lives because of speedy and effective medical intervention. The first century situation of Jesus being raised from the dead, however, is more than simply being brought back to life. Resuscitated people will eventually die. Resurrection is about a transformation of the bodily life we know in this world into a new, transformed, and eternal existence with God.

The concept of resurrection is complex and confusing to many people, and the way the biblical story develops makes rational explanation difficult – earthquakes and angel messengers, sealed tombs mysteriously opened, a man seen to be dead and buried now seen alive again in a new and wonderful way – the rational mind has difficulty accepting these things. There is no denying that the story offers a strange mixture of fear and joy, along with an equally strange mixture of broad promise and precise detail.

Mary Magdalene and the other Mary had gone to see the tomb where the body of Jesus had been placed. Their journey was interrupted by a sudden earthquake, and just as unexpectedly an angel of the Lord descended from heaven and rolled back the stone covering the entrance to the tomb and sat on it. This dazzling creature spoke to them in precise detail about the amazing promise of the resurrected Jesus going ahead of them to Galilee. And this precise geographic detail is repeated as Jesus himself met them and tells them: "Do not be afraid; go and tell my brothers to go to Galilee; there they will see me."

In Matthew's telling of the story Jesus doesn't appear to the disciples in Jerusalem, or in the Upper Room, or on the road to Emmaus. Jerusalem, the center of political and religious authority, is intentionally downplayed in what may be another example of the amazing reversals in the story of the life and ministry of Jesus.

In an overview of the Gospels, it was a reversal of expectation that the birth of the Savior would take place in a humble stable. It was a visible reversal of expectation that Jesus entered Jerusalem, humbly, riding on a donkey. It was another overt reversal of expectation that the Teacher and Master took on the role of servant in washing his disciples' feet. And now, with the great reversal of victory over death, the risen Christ gives precedence to out-of-the-way Galilee.

Galilee was home territory to Jesus, but Galilee was not seen as important in his day, especially when compared to the power and prestige of the capital city, Jerusalem. Galilee was seen as a backwater place, and Galileans were thought of as country bumpkins. The story (Mt 26:69-75) of Peter's denial of ever knowing Jesus begins with Peter being identified as a Galilean. His country "look" or accent must have given him away.

The name Galilee comes from the Hebrew *galil* which means "border," with the connotation of being a boundary area between the known and the unfamiliar. To those at the perceived center of power and influence in Jerusalem, Galilee was distant, strange, and unimportant.

This strangeness was heightened by the fact that many Gentiles lived in that region. It was a trade route and crossroads area populated by Greeks, Phoenicians, Syrians, and other non-Jewish people, worshippers of other gods, aligned with the Roman Empire, the occupier and oppressor. And yet, Jesus tells his disciples to go to Galilee to meet him. Galilee is where he gives them the Great Commission to go and "make disciples of all nations" (Mt 28:19). How appropriate it is that this new mission is initiated in Galilee, a Jewish place, but with people of many countries and nations.

In the midst of all that was strange and amazing about the events in Jerusalem, the risen Jesus took his disciples back to what was familiar to many of them, back to Galilee, in order to prepare them for something new and wonderful. This journey took them away from Jerusalem and their fear and hiding behind closed doors. In going to Galilee they moved out of the thrall of speculation and second-guessing their situation. They went back to Galilee and were given work to do – important and world-changing work. They didn't isolate themselves in a closed, exclusive circle of "first disciples," but they drew that circle of awareness wide enough to include "all nations."

Matthew's Gospel reminds and reassures us that Jesus goes ahead of us and will meet us in whatever is our equivalent of Galilee. We don't have to go to some out-of-the-world place to encounter the risen Christ. We don't have to go into some hyper-spiritual zone or to accept some incomprehensible abstract theological concept. We can go to whatever is home and known or new and different and Jesus meets us there.

Part of the joy of celebrating Easter is the realization that resurrection is not just a strange and awesome event recorded as happening some 2000 years ago, but something that happens to us here and now and continually. Christ makes us new creatures, and with God's help we overcome despair, make new friends, let go of old hurts and prejudices, enter new relationships, and learn new ways of faithful living.

Again this Easter, and every day, we can know ourselves to be loved, forgiven, accepted, and included in Christ's ongoing ministry. In that awareness we are changed, and living this new life we go with Jesus to change the world by loving, forgiving, accepting, and including, as Jesus did. Amen.

– Gordon Timbers

Hymns
Opening Hymn
Jesus Christ Is Risen Today
At the Dawning of Salvation
Sermon Hymn
Now the Green Blade Rises
Christ Has No Body Now But Yours
Closing Hymn
Christ Is Alive
This Joyful Eastertide

May 1, 2011

2nd Sunday of Easter

Lessons

RCL	Roman Catholic
Acts 2:14a, 22-32	Acts 2:42-47
Ps 16	Ps 118:2-4, 13-15, 22-24
1 Pet 1:3-9	1 Pet 1:3-9
Jn 20:19-31	Jn 20:19-31

Speaker's Introduction for the Lessons
Lesson 1
Acts 2:14a, 22-32 (RCL)
As a sign pointing to God's Messiah, Peter uses words of Psalm 16 to illustrate prophecy fulfilled in David's descendant, Jesus, not being abandoned in death but raised by the power of God.

Acts 2:42-47 (RC)
The gift of the Holy Spirit enables Christians to build community and live in a way that makes a positive witness and difference to the world around them.

Lesson 2
Psalm 16 (RCL)
The psalmist expresses thanks for God's protection, provision, and presence: "You show me the path of life."

Psalm 118:2-4, 13-15, 22-24 (RC)
These verses of Psalm 118 are almost exactly the same as the psalm reading for Easter Sunday, continuing the "glad songs" of praise.

Lesson 3
1 Peter 1:3-9 (RCL/RC)
Peter offers assurance that in Christ's resurrection Jesus' presence and power encourage Christians to hold firm to their faith.

Gospel
John 20:19-31 (RCL/RC)
In an echo back to the creation story, Jesus uses breath and wind as powerful metaphors of new life in and through the gift of the Holy Spirit.

Theme
Thomas deserves a new reputation to reflect the new life Jesus gave him.

Thought for the Day
By the grace of God, those who come to faith through the testimony of others are truly blessed.

Sermon Summary
Because Jesus understood and accepted Thomas's questions, Thomas gains a fuller picture of who Jesus was and what it means to be his disciple. This is an encouragement to us in our own growth in discipleship.

Call to Worship
One: On the first day of the week, Jesus came and stood among them.
All: The disciples rejoiced when they saw the Lord.
One: Blessed be the God and Father of our Lord Jesus Christ.
All: We have been given new birth through the resurrection of Jesus Christ from the dead.
One: In thanksgiving and praise let us worship God.
All: Alleluia! Alleluia!

Pastoral Prayer
God, you are the strength of those who believe and you are the hope of those who seek. We claim that strength and hope as we move forward in this Easter season. Like those first disciples we no longer look for Jesus among the dead because we know him to be alive in a new and wonderful way. We know him to be present with us, and we pray that this knowledge will sustain and guide us through whatever doubts or difficulties may lie ahead. As your love is new every morning, renew our faith day by day. Help us to grow into the promise and potential that is ours as people who have been given new life, brothers and sisters in Christ. Amen.

Prayer of Confession

Almighty God, we have celebrated Easter. We have sung our hallelujahs with energy and enthusiasm and have listened again to the familiar and amazing story of our Lord's resurrection. Help us to maintain the awareness of the great gift of new life that is ours to claim on Easter, and every day. Let the hope and joy of this season give us assurance and confidence to live as those who claim the presence of your Spirit. May our words and actions give powerful witness to our claim that Jesus Christ lives and reigns with you and the Holy Spirit, one God, now and forever. Amen.

Prayer of Dedication of Gifts and Self

Ever-living God, let the resurrection of your Son transform our lives in gratitude for what you have done for us. In confident faith may we be creative and courageous in serving you and bringing other people your good news of salvation and new life. Amen.

Hymn of the Day
We Walk by Faith and Not by Sight

This hymn was written by Henry Alford and first published in *Psalms and Hymns, adapted for the Sundays and Holidays throughout the Year* (1844) and then in *Year of Praise* (1867). Alford was a writer of poetry and hymn texts, a Greek scholar, and an ordained priest in the Church of England. He was dean of Canterbury Cathedral for the last 14 years of his life. This text is an interesting "contemporary commentary" on our lives in comparison to those of the disciples following Jesus' death. There are a number of tunes associated with this text – DUNLAP'S CREEK by Samuel McFarland, MARTYRDOM attr. to Hugh Wilson, and ST. BOTOLPH by Gordon Slater being the most common.

Children's Time: Hard to Believe

Talk with the children about questions. What are some big things in the world they have questions about? *(Prompt them, as needed, with questions like "Why is the world round?" or "How do airplanes fly?" Be prepared for some amazing questions, and possibly some amazing answers! Don't feel the need to answer the children's questions; just celebrate them.)*

We all have questions. We all have things we wonder about. We all have things we're not sure of.

Last week was Easter Sunday, and we celebrated Jesus coming back to life. In fact, the Easter season goes for several weeks, and we keep celebrating that Jesus is alive and with us forever.

But it was hard for people to believe in those early days that Jesus was alive again. This had never happened before, and it was hard to understand. Most of the disciples got to see Jesus alive right away, but one of them wasn't there. His name was Thomas, and when the other disciples told him Jesus was alive, he just couldn't believe it.

A week later, Jesus came to see Thomas. Thomas wanted to believe it was Jesus, but he just couldn't – until he reached out and touched him. Then he knew.

It is all right to doubt, and to wonder, and to have questions. God is patient, and God understands our questions.

Prayer: Patient God, when we have questions, remind us that it is okay to wonder, even to doubt. Amen.

The Sermon: Rehabilitating a Reputation
Scripture: John 20:19-31
(For sermon materials on Acts 2:14a, 22-32, see the January/February 2011 issue of *The Clergy Journal*; for sermon materials on John 20:19-31, see the May/June 2010 planning issue of *The Clergy Journal*.)

Nicknames have a way of focusing on one aspect of a person's appearance or character, or on one incident in a person's life. In history classes we learned of people like Eric the Red, Richard the Lion-hearted, and the Mad King Ludwig, and in church we sing the carol about Good King Wenceslas.

We see something of the same kind of naming applied in our own life experience. A child fumbles a ball in a schoolyard baseball game and for long after is known as "Butterfingers." The smallest kid in the neighborhood is tagged "Pee-wee" and the name sticks. The roughest kid in town is known as "Bruiser," at least by those afraid of him. Few people get to choose their nicknames, and it's likely that few people are happy with how they are named and known in this way.

The disciple Thomas would very likely be upset at the way he has been remembered. Thomas is a disciple who showed great loyalty and bravery. When Jesus announced that he was going back to Judea, even though people there had previously tried to stone him, Thomas is the first to say, "Let us go with him." He was ready to stand by Jesus in the face of danger. Thomas is said to have brought Christianity eastward as far even as India. And yet, mention this disciple and most people will name him as "doubting Thomas."

The perception is so well entrenched that we may not hear or see anything else in this exciting and important story about the risen Christ appearing to the disciples. Thomas wasn't with the other disciples when Jesus first appeared. The Gospel tells us that they were hiding behind locked doors. Their teacher had been arrested, tried, and executed. Their world had been shaken, and they were afraid for their own lives.

We might wonder where Thomas was at this time. Perhaps he was less frightened. At any rate, he joins them later and hears their report that they have seen the Lord. The way the text is written the conversation flows immediately to Thomas saying that he needs to see the mark of the nails in Jesus' hands and the wound in his side. We have no information about what else might have been said or about tone or inflection in the voices, but we can consider that in asking to see the nail marks and the wound, Thomas was no more disbelieving than the other disciples had been in hearing the women tell of their experience at the empty tomb. The other disciples had heard Mary Magdalene's account of meeting the risen Christ, but her story hadn't convinced them. They were still hiding in fear behind locked doors.

If we look at this story with fresh eyes, we may see something quite wonderful in the interaction between Jesus and Thomas. It is a great reassurance to us with our own questions and hesitations that Jesus does not rebuke Thomas when he asks to see the nail marks and the wound. Thomas is expressing a heartfelt need, and Jesus graciously responds to that need. Jesus' first words spoken in this second appearance to his disciples are the same words spoken earlier to this group of shaken and fearful men: "Peace be with you." Not words of accusation or condemnation, but words of blessing and benediction.

We can try to imagine the tone of voice in which these words were spoken. We might hear the words spoken gently and lovingly, encouraging Thomas to move forward in his quest for reassurance. Jesus said to Thomas, "Put your finger here and see my hands. Reach out your hand and put it in my side." And in that same tone and manner, without rebuke or condemnation, Jesus offers invitation and encouragement: "Do not doubt, but believe."

It is also possible to imagine these words spoken just as lovingly but gushing forth, bursting with energy and enthusiasm. The word translated in English as *put* – as in Thomas saying that he must "put my finger in the mark of the nails and my hand in his side" – can be translated as *throw* in the original Greek. That word gives a sense of vitality and action to what Thomas asks and to how Jesus responds. We know what it means to "throw" ourselves into some cause or effort or mission or ministry. Thomas has "thrown" himself into his search for the truth of the Easter promise, and the risen Christ offers all of himself as the expression of God's love and grace and mercy and forgiveness.

There is an intimacy of relationship here that goes beyond the physical proximity of that particular gathering, at that particular time, in that particular room. In inviting Thomas to "reach out" his hand, Jesus is bridging all space and time to connect with us and our questions, our doubts, and our need to "see" Jesus and "feel" a connection with him. Whether Thomas actually followed through on the physical action of touching Jesus' hands and side, the story declares a spiritual and personal connection that enables Thomas to say, "My Lord and my God!"

The interaction between Thomas and Jesus is a powerful invitation and encouragement for each of us to ask questions, to present our spiritual needs, and to persevere until a helpful response is given. Thomas shows us how to ask bold questions and how to be ready and willing to take bold actions. Jesus shows us how to listen to what is really being said when difficult questions are put forward and how to bless the questioner with acceptance and inclusion.

We may not want to be associated with "doubting" Thomas, but we can be attracted by the strength and conviction of a faithful disciple who can ask a question and articulate a spiritual need, and respond with joy and gratitude when the question is heard and the need is met. Rather than this being a story about doubt, casting guilt upon those who may have their own questions, this is a story about new life. The risen Jesus, for a third time, says, "Peace be with you." Thomas, who has seen Jesus' hands and side, now sees something more in himself and responds in faith and trust: "My Lord and my God." May we do likewise.

– Gordon Timbers

Hymns
Opening Hymn
The Day of Resurrection
Alleluia, Alleluia, Give Thanks to the Risen Lord
Sermon Hymn
Jesus, Stand among Us
Where Charity and Love Prevail
Closing Hymn
Thine Be the Glory
Grateful for the Life You Give Us

May 8, 2011

3rd Sunday of Easter

Lessons

RCL	Roman Catholic
Acts 2:14a, 36-41	Acts 2:14, 22-28
Ps 116:1-4, 12-19	Ps 16:1-2, 5, 7-11
1 Pet 1:17-23	1 Pet 1:17-21
Lk 24:13-35	Lk 24:13-35

Speaker's Introduction for the Lessons
Lesson 1
Acts 2:14a, 36-41(RCL); 2:14, 22-28 (RC)

The narrative begun in the Gospel of Luke continues in the Acts of the Apostles, the second half of what scholars consider to be one volume together. The story of the early church begins here.

Lesson 2
Psalm 116:1-4, 12-19 (RCL)

This psalm of thanksgiving in the face of death would have been offered publicly as a thank offering when the suffering was complete. A portion of this psalm is also included in thanksgiving after childbirth.

Psalm 16:1-2, 5, 7-11 (RC)

This psalm is placed in a group of psalms called songs of trust. It features prominently a confidence in the faith in God.

Lesson 3
1 Peter 1:17-23 (RCL); 1:17-21 (RC)

First Peter is a pastoral letter written to Gentiles, resident aliens, and household slaves somewhere in Asia Minor. Being outsiders all, they are encouraged to find their identity in Christ.

Gospel
Luke 24:13-35 (RCL/RC)

Following the discovery of the empty tomb, the disciples scatter. The women wonder at what they'd seen, Peter checks on their report, and two disciples leave Jerusalem, believing that it is all over.

Theme

Truth is revealed when our stories are reinterpreted in the presence of Christ.

Thought for the Day

When have you experienced your "heart burn" with the recognition of God's presence?

Sermon Summary

Following his resurrection, Jesus meets two disciples on the road to Emmaus and invites them to tell the story of the events of the past days. Not knowing with whom they speak, they offer their limited explanation. Jesus listens patiently, then reinterprets the story and is revealed to them.

Call to Worship

One: What shall I return to the Lord for all his bounty to me?

All: I will lift up the cup of salvation and call on the name of the Lord.

One: I will pay my vows to the Lord in the presence of all his people.

All: In the courts of the house of the Lord, in your midst, O Jerusalem. Praise the Lord!

– Based on Psalm 116

Pastoral Prayer

We come before you, our loving God, like the psalmist in need of the refuge of your shelter; like the disciples, alone and uncertain, on the way to Emmaus so long ago. We come giving thanks for the mercy we have received from your presence revealed in ways that are beyond our comprehension. We seek your wisdom as we pour out the stories of our own hearts before you, trusting in your grace and vision for us. Reveal yourself to us as we gather in this hour, and open us to understanding ourselves and your story anew. Bless us as we strive to be faithful. Amen.

Prayer of Confession

Merciful God, we confess our weaknesses before you. Too many times we have been so consumed with our own needs, we failed to see the needs of others or of you. Too many times we have not believed, even though the truth was here among us. Open our eyes to see the suffering and opportunities around us. Open our hearts to receive the truth of your presence in the world. Forgive us, we pray, and strengthen us to live more faithfully. Amen.

Prayer of Dedication of Gifts and Self
Generous God, who gives so freely the gifts of love and grace that we may have new life, accept the gifts of our resources and of our lives this day. Like the psalmist, we dedicate our lives to you and offer this sacrifice of thanksgiving for your work here and in the world. Amen.

Hymn of the Day
I Want Jesus to Walk with Me
There is some disagreement as to the origin of this song of faith. Most scholars believe it to come from the African American slavery culture; however, some scholars believe this song to be a "white spiritual" coming from rural Appalachia. Whatever its origin, this is a strong song of faith – a faith that Jesus walks with us at all times, in all places, and in all circumstances. There is a stanza, left out of most denominational hymnals, that is very familiar to most African American assemblies – "He walked with my mother, he'll walk with me." This statement alone supports the case that this is not a questioning song but one of bold and steadfast faith. It should be sung with conviction.

Children's Time: Coming to Understand
(Preparation: Bring a large picture that you have covered with sticky notes that can be easily peeled off. Arrange the notes in a grid, so the picture is entirely covered and can slowly be revealed as the notes are removed. Alternatively, if you are able to obtain a camera that takes instant pictures – the kind that take a moment or two to appear – you could bring that.

Plan to take a photograph of the children, or of something in the church, and then wait together for the picture to appear. Or, show the large picture you have brought. Share the following story, and remove a tag after each sentence or more often as needed.)

Long ago, on that first Easter, a couple of disciples were walking to a town called Emmaus. They couldn't really understand what had happened, and they had not heard that Jesus was risen. They noticed a stranger come along, and mentioned about Jesus dying. The stranger told many of the things God had done through history. Slowly, the two disciples realized something incredible: it was as if Jesus was right there, walking with them! They were not alone anymore; Jesus was risen. When they got to Emmaus they could not wait to tell their friends.

(Continue to remove the sticky notes, or look again at the photograph, and talk about how sometimes it takes a while for things to appear, but when they do, it's a wonderful thing.)

Prayer: Thank you, God, for wonderful surprises. Thank you for the many ways we can feel Jesus alive and with us even today. Amen.

The Sermon: Telling the True Story
Scripture: Luke 24:13-35
(For sermon materials on Acts 2:14a, 36-41, see the January/February 2011 issue of *The Clergy Journal*; for sermon materials on Luke 24:13-35, see the May/June 2010 planning issue of *The Clergy Journal*.)

"Read me the story again," is a frequent refrain in many households as kids are growing up. Many parents read daily to children, often each night before they go to bed. Kids, like many of us, have favorite stories, and so you might find yourself sitting on the couch or in a favorite chair, night after night, turning the pages of stories you can recite by heart because of its familiarity. While some nights this clearly may be an intentional tactic to delay going to bed, one cannot deny the power of story to engage the heart and awaken the imagination.

Storytelling has long been at the center of the Judeo-Christian experience. In fact that is just what two disciples were doing as they walked the road from Jerusalem to Emmaus following the death and resurrection of Jesus. As they walked they talked about all the things that had recently happened and, unbeknownst to them, Jesus fell into step beside them. His question about their discussion launches them into a story, a story ironically that they expected he'd already heard (not knowing that the story they told was his own). And so at his insistence they begin again, relating the hopes and heartaches that had been played out over the past few days.

Telling the story – of our lives and of our congregations – is important work as we journey through life. Our story, and our perspective on it, is unique. It represents not only the facts or truth about what happened, but it also reveals something of our nature and our response to life's encounters.

The story of our congregation is the story of our faith. It is the story of how we have, over the years, striven to be good stewards of the resources of people, gifts, energies, time, and opportunity to tell the good news of Jesus Christ.

How effectively we tell our story influences how people will receive it. With words, pictures, video, in person, online, in printed materials, we tell the story of God's interaction with us and our call to be in service to the world. So as Jesus joins these disciples, it is no wonder this is where he begins, by asking them to tell their story. And he falls into step with them as they begin.

This is how the narrative process works! There is the storyteller, yes, but just as importantly, there is also the listener. Jesus listens as they tell their story and when they are finished he says, "How foolish you are, and how slow of heart to believe all that the prophets have declared!" It's like he says, "Oh, come on, folks! Get with the program! Is this *really all* you believe?" Jesus listens to their story and then he starts back near the beginning, with Moses and the prophets, and "interpreted to them the things about himself in all the scriptures." Jesus hears their words and he puts them in a different context, sheds new light. They tell their story and he brings fresh perspective! He re-interprets for them the things they *thought* they already knew.

As we tell our stories, either personal or communal, it is important for us to take the time to listen, to really hear what we are saying. It's important for us to ask ourselves, what is it that we are *really* communicating? When we tell the story of our congregation, what and who do we talk about? What places in our congregational story are missing or are told so many ways it's not clear what is actually true? What part of the story do we tell without fully understanding its meaning? The disciples told their story but failed to see what they told actually meant. We need to ask: do we understand the meaning of our own story? What of it remains a mystery? What of it rings true?

One of the difficult things about hearing a familiar story *is* discovering something new. The more familiar we are with the story the less able we are to step back from it, to hear it as if for the very first time. The more conditioned we are to hear the story told in the same voice, at the same pace, with the same language, the more innocuous it becomes! The surer we are that we know the outcome, that we've memorized the script, the less engaging, the less transformative its power!

It is like the times some of us have read to children who have memorized the book. After reading the same story night after night, you can (and many do) close your eyes and say the words while they flip the pages! But what happens if you skip a word or drop a line? You can be sure they will notice. We don't dare change the words or the rhyme or the rhythm. The surer we are of the story the less open we are to hearing it a new way. Interestingly enough, Jesus meets the disciples on the road and tells them their *own* story in a new way. And sure enough, they heard something that they had not heard before.

What makes a story transformative is the power it has to connect with and change our lives. Luke tells us that the disciples can go no farther alone; I suspect that is both a literal and figurative truth. They invite Jesus to stay with them to bless and break of bread. And the connection was made. What was familiar, this table ritual, became new again. What was hidden, revealed. What was lacking, complete. The story became clear and the truth it held evident. In that moment, their eyes are opened and they see Jesus, and likely themselves, in a whole new light.

People of God, listen to your own story with open hearts, with attentive spirits. What is compelling about the words we speak? Where in the story do we invite others to make a connection, to find their place? In the familiar rituals of worship, education, service, can we find fresh insight? In the words we say and live, can we find nourishment for our souls? It wasn't until the disciples invited Jesus to *stay with them* that their eyes were opened, that they experienced true communion, that their "hearts burned" within. May this Living Christ stay with *us* in this Easter season, that *our* eyes might be opened, that *we* might experience true communion, that *our* hearts might burn with story of our own vision for the story that gives us life.

– Marcia Bailey

Hymns
4/30/17
Opening Hymn
He Lives
I Want Jesus to Walk with Me
Sermon Hymn
Jesus, Sovereign, Savior
Be Known to Us in Breaking Bread
Closing Hymn
Abide with Me 97
Lead On Eternal Sovereign

May 15, 2011

4th Sunday of Easter

Lessons

RCL	Roman Catholic
Acts 2:42-47	Acts 2:14, 36-41
Ps 23	Ps 23
1 Pet 2:19-25	1 Pet 2:20-25
Jn 10:1-10	Jn 10:1-10

Speaker's Introduction for the Lessons
Lesson 1
Acts 2:42-47 (RCL); 2:14, 36-41 (RC)

Koinonia is the Greek word for what is described in Acts 2. The early believers shared a common life, not only out of economic necessity but also out of a belief that they shared a common relationship in the love of Jesus Christ.

Lesson 2
Psalm 23 (RCL/RC)

This well-known "shepherd's psalm" dates from the postexilic period when focus on an individual's relationship with God was common. It is perhaps its personal nature that has drawn so many to its poetic beauty.

Lesson 3
1 Peter 2:19-25 (RCL); 2:20-25 (RC)

These verses are addressed to slaves and present some difficult ideas, especially in light of our own view of slavery today. The fact the Christ is used as an example to slaves for living their plight makes this interesting imagery for both.

Gospel
John 10:1-10 (RCL/RC)

Jesus' descriptive use of an actual sheepfold must have made vivid connections with his livestock-tending hearers, though it may be more difficult for us to imagine today. Regardless, the Shepherd reaches out to all the "sheep."

Theme

Jesus is both our protector and our source for abundant life.

Thought for the Day

In what ways do we facilitate or deny others access to God?

Sermon Summary

Jesus' description of himself as the "gate" is both a model for and a challenge to our own welcome of those who would follow him. There are many ways we put barriers in the paths of believers, in contrast to the freedom of the welcome Jesus offers us all, a welcome that includes the gift of abundant life.

Call to Worship

One: Jesus says, "I am the gate."
All: "Whoever enters by me will be saved and will come in and go out and find pasture."
One: "The thief comes only to steal and kill and destroy."
All: But Jesus came that we may have life, and have it abundantly!

– Adapted from John 10:9, 10

Pastoral Prayer

O God of life, we celebrate the gift of your presence with us this day! We hear your invitation to follow you, to know your guidance, love, and protecting care. Help us to be faithful to you. Open to us the gate of welcome; teach us what it means to have life that is full. May our words and actions be a welcome gate for others, that each one might know your tender care and call your presence "home." Amen.

Prayer of Confession

O God who gathers us into your care, we confess that more times than not, we have strayed from you. We have wandered into places of our own choosing, rather than heeding your call to follow you. We have gotten lost, hurt, waylaid all because we failed to hear you call our names. At times, we have even blocked the path of others who seek you. Be merciful to us, we pray. Welcome us into your presence once again, and remind us that nothing we do can keep us away from you. Amen.

Prayer of Dedication of Gifts and Self

You call us by name, Good Shepherd, and invite us to follow you, both into the safety of the fold and into the challenge of the world. Accept the gifts we bring – both of our resources and ourselves – that we might respond with joy and thanksgiving to all that you offer to us. Amen.

Hymn of the Day
You Satisfy the Hungry Heart

Omar Westendorf's text, paired with Robert Kreutz's tune, Finest Wheat, was the winning hymn in a competition for a theme hymn for the 41st Eucharistic Congress of the Roman Catholic Church held in Philadelphia in 1976. Originally named Bicentennial for the year of its composition, the tune was renamed to more closely match the text. As with other hymns that start with or have a refrain, stanzas may be sung by a soloist or the choir while the refrain is sung by the whole congregation. The tune lacks a common time signature; rather it moves between four and three beats per measure, according to the rhythm of the text. Sing with flexibility, yet with a steady pulse. Use a moderate tempo to allow both the text and the music time to breathe.

Children's Time: Jesus Is Our Shepherd

(Preparation: You could bring a picture of Jesus with children, and/or a picture of Jesus as a shepherd – preferably a more modern one; however, neither picture is necessary. If you bring them, use them to illustrate the conversation as appropriate.)

Talk with the children about who takes care of them. They might say parents, teachers, daycare providers, grandparents, and so forth. What kinds of things do these people do? How do they care for us? How do they help us get the most out of life?

Jesus talked about how he wanted to care for us. He knew that people of all ages need to feel loved and cared for. Jesus also wanted us to know that God loves us very much.

Jesus said he was going to be like a shepherd. What does a shepherd do? *(The children may have varying awareness of this image. Share with them that a shepherd looks after sheep, feeding them, giving them water, keeping wild animals away, tending to their injuries, and generally watching over them.)* Jesus knew that the people he was talking to would understand what he was saying because where Jesus lived there were lots of sheep.

Jesus might have said he wanted to be like our parents or our teacher or our babysitters. What Jesus wants us to understand is that he cares for us. He wants us to have enough to eat and drink. He wants us to feel loved and cared for and safe.

Jesus is our shepherd. Jesus is our best friend. Jesus is someone who watches out for us and wants us to have the best life we can have.

Prayer: Thank you, God, that you have sent Jesus to be our shepherd and friend, to care for us and show us your love always. Amen.

The Sermon: Easy Access
Scripture: John 10:1-10
(For sermon materials on Acts 2:42-47, see the January/February 2011 issue of *The Clergy Journal*; for sermon materials on Psalm 23, see the May/June 2010 planning issue of *The Clergy Journal*.)

My Dad sat beside me a few weeks ago as I drove through the southern Adirondacks. We were looking for a place to have dinner and as we came into view of a restaurant he said, "We could try that place; we've never been there before." Slowing down, I quickly looked the place over. "I don't think so Dad," I found myself saying. "There isn't any access; we can't get you in." In silence we drove on.

You see, my father uses a wheelchair. Three more times as we continued on that road that afternoon, the conversation repeated itself: you can't go there; there is no way for you to get in. I was saddened, struck again by the limitations placed on him, on any, who for whatever reason can't negotiate flights of stairs, narrow doors, walkways cluttered by merchandise – all barriers that told us at worst, we were not welcome; at best, no one thought that someone like us might want to come.

The text this morning seems to be all about shepherds and sheep and things disconnected from where most of us find ourselves today. Jesus speaks first about the nature of a sheepfold – a place where shepherds gathered their flocks overnight, where the intimacy of knowing and being known was experienced, where the shared protection of walls and other shepherds ensured the flock was safe. "He calls his own sheep by name," Jesus says, "and leads them out. When he has brought out all his own, he goes ahead of them, and the sheep follow him because they know his voice" (Jn10: 3b, 4). The sheepfold was a place of welcome, of community, of security and rest. But that didn't seem to clarify anything for the Pharisees who were listening, so Jesus tries again.

"Very truly, I tell you, I am the gate for the sheep." And again in verse nine, "I am the gate. Whoever enters by me will be saved, and will come in and go out and find pasture." And in verse 10, "I came that they may have life," Jesus says, "and have it abundantly" (Jn 10: 7a, 9, 10b).

Jesus is the gate! The way in . . . and the way out! The entry point, the access, the one through whom one must pass in order to find safety and respite. For religious leaders who thought *they* set the criteria for who had access to the benefits of God, this only added to their shock and confusion.

Think about gates for a moment. Some gates are made to keep people or things in: children in playgrounds, pets in backyards. Other gates are there to keep us out: gates at the end of long, private driveways, gates around businesses, gates around properties. A garden gate draped with flowering vines can welcome us into a place of beauty and delight. Gates topped with barbed wire send an entirely different message.

And then there are gatekeepers, those who monitor the gate, deciding who gets through, who has access to what or whom. Watch dogs and security personnel are the most obvious gatekeepers we might think of, but what about the person who stands between you and your next promotion? What about boards or committees with excess power and influence? How about the folks who say "we don't do it that way around here" or "you don't belong here" because of what you believe or who you love, the color of your skin or your gender or your age?

But notice Jesus doesn't say he's a *gatekeeper*. Jesus says "I am the gate." He is the gate itself, inviting "whoever" to enter, and "be saved," allowing easy access, in and out, safety, and life (vs. 10). Jesus is the gate, the *way* to relationship and intimacy with God. Jesus is the gate, the place of welcome, security, freedom, and rest. Jesus says to the Pharisees and any others listening that he isn't about restricting or stealing or harming but about offering life – abundant life; life that is sweet and whole and full.

And so I wonder about this kind of easy access . . . do if we find or offer it in our own lives, in our own church? I wonder about this kind of unfettered welcome where folks can come and go, where *abundance* is what life is all about.

There are lots of churches where multiple gatekeepers obscure the welcome of the "Jesus gate," plenty of places where folks who don't fit the theological, physical, or spiritual mold aren't invited in. Making churches handicap accessible is a great challenge for many with old buildings; it can be nearly impossible to invest the money necessary so that all can literally come in.

But churches can be inaccessible in many other ways as well. In recent visits to churches I was surprised to see all the ways we limit people's access to our communities, even to God. We abbreviate things in the bulletin (to save space we say) so that only those who "know" get the message. We say "everyone's welcome," but we don't say *where* we're meeting or *how* to get there or *what* we're really about. We give lip service to wanting everyone to feel "at home" but we don't *really* mean we want homeless people, or sexual minority people, or people who are more conservative or more liberal than us, or deaf or blind people, or people who speak another language holding our babies and teaching our children and serving as church officers, do we?

If we *are* open to these ones, then we need to ask ourselves: "How will these people *know* they are welcome here?" And if we aren't open to them, we need to ask: "What is it about these persons that we are afraid of? What makes us withhold the welcome of Jesus to them?"

"I am the gate," Jesus says. "Whoever enters by me will be saved, and will come in and go out and find pasture (refreshment, relaxation, peace, rest). I have come that they may have life, and have it abundantly." Easy access, a genuine welcome, abundant living.

May we hear this word of welcome to *each of us*, and may *our faith* be lived in such a way that we grant easy access to any and all who seek the Jesus gate and with it, abundant life!

– Marcia Bailey

Hymns
Opening Hymn
God Is My Shepherd
Savior, Like a Shepherd Lead Us
Sermon Hymn
My Shepherd Is the Living God
My Shepherd Will Supply My Need
Closing Hymn
We Cannot Own the Sunlit Sky
Won't You Let Me Be Your Servant?

May 22, 2011

5th Sunday of Easter

Lessons

RCL	Roman Catholic
Acts 7:55-60	Acts 6:1-7
Ps 31:1-5, 15-16	Ps 33:1-2, 4-5, 18-19
1 Pet 2:2-10	1 Pet 2:4-9
Jn 14:1-14	Jn 14:1-12

Speaker's Introduction for the Lessons
Lesson 1
Acts 7:55-60 (RCL)

This passage depicts the death of Stephen, a martyr for the Christian faith who was charged with prophesying against the temple. His outspoken witness is the first which separates the early Christian believers from Judaism, and this cost him his life.

Acts 6:1-7 (RC)

As the church grew in numbers, caring for its members became an issue. The apostles led by bringing the church together and working together to solve the problem. And "the word of God continued to spread."

Lesson 2
Psalm 31:1-5, 15-16 (RCL)

This psalm is a combination of three laments: the first a "protecting psalm," the second a lament of one who is sick, and the third a lament of one who is falsely charged.

Psalm 33:1-2, 4-5, 18-19 (RC)

In this hymn the just are invited to praise God, for the greatness of human beings consists in God's choosing them as a special people.

Lesson 3
1 Peter 2:2-10 (RCL); 2:4-9 (RC)
>1 Peter is believed to be written by the Apostle Peter with the influence and help of Silvanus. In this passage, a mixture of images is presented. The first are used to characterize believers who are exhorted to faithfulness. The imagery then turns to Christ and the church.

Gospel
John 14:1-14 (RCL); 14:1-12 (RC)
>This familiar passage begins what is known as Jesus' farewell discourse and prayer found in John 14-17. It is John's interpretation of Jesus' finished work and the connection it has to believers when he is no longer with them.

Theme
We know the way of Jesus through the faithfulness of those who believe.

Thought for the Day
Each of us, by word and deed, points out the way of Jesus in the world.

Sermon Summary
In a time of uncertainty, the disciples struggle to understand Jesus when he speaks of leaving, preparing a place for them, and coming again. Not knowing where he's going, Thomas asks, "How can we know the way?" That's a question many of us ask today. Jesus invites them to see God in the words and works he has performed, believing that he is the way, truth, and life. Like Jesus, believers today show the way by the witness and actions they take in the world, pointing others on the path to God.

Call to Worship
>One: People of God, come follow the Way!
>**All: We want to walk in the footsteps of Jesus.**
>One: People of God, come seek the Truth!
>**All: We desire to live lives that reflect the love and mercy of our God.**
>One: People of God, come embrace the Life!
>**All: Jesus is our way, truth, and life! We live our lives in Him!**
>– Adapted from John 14:6

Pastoral Prayer

With gratitude and praise, we give thanks, O God, that you are the way and the truth and the life. In the midst of uncertain times, in trouble and turmoil, confusion and unrest, you point the way to love and life, and we seek to follow on your path. We ask for your guidance as we live our lives in you. Help us to love as you love, rejoice as you rejoice, forgive as you forgive, enact justice when you would speak. Just as you were revealed in the mission and ministry of Jesus, so may our lives show forth your presence each day. May others look at us and see your face, hear your voice, know your touch, experience your peace, because we live and love because of Jesus. Amen.

Prayer of Confession

O God, we confess that we have lost our way. We have not followed in your footsteps; we have not helped our sisters and brothers to find your path. Forgive us our distractions and set our feet on your path again. Empowered by your grace, direct us as we seek to follow you once again, walking in your truth and bringing to light your life. Amen.

Prayer of Dedication of Gifts and Self

We return to you, O God, gifts that are not our own. We gratefully know that they come from your generous hand. As we follow in your way, may all that we have and all that we do be an expression of our gratitude to you. Amen.

Hymn of the Day
Come, My Way, My Truth, My Life

The text, based on part of the Gospel for the day, is from *The Temple* (1633), a collection of poetry by George Herbert. It was published after the poet's death in 1633 by Nicholas Ferrar. The tune, THE CALL by Ralph Vaughan Williams, is based on one of his *Five Mystical Songs* (1911). The hymn arrangement was created by E. Harold Geer and published in *Yale Hymnal for Colleges and Schools* (1956). This well-known text takes some thought and effort to reveal its full meaning. During the preparation time before the congregation sings this hymn, introduce the tune and text in a number of ways: as an organ solo or in its original form as a vocal solo from the song cycle. This hymn is worth whatever effort it takes to introduce it to your congregation.

Children's Time: The Way, the Truth, and the Life

Talk with the children about how we are still in the season of Easter. We're celebrating that Jesus is alive and with us always. It's a very special time.

In one of our Bible readings today Jesus says, "I am the way, and the truth, and the life." Kind of a funny thing to say, isn't it? Let's look at what it might mean:

Jesus said, "I am the way." Jesus showed us how to live in God's way. Jesus showed us how important it was to love others, especially those who other people say aren't worth it. Jesus showed us how to forgive others, and how to get along with people. He wants us to follow his example and live the way that God wants.

Jesus said, "I am the truth." We can trust the things that Jesus tells us. He tells us that God loves us. He tells us that God promises us life that never ends. Even when we die, we'll live forever with God. Jesus tells us that we can trust that.

Jesus said, "I am the life." When Jesus is our friend, life is better. We know that whatever happens to us, we won't be alone because Jesus is with us, even though we can't see him. He reminds us that God loves us always. That makes life special.

Jesus is the way, the truth, and the life. Hallelujah!

Prayer: Loving God we thank you that Jesus has shown us about your love, and how you want us to live. Amen.

The Sermon: How Can We Know the Way?
Scripture: John 14:1-14

(For sermon materials on Acts 7:55-60, see the January/February 2011 issue of *The Clergy Journal*; for sermon materials on 1 Peter 2:2-10, see the May/June 2010 planning issue of *The Clergy Journal*.)

Recently, a friend of mine who is not good with directions purchased a car with a GPS. Although traveling a familiar road, he decided to try it out. It just so happened that there had been recent road construction in the area, but the work had been finished for several months. As he made a turn onto a section of the newly constructed road, the GPS began to "speak" loudly, repeatedly imploring, "Stop! You are off the road! You are off the road!" The further my friend drove, the louder and more insistent the automated voice became. "You are OFF the road!" Knowing full well he was indeed, not off the road, he switched off the GPS, not at all convinced that he had found anything that could show him the way.

How can we know the way? It's a fitting and unsettling question for times such as these. In the last few years, with no outline, no road map, no blueprint before us, we have found ourselves propelled onto the landscape of economic meltdown, global warfare, and political standoffs. We are "off the road!" Most of us have not traveled this way before and feel as if we are being swept along in directions without clear courses. We find ourselves on new roads, discover we are in unfamiliar territory, arriving at destinations not of our own choosing. As we seek to make sense of the landscape we wonder which path to take. Which direction is correct? How *can* we know the way?

How can we know the way? That is the question the disciples ask Jesus. While they have been with Jesus nearly his entire ministry, they don't understand what he means when he speaks of his departure; he told them that where he is going they cannot follow now (Jn 13:36). But then he speaks of places prepared for them. This idea that their communion with him might continue after he is gone baffles them. They fail to comprehend what dwelling places with God have to do with their lives in the present. His assumption that they know where he is going compels Thomas to express their ignorance and uncertainty: "Lord, we do not know where you are going. How can we know the way?" Jesus' answer seems about as helpful as my friend's GPS: he tells them that if they know God, then they know him. But even that is not clear enough.

In a world of GPS, I continue to be fond of road maps. I find maps fascinating because they show the relationships things have to each other. Distances and landmarks, choices of routes and other possible destinations, all become clear on a road map. Maps locate us in the large scheme of things; they remind us that we are not isolated, and that the distance and geography between us has tangible effects on the choices we make. But what maps don't tell us is which route to take; we get to make that decision ourselves. And it is that choice that seemed to trouble the disciples as Jesus prepares to leave them.

How can we know the way? In uncertain times – like those of the disciples and we ourselves – many look for direction and guidance on the way. Jesus declares himself the "way, and the truth, and the life," opening up new possibilities for relationship and communion with him. He speaks about knowing him by his words and works, thus revealing not only himself, but the very heart of God. Perhaps more like a road map than a GPS, Jesus does not declare us "off the road" but instead invites us to the way as a path of action and witness, discovered as we look at him, and as we look *like* him.

Like a road map, it is the relationship to others that mark the works of Jesus, pointing the way to God. When he fed the hungry, healed the sick, spoke to outsiders, Jesus revealed not only his own loving, justice-driven nature but that of God's. He says to the disciples, If you want to know what God looks like, look at my relationships with others, then you'll see God. Just as a road map reveals relationships between places and people, our own actions reveal the relationships we have with the world in a way that can point others to God.

We show the way when we incarnate the love and mercy of Jesus in our own lives, in our own surroundings. When we serve soup in the men's shelter, comfort women who've experienced abuse, give clothing to children who don't have enough, we become the way for others who are searching for God. When we gather for worship, stand for justice, weep with the oppressed, and welcome the stranger, then we are become the path that leads to love, that leads to God. Jesus tells the disciples to believe that he and God are one, but if they cannot, then "believe me because of the works themselves" (v. 11b). Likewise, if others cannot believe the words we say, then the lives we live must point the way.

We have lived in our present home for 15 years and yet one of the more popular search engines for finding directions has yet to realize that we are here. Folks looking for our home are quick to point out that we aren't even on the map! While it's merely inconvenient for them and us, think how tragic such a reality could be if we who believe aren't demonstrative enough in our faith to be "on the map." Just as the disciples looked to Jesus to discover the way, others are looking at us today. As people of faith, we have a responsibility to translate our belief into action so that others may see what we do and find themselves invited to follow the way.

How can we know the way? We know the way when we allow our hearts to be captured by the love and grace of God demonstrated in the tangible ministries of Jesus. We *become* the way for others when we live lives that incarnate that mercy in the world around us, followers of the way giving light to others on the path.

– Marcia Bailey

Hymns
Opening Hymn
Jesus the Christ Says
Sekai no Tomo (Here, O God, Your Servants Gather)
Sermon Hymn
Come, My Way, My Truth, My Life
You Are the Way
Closing Hymn
O Jesus, I Have Promised
Teach Me, O Lord, Your Holy Way

May 29, 2011

6th Sunday of Easter

Lessons

RCL	Roman Catholic
Acts 17:22-31	Acts 8:5-8, 14-17
Ps 66:8-20	Ps 66:1-7, 16-20
1 Pet 3:13-22	1 Pet 3:15-18
Jn 14:15-21	Jn 14:15-21

Speaker's Introduction for the Lessons

Lesson 1
Acts 17:22-31 (RCL); 8:5-8, 14-17 (RC)

It has been said that a better title for "The Acts of the Apostles" is "The Acts of the Holy Spirit." Whether preaching, teaching, healing, or baptizing, the Spirit causes the young church to grow.

Lesson 2
Psalm 66:8-20 (RCL); 66:1-7, 16-20 (RC)

The psalmists almost always begin with their experience – in their history and the history of their people, they testify to God's presence or absence, and speak their praise, their petition, or their lament.

Lesson 3
1 Peter 3:13-22 (RCL); 3:15-18 (RC)

First Peter was written to believers living in Asia Minor whose faith was tested by periodic hostility toward and persecutions of Christians.

Gospel
John 14:15-21 (RCL/RC)

On the last night with his disciples, Jesus prepares the disciples for life without him.

Theme

Jesus does not leave us alone in our discipleship.

Thought for the Day
Love has little meaning outside of a commitment.

Sermon Summary
Jesus calls his disciples to demonstrate their love by keeping his command-ments. Jesus does not abandon us to honor this commitment on our own. He sends the Spirit to abide in us and remind us of everything he taught us.

Call to Worship
One: Make a joyful noise to God, all the earth!
All: Sing the glory of God's name.
One: Come and see what God has done. God is awesome in his deeds among mortals.
All: Sing the glory of God's name.
One: Bless our God, O peoples, let the sound of praise be heard.

– Adapted from Psalm 66

Pastoral Prayer
Commandment is not often the word we want to hear from you, covenanting God. We are wary of being told what to do. And yet your command to love one another is the key to our greatest joy and our greatest challenge. Help us to embody that commandment each day. Send us your Spirit to strengthen us to serve as you served, to give as you gave, to trust as you trusted, to love as you loved. Abide in us so that we might abide in you. Walk alongside us so that we might walk alongside you. Give us courage to keep our commitment to love one another so that your love might be known in every corner of our world. Amen.

Prayer of Confession
Forgive us, loving God, for the times when we have not loved as you have commanded. Forgive us when we have neglected this commitment to you. Forgive us for times when our talk of love has been cheap. Open us to your Spirit each day so that we might have courage to lead lives worthy of your calling. Deepen our capacity to love one another in our church, in our families, in our workplaces, and everywhere you send us. In Christ's name we pray. Amen.

Prayer of Dedication of Gifts and Self

We thank you for the gifts of the earth, the works of our hands, and the voices that you gave to us to share in song together. We thank you especially this day for your commitment to love us, a commitment that you honor and keep. Use these gifts, and use us to love our neighbors here in this community and around the world, so that more may know of your healing, your love, and your hope. Amen.

Hymn of the Day
Wa wa wa Emimimo/Come, O Holy Spirit, Come

This song was first presented at a World Council of Churches and then paraphrased by ethnomusicologist and professor of church music, I-to Loh. It is easy to attain a reasonably authentic presentation of this African song. The singing should be unadorned and unaccompanied with the use of hand percussion. The part singing – women sing the call and men sing the response – is very important but not difficult. With a little encouragement, the men will enjoy singing their own part. Once the meaning of the song has been conveyed, sing in the original Yoruba. It makes the singing more authentic, but also easier, as syllabic stress fit the music.

Children's Time: The Spirit of God

(Preparation: Bring a feather.)

Jesus' disciples knew that, even though he had risen from the dead, he would not be with them always. They seemed worried that they would be left all alone again, so Jesus told them something important.

"I'm going to ask God to send you a Spirit, who will be with you forever."

We cannot see a spirit, but we can often know it's there. It's a little bit like the wind: we cannot see it, but we can feel it. *(You may want to blow gently on the feather, and/or invite the children to blow on their hands.)*

We can see what the wind does. We can feel it. And because of that, we know that air exists.

Jesus said God's Spirit would be like an advocate. That's someone who speaks for you and defends you. It was if Jesus wanted us to think of God's spirit as our friend, as one who would help bring us closer to God, just as Jesus had done.

God's Spirit is with us always. We may not see it, but often we can feel it *(blow again on the feather).*

Prayer: Thank you, God, that you sent your Spirit to be with us always. Amen.

The Sermon: Here to Stay
Scripture: John 14:15-21

(For sermon materials on Acts 17:22-31, see the January/February 2011 issue of *The Clergy Journal*; for sermon materials on 1 Peter 3:13-22, see the May/June 2010 planning issue of *The Clergy Journal*.)

I've never been big on obedience theology. The concept of obedience carries negative connotations for me. It takes knowing only one battered wife who was told to be "obedient" to her husband, or one abused child who was told he must be "obedient" to his parents to convince me that obedience is a dangerous concept. So when Jesus says, "If you love me, you will keep my commandments," the red flags are waving.

Just to make sure I wasn't overreacting, I tried this out on my partner in marriage. I told her, "If you love me, you will clean out the cat's litter box." I didn't get a very positive response. Things didn't work out as well for me as they did for Jesus.

"We love God because God first loved us" – that's what I've always been taught. God loves us before we know it, before we are able to claim or respond to that love. Here in John, Jesus seems to flip that on its head. "They who have my commandments and keep them are those who love me; and those who love me will be loved by my Father, and I will love them and reveal myself to them." If you love me, you will do what I tell you to do.

I was feeling a familiar resistance to the whole commandment thing until I remembered a conversation I had with a teenager about his drug-addicted mother. "I used to believe her when she told me that she loved me," he said, "until she started selling our food stamps to buy her drugs. Then I knew the truth – that she loved her drugs more than she loved us." For this teenager, talk of love was cheap without a commitment to go along with it. That's true for parents, true for spouses, true for followers of Jesus. Love is not good intentions. It is a commitment, a commitment that Jesus *requires* from his followers.

That commitment isn't manipulative on Jesus' part. Jesus doesn't tell his disciples to clean out the litter box. He doesn't command them to stand in for him when the crowds get rough, or the empire comes calling. He doesn't command them to take his place on the cross. He doesn't ask them to do anything that he's not willing to do himself. He doesn't take advantage of his power to force them to do something against their will.

He simply defines what it means to love him, making clear that love is unintelligible without concrete acts of commitment to define it. He commands them to love God and to love each other – to make that commitment and to keep it.

This kind of commitment seems increasingly scarce today. Financial institutions that are "too big to fail" come crashing down. Workers who have given decades of their lives have their loyalty repaid with layoffs. Relationships that once felt invincible suddenly crumble. Then we wonder if all talk of commitment is cheap.

Only then do I realize just how important this obedience theology is for our faith. Following the one who laid down his life for his friends, we don't have to wonder whether God's commitment to us can be trusted. We don't have to wonder whether God's talk of love is cheap. Jesus has already kept every commitment he made to the Father and made to us. The commitment that Jesus requires from his followers is a commitment that Jesus has already kept. God's love for us is proven and palpable.

Perhaps this is why, in the wake of Jesus' commandment to be obedient, the disciples seem to be worried. "Do not let your hearts be troubled," Jesus says. And later, "I will not leave you orphaned." And still again, "Do not let your hearts be troubled, and do not let them be afraid." Perhaps the disciples know just how difficult it is, and will be, to keep Jesus' commandments. Perhaps they know that they are not able to keep this commitment as Jesus did. Perhaps they are worried that in the absence of Jesus they are not up to the task.

If so, it's not an unreasonable worry. All through the Gospels, the disciples demonstrate again and again their inability to do what Jesus asks of them. The have trouble healing like he heals. They turn children away when they ought to welcome them. They fall asleep when he tells them to stay awake. They doubt when he commands them to trust. The disciples have a checkered record when it comes to keeping Jesus' commandments – and that's when he's with them. It's not unreasonable to fret over how they'll perform when he's gone.

Jesus, who is in the better position to judge their fitness for discipleship, doesn't seem worried at all. There is another "advocate," the Spirit, who will come to them. This Spirit will function like a steadfast tutor, reminding them of everything that Jesus taught them. They will know this Spirit because "he abides with you, and he will be in you." It's hard to overstate the importance of that promise to those early disciples. The death or departure of most teachers surely would have meant the end of the community they spawned. If not for the Spirit, it's likely that the disciples would have returned home to start over. If not for the Spirit, they might have never dared to continue what their teacher had taught them.

That's good news for those of us who know that we are more like the disciples than we'd like to admit. When you make the commitment to keep Jesus' commandments you're not going to be left alone to make good on your promises. When you make the commitment to love one another just as God has loved us, you don't have to navigate that commitment on your own. Your knowledge of just how difficult it is to keep Jesus' commandments need not dissuade you from making that commitment.

On the last night with their teacher before his death, I doubt the disciples understood who this Spirit was or what this Spirit would mean for the community of faith. Apparently, their lack of understanding didn't dissuade them from trying to make good on the commitment they had made to Jesus. What they did seem to hear clearly and understand completely was that the coming of the Spirit meant Jesus would never leave them orphaned – love was here to stay. Maybe that is the most important thing that any follower of Jesus needs to know.

– Andrew Foster Connors

Hymns
Opening Hymn
> O God the Creator
> Great God, Your Love Has Called Us Here

Sermon Hymn
> More Love to Thee, O Christ
> Spirit of God, Descend Upon My Heart

Closing Hymn
> Love Divine, All Love Excelling
> Let Every Christian Pray

June 2, 2011

Ascension Day

Lessons

RCL	Roman Catholic
Acts 1:1-11	Acts 1:1-11
Ps 47 or Ps 93	Ps 47:2-3, 6-9
Eph 1:15-23	Eph 1:17-23
Lk 24:44-53	Mt 28:16-20

Speaker's Introduction for the Lessons
Lesson 1
Acts 1:1-11 (RCL/RC)

Luke's Gospel closes with Jesus giving final instructions to his disciples before ascending to heaven. But Acts, the sequel to Luke's Gospel, opens with a different version of the same event.

Lesson 2
Psalm 47 (RCL); 47:2-3, 6-9 (RC)

Sometimes we are deluded into thinking that earthly powers have the last word. The psalmist retells the narrative with God at the center.

Lesson 3
Ephesians 1:15-23 (RCL); 1:17-23 (RC)

Unlike other Pauline epistles, Paul's letter to the Ephesians does not appear to address any particular concern other than a plea for unity in Jesus Christ.

Gospel
Luke 24:44-53 (RCL)

In this final post-resurrection gathering with his disciples, Jesus gives them final instructions before ascending to heaven.

Matthew 28:16-20 (RC)

The end of Matthew's Gospel signals a new beginning in the ministry of the disciples and of those of us who come after them.

Theme

God gives us space to grieve our losses.

Thought for the Day

In times of loss, rather than willing our way into hope, Jesus invites us to wait for it, trusting that it will come.

Sermon Summary

The disciples are not prepared to lose Jesus a second time. Jesus does not tell them to get over it. He gives them space to grieve their losses. This time of waiting is what prepares them to receive the new thing – the presence of the Holy Spirit.

Call to Worship

> One: Come into the presence of the living God. Bring your whole being to worship our Lord.
>
> **All: We bring it to the Lord.**
>
> One: Bring your anger.
>
> **All: We bring it to the Lord.**
>
> One: Bring your hatred.
>
> **All: We bring it to the Lord.**
>
> One: Bring your sorrow.
>
> **All: We bring it to the Lord.**
>
> One: Bring your deepest wound.
>
> **All: We bring it to the Lord.**
>
> One: Bring your whole being to the living God. Wait here for healing. Wait here for justice. Wait here for freedom. Wait here for peace. Come into the presence of the living God.

Pastoral Prayer

You know what it means to suffer loss, crucified God. So we turn to you in the worst of transitions in our lives. When the cancer comes back, we turn to you. When we lose our direction, or someone we love, or lose our way in life, we turn to you. We thank you that even in your departures, you do not leave us alone. You send your Spirit to come and shelter us, to come and nurture us, to come and nudge as back into the wounds of the world bearing gifts that you have given to us. We praise you for this gift and for the healing that your Spirit brings. Strengthen us through every loss so that we may strengthen others. Amen.

Prayer of Confession

Healing God, we do not always grieve well. Sometimes we ignore our losses as if they do not affect us. Sometimes we despair over them, convinced that we are a people without hope. Give us space to speak our losses in prayer and in community with fellow disciples. Give us time to grieve so that we might be prepared to receive a new kind of power, not to replace what we have lost, but to remake us into your people – wounded healers, sent out into the world to share the good news of your forgiving love. Amen.

Prayer of Dedication of Gifts and Self

You have shared your breath, your life, and your heart with us. Now we give ourselves back to you. Use these gifts of money and music, and use us to do the work of your Spirit in this congregation, in this city, in every place where you send us. Amen.

Hymn of the Day
Hail the Day that Sees Him [Christ] Rise

This text was written by Charles Wesley and first appeared in *Hymns and Sacred Poems* (1739). It was written for Ascension Day; however the original text did not have any alleluias. They were added in 1852 by G.E. White. There are several tunes associated with this text. The most common are LLANFAIR by Robert Williams, ASCENSION (MONK) by William H. Monk, and GWALCHMAI by Joseph D. Jones. All are strong tunes that suit this text. Sing with vigor. A suggestion is that everyone sings the first stanza in unison before having experienced singers move into harmony. Brass will add greatly to the presentation; however, organ would be considered the standard instrument for accompaniment.

Children's Time: The Church Is Jesus' Body

(Preparation: Bring a whiteboard or newsprint pad and marker.)

Today is Ascension, the day we remember the story of Jesus going back to heaven to be with God. *(Invite the children to explore with you how the disciples might have felt about this.)* The disciples might have felt kind of lost and alone, and not sure what to do, now that Jesus was gone.

However, Jesus wasn't really gone. His Spirit was still here – his Spirit is still here today. It guides us and helps us to know what to do. And the Bible tells us that Jesus' body is here, too. Do you know how? Well, it says that the church is Jesus' body.

That might sound kind of strange, but it's very true. *(Draw a simple body outline on the board or newsprint.)* Let's imagine how we might be the body of Jesus. What kinds of things did Jesus do with his hands? *(He healed, welcomed people, clapped them in praise and celebration, and so forth. Depending on your creativity, draw images of the church doing these things, or illustrate them on the body outline. Alternately, write some key words beside the body parts mentioned, or invite the children to draw or write.)*

Continue the conversation and drawing, exploring what Jesus did with his feet *(visited people, traveled around telling the good news)*, his mouth *(taught how to live in God's way, told the good news)*, heart, mind, etc. Make the conversation as simple or as elaborate as you would like, exploring with the children how we are the body of Christ.

The Bible says that God has filled us with the same power that Jesus was filled with, so we, too, can do the things he did.

Prayer: God, you have told us we are the body of Christ. Help us and our church to do the things you want in the world today. Amen.

The Sermon: Left Behind
Scripture: Acts 1:1-11
(For sermon materials on Acts 1:1-11, see the January/February 2011 issue of *The Clergy Journal* or the May/June 2010 planning issue of *The Clergy Journal*.)

Second chances do not come like this to most of us. "If only I could see him again," I've heard spoken at the grave of a family member. "If only I had told her this," I've heard from a grieving spouse outside the E.R. "If I could just hold his hand one more time," I've heard from the parent of a child departed too soon, too young.

Unlike most of us, the disciples get their second chance: a chance to see Jesus again, a chance to say what needed to be said, a chance to hold his hand one more time. His resurrection gave them precious time they had not anticipated. Forty days to say goodbye. Forty days to find the answers to the questions they had never asked. Forty days of preparation for his second and final departure. But even their second chance wasn't enough. Even 40 days beyond the grave were not enough.

Despite our graveside supplications, most of us who have lost someone know deep down that it wouldn't be enough for us either. One more conversation wouldn't be enough for a family member, one more embrace wouldn't be enough for a spouse, one more hold of the hand wouldn't be enough for any parent. There is never enough time to say goodbye.

Maybe that is why the disciples, huddled together, watching Jesus rise to the heavens, seem so unprepared for his absence. Unprepared *again*. Grieving *again*. Fearful *again*. Forty days were not enough. No time would be enough to prepare for a loved one's departure. It is never enough.

Christians have been instructed since the fourth century to celebrate the day of the Ascension as a Feast Day, the day when Jesus "ascended into heaven," but the disciples don't appear to be celebrating. They do not want to see Jesus go. They do not want to see him leave them again. They do not want the 40 days to end, the friendship to be a memory of the past, the leader they have finally come to follow taken from them again. They do not want to say goodbye. They do not want their second chance to end.

Even though Jesus does not die, I think they grieve. They grieve their loss. They grieve their separation. They grieve the end of a way of life they have come to expect, to count on, to trust. And we are no different. Every one of us will have to deal with loss at some point in our lives. Whether we lose our way, or lose our vocation, or lose our innocence, or lose the ones we love, we grieve our loss. We grieve separation from the familiar. We grieve no longer holding a hand that we know as well as our own, no longer finding our way that once led us, separated from some way, or someone too early, too soon. The separation always comes too early. Few of us are ready.

Jesus could have told the disciples to trust in him and their sadness would go away. He could have told them that as those who have seen how God defeated death in the past, they should be happy, they should celebrate. He could have told them that they should "rejoice, now that he is in a better place." He could have told them not to worry that things will get better, or that sometimes God's will is difficult for us to accept.

But unlike our liturgical calendar, Jesus does not tell the disciples to get over it. He does not tell them to cover their pain with songs of joy. He does not deny the loss they experience. He does not expect them to celebrate his departure. Perhaps he knows that between the end of something they have loved and cherished and the beginning of something new and fulfilling, they need the time and the space to rest in their grief, to savor their loss, to know their despair before they dare to hope for something new.

The words that Jesus does give to them are words about the future. "You *will receive* power when the Holy Spirit has come upon you; and *you will* be my witnesses in Jerusalem, in all Judea and Samaria, and to the ends of the earth." It is almost as if Jesus knows that none of the disciples feel like being witnesses in this moment. None of the disciples feel like running out in joy to fulfill the calling they have received. None of the disciples have the strength to envision the possibility of feeling a new power in this – not in this time of loss. The words he gives them are words for the future, words that will guide them when they are ready.

Next week we will celebrate the coming of something new – the power of the Holy Spirit. But this week we wait. We are left behind in this quiet place, timid and grieving, waiting to figure out what to do next, where to go next, waiting to figure out how we can keep on keeping on in the face of losses that we all have to face, some that seem too big to get beyond, that cut too deep to heal. Thankfully, God gives us time and space to gaze up toward heaven, longing for that which we have lost, waiting for something that is stronger than our grief to help us to do the work, to live the life to which we've been called.

There is no quick fix for the disciples – no way around the grief, no way to avoid the despair, no way to pretend their loss is somehow insignificant. All they have is each other and an upper room to pray. I don't know what they prayed for. I don't know whether they prayed for Jesus, or for each other, or for their loss, or for the coming of the Spirit that Jesus had promised. I don't know whether they asked God to speed the coming of the kingdom or the coming of something new in their lives. I can only imagine that among those left behind in their loss, gathered together in the quiet space of the upper room, familiar hands held onto each other that night, words of comfort were shared, loss was not hidden. And their grief began to prepare a place for a power they could not yet imagine.

– Andrew Foster Connors

Hymns
Opening Hymn
Alleluia! Sing to Jesus
A Hymn of Glory Let Us Sing
Sermon Hymn
Holy Ghost, Dispel Our Sadness
If Thou but Trust in God to Guide Thee
Closing Hymn
Alleluia! Sing to Jesus
Let Every Christian Pray

June 5, 2011

7th Sunday of Easter

Lessons

RCL	Roman Catholic
Acts 1:6-14	Acts 1:12-14
Ps 68:1-10, 32-35	Ps 27:1, 4, 7-8
1 Pet 4:12-14, 5:6-11	1 Pet 4:13-16
Jn 17:1-11	Jn 17:1-11

Speaker's Introduction for the Lessons
Lesson 1
Acts 1:6-14 (RCL); 1:12-14 (RC)

Just as Jesus spent 40 days in the wilderness preparing for the beginning of his ministry, now he spends 40 days preparing his disciples for the beginning of their ministry together.

Lesson 2
Psalm 68:1-10, 32-35 (RCL)

The good news of God's justice, God's deliverance of God's people, and God's provision for the needy is the foundation for our joy.

Psalm 27:1, 4, 7-8 (RC)

The Bible makes a strong case that the opposite of love is not hate, but fear. In times when fear overtakes us, an honest cry to God for help leads to courage and to faith.

Lesson 3
1 Peter 4:12-14, 5:6-11 (RCL); 4:13-16 (RC)

The writer of 1 Peter is less concerned over why Christian disciples suffer, and more concerned with strengthening their witness for love, peace, and justice in a world hostile to this way of living.

Gospel
John 17:1-11 (RCL/RC)

Traditionally referred to as "the highly priestly prayer," this is the final prayer Jesus speaks in John's Gospel before his betrayal, arrest, and crucifixion.

Theme

To survive and thrive in the in between times, disciples of Jesus need each other.

Thought for the Day

The church is not a building, but a gathering of disciples who depend on each to stay faithful to the work that Christ has given them.

Sermon Summary

Jesus prays for the disciples in their hearing. He prays for the disciples. To live eschatological lives – in between the world as they know it and the promised one to come – they need each other. Jesus prays for their unity.

Call to Worship

One: Let the righteous be joyful; let them exult before God; let them be jubilant with joy.

All: **Sing to God, sing praises to God's name!**

Leader: Parent of orphans and protector of widows, God gives the desolate a home to live in; God leads out the prisoners to prosperity.

All: **Sing to God, sing praises to God's name!**

– Adapted from Psalm 68

Pastoral Prayer

We do not often know what to expect in our world, Holy God, and we are painfully aware that we are not in control. Wars begin or continue despite our efforts for peace. The poor are still poor despite our efforts to proclaim good news. Friends, colleagues, and family members still fall ill despite our efforts for healing. We still face death despite our faith in your resurrection hope. So we thank you that in our struggle to live and to serve, you do not leave us alone. You bring us together in this community called the church. Deepen our trust in one another, so that in our living and in our serving, we may support each other as one community. Amen.

Prayer of Confession

Loving God, you gift us with life and we sometimes make a mess of ours. We spend our time on things that do not satisfy. We spend our money on stuff that does not fill us up. We turn from each other, and in so doing, turn from you. Share with us again your vision for a world with bread and joy for all. Entrust to us again the joy and the privilege of pursuing that vision. Draw us together for support so that as we learn to live with each other, as we learn to share your work together, we may see glimpses of your coming reign already present with us in this community. Amen.

Prayer of Dedication of Gifts and Self

From the treasures of our lives and the treasures of our hearts, we bring these gifts, Almighty God. Bring us together so that we might spend our money and spend our lives in common purpose: healing the sick, binding up the brokenhearted, delivering good news to the poor, and proclaiming the arrival of your reign. Amen.

Hymn of the Day
O Love, How Deep, How Broad, How High

The source of this text is a 23-stanza poem "Apparuit benignitas," attributed to Thomas à Kempis. It was translated and published in *The Hymnal Noted, Part II* (1854) and *Hymns Ancient and Modern* (1861). The text is basically the life of Christ in miniature. *The New Century Hymnal* (1995) has provided a new translation, "O Love, How Vast, How Flowing Free," using alternatives for spatial language. The choice of tunes to partner this text depends on the country that sings it. In the United States Deo Gracias (the Agincourt Hymn) is most common. In Canada Puer Nobis Nascitur, a 15th century tune, is used. Either tune makes a great partner for this text; however, the melodic shape of Puer Nobis Nascitur tends to follow the intent of the word more exactly, giving a wonderful sense of word painting.

Children's Time: Caring for Our Friends

Talk with the children about their friends. You might ask questions such as: What are their friends like? Do they always get along, or are there times when they disagree? What are things you like to do with your friends? Do you have one special or "best" friend? Are you friends with your brothers and sisters?

How do friends care for one another? What are some ways you and your friends show you love and care for each other?

Jesus had some very good friends; they were called the disciples. There were 12 very close friends, and many, many others – men, women, and children. Jesus loved them very much.

Just before leaving this world, Jesus said a special prayer. He asked God to take care of his friends. It was a wonderful way Jesus could show he cared about them. It was also a wonderful way Jesus showed us how to care for our friends.

Prayer: God, we thank you for all our friends. We especially thank you for our friend Jesus, who has showed us to love others. Amen.

The Sermon: Prayer for the People
Scripture: John 17:1-11

(For sermon materials on Acts 1:6-14, see the January/February 2011 issue of *The Clergy Journal*; for sermon materials on 1 Peter 4:12-14, 5:6-11, see the May/June 2010 planning issue of *The Clergy Journal*.)

Like many churches, in the evening of September 11, 2001, we gathered with stunned families to pray. At some point that evening the staff of the church I served shared different perspectives on how to cope and how to grieve in the wake of the tragedy. One of the pieces of wisdom that stands out for me came from the Christian educator. She counseled parents to stand within earshot of their children at night after they had tucked them in and kissed them good-night. "Let your children overhear you praying for them," she said.

Though my own daughter was too young to know what was happening in the world, the educator's advice struck me as the most helpful that night. Standing near my daughter's door I prayed not only for her safety but that the world she was growing into would turn from violence to peace.

Jesus prayed for his disciples *in their hearing*, in a world with at least as much danger as our own. All through the Gospel of John, the conflict between Jesus and the authorities has been building. The cross moves into view. Grief is already apparent in the hearts of the disciples as Jesus talks incessantly of his death and his departure, giving final admonitions to his followers. At the end of all the preparations, the admonitions, the commands, it's easy to imagine the dread that the disciples must feel. Jesus will be betrayed. Peter will deny him. The world will hate them for following him. It's not the kind of joy that we would like to celebrate in the season of Easter.

It's not clear what effect his prayer has on the disciples. On the one hand Jesus doesn't mince any words about the world the disciples are facing. They will know sorrow. They will know persecution. Life isn't going to be easy. On the other hand, he knows that the world has already been brought under the dominion of the Father. War will cease. Peace will come in the world and in their hearts. The commandment to love – so unrealistic in the world in which they live – will be established as the governing law and ethic of this new realm. The disciples are left in between these two realities, the harsh reality of the world in which we live, and the new realm that has already emerged in the life of Jesus.

Jesus stands where he can be overheard and prays. He prays for the disciples who are "in the world." Standing in the doorway, between this world and the next, he prays where he can be overheard. The prayer is for protection, but it is also for Jesus to be glorified. "Glorify your Son so that the Son may glorify you." *Glory* is a tough word to unpack, and Jesus doesn't make it any easier here. "I glorified you on earth by finishing the work that you gave me to do." That is, Jesus manifested God's presence by doing the work that was given to him to do. By doing God's work, the world was able to see the full presence of God in Jesus. Now that work is almost complete, and Jesus prays for a kind of return to the presence of God that he had known before the world existed.

This is all very confusing for most of us, at least those of us who do not spend a great deal of time pondering the architecture of the Triune God. There is a mysterious interchange between "Father" and "Son" that is not fully explainable. "Everything you have given me is from you." "All mine is yours and yours are mine." The language is so puzzling that it's easy to imagine that we are bystanders, watching the Triune God discuss matters that do not pertain to us. But the disciples are at the center of this prayer. They are the ones for whom Jesus appeals for the gift of eternal life (v. 3). They are the ones who know that everything that Jesus taught them is from God (v. 7). They have believed that Jesus was sent by the Father (v. 8). The prayer, then, is asked on behalf of the disciples (v. 9). Protect them in Jesus' name so that they may be one.

Jesus does not pray for them to be rescued from suffering. He does not pray for them to have magical powers to overcome evil. He does not pray for them to avoid suffering, pain, hurt, or even death. He prays for them to be one, to be unified in his name. This is the way that the disciples will find protection from evil. This is the way they will endure suffering. This is the way they will find courage even in the face of death – by coming together as one in the community that gathers in Christ's name; the community that houses the presence of Jesus Christ himself.

If you've spent any time in a church, this final request can be a bit disappointing. The church does not always seem to be the place where

Christ is most palpable. It does not always seem like a place of protection. A prayer for the community unified in God's name might not be the first prayer that we would choose to offer in this Easter space in between the world that we live in and the world that we know is coming.

Then yesterday I received the news that a friend died suddenly while jogging – a young man – leaving behind a wife and four young children. How will this family endure? Sunday morning I heard news that our sister parish in El Salvador had turned itself into a relief shelter for hundreds of people made homeless by the most recent tropical storm. How will they get through it? A week ago I joined other pastors on the playground of a local school where gunshots and drug needles have threatened to desecrate this sacred space. How will we change the situation?

A prayer for followers of Jesus to be one seemed more like grace than I had first imagined. There is more to this community that we call church than we sometimes care to admit. This is a gift that God gives to us, to protect us while we stand in the doorway between the harsh reality of the world in which we live and the new realm that has already emerged in the life of Jesus. Amen.

– Andrew Foster Connors

Hymns
Opening Hymn
The Church's One Foundation
Here, O Lord, Your Servants Gather
Sermon Hymn
Blest Be the Tie That Binds
In Christ There Is No East or West
Closing Hymn
Come Sing, O Church, in Joy!
Today We All Are Called to Be Disciples

June 12, 2011

Day of Pentecost

Lessons

RCL
Act 2:1-21 or Num 11:24-30
Ps 104:24-34, 35b
1 Cor 12:3b-13 or Acts 2:1-21
Jn 20:19-23 or 7:37-39

Roman Catholic
Acts 2:1-11
Ps 104:1, 24, 29-31, 34
1 Cor 12:3-7, 12-13
Jn 20:19-23

Speaker's Introduction for the Lessons
Lesson 1
Acts 2:1-21 (RCL); 2:1-11 (RC)

The day of Pentecost text is a re-interpretation and claiming of one of Judaism's high and holy days as part of the new and unfolding story of Jesus.

Lesson 2
Psalm 104:24-34, 35b (RCL); 104:1, 24, 29-31, 34 (RC)

The psalm is a song of praise justifying itself, as it invites us to affirm that to acknowledge the Creator and the Sustainer is to proceed appropriately into praise.

Lesson 3
1 Corinthians 12:3b-13 (RCL); 12:3-7, 12-13 (RC)

This is Paul's celebration of diversity, not for the sake of diversity, but for the sake of accomplishing the will and the work of God.

Gospel
John 20:19-23 (RCL/RC)

Today's Gospel is the Johannine record of the Great Commission and Pentecost.

Theme

Our deep longing for home is ultimately met only in the good news of God.

Thought for the Day

What the ears of those with faith hear as good news, sounds like just so much absurdity to the ears of those without faith.

Sermon Summary

At the festival of Pentecost, Jews gathered from around the world in Jerusalem. There had to have been an odd disjointedness between what they hoped and what they experienced. Hearing the good news of God in the languages of their homes was a wonder-filled opportunity to hope again.

Call to Worship

> One: They spoke in the language of the Parthians, the Medes, and the Elamites.
>
> **All: They spoke in the language of the Germans, the Italians, the Arabs, and the Chinese.**
>
> One: They spoke in the language of Mesopotamia, Judea, Cappadocia, Pontus, and Asia.
>
> **All: They spoke in the language of the Russians, the French, the Spanish, and the Indians.**
>
> One: They spoke in the language of Phrygia, Pamphylia, Egypt, and Libya.
>
> **All: They spoke in our language.**
>
> One: They shouldn't have been able to.
>
> **All: It was amazing. But more amazing by far**
>
> One: Was what they said.
>
> **All: Thanks be to God.**

Pastoral Prayer

Take our strongest sense of home, God, our best memories, our most treasured hopes – take that which is richest, deepest, most beautiful, and most profound in our experience, and craft of all that, a yearning for our true home that will leave us frustrated until we rest in you. Shape of what we know, a hope for that which we cannot know, that will keep us pointed in your direction – that will grace us with the stick-to-itness we need as we are directed in your way. This we pray, in the name of the one who is the way, and on the way with us, leading us and pushing us, always by our side. Amen.

Prayer of Confession

We confess, our God, even as believers, to disbelieving the fullness of your good news. We affirm the holiness of your way, but don't fully lean into the wholeness of it. We celebrate your story, but don't rely on it enough to risk living it. We say our prayers, but count our money. We know the stories and we sing the hymns, but we won't risk trusting the implications of those stories and songs at the workplace or at the gym or at home. Blow away our half-heartedness, God. Breathe into us and fill our hearts with hope and possibility and commitment. We can't do it breathing for ourselves. Breathe in us, we pray. Amen.

Prayer of Dedication of Gifts and Self

We give our money, O God. Some of it, anyway – a little, relatively speaking. What if, instead, we were to give ourselves completely with utter abandon to your good news – to your way of being? What if we just said, "Oh, to heaven with it!" and went for it? All or nothing. We're going to wager ourselves on you, God. What if we were to do that? We give our money – some of it – a little, relatively speaking. It's a start. We pray for the possibility of more in the name of the one who gave himself completely. Amen.

Hymn of the Day
Like the Murmur of the Dove's Song

Carl P. Daw Jr. wrote this text for *The Hymnal 1982* and specifically to be sung to the tune BRIDEGROOM. Peter Cutts, originally from Great Britain, served as music director for churches in New England and then on the faculty of Andover Newton Theological Seminary. The tune was originally published in *100 Hymns for Today* (1969). This is a hymn that must soar and be sung with long expressive lines. Notice the hemiola (change in rhythm) in the last line. Help the congregation to sing this accurately as the rhythm helps emphasize the text "come, Holy Spirit, come."

Children's Time: Pentecost

(Preparation: You might wish to make simple "flame" hats for all the children. Cut lengthy strips of paper – about 20 inches/51 cm long by 1 inch/2.5 cm wide. Join into loops, and add paper flames – cut out of red, orange, or yellow paper. Make the flames whatever size you wish. These hats are optional.)

You will tell a shortened version of the Pentecost story – dramatize it and include the children as much as possible. Whenever you say the word spirit invite the children to blow softly.)

The disciples had all gathered in Jerusalem, because it was an important Jewish festival called Pentecost. Suddenly, there was a great wind. *(Blow, and invite the children to blow with you.)* After the wind, something that looked like fire landed on everyone's head. *(Distribute the flame hats, or invite the children to pat the tops of their heads.)*

They all started to speak in their own languages and, amazingly, they could all understand each other – God's *spirit* made it work. Everyone was amazed and confused.

"They must all be drunk," some people said.

So Peter stood up to explain. "We're not drunk," he said. "No, friends, this is God's *spirit*. Remember how long ago the prophet Joel said God's *spirit* would come upon everyone? Well, it's happening. God's *spirit* is helping us understand each other. It's what Joel promised, and what Jesus spoke about."

Even today in the church, we celebrate that God's *spirit* is always with us. It's upon everybody – young, old, men, women, tall and short: everyone!

Prayer: Thank you, God, that you sent your Spirit to guide us and give us all new life. Amen.

The Sermon: The Language of the Heart
Scripture: Acts 2:1-21
(For sermon materials on John 20:19-23, see the March/April 2011 issue of *The Clergy Journal*; for sermon materials on Acts 2:1-21, see the May/June 2010 planning issue of *The Clergy Journal*.)

It's eight weeks after Jesus' resurrection – a little over a week after Jesus' ascension, and there are all these devout Jews in Jerusalem for Pentecost. Pentecost was, after all, a Jewish holiday – or holy day – before it was a Christian one, and in terms of people making pilgrimages, it was quite possibly the most popular (John B. Polhill, "Acts: An Exegetical and Theological Exposition of Holy Scripture" in *The New American Commentary*, Nashville: Broadman Press, 1992, 97.

Pentecost was a festival celebrating the spring harvest, the goodness and bounty of God. It was also a time of remembering the covenant –

God's gift of the law – the promise God made to be home for the people, and the people's promise to live accordingly. Pentecost was a time of reaffirming the covenant and recommitting to it.

Among all these devout Jews in the city, there was a large number of Diaspora Jews – Jews who had fled Israel – who had dispersed, and for the last 620-some-odd years, had made their homes in diverse lands where they had established synagogues, had raised their children. Those children had learned the languages of these places. And their children's children went to the local symphony and museums and libraries. Their children got involved in local politics. And Hebrew became a taught language – learned from books and lessons – not on the playgrounds and streets. Israel became a memory – a story of where they came from, of their ancestors – and their ancestors in the faith. At worst, Israel became just a story of a past home long ago; at best, a dream of home as it was supposed to be.

Now, a number of these Jews are in Jerusalem. Some, no doubt, just in for the festival; some who had actually relocated to Jerusalem. Some spoke the language fluently; others were trying to reconcile what they heard on the streets around them with their books on tape. And however overjoyed they were at being in the land of their ancestors, however much they reveled in seeing the places they had only read about, there was this inescapable sense of how far they were from where they grew up – how far they were from familiar places where the language with which they grew up was the one they heard around them.

There had to have been an odd dynamic – being in a place they had called home, being in a place they had longed to get to, so they could finally be at home – and feeling like a stranger. No one there with whom they grew up. No one who knew their nicknames from grade school. No one who even spoke their language, not the one they learned on the playgrounds and streets.

Then, all of a sudden, each head turned, as each heard, each one of them, the language of his or her own heart, being spoken in this place that was supposed to be home to them, but wasn't – not the way they had hoped it would be. And they turned with suddenly brighter eyes. They turned with a smile. They turned with some undefinable hope – not just because it was a familiar language, but because now *this* was the opportunity for everything to be perfect. *This* was now the dream of things as they're supposed to be. *This* became the opportunity for home.

What reaction does scripture record these Jews had to hearing their own language? Scripture tells us that they were bewildered, amazed, and perplexed. Some were probably intrigued. Some listened. And then scripture says that some mocked the disciples and accused them of being drunk.

It is somewhat odd, don't you think, that they would call the Galileans drunk? It's not, as many might assume, that they were babbling in different languages. Why would they be mocked for that? Why would they be called drunk because of that? I've been around drunks. If drunks make sense, you don't mock them! If drunks are speaking clearly in a language you didn't even think they knew, that's no reason to mock – marvel maybe, but not mock. No, it couldn't have been that they were speaking these foreign languages – there was no denying, no mocking that. No, it had to have been *what* they were saying. And what *were* they saying? They were speaking of God's deeds of power.

Given that it was the disciples, they could have been noting any of the acts of power that we read in what we call the Old Testament. Jesus taught them well. But if this was a festival commemorating the covenant, then surely there were many recounting the story of the Exodus and the God who liberated the children of Israel and led them home to the promised land. Surely many were talking about the God of power who appeared at Sinai in smoke and fire and thunder. So no one would mock that.

It may be more likely that the disciples were talking about acts of power to which they were witnesses. They were probably talking about things Jesus did, and they probably mentioned the death and the resurrection. They may have talked about the new life we can have in Christ Jesus. They may have talked about being born again, and the implications of being born again for the kind of lives we are called to live. They may have talked about the last being first – about the master serving. They may have talked about dying to self in order to find the life that is life. Because the transformation of a human life – the rebirth of a sinner into an acknowledged child of God – that, too, was considered an act of power.

And here, some might mock. Those whose dreams had crashed around them – or those whose dreams had just kind of faded away – now confronted with these – these – what? Idealists? Dreamers? Still hoping. Still talking about love and peace in a world in which violence and terror are viable alternatives to so many. Still talking about justice and righteousness in a world shaped by profit margins and ends that justify means. Ah, they're drunk. They'd have to be to keep believing.

But there were some, and still are some, who say, "Whatever it is they're having – that's what I want!"

– John Ballenger

Hymns
Opening Hymn
On Pentecost They Gathered
God of Grace and God of Glory
Sermon Hymn
There's a Spirit in the Air
Amarte Solo a Ti, Senor
Closing Hymn
Spirit of God, Descend upon My Heart
Breathe on Me, Breath of God

June 19, 2011

Trinity Sunday

Lessons

RCL	Roman Catholic
Gen 1:1—2:4a	Ex 34:4-6, 8-9
Ps 8	Dan 3:52-56
2 Cor 13:11-13	2 Cor 13:11-13
Mt 28:16-20	Jn 3:16-18

Speaker's Introduction for the Lessons
Lesson 1
Genesis 1:1—2:4a (RCL)

The beginning of every biblical story resonates with the words "in the beginning."

Exodus 34:4-6, 8-9 (RC)

Here Moses does as he is commanded to bring two tablets like the ones he has broken on Mount Sinai to the Lord.

Lesson 2
Psalm 8 (RCL)

In our worship we celebrate the majesty and glory of our God, and of the human beings created in the very image of God.

Daniel 3:52-56 (RC)

These verses are inspired additions to the Aramaic text of Daniel, translated from the Greek form of the book. The church has always regarded them as part of the canonical scriptures.

Lesson 3
2 Corinthians 13:11-13 (RCL/RC)

The closing words of Paul's letters deserve close attention. Hear this exhortation and benediction.

Gospel

Matthew 28:16-20 (RCL)

The end of Matthew's Gospel is the beginning of another story, in which we find and take our places.

John 3:16-18 (RC)

It is typical of Johannine thought for this to be presented as two extreme options: either perish or have eternal life.

Theme

We are sent out in all humility to change the world!

Thought for the Day

The triumph of the gospel, the good news of God, is what God does with the faithfulness of those who live in the way of God.

Sermon Summary

The context of a biblical text informs its meaning, and our text at the end of Matthew's Gospel takes its place within the larger context of the rest of the gospel and, indeed, the larger biblical story. The resonance of our text within the larger gospel framework can protect it from certain misinterpretations.

Call to Worship

One: You commanded us to gather in your name,

All: And here we are.

One: You promised us the Spirit would be present and guide us into all truth,

All: And here we are.

One: You named us your body, your hands and feet, heart and voice,

All: And here we are.

One: You tell us to learn more of your teaching, to obey and to live your life,

All: And here we go.

Pastoral Prayer

May we embrace the grand adventure, God, of life lived in your name – the quest to follow you closely enough that we might lead others in your way of being. In our service and in our worship, may we come to know ever more the depths of the wonder and the joy that allow us to face the challenges of life with the assurance that our faithfulness matters. That when we walk in our integrity as believers, you make a difference in, through, and beyond us. This we pray in the name of the one who made all the difference. Amen.

Prayer of Confession

Our God, we confess to running away from you, to denying you, to valuing our expectations of you more than your expectations of us. We confess to wanting the immediate and the easy success – the vindication that doesn't cost us much. Forgive us, God, we pray, and thank you for trusting us still with the charge to live the life we see in Jesus – to offer the invitation of your grace to all who witness our living. This we pray in the name of the one who lives your life. Amen.

Prayer of Dedication of Gifts and Self

At this time, set apart in worship for the giving of our gifts to you, our God, we offer you, too, our hope to learn ever more about you and your way in the world. We offer you our obedience to your teaching, our commitment to following your lead, our intent to be consistent, and our desire to always place ourselves where we might encounter you even when we have failed. These things, along with our gifts, we offer you, in the expectation that you will take what we give, and multiply it all within your blessing. Amen.

Hymn of the Day
Lord, You Give the Great Commission

Jeffrey Rowthorn wrote this hymn specifically for the tune ABBOT'S LEIGH. At the time, Rowthorn was Episcopal suffragan bishop of Connecticut and professor at Yale Divinity School. The graduating class of 1978 requested a new hymn to be sung at their graduation service. It was first published in *Laudamus* (1984), a supplement to the Yale hymnal. The tune was composed by British hymn writer Cyril V. Taylor in 1941 while he was working at Abbot's Leigh near Bristol. This hymn stresses the ministry for all Christians, sharing Christ's tasks both corporately and individually. This is a vigorous text paired to an equally vigorous tune. Encourage strong, energetic singing. Allow each line to build to the next, like waves.

Children's Time: Jesus Is with Us

Do you ever get scared? What are some things that might scare you? Is it sometimes hard to do things, because you don't know how people will respond?

Most of us have had tough times like that. We might feel all alone, or that no one cares about us or loves us.

Sometimes we might do something that makes us feel bad, and we are scared to admit it. Or we might even get in trouble for doing something, and feel bad.

Did you know that in those times, we are not alone? That's right. No matter what is going on in our lives, Jesus is with us. We cannot see him, but we can know he is there.

Long ago, Jesus met with his friends – the disciples – and told them to travel the world and tell people about Jesus. That was probably very scary for some of them, because they had seen how some people didn't like Jesus. What would it be like? What might happen?

Then, Jesus told them something very, very special: "Remember," Jesus said, "I am with you always. To the end of time."

No matter where we go, or what we do, or what happens to us, we can know that Jesus is with us. Jesus loves us and cares for us. Always.

Prayer: God, we thank you that Jesus is always with us. When times are tough, help us to remember that. Amen.

The Sermon: The Bookends of God's Promise
Scripture: Matthew 28:16-20

(For sermon materials on Psalm 8, see the March/April 2011 issue of *The Clergy Journal*; for sermon materials on Matthew 28:16-20, see the May/June 2010 planning issue of *The Clergy Journal*.)

Because of church history, part of our text – the part popularly known as the Great Commission – the part typically extracted from its context and proclaimed and heard on its own, has become associated for many with the arrogance and self-righteousness of a colonial approach to missions. We have been entrusted with the truth and we will export it, along with our culture, to the natives of lands we wish to exploit – always maintaining control, of course, of orthodoxy and all church property.

There is much in our text to seriously undermine any such reading, and we begin with the recognition that "[t]his is the first scene in which the

disciples have appeared since they fled during the arrest of Jesus (26:56)"
(M. Eugene Boring, "The Gospel of Matthew" in *The New Interpreter's Bible*, Nashville: Abingdon Press, 1995, 502), and there are 11 of them. We start, in other words, with the reminder that Jesus was betrayed from within and not by one, but by all of his disciples. We are reminded of all that Jesus suffered because of, if not ultimately, at least immediately – because of one of his own disciple's frustration that he did not live up to that disciple's hopes and expectations.

Next, we note that even looking in the very face of the resurrected Jesus, the remaining 11 disciples worshiped *and* doubted. That final clause of verse 17 is written in such a way that one can legitimately argue (and translate) the "some" who doubted as other, unnamed persons, or as some of the disciples, or as all of the disciples. But given Matthew's own presentation of discipleship throughout the Gospel, it's the last reading that's the most consistent (Boring, 502). All the disciples worshiped and doubted.

So the context established for the so-called Great Commission, often omitted (and we can see why!) is one of failure and betrayal, and one that doesn't just so significantly validate the experience of doubt – of ambivalence, but that also raises questions about anyone with too much certainty. If Jesus' own disciples, looking the resurrected Jesus in the face, had doubts, who are we not to?

This was the context into which the resurrected Jesus came, noting that all authority had been given him. Whatever questions have been raised about the authority of the disciples, the authority of Jesus is quickly affirmed as uncompromised and universal.

But as we come to the end of Matthew's Gospel, this very conclusive affirmation of Jesus' authority points us back to an early Jesus story: the temptation story, in which the devil took Jesus up a mountain and offered him the kingdoms of earth, offered him authority on earth. And Jesus responded, "Worship the Lord your God, and serve only him" (Mt 4:8-10). Jesus rejected the preliminary offer of authority on earth in order to receive all authority (on earth and in heaven) from God, in the fullness of time, and in response to his commitment to serve God and God alone.

What we find having unfolded in the story is the same affirmation we find in the poetry of the Philippian hymn (Phil 2:5-11): the affirmation of faithfulness unto and through suffering and humiliation, with consistent and obedient faithfulness leading God to invert humiliation and suffering.

Because Jesus has this legitimate authority, he uses it, and tells his disciples to go. And the end of the Gospel points us back to one of the earliest Bible stories. Jesus tells the disciples to go as God told Abram to go (Gen 12:1-3). And as God promised Abram, "by your offspring shall all the nations of the earth gain blessing for themselves, because you have obeyed my voice" (Gen 22:18), so Jesus seeks to fulfill the ancient promise of God in the mission of the disciples and the church.

Since that story of Abraham, since the earliest stories of Israel's beginning, it's been a part of the faith tradition of Israel that Israel will shine as a light to the nations – that through Israel, all the world shall be blessed. But here we find a reversal of the prophetic expectation that the nations would flock to Zion, and just as Jesus took the initiative and came to the disciples, so too are they to take the initiative and go to the nations.

And they go to the nations to disciple. Not to count converts, not to be welcomed with flowers and open arms, but to make disciples, and to teach obedience – to teach the obedience they have themselves learned. There's a reciprocal nature to their mission. Jesus had told them to go to the mountain in Galilee (unrecorded), and they went. Now on that mountain, Jesus tells them go, and the implication is that just as they have obeyed, they will again. They go to model what they were taught, what they now teach. They go to live the life they saw lived. They go, obedient and faithful, to earn an authority they do not have.

And Jesus commands them to baptize new disciples in the name of the Father and of the Son and of the Holy Spirit. Most of the New Testament record of baptism is in the name of Jesus (Acts 2:38; 8:16; 10:48; Rom 6:3; 1 Cor 1:13; 15; 6:11; cf. 10:2) (Eduard Schweizer, *The Good News According to Matthew,* Atlanta: John Knox, 1975, p. 530). So there's an argument to be made that the trinitarian formula was not necessarily original to Jesus, but composed by Matthew in the context of the later Matthean church. With the trinitarian formula now the norm, it's less necessary to deny a trinitarian baptismal formula early in the stories of the early church, than to acknowledge that it wasn't the only way in which people were baptized.

Several times, the end of Matthew's Gospel has pointed us back (back to the temptation story, back to Abram). So, in conclusion, Matthew begins his Gospel in anticipation. "Look, the virgin shall conceive and bear a son, and they shall name him Emmanuel" (Mt 1:23). Emmanuel meaning, of course, "God with us." Matthew ends his Gospel with the assurance of God's promise answered – with anticipation fulfilled – as Jesus says, "Remember, I am with you always, to the end of the age." It's not just a high christology, though it certainly is that; it's also the promise of prophecy fulfilled, the promise that God honors and celebrates faithfulness. May it be so, in our failures and doubts as in our worship and obedience. Amen.

– John Ballenger

Hymns
Opening Hymn
> Break Out, O Church of God
> Called as Partners in Christ's Service

Sermon Hymn
> We've a Story to Tell
> I Love to Tell the Story

Closing Hymn
> I Will Go Wherever God Calls
> *Sois la Semilla*

June 26, 2011

2nd Sunday after Pentecost (Proper 8 [13])
RC/Pres: 13th Sunday in Ordinary Time

Lessons (See p. 10 for guidelines)

Semi-continuous (SC)	Complementary (C)	Roman Catholic (RC)
Gen 22:1-14	Jer 28:5-9	Deut 8:2-3, 14-16a
Ps 113	Ps 89:1-4, 15-18	Ps 147:12-13, 14-15, 19-20
Rom 6:12-23	Rom 6:12-23	1 Cor 10:16-17
Mt 10:40-42	Mt 10:40-42	Jn 6:51-58

Speaker's Introduction for the Lessons
Lesson 1
Genesis 22:1-14 (SC)

This story is so fundamental to the Judeo-Christian tradition and the Muslim tradition that the identity of Abraham's son in the story changes in the traditions from Isaac to Ishmael!

Jeremiah 28:5-9 (C)

Prophesies of dire tidings often come to pass, but the prophesies of peace can only be made to pass by the living God.

Deuteronomy 8:2-3, 14-16a (RC)

God takes care of those who love him even when natural means seem to fail them.

Lesson 2
Psalm 113 (SC)

The praiseworthiness of our God is always made most manifest in God's care for the poor.

Psalm 89:1-4, 15-18 (C)

The psalmist Ethan sings of God's promise that someone from David's family would be king. Jesus will be that king.

Lesson 3
Romans 6:12-23 (SC/C)

Paul's existential questions prompt his theological thinking.

1 Corinthians 10:16-17 (RC)

We are one in the body and blood of Christ.

Gospel
Matthew 10:40-42 (SC/C)
God participates in the interactions of life, within relationships and through actions.

John 6:51-58 (RC)
Jesus tells the Jews who dispute he is the living bread that his flesh and blood is the true food and drink. Jesus says, "Those who eat my flesh and drink my blood will have eternal life."

Theme
The reality of sin pervades even the powerful imagery of new life.

Thought for the Day
God's word celebrates the joy of beginning but encompasses all of what it takes to work through disappointing failure.

Sermon Summary
Paul affirms and celebrates the life-changing dimension of baptism while acknowledging that our lives aren't always changed in the ways one might and should expect. How do we explain the sin of the old life that persists in the new life?

Call to Worship
One: We were, each one of us, taken below the waters.
All: We, each one of us, died with Christ in baptism.
One: And we were, each one of us, raised, dripping, to newness of life.
All: We were, each one of us, born again,
One: Breathing in for the first time the breath of God,
All: The life-creating Spirit that dreamed us, each one, into being.
One: And we, each one of us, live in the hope of living up to this newness and of not letting it down.
All: May it be so,
One: And when it isn't,
All: May we breathe in God and dream again.

Pastoral Prayer

Remind us this day, God, of the moment we first believed – that first moment your presence lit us up, your word shined, and your way extended so clearly illuminated before us. Remind us of our wonder and our excitement and the boundless hope we had for our future and for our world. Remind us of all we thought and felt, believed, and wanted. And as we remember, inspire us, God, to want that again, to look for that, to expect that, and to live that again as many times as it takes. This we pray in the name of the one who offers us new life – always. Amen.

Prayer of Confession

Our God, we confess that though our old selves died with Christ in baptism and that we were then raised to newness of life, there is much of our old selves that yet lingers – that still determines some of our attitudes and some of our behavior. We confess to a certain half-heartedness, to a certain double-mindedness. Led out of bondage from our various Egypts, we look back to that from which we were freed. We yearn for what we knew, as bad as we know it to be. Lead us on, we pray, into our future. Grant us the courage to face the unknown with you rather than return to what we know without you. This we pray in the name of the one who, celebrating his faith, walked into his future that is your present to and for us all. Amen.

Prayer of Dedication of Gifts and Self

Our God, we collect our gold, we collect our jewelry, and intentionally give enough of it to you in our worship, that there's not enough left with which to construct a golden calf – even if we wanted to, even when we want to. We give because you expect it. We give because we believe in you, your way, your people. And we give because it's good for us – because the more we give you, the more we invest in you, the less there is to invest in anything else. Accept these our gifts, and bless our giving, in Jesus' name. Amen.

Hymn of the Day
Amazing Grace

This well-known and well-loved hymn was published in *Olney Hymns* (1779). The first four stanzas were written by John Newton, an Anglican priest who had a conversion experience after leading a life as a slave trader. The fifth stanza, "When we've been there . . . " has been identified by William

J. Reynolds as one borrowed from an anonymous 19th century American hymn, "Jerusalem, my happy home," published in *A Collection of Sacred Ballads* (1790). This hymn is a specific favorite with the first nation's people of North America and has been translated into many aboriginal languages. The tune, AMAZING GRACE (NEW BRITAIN), was first printed in *Virginia Harmony* (1831). Its actual origin is unknown. Edwin Excell arranged the tune to suit the text in 1900.

Children's Time: Starting Over

Have you ever heard of the word *sin*? It's a word that gets used a lot in the Bible, and people in the church often talk about it. Sometimes it means different things to different people. One of the reasons is that in the original languages of the Bible they used different words that we translate as sin.

The most common word for *sin* in the Bible is a Greek word that goes *hamartia* (ham-ar-TEE-uh). You don't have to remember how to the say word, but the meaning is interesting. It's a term that comes from archery, and it means "to miss the mark." You know how, when you're trying to shoot an arrow, or toss darts or horseshoes, you can miss the target or the post? That's *hamartia*. That's "sin." Those times when we try to do what God wants, but we don't quite get it right. It might be because we can't, or because we don't really want to.

St. Paul tells us something very special about sin. Paul said we could "repent." That's another word that comes from the Bible, and it means to turn away from one thing and turn toward another.

It means that, when we have done things wrong, or just not gotten it right, we can turn away from that, and turn toward God. When things aren't going the way they should, we can start over.

Prayer: Sometimes, God, we miss the mark and do not do what is right. Thank you for the gift of repentance, and the chance to start over again. Amen.

The Sermon: The Tipping Point
Scripture: Romans 6:12-23

(For sermon materials on Matthew 10:40-42, see the March/April 2011 issue of *The Clergy Journal*; for sermon materials on Genesis 22:1-14, see the May/June 2010 planning issue of *The Clergy Journal*.)

A text that begins with "therefore" forces you to look back to figure out "wherefore" before you can move on. In this case, looking back at the first 11 verses of Romans 6, we read about baptism as a tipping point in a person's life. Do you know what a tipping point is? According to Malcolm Gladwell, staff writer for the *New Yorker* and author of *The Tipping Point: How Little Things Make a Big Difference*, the "word 'Tipping Point' . . . comes from the world of epidemiology. It's the name given to that moment in an epidemic when a virus reaches critical mass" (http://www.gladwell.com/tippingpoint/index.html). More generally, tipping points are "the levels at which the momentum for change becomes unstoppable" (http://en.wikipedia.org/wiki/The_Tipping_Point).

And in a person's spiritual life, baptism, as the tipping point, is the point after which everything is different. Baptism creates a sharp and absolute duality expressed in juxtapositions of the old self and the new self, of death and life, of sin and God. "Because of your baptism," Paul writes, "because you died to self with Christ and were raised to newness of life in Christ – because you reached a tipping point – because everything is different, *therefore*, do not let sin reign in your body and allow your body to make you obey it.

Now with Paul, you always have to pay such close attention. He packs so much insight and so much information so subtly into his writing. Often blamed for blatancy, notice what he does here. He exhorts, "Do not let sin reign in your body," and goes on to suggest that if sin does reign in your body, it allows your body to make you obey it. So here's the question: who reigns? Because if sin reigns, you obey your body – not sin. You obey your body, as if sin is, in and of itself, nothing – just something causing inappropriate prioritizing in people's lives. If sin reigns, you don't obey sin. It merely encourages you to obey something, anything other than God's way of being. Paul juxtaposes sin with God in his dualities, and yet, sin is nothing! Not a competing force, not an evil spirit. Misdirection.

Paul goes on. Because you reached a tipping point – because everything is different – don't let anything stay the same. This is, somewhat problematically, by no means automatic, but rather a decision you have to make and a discipline you have to maintain. Paul remains so aware of the question, if the tipping point is passed, if everything is different, then how and why does sin remain a reality in my living? It is Paul, after all, who confesses, "I do not do what I want, but I do the very thing I hate" (Rom 7:15). Misdirection.

Paul wants and needs to affirm simultaneously the fact that baptism is a tipping point, after which everything is different, *and* the fact that after baptism, there's too much that is just the same old, same old. And so he writes in one verse, "do not let sin exercise dominion in your mortal bodies" and in another, "sin will have no dominion over you." And the question is not, "well, which is it?" but rather the affirmation, "it's both."

If all you hear is the exhortation not to let sin exercise dominion, you live in fear without the assurance that grace has enabled a new you. But if all you hear is that sin has no dominion, then you deny the profound challenge that is the living of your new life in Christ. Jesus came in grace and truth (Jn 1:14), and Paul wants to make sure we don't lose either the grace that is who and how we've been raised to be, or the truth that is who and how we can nonetheless still be. The grace that is the teaching of Jesus, as it is the life of Jesus into which we're raised, allows us to do righteousness, but it doesn't force us to.

Somewhat oddly then, and indeed somewhat offensively, to our ear, Paul uses the institution of slavery as metaphor here. He even offers an apology for the imagery (blaming the limitations of thought and language), but apology aside, it all does fit into his thinking. For the background to our text lies in the Exodus story. Not in its easy, culturally accepted, normative interpretation: we were enslaved, but now we're free, but in the deeper truth known to careful students of the scriptural stories. Those who know that when God said, "let my people go," God actually said, "let my people go that they might worship me," and that between God's first "let my people go that they might worship me" (Ex 3:12) and Pharaoh's final, exasperated, "go worship" (Ex 12:31), the call to worship is a consistent refrain (Ex 5:1; 7:16; 8:1, 20; 9:1, 13; 10:3, 7, 8, 24).

God leads the children of Israel out of slavery and into worship. Not from being told by Pharaoh what to do to doing whatever they wanted (which some of them were hoping for), but from being told by Pharaoh what to do to doing what God would have them do. Not because they had to, but because they wanted to, because they chose to.

It is awkward for Paul to claim you will be a slave to someone or something. But in his larger thought frame, sin isn't a master, sin simply elevates something – anything other than God to an inappropriate level of importance. Whether that's a golden calf or your self-esteem, your family, your job, your appetite, your childhood, your dreams, your sense of security. Choosing God as ultimate priority, as master, simply allows all else to fall into an appropriate order, whereas choosing anything other than God (which is sin), necessarily disorders everything.

And the children of Israel were led out of bondage into worship, out of an enforced obedience to Pharaoh into a chosen obedience to God. And yet how well did that work out for them, or for God? The Old Testament is one ongoing story of the people letting God down, of God's anger and rejection, and then of the grace of the ongoing story of relationship. "Do not let sin exercise dominion in your mortal bodies," *and* "sin will have no dominion over you."

We live at the tipping point. We always have. We're always there at the critical moment, the decisive moment, because each moment brings a choosing between God and something – God and anything. Choose wisely.

– John Ballenger

Hymns
Opening Hymn
God of Grace and God of Glory
Dear God, Embracing Humankind
Sermon Hymn
My Shepherd, You Supply My Need
In These Dark Uncertain Moments
Closing Hymn
In Water We Grow
Where Charity and Love Prevail

July 3, 2011

3rd Sunday after Pentecost (Proper 9 [14])
RC/Pres: 14th Sunday in Ordinary Time

Lessons (See p. 10 for guidelines)

Semi-Continuous (SC)	Complementary (C)	Roman Catholic (RC)
Gen 24:34-38, 42-49, 58-67	Zech 9:9-12	Zech 9:9-10
Ps 45:10-17 or Song 2:8-13	Ps 145:8-14	Ps 145:1-2, 8-11, 13-14
Rom 7:15-25a	Rom 7:15-25a	Rom 8:9, 11-13
Mt 11:16-19, 25-30	Mt 11:16-19, 25-30	Mt 11:25-30

Speaker's Introduction for the Lessons
Lesson 1
Genesis 24:34-38, 42-49, 58-67 (SC)
Within the ritual of marriage negotiations, love and comfort await Isaac.
Zechariah 9:9-12 (C); 9:9-10 (RC)
This passage, which becomes a model for Jesus' triumphal entry into Jerusalem, is a pronouncement of a peace that is not dependent on the violent submission of one's enemies.

Lesson 2
Psalm 45:10-17 (SC)
Within the imagery of the royal consort, we are invited to make ourselves beautiful for our God.
Psalm 145:8-14 (C); 145:1-2, 8-11, 13-14 (RC)
In God's name and as the hands and feet and heart of God, we are to support those who are falling.

Lesson 3
Romans 7:15-25a (SC/C)
We can't live life in the way of God as we want to on our own, but within our subsequent fear and frustration, we are invited into the embrace of Jesus.
Romans 8:9, 11-13 (RC)
Paul speaks of life in the flesh and life in the Spirit.

Gospel
Matthew 11:16-19, 25-30 (SC/C); 11:25-30 (RC)

We miss the word of God unfolding in the world around us, and are yet invited into the embrace of Jesus.

Theme

Sin is the tendency and the encouragement to prioritize other people and things over God.

Thought for the Day

It's not just the moral or ethical dimension of behavior that determines sin. We mustn't allow the more socially acceptable distractions from God to escape being defined as sin.

Sermon Summary

Paul's assessment of his own inability to live in the way of God leads to his assessment of the law as a valuable tool in knowing right from wrong. But along with everything but Jesus, he finds it woefully inadequate in making a difference in the way we live into that knowledge.

Call to Worship

One: We, as your followers, God, know the way in which you lead.
All: We know your teaching, and so we know your expectations.
One: We know the example you lived in Jesus.
All: Even as we are always coming to know you, we are also coming to know ever more how you would have us be as those created in your image.
One: We know all this,
All: And yet it doesn't seem to make a difference in the way we live.
One: We yoke ourselves to Jesus
All: In hope, and in the prospect that he will make the difference.

Pastoral Prayer

Our God, fill us with the assurance of your grace. We need such assurance because we are so full of the sense of failure – so full of memories of having fallen short, of having let you down. We're so full of compromise – so full of poor choices and wrong decisions. We've been cruel and mean. We're full of words we said and wish we hadn't, as well as full of words we didn't say and wish we had. We're so full of it. Fill us with the assurance of your grace – the possibility of being full of you. This we pray in the name of the one full of you. Amen.

Prayer of Confession

Our God, we confess to knowing more about how you would have us be than actually being that way. We confess to professing more in our statements of faith than we make manifest in our living. We confess our ambivalence, our confusion, our frustration and our apathy about the discrepancy between what we believe and what we do. We confess to justifying our compromises. But we also confess to trusting you in and through our failures. We confess to clinging to your grace. For our most honest confession, we confess, is our confession of deepest gratitude for your grace in Christ Jesus, in whose name we pray. Amen.

Prayer of Dedication of Gifts and Self

Our God, we give to you this day, along with our gifts, our consistent attempts to live in your way as many times as we fall short. We give you our sense of what's right and what's wrong – as many times as we don't live into that knowledge. We give you our trust in your grace – as many times as we let you down. For we trust you, our God, to love us, more than we trust ourselves to live your love. This we pray, our God, in the name of the one who was and is your love lived. Amen.

Hymn of the Day
Creating God, Your Fingers Trace

Jeffrey Rowthorn's paraphrase of Psalm 148 was one of two winning entries in a competition for new psalm texts sponsored by The Hymn Society in the United States and Canada in 1979. Rowthorn actually did not know his text had been entered until he was notified of the win. The text first was published in *The Hymnal 1982* and has been included in most hymnals since. The most common tune associated with this text is HANCOCK, by Eugene W. Hancock, an organist, composer, and educator. It was first included with this text in the *Presbyterian Hymnal* (1990). Other tunes, including CANONBURY and CREATION, are also used, but HANCOCK is a strong tune that is well worth learning.

Children's Time: I'll Be with You

Talk with the children about doing something difficult. You might share a story of a job that was very tiring, or a long hike that exhausted you. Ask the children if they've ever had to do something that was really hard. What did it feel like to stop and have a rest? Or how did they feel when it was all over? What sort of things did you or they have for refreshment during the task or journey?

Sometimes when we are doing a hard task, it's a lot easier if someone works alongside us and helps us. Or if we're going on a long walk, someone might hold our hand, and that can make it easier.

Jesus knew that, as we journey through life, we might get tired or overwhelmed from time to time. We might think, "This is really hard. I don't know if I can go on."

Jesus said that we could turn to him, and he would give us rest. If we're feeling overwhelmed, we can talk to Jesus about it. When we're not sure how we're going to get through something, Jesus says, "I'll be with you. I'll help you through."

Long ago, St. Paul was struggling. He knew he wanted to do things well, but he didn't always manage it, and it was driving him crazy. Then he remembered that Jesus promised to be with us always and help us, and Paul felt a lot better.

Prayer: When we get stuck or worried or scared, O God, remind us that Jesus will help us always. Amen.

The Sermon: Sin in Me
Scripture: Romans 7:15-25a

(For sermon materials on Matthew 11:16-19, 25-30, see the March/April 2011 issue of *The Clergy Journal*; for sermon materials on Genesis 24:34-38, 42-49, 58-67, see the May/June 2010 planning issue of *The Clergy Journal*.)

Our text today begins with the very familiar verse: Paul's cry, "I do not understand my own actions." Within the context of trying to live in the way of Jesus, that's something with which we can all identify, for we all act in ways contrary to our professions of faith.

Paul's statement is even stronger in the Greek, literally translated, "What I do, I do not know" (N.T. Wright, "The Book of Romans" in *The New Interpreter's Bible*, Nashville: Abingdon, 2002, pp. 566-567). More than just being puzzled at the discrepancy between faith and life, Paul claims here a genuine ignorance about what he does. Remember, Paul remembers persecuting the church. "I didn't know what I was doing. I thought I was obeying God."

And we remind ourselves not only that the law of unintended consequences is always in effect (we never know the fullness of what we do), but also that these days, with our inevitable and typically unquestioned participation in all the systems of the status quo, we all too often, literally, do not know what we do. When we buy this or buy into that, we don't know what we support and encourage and justify, and in our ignorance, we do what we would never choose to do.

Paul goes on, "I also do what I don't want to do." It's not that that puzzling discrepancy between our beliefs and our lives doesn't have a place in our text; it's that Paul doesn't say the same thing twice. First, he addresses acting out of ignorance, then, acting out of that discrepancy.

Paul, often known for condemning the law, goes on to point out, "If I know what's right, if my faith and my understanding of the scriptures and the teachings of Jesus have led me to know what I should do (whether I do or don't), then the word of God, God's law – it's all good." It orients us within our living. It just doesn't get us where we need to go in terms of being able to match our actions to our knowledge of good and evil. I can want to do the right thing; I just can't do it.

"And here's what I've noticed," writes Paul. "The more I approach the possibility of living into love, the more other options appear – easier options, more immediately gratifying options. Not always bad options either. Some good options." As followers of God, we are often called not to choose good over evil, but to choose the ultimate over what's good and important. And though we know that, we can't always do it. So what is it that keeps us from doing what's right? Sin.

When we think of sin purely in moral and ethical terms, we think of evil behavior. But we then risk losing sight of the fact that good can be just as much a temptation to subvert the way of God. And in some ways, the more morally acceptable the distraction, the more of a distraction it can be. There's God, for example. We know, as does Paul, that commitment and dedication to God can be distorted and perverted. And that's sin. There's country. Calls to patriotism often demonstrate an empire's way of being subverting God's. And that's sin. There's family. We see in love of and allegiance to family a priority that can undermine commitment to God's way of being.

We know, as readers of scripture, that Jesus demands an allegiance that will not allow even family to compromise its radical call, for that, too, is sin. There's church. Clarence Jordan bemoaned the fact that the church itself all too often encourages young people to say "yes" to God, but then "no" to the consequences of that "yes." And that's sin.

411

It's certainly easier to talk about, think about, and preach against sin by condemning socially unacceptable or questionable behavior. But if sin is the mis-ordering of life as God would have life be ordered, we all participate in that mis-ordering, and the more socially acceptable our behavior is, the easier it is never to identify the sin in our living. Regardless of what it is that draws our allegiance away from God's way of living, sin should have a more confessional and a less judgmental tone.

For if sin is the tendency and the encouragement to take one of those easier options – one of those more immediately gratifying options, then it is always within us and always surrounds us, and the more we approach the possibility of actually living into love, the more those other options appear. As much as we want to live in the way of God, we can't. We don't. Not consistently. Not reliably.

Paul bemoans this state of affairs and demands who will save him, answering his own question in giving thanks to God for Jesus. Now one way of understanding Paul's gratitude for Jesus is that we've failed trying to make it on our own. What we've needed is some kind of transformation: a new heart (Jer 31:33), a rebirth (Jn 3:3). We've needed Jesus. For Jesus is affirmed as not just a man who made the right decisions – someone who got it all right – who faced all the temptation we face without succumbing; Jesus is not celebrated as the essence of the truly human, but as one who is more than we are. Because part of what being truly human means is that we can't live like God. Jesus will help us be more than we are.

So it is that with Jesus, we have hope. In Jesus, we have hope. But then, we run into the reality that once we are transformed, once we have a new heart, once we are reborn, once we know Jesus, once we are baptized, we *still* sin. And then we have to understand Paul's praise of Jesus not as the one who enables me to live the way I've not been able to, but Jesus as the one who ultimately makes it okay not to be able to. Not as an excuse. Not to minimize the importance. But Jesus as the one in and through whom the grace of God extends to us as sinners, saying, "In your ignorance, in your ambivalence, in your frustration, in your failures to live into the way of God, nonetheless, if you continue to want what God wants and if you continue to try, if you consistently orient yourself by the way of God, then you are forgiven. You are always loved. Be at peace."

– John Ballenger

Hymns
Opening Hymn
How Firm a Foundation

Sing My Song Backwards

Sermon Hymn
In Ancient Times the People Yearned

God of the Sparrow, God of the Whale

Closing Hymn
I Cannot Dance, O Love

Wonderful Grace of Jesus

July 10, 2011

4th Sunday after Pentecost (Proper 10 [15])
RC/Pres: 15th Sunday in Ordinary Time

Lessons (See p. 10 for guidelines)

Semi-continuous (SC)	Complementary (C)	Roman Catholic (RC)
Gen 25:19-34	Isa 55:10-13	Isa 55:10-11
Ps 119:105-112	Ps 65:(1-8), 9-13	Ps 65:10-14
Rom 8:1-11	Rom 8:1-11	Rom 8:18-23
Mt 13:1-9, 18-23	Mt 13:1-9, 18-23	Mt 13:1-23 or 13:1-9

Speaker's Introduction for the Lessons
Lesson 1
Genesis 25:19-34 (SC)
Just as Jacob and Esau are born into conflict with one another, so we continue to struggle against ourselves, each other, and God.

Isaiah 55:10-13 (C); 55:10-11 (RC)
When we hear and heed God's word in the world, our lives can be full of joy and abundance.

Lesson 2
Psalm 119:105-112 (SC)
Though the world holds affliction and conflict for us, God's word always offers guidance.

Psalm 65:(1-8), 9-13 (C); 65:10-14 (RC)
While we affirm the sovereignty of God, we understand that we work in partnership with God and all of creation.

Lesson 3
Romans 8:1-11 (SC/C)
Writing to a congregation that he did not found and never visited, Paul reassures them that their "sins of the flesh" have been replaced by the indwelling Spirit.

Romans 8:18-23 (RC)
Paul reassures the Christians in Rome that though they face struggles and trials, the Holy Spirit is always interceding on their behalf. The same remains true for us today.

Gospel
Matthew 13:1-9, 18-23 (SC/C) 13:1-23 (RC)

Jesus most often taught in parables, including today's parable of the sower, to help us turn our focus from our ordinary world to God's extraordinary world of hope.

Theme

We live life to the fullest only when we embody the Holy Spirit in the world.

Thought for the Day

Christianity overcomes law and despair by the certainty that we are the children of God. There is nothing higher than this.

– Paul Tillich (*The Shaking of the Foundations*,
New York: Charles Scribner's Sons, 1948, p. 135)

Sermon Summary

The Apostle Paul warns that when we pursue the trappings of this world, we ultimately will fail, even if we succeed by the world's standards. Christ calls us to wholly and fully embody the Holy Spirit and bring life and peace to a hurting and dying world.

Call to Worship

One: Holy One, we come offering thanks and praise.
All: Your word is a lamp unto our feet!
One: Holy One, we come seeking relief from our despair.
All: Your word is a lamp unto our feet!
One: Holy One, we come seeking your will for our lives.
All: Your word is a lamp unto our feet!
One: God, guide our hearts this day and always.
All: Your word is a lamp unto our feet!

– Adapted from Psalm 119

Pastoral Prayer

Holy God, we come before you today with thanks and praise. Even in a world of conflict, a world where we're told that we're failures unless we have more, do more, or make more than others, we know that worldly pursuits are ultimately a dead end. We ask, Lord, for your guidance, for your mercy, and for your grace. Prepare our hearts so that the good seed of your Spirit may fall afresh on us today. Amen.

Prayer of Confession

Patient God, we have missed the mark. Instead of seeking after your Spirit, we have sought out the spirit of this world. We have worked to gain the world's recognition, but have failed to think and act in ways that glorify your name alone. Loving God, we ask for forgiveness for our failings and for strength to walk the path you have set out before us. Guide us away from conflict, from pettiness, from competition, and greed, and guide us in your paths of righteousness and compassion. Amen.

Prayer of Dedication of Gifts and Self

God of abundance, we come giving you thanks and praise for many gifts you have bestowed upon us. We are a blessed people – blessed in material and spiritual gifts that we offer to you now. We ask that you take these gifts and multiply them to your glory. May our blessings from you go forth and not return to us empty. Amen.

Hymn of the Day
Breathe on Me, Breath of God

Edwin Hatch was born and raised in England. After eight years teaching in Canada, he returned to England. This text was first published in a leaflet *Between Doubt and Prayer* (1878). TRENTHAM was composed by Robert Jackson, an organist and tune writer in Lancashire, England. It was originally published in 1894 paired to another text. In the early 1900s it was matched to the Hatch text and they have remained together ever since. Sing this favorite with simplicity yet conviction. Within its quiet "exterior" there are some very powerful, faith-based phrases (basically the second and fourth line of each stanza).

Children's Time: Planting Seeds

Retell the story of the sower and the different kinds of soil. Mime the story with your hands as indicated.

Jesus once told a story about planting seeds in different kinds of soil. Someone went out to plant some seeds. They scattered seeds all over. *(Mime this action as you describe it.)* Some of the seeds fell on the road, and birds came and ate them up. *(Swoop one arm like a bird over the palm of the other hand.)* Some of the seeds fell on thin, rocky ground. They tried to grow *(hold arm vertical, wriggling fingers as if they are growing)*, but the sun came out and because the plants didn't have enough ground to put down roots, they dried up. *(Fold fingers back down.)*

Some of the seeds grew up among weeds *(wriggle fingers of both hands as if growing)*. But the weeds grew strong, and they choked the plants *(fingers of one hand "choke" the other fingers)*. But some of the seed fell on good soil, and grew tall, and produced a wonderful crop *(finger of both hands "grow" tall – reach arms up)*.

Jesus wasn't really telling a story about planting seeds; he was telling a story about God's love. *(Repeat the above actions as you tell the allegorical meanings)*. Some people hear the message of God's love, but they don't understand it because other things gobble up their time and interests. Some people get all excited when they hear it, but then they get bored easily and forget about God's love. Some people hear the message, but then they start worrying about other things, and the other things just sort of take over.

But some people hear the good news, and it changes their life. They are so pleased to hear about God's love, they decide to follow Jesus all their lives.

Prayer: God of wonder, you plant seeds of your love all over the world. Help us to grow as you would like. Amen.

The Sermon: We've Got Spirit, Yes We Do!
Scripture: Romans 8:1-11
(For sermon materials on Matthew 13:1-9, 18-23, see the March/April 2011 issue of *The Clergy Journal*; for sermon materials on Genesis 25:19-34, see the May/June 2010 planning issue of *The Clergy Journal*.)

"We've got spirit, yes we do! We've got spirit, how about you?"

This is the cheer I remember most from my high school days. It's a classic in call-and-respond liturgy in the ritual of high school football. Our cheerleaders would jump, shake their pom-poms, and lead the crowd on our side of the field in the chant directed at the crowd on the other side of the field, challenging them to respond in kind.

And they would: "We've got spirit, yes we do! We've got spirit, how about you?"

Our side would respond again with the same chant. It would go on for a few rounds back and forth, each time the crowd getting louder and louder, clapping their hands and stomping their feet on the wooden bleachers, hoping that sheer volume would finally prove who, indeed, had the most spirit.

I've often marveled at the tenacity and ferocity of sports fans, whether it's a high school, college, or professional level team. The most dedicated fans are as loyal to their team as the most pious person is loyal to their religion. For some, sport is a religion. Each Sunday or Monday night, they perform familiar rituals of gathering with friends in front of a big screen television or in the actual stadium with reverence many feel coming into a church. They perform a ritual of breaking bread – or nacho chips – together, bonding in a rite of eating and drinking, sometimes to excess. They mourn together when their team loses, commiserating over bad seasons, falling stats, or poor coaching. They rejoice when their team is victorious, recounting stories of athletic glory for years, memorizing and repeating stats in the same way some people memorize and recite Bible verses.

The apostle Paul would recognize this behavior but probably not approve. What these rabid sports fans exude – which some may mistake for obsession – is spirit. They truly have captured the spirit of the game, the spirit of their favorite team. They fully embody the team that inspires them, whether by wearing team colors, or sporting team logos on their cars, or simply having some uncanny ability to spot another fan even without such labeling.

While Paul might dismiss devotion to a sports team as pursuit of a "fleshly desire" – something wholly of this world – he would approve, I believe, of the zealousness of sports fans. Perhaps if Paul had been one to carry pom-poms, he might have come up with the same cheer for the Romans to repeat back to him.

"We've got spirit, yes we do! We've got spirit, how about you?"

The beginning of Romans 8 is Paul's version of this chant as he challenges the Romans "to set the mind on the Spirit" instead of things of the "flesh."

The Greek words for "to set" and "mind" are the same: *phronema*, which means "thoughts and purpose." The King James Version makes this relationship clear: "For to be carnally minded [is] death; but to be spiritually minded [is] life and peace."

The verb "to be" here is *phronema* just as the word *minded* is – which means that our thoughts and purpose *are* who we are. If we are to be *phronema*, then we are to *be* our thoughts and our purpose. Paul knows that too often our thoughts and our purpose are set on things of the flesh or *sarx* – meaning our imperfect human nature.

Our mind is usually consumed with "fleshly" things like how we can get ahead in the world, how we can get more than, or at least exactly what, our neighbor has, how we can get more money, how we can get a better car, a better house, a better job, a better partner. Like Esau plotting against Jacob, our minds are spinning continuously, hatching some plot to get ahead in this life, to outdo one another in worldly competition, even if that means stepping on someone else or cheating another out of what may be rightly theirs.

Paul knows how single-mindedly dedicated human beings can be to things of the flesh. After all, it feels so good when we get them – and for still others, even the pursuit of them spells pure happiness. However, when we embody those worldly desires of fame, fortune, or power, it can lead, ultimately, to nothing good. Indeed, we have seen how fleeting all three can be in this world as celebrities become has-beens, the rich are reduced to rags through corruption or greed, and the powerful brought down by their own hubris. Embodying worldly desires, Paul tells us, can only end in one way: death.

Seeking to put our thoughts and purpose in tune with God's Holy Spirit, however, brings both life and peace. The Greek word for life is *zoe*, which means more than just being physically alive. It also means to live life to the fullest, to live authentically as God has called us to live. This kind of life may or may not have some of the trappings of fame, fortune, or power, but they are not the goal of this Spirit-led life. The goal of this life is to embody God's Holy Spirit in our thoughts and purpose. In doing so, we live an abundant life full of peace, or *eirene*, which not only brings personal peace to our mind, body, and spirit, but manifests itself also in a corporate tranquility. We cannot make war on others if the Spirit is in us because the Spirit also brings with it gifts of compassion, love, and mercy.

For us to be able to embody that Spirit, however, we must be open to hearing God's call to us away from our "fleshly" nature that craves competition and domination over others. The soil of our hearts and minds must already be tilled and ready for sowing, otherwise the seeds of the Spirit will fall along the path and be eaten by the birds.

Examine the Spirit you are embodying today. Is it a "fleshly" spirit that drives you to "keep up with the Joneses" or seek accolades from this world? Are you ready to put the world's pursuits out of your mind and instead "set the mind on the Spirit"?

Listen as God calls to you today:

"We've got spirit, yes we do! We've got spirit, how about you?"

– Candace Chellew-Hodge

Hymns
Opening Hymn
    All Creatures of Our God and King
    Spirit
Sermon Hymn
    Lord Be Glorified
    Take My Life and Let It Be
Closing Hymn
    Come Share the Spirit
    Isaiah the Prophet Has Written of Old

July 17, 2011

5th Sunday after Pentecost (Proper 11 [16])
RC/Pres: 16th Sunday in Ordinary Time

Lessons (See p. 10 for guidelines)

Semi-continuous (SC)	Complementary (C)	Roman Catholic (RC)
Gen 28:10-19a	Wis 12:13, 16-19 or Isa 44:6-8	Wis 12:13, 16-19
Ps 139:1-12, 23-24	Ps 86:11-17	Ps 86:5-6, 9-10, 15-16
Rom 8:12-25	Rom 8:12-25	Rom 8:26-27
Mt 13:24-30, 36-43	Mt 13:24-30, 36-43	Mt 13:24-43 or 13:24-30

Speaker's Introduction for the Lessons
Lesson 1
Genesis 28:10-19a (SC)
Esau may have lost his father's blessing because of his brother Jacob's deceit, but at Bethel, Jacob learns the true meaning of blessing as he encounters God's presence and promise.

Wisdom of Solomon 12:13, 16-19 (C/RC)
The author of this book contemplates the nature of God's power, especially when it seems that the righteous are constantly under attack.

Lesson 2
Psalm 139:1-12, 23-24 (SC)
Though we grow in love and knowledge of God in community, God knows us each intimately as individuals. Indeed, we are "fearfully and wonderfully made."

Psalm 86:11-17 (C); 86:5-6, 9-10, 15-16 (RC)
When we are in distress, we can cry out to our God who will "give ear" to our prayer.

Lesson 3
Romans 8:12-25 (SC/C)
We may face suffering and evil in this world, but ultimately, we are not children of earthly parents, but God's children, adopted through our relationship with Christ.

Romans 8:26-27 (RC)
Often when we go to God in prayer, we find ourselves speechless. In these times, we are assured that the Holy Spirit lifts our deepest longings to God.

Gospel
Matthew 13:24-30, 36-43 (SC/C); 13:24-43 or 13:24-30 (RC)
Farmers in Jesus' time were familiar with the "tares" in their field. In their early growth these tares were hard to tell apart from the wheat, but ultimately the two must be separated.

Theme
Don't be quick to judge the "weeds" of this world; they could be wheat in disguise.

Thought for the Day
Develop your sense of perspective. When everything around you looks like weeds, remember: From the heavens, all is a garden.

–Philip Toshio Sudo (*Zen Guitar*, New York, Simon & Schuster Paperbacks, 1997, p. 118)

Sermon Summary
When we think about weeds, we conjure up images of ugly plants choking out the beautiful plants in the garden. But, those weeds exist for a reason, and God can bring us blessings through "some good weed."

Call to Worship
One: Rejoice, people of God! The Lord knows you completely.
All: You know when we sit down and when we rise up.
One: Rejoice, people of God! The Lord knows you completely.
All: Where can we go from God's spirit?
One: Rejoice, people of God! The Lord knows you completely.
All: God's hand leads us no matter where we go, near or far.
One: Rejoice, people of God! The Lord knows you completely.
All: Search us, God. Know our hearts.

– Adapted from Psalm 139

Pastoral Prayer

All encompassing God, we come before you with hearts full of thanks and praise. We give you thanks for this day, for this community of faith, for the people in our lives who challenge us, bless us, and make us grow in faith. Assure us now, God, that we are your beloved children, adopted into the holy family of faith through Christ Jesus. Give us the strength we need this day and every day. Guide our lives so that we may be a blessing and bring honor and glory to you. Amen.

Prayer of Confession

God of love and mercy, we come to you today, our hearts heavy with the words we have spoken and the deeds we have done that have disappointed you. Bring our awareness to you, God. Help us to remember that wherever we are and whatever we are doing, you are there with us. Search our hearts this morning, God, and weed out those thoughts and deeds that bring dishonor to you and to us. Forgive us where we have failed you and make your presence so real to us in each moment of our lives so that our thoughts and actions will be filled with your spirit. Amen.

Prayer of Dedication of Gifts and Self

God you have granted us many blessings, whether it is material or spiritual wealth. For this we offer thanks and return a portion of those blessings for your mission in our world. Generous God, help us to understand the true meaning of your blessings – that they are not in earthly possessions, but in your presence and your promise in our lives. Use us to bless still others. Amen.

Hymn of the Day
Sois la Semilla/You Are the Seed

This hymn was written by Spanish theologian and composer Cesáreo Gabaraín. It first appeared in a collection *Dios con nosotros* published in Madrid. The tune name, ID Y ENSEÑAD, literally means "go and teach." There is a very strong sense of empowerment found in the text which makes it an ideal commissioning, ordination, or renewal hymn. The tune is spirited with repeated motives in the refrain. At first, teach the congregation the refrain and have the stanzas sung by soloists. Soon everyone will want to sing this infectious hymn. Guitar with percussion is the preferred accompaniment, however, if piano is used keep the playing light and very rhythmic.

Children's Time: Judging Others

Do you ever feel like you're not useful? Do you ever feel like people are judging you? Do you think you ever judge others?

We probably all judge other people at one time or another. If someone is mean to us, we might call them a "meany," and that's judging them. Or someone might stutter, and we look down on them.

Jesus told his disciples something very important about judging others.

"Imagine," Jesus said, "someone who planted some seeds. But in the night, some weeds came up. The yard workers said, 'Gee, you planted good seeds, and now there are all these weeds. Let us pull them out.' But the landowner said, 'No. Let's wait and see that they are like.'"

It's as if Jesus was trying to say, "Don't judge other people too quickly. Get to know them. Give them a chance to live and act, and then you'll get an idea of what they are really like."

Judging others can be hurtful; it also hurts when we are judged.

Prayer: Help us, gracious God, not to judge others, but to give everyone a chance. Amen.

The Sermon: Some Good Weed
Scripture: Matthew 13:24-30, 36-43

(For sermon materials on Genesis 28:10-19a, see the March/April 2011 issue of *The Clergy Journal*; for sermon materials on Romans 8:12-25, see the May/June 2010 planning issue of *The Clergy Journal*.)

The world is a scary place, full of war, famine, corruption, murder, violence, and indifference. We live, however, in a world of paradox, full of evil but also full of beauty and grace, where people love their families but do not hesitate to kill their enemies.

My guitar teacher's 25-year-old son died a couple of years ago in a car accident. A good man is gone while evil people continue to thrive. Babies die every day, while dictators and oppressors live full and healthy lives. We don't understand the world. Didn't our maker sow good seeds? Where did all this evil come from? Like Jacob, we feel that we have somehow been cheated out of our worldly blessings by a conniving brother. We begin to wonder how so many weeds sprung up in our good garden.

Even in our anxiety over the weeds in our garden, we get a little excited when we hear this parable. There are weeds in the wheat? Great! I've got my gloves on, let's get to weeding! We're certain that we can tell the difference between the good people and the bad people in the world! We know the wheat from the weeds!

But Jesus puts a damper on our enthusiasm. He tells us to leave the weeds among the wheat – let the good and the evil mix. We are not wise enough to know the difference between what's good and what's evil. What we call weeds, God may call wheat – only God can finally judge anyone, or any thing, or any situation in our world. If we appoint ourselves as judges, we may destroy some good weed.

Let us consider that good weed – that cannibas, Mary Jane, pot, weed, reefer, dope – it goes by many names. It's gotten a bad rap in our society's war on drugs. Marijuana has been grown for fiber for thousands of years. Hemp fabric is one of the strongest natural fibers out there. The plant – this good weed – also has many medicinal uses. The plant, and its derivatives, can be used to treat everything from glaucoma to multiple sclerosis, from cancer to migraines. It can also be turned into a bio-fuel and used to power our cars without even giving us a contact buzz. I'm not advocating using marijuana as a mind-altering drug, but we've demonized a weed that is useful in many ways. It is indeed a "good weed."

If you've ever been to Charleston, South Carolina, you've probably seen another plant often considered a weed – seagrass. This plant may not seem beautiful to us, but it plays an important role in the ocean by providing oxygen, food, and a place to live for many ocean animals. But, that good weed, in the hands of a skilled basket maker, can be transformed into something beautiful. The tradition of making seagrass baskets dates back to the 1700s. This is an ancient use of "some good weed."

God can transform the ugly in the world to things of beauty. I don't know about you, but I'm glad it's God who does the final judging and not me. Whenever someone flies past me on the highway, I "wish them troopers." In other words, they are my "cop bait," and I want to see it when the cop nails them. I want to be there to witness justice being meted out. I want to drive by and laugh! In fact, if it were up to me, doing stupid things in traffic would get you the death penalty. Thank God it's not up to me because I wouldn't live through my own rules.

But, we want to see people get their comeuppance, don't we? We want to see the speeder nailed, the thief punished, the cheater caught, the murderer condemned. We want our thirst for vengeance satisfied. We're so stuck on this idea that we make movie after movie after movie on just such a theme – the bad guy getting his due – usually violently.

You see, there are not just weeds in the world, but weeds in our own hearts. The Apostle Paul told the Romans that it's not just the whole creation that groans in pain, but we do as well. We groan inwardly while we wait for redemption, not just for this world but for ourselves.

Vengeance is just one of those weeds; there are others: pride, envy, gluttony, dishonesty, indifference, cheating, stealing, lying, anger. They're all there – all within each of us – weeds among the wheat of our good works, our good thoughts, our love, our caring, our compassion, and our hope. We have tons of self-help books ready to help us weed our inner gardens, but what if we stopped and gave thanks for our weeds instead of seeking to rip them up by the roots?

It has been my anger that has caused me the greatest pain and the greatest joy. My anger has harmed relationships, driven people I love away from me, held me hostage, and caused damage to people and things. But, it has been in tending the good weed of anger that I have grown to be a stronger, healthier, and happier person. I have learned the art of forgiveness. I have learned the art of compassion and self-control – all because of that good weed of anger. That good weed of anger has also led me to get involved in causes that seek to do good in the world – that seek to grow the good wheat stronger.

Think of your own weeds. Think of those things about yourself that you're ashamed of, that you don't want anyone else in the world to know about. Think about your weaknesses, your addictions, your guilty pleasures. Now, give thanks for them. That's some good weed you've got growing there. Don't be so quick to yank those up by the roots. Those good weeds challenge you to grow stronger wheat, to make your wheat outgrow all the weeds in your inner garden. Use the weeds wisely and God can redeem them – and create something beautiful in your life.

– Candace Chellew-Hodge

Hymns
Opening Hymn
You Are the Seed
Come, Ye Thankful People, Come
Sermon Hymn
Standing on the Promises
Here I Am, Lord
Closing Hymn
Rejoice Ye Pure in Heart
O Christ, the Healer, We Have Come

July 24, 2011

6th Sunday after Pentecost (Proper 12 [17])
RC/Pres: 17th Sunday in Ordinary Time

Lessons (See p. 10 for guidelines)

Semi-continuous (SC)	Complementary (C)	Roman Catholic (RC)
Gen 29:15-28	1 Kings 3:5-12	1 Kings 3:5, 7-12
Ps 105:1-11, 45b or Ps 128	Ps 119:129-136	Ps 119:57, 72, 76-77, 127-130
Rom 8:26-39	Rom 8:26-39	Rom 8:28-30
Mt 13:31-33, 44-52	Mt 13:31-33, 44-52	Mt 13:44-52 or 13:44-46

Speaker's Introduction for the Lessons
Lesson 1
Genesis 29:15-28 (SC)

After tricking Esau out of his father's blessing, Jacob flees to his mother's homeland to live with his uncle Laban to escape Esau's plan to kill him.

1 Kings 3:5-12 (C); 3:5, 7-12 (RC)

King Solomon is known for his wisdom, but it didn't just appear. He specifically asked God for an understanding mind to discern between evil and good.

Lesson 2
Psalm 105:1-11, 45b (SC)

God has done wonderful works, not just for Israel, but for all people on earth. Let us give thanks to the Lord.

Psalm 119:129-136 (C); 119:57, 72, 76-77, 127-130 (RC)

The longest psalm in the Bible makes a poetic plea for God to show us his will for our lives and to help us follow God's ways.

Lesson 3
Romans 8:26-39 (SC/C); 8:28-30 (RC)

The Christians in Rome faced much oppression from their Roman rulers, but Paul assured them that their justification from the God of creation was more powerful than any earthly ruler.

Gospel
Matthew 13:31-33, 44-52 (SC/C); 13:44-52 or 13:44-46 (RC)

Speaking in parables, Jesus reveals God's realm as from small, even insignificant beginnings, but worth sacrificing everything we are and own to possess.

Theme

We say we understand Jesus' commands to us, but do our actions prove it?

Thought for the Day

Like Jacob, some of us have found the worst parts of ourselves converted into something better, our small expectations shattered in the presence of God's great abundance.

– Kathleen Norris (*Amazing Grace: A Vocabulary of Faith*, New York, Riverhead Books, 1998, p. 299)

Sermon Summary

Jesus often spoke in parables that could be confusing. He likens God's realm to a mustard seed, yeast, and expensive pearls. We prove that we have understood Jesus' words when we realize nothing is more valuable than being God's servants in this world.

Call to Worship

One: We sing praises to our Lord,

All: Give thanks to the Lord, call on God's name.

One: We rejoice in God's holy name,

All: Give thanks to the Lord, call on God's name.

One: We seek our strength in God,

All: Give thanks to the Lord, call on God's name.

One: We remember the blessings God has granted us,

All: Give thanks to the Lord, call on God's name.

One: God will never forget his promises to us,

All: Give thanks to the Lord, call on God's name.

– Adapted from Psalm 105

Pastoral Prayer

Living God, we approach you in our weakness, asking for strength for our journeys from the only place it is available – your Spirit. Fill us, God, with your Holy Spirit, especially when our worldly burdens seem heavy and our hearts fill with despair for our world. We know, God, that you are always at work, bringing good things out of things that may seem random, or even evil, to us. Help us to trust you, holy one. We are justified in you, God. Help us to know, without a doubt, that nothing in this world can separate us from your love. Amen.

Prayer of Confession

God of all knowledge, we confess that too often we rely on our own understanding and not on your wisdom. We often forget the blessings you have bestowed on us and instead focus on the problems and obstacles we face. Forgive us, God, for our lack of faith, for our shortsightedness, and for our failure to call upon your name whenever we feel challenged or inadequate. Remind us, God, that we are a forgiven people, a loved people, and that you are always available to show us grace and love. Amen.

Prayer of Dedication of Gifts and Self

We give thanks to you, Lord, for the abundance you have bestowed upon us. Whether it's an abundance of money, an abundance of time, an abundance of spirit, an abundance of love, an abundance of patience, we understand that all blessings, monetary and spiritual, come from you. It is in that spirit that we offer these gifts back to you for your blessing, knowing you will increase them according to your will and use them for your purposes in our world. Amen.

Hymn of the Day
Seek Ye First the Kingdom of God

Karen Lafferty wrote the first stanza and tune for this popular song after attending a Bible study on "Seek ye first the kingdom of God." Stanzas two and three, which have become an essential part of the song, were added later from unknown sources. The tune LAFFERTY is also known as SEEK YE FIRST. Sing this folk-style hymn with energy and sustained power. The descant, often not used, is really a very integral part of the song. It can be used as a descant or the song can be sung as a two-part round, the text being part one and the descant alleluias being the second. Guitar is the instrument of choice, however if piano is used, fill in the harmonies with light improvised broken chords.

Children's Time: The Realm of God

Jesus used to speak a lot about the realm or kingdom of God. People wanted to know what it was like. Some thought it meant heaven, or a place we go far in the future. Jesus told people over and over that the realm of God was here and now. Jesus tried to give the people some images of what the realm of God might be like. Here are some:

It's like mustard seed. It may not seem like much, but when you plant it – wow! It becomes a big tree, and birds come to its branches. The realm of God starts small, but it grows. And there's room for all in it.

It's like yeast that someone kneaded into bread – you can mix it into your life and it makes things grow.

The realm of God is like a treasure in a field. When you discover it, you're so excited you sell all you have to buy that field.

It's like someone who found a wonderful pearl, and sold everything to buy it. The realm of God is valuable!

Jesus told the people other things as well. More than anything else, he simply wanted us all to know that the Realm of God is something wonderful, it is all around us, and it is something we should celebrate.

Prayer: God, help us to notice and celebrate your realm that is everywhere. Amen.

The Sermon: Do You Understand?
Scripture: Matthew 13:31-33, 44-52

(For sermon materials on Genesis 29:15-28, see the March/April 2011 issue of *The Clergy Journal*; for sermon materials on Romans 8:26-39, see the May/June 2010 planning issue of *The Clergy Journal*.)

I nodded slowly, not sure exactly what else to do. My partner had spent the last few minutes excitedly describing what she wanted to do to renovate one of our bathrooms. I had tried to listen attentively, but she had lost me shortly after saying, "Here's what I want to do with the bathroom . . . "

The problem is that I am not the kind of person who can visualize things that aren't there. You can't point at something and say, "Imagine that wall gone and the tub over there." I can't make it happen in my head. I see a wall and the tub in the other spot and that's all it will ever be until you physically change the layout and show it to me again.

Truthfully, I had not understood a word she had said, but admitting that would mean she would simply repeat everything she had said, and again ask, "Now, do you understand?"

Simply nodding the first time around and adding, "That sounds great" let me right off the hook and saved us some time. I trusted her that whatever she had planned would look fantastic and found it easier to affirm her than to understand her.

When I read today's Gospel, I had to wonder about those disciples. Were they treating Jesus the way I treat my spouse – simply nodding their assent without really understanding just so Jesus would move on to something they really did get?

Jesus asks the disciples, "Have you understood all this?" after telling them several obscure parables to describe God's reign in the world. He told them the kingdom was like a mustard seed, like yeast, like treasure hidden in a field, like fine pearls, or like net tossed out to sea where the good catch is sorted from the bad afterward.

I imagine the disciples' heads were spinning at this point. The kingdom is like, what? They, like we, wanted to know how Jesus was going to change the world. They wanted to know how Jesus was going to help them get rid of their oppressors. They wanted to know how Jesus was going to bring about a revolution that would change the world as they experienced it. In short, they wanted to know how Jesus would overthrow the worldly government that ruled over them. How could a mustard seed, some yeast, some hidden treasure, pearls, and sorting out the catch of the day accomplish any of this?

But, Jesus wasn't concerned with revolution against the earthly powers. Replacing one human institution with another human institution, even if the new institution is more benevolent and generous to the least of these than the previous one, would not usher in God's realm. Jesus would have understood the sentiment expressed by the 1960s rock band The Who when they sang: "Meet the new boss, same as the old boss."

Instead, Jesus was inviting his disciples, and us, to view the world in a different light – to change our perspective. It's not big revolutions that change the world, but little revolutions with the hearts and minds of every human being in the world. Small things like mustard seeds become imposing bushes. Just a tiny bit of yeast can yield an enormous amount of bread – enough to feed multitudes. The kingdom is of such great value that when we find it, we'll sell all we have to own it. Worldly goods are nothing when compared to the spiritual riches God's realm brings to us and to the world. God helps us sort out our daily catch – tossing the bad things aside that would distract us from working to accomplish God's will in our lives and in the world.

I'm reminded of another parable, one not told by Jesus but by other traditions that tells the story of a woman who had found a precious stone. She put the stone in her bag and went on her way. The next day, a hungry traveler came by her on the road and asked if she had anything to eat. As she rummaged in her bag, the man spied the precious stone she had. "Instead of food, would you give me that stone?"

Without hesitation, the woman smiled and handed over the stone. The traveler left feeling elated. He had something better than food. He had something that he could sell and end all of his earthly troubles. He hurried off to town to enjoy his newfound riches.

A couple of days passed and again the woman was traveling the same road, and she ran into the same man. He approached her and handed her the precious stone.

"I had intended to sell this stone and become rich," he told her, "but after I thought about it, I realized that you can give me something even more precious."

"What is that?" asked the woman.

"I want whatever it is you have that made you able to give me that stone," he said.

"Have you understood all this?" Jesus asked his disciples and continues to ask us. Have we understood that God's realm is not about worldly riches, but about the abundant riches of the Spirit? Have we understood that God's realm is about gladly giving away ourselves and all we have to anyone and everyone who asks it of us? Have we truly understood, as Paul told the Romans, that no earthly power finally separates us from God's realm?

The disciples *said* they understood. But, then they, and those who came after them, spent the next few hundred years proving that they *didn't* really get it. Church fathers spent centuries arguing over Jesus' divinity and humanity, over how or why his death was redemptive, over whether his mother was a virgin, and over a myriad of other doctrinal arguments instead of paying attention to the mustard seed, the yeast, the hidden treasure, or the pearl of great value that needed to be cultivated in their own hearts. While they argued, people starved.

"Have you understood all this?" We have, only when we spend less time arguing about who Jesus is and what he means and instead get to work obeying his commandment to love each other and stop pursuing worldly ways to bring about God's realm.

"Have you understood all this?"

– Candace Chellew-Hodge

Hymns
Opening Hymn
Let Us Talents and Tongues Employ
Colorful Creator
Sermon Hymn
We Plant a Grain of Mustard Seed
Enter in the Realm of God
Closing Hymn
O Master, Let Me Walk with Thee
Make Me a Blessing

July 31, 2011

7th Sunday after Pentecost (Proper 13 [18])
RC/Pres: 18th Sunday in Ordinary Time

Lessons (See p. 10 for guidelines)

Semi-continuous (SC)	Complementary (C)	Roman Catholic (RC)
Gen 32:22-31	Isa 55:1-5	Isa 55:1-3
Ps 17:1-7, 15	Ps 145:8-9, 14-21	Ps 145:8-9, 15-18
Rom 9:1-5	Rom 9:1-5	Rom 8:35, 37-39
Mt 14:13-21	Mt 14:13-21	Mt 14:13-21

Speaker's Introduction for the Lessons
Lesson 1
Genesis 32:22-31 (SC)

Just as God gives Jacob a new name and future of hope, so does God daily renew our lives and call us God's beloved children.

Isaiah 55:1-5 (C); 55:1-3 (RC)

A community in exile is invited to "come, buy, and eat," but they have no money. Instead, it is God's word that fills and enriches our lives.

Lesson 2
Psalm 17:1-7, 15 (SC)

When we feel that we have been treated unjustly by the world or the people in our lives, we are assured of God's justice in all situations.

Psalm 145:8-9, 14-21 (C); 145:8-9, 15-18 (RC)

This psalm is written as an "acrostic," meaning each verse begins with a successive letter from the Hebrew alphabet, literally covering God's greatness from "A" to "Z."

Lesson 3
Romans 9:1-5 (SC/C)

The Apostle Paul finds himself in great pain over the fact that despite his preaching, many Jews still rejected the gospel of Jesus Christ. Here he swears to the veracity of his message.

Romans 8:35, 37-39 (RC)

Paul rounds out this part of his letter to the Romans with a doxology praising the ultimate power of God to reconcile us to him no matter what obstacles we may encounter.

Gospel
Matthew 14:13-21 (SC/C/RC)

Just as Isaiah urges the Israelites to rely on God for sustenance, so too the crowd gathered around Jesus are fed, their bellies and their hearts filled with God's grace.

Theme

No matter how small we may feel our gifts are, God has the power to increase them.

Thought for the Day

Never hesitate to bring your gifts to God. No matter how small, God will transform your gifts into blessings that feed the multitude.

Sermon Summary

Whenever we encounter miracle stories in the scriptures, we often get bogged down arguing over whether it literally happened or not and miss the power of the stories. Here, Jesus tells us that there is no gift too small to offer to God. All of our gifts will be transformed into something that can bless and change the world.

Call to Worship

One: Have you come here thirsty?
All: Come, buy, and eat.
One: Have you come here hungry?
All: Come, buy, and eat.
One: Have you come here tired from labor?
All: Come, buy, and eat.
One: Though you have no money,
All: Come, buy, and eat.
One: God provides all that is good.
All: We listen to our God, so that we may live.

– Adapted from Isaiah 55:1-5

435

Pastoral Prayer

Holy One, we come to you hungry, wanting to be fed from your spirit, from your word, from your community. We come thirsty and tired from our journeys. We come with empty pockets, with nothing to buy what we truly seek. We come expecting miracles. We come expecting to leave with a full heart and mind. We come with praise in our hearts. We come with our gifts, whether large or small. We come with our faith, whether weak or strong. Most importantly, God, we have come. We have come to this place to worship you and grow in love and community. We seek your blessing. Fill us. Amen.

Prayer of Confession

O God, we call upon you; we ask that you hear our words. We cry to you words of anguish, words of despair, words of hopelessness and helplessness. We have failed you, God, in so many ways. The weight of the world is upon us and we feel as though we are being crushed. But, just as you have forgiven Jacob and given him a new name, you are faithful to us as well. Renew us this day. Forgive us for how we have failed you and others. Thank you for calling us your beloved, forgiven children. Amen.

Prayer of Dedication of Gifts and Self

Generous and loving God, we come before you today offering our small gifts, knowing that you have the miracle-working power to take even our smallest offerings and multiply them. God, we entrust these gifts to you and wait with anticipation to gather the leftover blessings after the multitude has been fed. We give you thanks and praise for your blessings great and small. Amen.

Hymn of the Day
Let Us Talents and Tongues Employ

This lively hymn first appeared as "Communion Calypso" in *Break Not the Circle* (1975), a collection of songs by Fred Kaan and Doreen Potter. In three short stanzas Kaan states some very basic truths about our beliefs and lives as Christians. Potter's tune, Linstead, is actually an arrangement of a Jamaican folk tune. This song is ideally suited for a hymn after communion or a sending forth hymn. It joyous rhythms and resounding last line (refrain) should send people forth with smiles on their faces and a willingness to face the world. Make sure that the syncopated rhythms are crisply executed. The use of hand percussion such as claves, bongos, and maracas will further enliven an already lively song.

Children's Time: Lots of Food!

(Preparation: If you wish, bring some fish-shaped crackers to share with the children as you tell the story. Bring a plate as well.)

One day, Jesus wanted to be alone. He just wanted some time to himself. But the people who liked to hear his stories followed him. Soon there was a huge crowd, and evening fell.

Some of the disciples came to Jesus and said, "We're in the middle of nowhere, and there are a lot of people here. Send them away so they can go home and eat. We don't have any food."

Jesus said, "Why don't you give them something to eat?"

"But we have only five buns and a couple fish," they replied. *(If you have crackers, carefully count a few onto the plate.)*

"Bring them to me," Jesus said. And he took them and gave them to the disciples, and they began to hand them out to everyone. Amazingly, there was enough for everyone to eat. *(Pour a bunch of crackers onto the plate.)* We're not sure how Jesus made it happen; some people think that maybe everyone had a bit of food but they didn't want to share it. When they saw Jesus and the disciples sharing, they began to take out their food and eat it.

However it happened, people remembered it forever. It was a wonderful reminder of how God cares for us, even in tough situations.

Prayer: Thank you, loving God, for the many ways you care for us and feed us. Amen.

The Sermon: From Small Things, Big Things One Day Come
Scripture: Matthew 14:13-21

(For sermon materials on Genesis 32:22-31, see the March/April 2011 issue of *The Clergy Journal*; for sermon materials on Romans 9:1-5, see the May/June 2010 planning issue of *The Clergy Journal*.)

Have you "backrubbed" today? I have; in fact, I "backrub" nearly every single day. It's both fun and educational. I learn a lot when I backrub – things I never knew before! I have been known to backrub friends, family, enemies, even strangers. I have even backrubbed famous people – names you would know! Occasionally, I backrub alone but I'll do it even in a crowd. I have backrubbed in the airport, at the office, in hotels, in coffee shops, and even in the privacy of my own home.

If you're honest, you too have backrubbed. Many of you do it daily. Many of you will backrub one another, or backrub this church, or backrub someone you're interested in, or even backrub something you're not interested in at all.

What does it mean to "backrub"? Well, back in 1996, that was the name of something many of us do now without even thinking about it. "Backrub" was the original name for the search engine "Google." The name was probably a reference to the underlying algorithm which counts back-links as affirmative votes. That's what makes a page popular in searches, and it's the same approach that Google now calls PageRank.

These days we use the word *Google* in all those sentences I used – we "Google" our friends, families, strangers, ourselves. We Google anywhere we can reach the Internet – airports, coffee shops, hotels. Employers regularly Google job applicants to check them out. Sometimes it's even better than a criminal background check at uncovering things you may not want your employer – or future employer to know.

"Google" has become such a common thing in our world, we don't even think about it any more. Google offers us everything from a search engine, to a Web browser, to email, to online books, to maps, news, and even a bird's eye view of Earth.

But, Google wasn't always this big. Originally, it was just an idea between two guys – Larry Page and Sergey Brin – at Stanford University. They were frustrated with the early versions of search engines on the Web and all the unrelated pages that would come up in searches. They set out to make the world's best search engine, and now they're a company that posts billions of dollars in profits every year.

The company started in a friend's basement in Menlo Park, California, before moving to Palo Alto. In 1997, they decided that the search engine needed a new name. Google's history page said the name is "a play on the word 'googol,' a mathematical term for the number represented by the numeral 1 followed by 100 zeros. The use of the term reflects their mission to organize a seemingly infinite amount of information on the web."

So, thankfully, now we're talking about "Googling" each other instead of "backrubbing" each other. Aren't you glad? I know I am.

The Google story is reminiscent of early stories of other companies that started small, in garages, like Microsoft and Apple. From these small beginnings, huge things have grown. Like tiny apple seeds that can produce an entire orchard of trees, like a bulb that becomes a beautiful flower or the hidden promise of a cocoon – from small things, big things one day come.

July 31, 2011
7th Sunday after Pentecost (Proper 13 [18])
RC/Pres: 18th Sunday in Ordinary Time

Today's Gospel reading is a familiar one where Jesus feeds 5000 people with just a few loaves of bread and some fish. In fact, it's one of the few stories about Jesus that makes it into all four Gospel accounts of his life. There are some parts that vary with each story, but overall the story is the same. That tells us that this event was pivotal to Jesus' followers and contains a message that is so important we still need to hear it today.

However, many churches and church people get sidetracked from the real message of this story because they get hung up arguing over whether or not a miracle really took place. Many people believe that miracle stories are literally true – that Jesus took these loaves and fishes and multiplied them so the crowd would be fed with much left over. Others believe that the miracle stories are more metaphor than fact – meant to point to a larger story outside of any literal sense.

What all the arguing misses, however, is the real, raw power of this story. What this story really illustrates is Jesus' power to take even our smallest gifts and infinitely multiply them with more than enough left over.

Jesus tells the disciples to bring the meager gift of five loaves and two fishes to him. The disciples were dubious about whether the small amount of food would feed such a large crowd, but Jesus knew that it wasn't the size of the gift that mattered. What matters is the giving.

What Jesus asks us to do is give whatever it is we have – and that doesn't always mean giving money. Jesus wants whatever you can offer, no matter how small. Perhaps it's the gift of time, the gift of an understanding ear, the gift of a ride to church, the gift of a smile for a stranger, the gift of old clothes for those in need. These are gifts that Jesus can take and multiply to infinity, blessing not just us, but the multitudes.

In the same way that God grows a small apple seed, or peach pit, into an entire orchard or grove of trees that produce even more fruit to feed the multitudes, so God can take our smallest gift of love, or time, or prayer, or generosity, and transform it into a gift that keeps on giving not just in our community, but in our state, our country, and around the world.

What small gift do you have that you have not brought to God yet because you feel ashamed, or you feel that it is not enough? What are you holding onto that could be blessing to everyone in this church, and everyone in the world?

The message of this Gospel passage is this: Whatever you bring to God will be more than enough. There is no lack in God. There is nothing but abundance. There is more in God than you could ever ask or imagine. God stands ready, every minute of the day, to transform even the smallest act of kindness, or mercy, or generosity, into a gift that will feed the multitudes and result in baskets and baskets of leftover blessings.

– Candace Chellew-Hodge

Hymns
Opening Hymn
I Sing the Mighty Power of God
Lord, Take My Hand and Lead Me
Sermon Hymn
Break Now the Bread of Life
Take My Gifts
Closing Hymn
Have Faith in God
Lord, Dismiss Us with Thy Blessing

About the Writers

May 8, 15, 22
Marcia Bailey is an ordained American Baptist pastor currently engaged in interim ministry in addition to teaching and writing. She is a full-time Assistant Professor at Temple University, Philadelphia, and a Faculty Associate at Colgate Rochester Crozer Divinity School, Rochester, New York. In addition, she has authored *Choosing Partnership, Sharing Ministry: A Vision for New Spiritual Community* (Alban Institute). She lives in Oaks, Pennsylvania.

June 12, 19, 26; July 3
John Ballenger pastors Woodbrook Baptist Church in Baltimore, Maryland, and savors his regular participation in worship with this congregation.

July 10, 17, 24, 31
Candace Chellew-Hodge is the associate pastor at Garden of Grace UCC in Columbia, South Carolina. She is the founder of *Whosoever* magazine, and the author of *Bulletproof Faith: A Spiritual Survival Guide for Gay and Lesbian Christians* (Jossey-Bass).

May 29; June 2, 5
Andrew Foster Connors is the pastor of the Brown Memorial Park Avenue Presbyterian Church in Baltimore, Maryland.

November 28; December 5, 12, 19, 24
Noelle Damico is an ordained minister in the United Church of Christ and an author of music and liturgy that places justice at the heart of faith. She currently serves as National Coordinator of the Presbyterian Church (U.S.A.) Campaign for Fair Food and as Catalyst of the University of the Poor School of Theology. She lives in Setauket, New York.

December 25, 26; January 2, 6, 9
David Albert Farmer is Pastor of Silverside Church in Wilmington, Delaware, and Adjunct Professor of Preaching and Worship at Palmer

Theological Seminary. He also serves as Adjunct Professor of Humanities and Speech at Wilmington University, teaching both face-to-face and online courses. He is editor of the online preaching journal, "Homilynk."

March 13, 20, 27; April 3, 10
Andrea La Sonde Anastos is an intentional interim minister and spiritual director. She is author of numerous articles, sermons, and prayers and is now exploring the intersection of color, texture, and language. Her most recent book is *Outside the Lines: Meditations on an Expansive God* (Pilgrim Press). She lives in Littleton, Colorado.

February 20, 27; March 6, 9
Paul Lundborg is a retired Lutheran (ELCA) pastor living in Olympia, Washington.

"How Preachers Become Disciples"
William Mangrum lives and writes and preaches in Durango, Colorado, where he serves as pastor of the First Presbyterian Church of Durango. Bill has worked in Baptist, Evangelical Free, Presbyterian, and Episcopalian congregations. He loves speaking with preachers about preaching and welcomes your correspondence at wmangrum@aol.com.

October 10, 17, 24, 31
Rebecca Messman is the Associate Pastor at Trinity Presbyterian Church in Herndon, Virginia, a suburb of Washington, DC. She is married, and she lives with her husband and newborn daughter in Arlington, Virginia.

September 5, 12, 19, 26; October 3
Frank Ramirez is the pastor of the Everett, Pennsylvania, Church of the Brethren. He is the author of *The Meanest Man in Patrick County and Other Unlikely Brethren Heroes* and *Brethren Brush with Greatness: 32 Stories*.

November 1, 7, 14, 21, 25; Children's Time
Donald Schmidt serves with the United Church of Christ in Washington. His book *Emerging Word: A Creation Spirituality Lectionary* has recently been revised and updated. He also writes regularly for *The Minister's Annual Manual* and *The Clergy Journal*. He lives in Bellevue, Washington.

April 17, 21, 22, 24; May 1

Gordon Timbers has been involved in team development of congregational education and worship resources and is currently ministering with the people of Unionville Presbyterian Church in Markham, Ontario.

August 1, 8, 15, 22, 29

Deborah Spink Winters is an Affiliate Professor of Biblical Studies at Palmer Theological Seminary at Eastern University and is a professional Clergy Coach. She lives in Reinholds, Pennsylvania.

January 16, 23, 30; February 6, 13

Nancy E. Topolewski is an ordained United Methodist minister, a member in Full Connection of the Wyoming Annual Conference (New York and Pennsylvania), currently on incapacity leave. She is attached to the Church of the Good Shepherd United Methodist Church of Newport, New Hampshire.

Hymn of the Day

Alan C. Whitmore was Music and Liturgy Editor of Wood Lake Publishing for almost ten years. He is currently Director of Music Ministries of the Episcopal Church of Our Saviour, Jacksonville, Florida, where he plays the organ, conducts the Parish Choir, and leads a graded music program for children and youth.

Four-Year Church Year Calendar

	Year C **2009**	Year A **2010**	Year B **2011**	Year C **2012**
Advent begins	Nov. 29	Nov. 28	Nov. 27	Nov. 25
Christmas	Dec. 25	Dec. 25	Dec. 25	Dec. 25
	2010	**2011**	**2012**	**2013**
Epiphany	Jan. 6	Jan. 6	Jan. 6	Jan. 6
Ash Wednesday	Feb. 17	March 9	Feb. 22	Feb. 13
Passion/Palm Sunday	March 28	Apr. 17	Apr. 1	March 24
Maundy Thursday	Apr. 1	Apr. 21	Apr. 5	March 28
Good Friday	Apr. 2	Apr. 22	Apr. 6	March 29
Easter	Apr. 4	Apr. 24	Apr. 8	March 31
Ascension Day	May 13	June 2	May 17	May 9
Pentecost	May 23	June 12	May 27	May 19
Trinty Sunday	May 30	June 19	June 3	May 26
Reformation	Oct. 31	Oct. 31	Oct. 31	Oct. 31
All Saints' Day	Nov. 1	Nov. 1	Nov. 1	Nov. 1

Calendars for 2010 and 2011

JANUARY					2010		FEBRUARY					2010		MARCH					2010		APRIL					2010	
S	M	T	W	T	F	S	S	M	T	W	T	F	S	S	M	T	W	T	F	S	S	M	T	W	T	F	S
					1	2		1	2	3	4	5	6		1	2	3	4	5	6						1	2	3
3	4	5	6	7	8	9	7	8	9	10	11	12	13	7	8	9	10	11	12	13	4	5	6	7	8	9	10
10	11	12	13	14	15	16	14	15	16	17	18	19	20	14	15	16	17	18	19	20	11	12	13	14	15	16	17
17	18	19	20	21	22	23	21	22	23	24	25	26	27	21	22	23	24	25	26	27	18	19	20	21	22	23	24
24/31	25	26	27	28	29	30	28							28	29	30	31				25	26	27	28	29	30	

MAY					2010		JUNE					2010		JULY					2010		AUGUST					2010	
S	M	T	W	T	F	S	S	M	T	W	T	F	S	S	M	T	W	T	F	S	S	M	T	W	T	F	S
						1			1	2	3	4	5					1	2	3	1	2	3	4	5	6	7
2	3	4	5	6	7	8	6	7	8	9	10	11	12	4	5	6	7	8	9	10	8	9	10	11	12	13	14
9	10	11	12	13	14	15	13	14	15	16	17	18	19	11	12	13	14	15	16	17	15	16	17	18	19	20	21
16	17	18	19	20	21	22	20	21	22	23	24	25	26	18	19	20	21	22	23	24	22	23	24	25	26	27	28
23/30 24/31	25	26	27	28	29		27	28	29	30				25	26	27	28	29	30	31	29	30	31				

SEPTEMBER					2010		OCTOBER					2010		NOVEMBER					2010		DECEMBER					2010	
S	M	T	W	T	F	S	S	M	T	W	T	F	S	S	M	T	W	T	F	S	S	M	T	W	T	F	S
			1	2	3	4						1	2		1	2	3	4	5	6				1	2	3	4
5	6	7	8	9	10	11	3	4	5	6	7	8	9	7	8	9	10	11	12	13	5	6	7	8	9	10	11
12	13	14	15	16	17	18	10	11	12	13	14	15	16	14	15	16	17	18	19	20	12	13	14	15	16	17	18
19	20	21	22	23	24	25	17	18	19	20	21	22	23	21	22	23	24	25	26	27	19	20	21	22	23	24	25
26	27	28	29	30			24/31	25	26	27	28	29	30	28	29	30					26	27	28	29	30	31	

JANUARY					2011		FEBRUARY					2011		MARCH					2011		APRIL					2011	
S	M	T	W	T	F	S	S	M	T	W	T	F	S	S	M	T	W	T	F	S	S	M	T	W	T	F	S
						1		1	2	3	4	5			1	2	3	4	5							1	2
2	3	4	5	6	7	8	6	7	8	9	10	11	12	6	7	8	9	10	11	12	3	4	5	6	7	8	9
9	10	11	12	13	14	15	13	14	15	16	17	18	19	13	14	15	16	17	18	19	10	11	12	13	14	15	16
16	17	18	19	20	21	22	20	21	22	23	24	25	26	20	21	22	23	24	25	26	17	18	19	20	21	22	23
23/30 24/31	25	26	27	28	29	27	28						27	28	29	30	31			24	25	26	27	28	29	30	

MAY					2011		JUNE					2011		JULY					2011		AUGUST					2011	
S	M	T	W	T	F	S	S	M	T	W	T	F	S	S	M	T	W	T	F	S	S	M	T	W	T	F	S
1	2	3	4	5	6	7			1	2	3	4						1	2	1	2	3	4	5	6		
8	9	10	11	12	13	14	5	6	7	8	9	10	11	3	4	5	6	7	8	9	7	8	9	10	11	12	13
15	16	17	18	19	20	21	12	13	14	15	16	17	18	10	11	12	13	14	15	16	14	15	16	17	18	19	20
22	23	24	25	26	27	28	19	20	21	22	23	24	25	17	18	19	20	21	22	23	21	22	23	24	25	26	27
29	30	31					26	27	28	29	30			24/31	25	26	27	28	29	30	28	29	30	31			

SEPTEMBER					2011		OCTOBER					2011		NOVEMBER					2011		DECEMBER					2011	
S	M	T	W	T	F	S	S	M	T	W	T	F	S	S	M	T	W	T	F	S	S	M	T	W	T	F	S
				1	2	3							1			1	2	3	4	5					1	2	3
4	5	6	7	8	9	10	2	3	4	5	6	7	8	6	7	8	9	10	11	12	4	5	6	7	8	9	10
11	12	13	14	15	16	17	9	10	11	12	13	14	15	13	14	15	16	17	18	19	11	12	13	14	15	16	17
18	19	20	21	22	23	24	16	17	18	19	20	21	22	20	21	22	23	24	25	26	18	19	20	21	22	23	24
25	26	27	28	29	30		23/30 24/31	25	26	27	28	29	27	28	29	30				25	26	27	28	29	30	31	

Index of Sermon Texts